Live & Work

IN

BELGIUM,

THE

NETHERLANDS

& LUXEMBOURG

Live & Work

— IN —

BELGIUM,

— THE —

NETHERLANDS

& LUXEMBOURG

André de Vries
Greg Adams

Published by Vacation Work, 9 Park End Street, Oxford

LIVE AND WORK
IN BELGIUM, THE NETHERLANDS
AND LUXEMBOURG
by André de Vries
& Greg Adams

Series Editor: Victoria Pybus

ISBN 1 85458 076 0 (softback)
ISBN 1 85458 077 9 (hardback)

Publicity: Roger Musker

Cover Design by
Miller Craig & Cocking Design Partnership

Printed by **William Gibbons & Sons Ltd**, Wolverhampton, England.

Contents
Belgium

SECTION I — LIVING IN BELGIUM

DAILY LIFE

RETIREMENT

SECTION II — WORKING IN BELGIUM

EMPLOYMENT

The Netherlands

SECTION I — LIVING IN THE NETHERLANDS

GENERAL INTRODUCTION

RESIDENCE AND ENTRY REGULATIONS

SETTING UP HOME

DAILY LIFE

SECTION II — WORKING IN THE NETHERLANDS

EMPLOYMENT

Living & Working in Luxembourg

GENERAL INTRODUCTION

RESIDENCE AND ENTRY REGULATIONS

SETTING UP HOME

DAILY LIFE

RETIREMENT

EMPLOYMENT

STARTING A BUSINESS

MAPS AND CHARTS

APPENDICES

INDEX OF ADVERTISERS

Foreword

Live and Work in Belgium, The Netherlands and Luxembourg is the fourth in a successful series of books which identifies the opportunities for work, starting a business, or retiring within the EC. The aim of the series is to provide an information base concerning the many and varied regulations and practicalities still involved in moving to continental Europe. Despite the promised freedom of movement of people, goods and services within the EC, there are still complications inherent in buying or renting a new home and starting a new job in another EC Member State where the laws and procedures are different from those to which one is accustomed. We hope that by using *Live and Work in Belgium, The Netherlands and Luxembourg* as a starting point, you will be able to take this major move in your stride. Each of the three countries in the book has two sections, one entitled *Living* and the other *Working*. These two sections cover all aspects of life, including how to find a job, work practices in the three countries, business opportunities, how to set up a business, renting and buying property, and retirement.

There are an estimated 60,000 UK nationals in the Benelux countries, many of whom work for British or multinational companies in the large cities such as Brussels, Antwerp, Rotterdam, The Hague, Amsterdam and Luxembourg-Ville. In Belgium, a considerable number of Britons work for the EC Commission and NATO. In The Netherlands, many work on short-term contracts in the fields of construction and engineering or to gain experience of the latest developments in horticulture. As the climate in the Benelux countries is much the same as in the UK, it can be assumed that Britons go there to work rather than to sit in the sun. The main motivating factors are professional and business opportunities, good working conditions, excellent social welfare systems and a high standard of living. While there is a certain touch of the exotic about any foreign country, Belgium, The Netherlands and Luxembourg have more in common with the UK on the cultural level than any other European countries. Those from English-speaking cultures will find it easy to form long-lasting relationships.

Out of the three countries, Luxembourg has very few economic problems and the highest proportion of foreigners. Belgium and The Netherlands, on the other hand, although not in the same league as France and Germany in terms of economic power, have excellent long-term growth prospects. The political situation in Belgium is disturbing, in that the extreme right is gaining considerable influence, and the regions are pulling away from the centre. Nevertheless, there is no likelihood of Belgium breaking up completely. The Netherlands is still one of the most progressive countries in Europe and leads the world in its determined effort to clean up its environment and develop renewable sources of energy.

The Benelux countries have always been pioneers in breaking down European trade and cultural barriers; the success of the Belgium-Luxembourg Economic Union (1922) and the Benelux Union (1948) contributed to a large degree in the creation of the Common Market. They will no doubt be the first to make the Single Market a reality. Those who are prepared to take the opportunities offered by these countries will be amply rewarded. This book tells you how, where and why to make it in Belgium, The Netherlands and Luxembourg.

André de Vries
Greg Adams
May 1992

Acknowledgments

We would like to thank the following for their invaluable help in compiling the Belgian section of this book: Dr I. de Vries, and René and Jacqueline Batslé for their hospitality in Belgium; Christel Mertens (Océ), Gordon McKay (Creyf's Interim), Mel Andrews (Brussels Relocation) and Robert Adams (Analysts International SPRL) for advice on setting up home and starting a business; and Michael Kingshott for information on buying and selling property in Belgium. Special thanks go to Michael Ingham OBE (De Keyser-Thornton) and Peter Burnett (EC Commission) for contributing their experience of living and working in Belgium to the case studies section. Thanks also to Katie Challans (Challans Design), Bernard Perry (Cotswold Nannies) and Mark Wilson (Green Express) for extensive interviews. The Belgian Embassy in London, and the National Institute of Statistics in Brussels were also very generous in providing prompt information.

For their generous assistance with the sections on The Netherlands and Luxembourg, we would like to thank: H.E. the Ambassador of the Grand Duchy of Luxembourg; Nicholas Braun for information on Luxembourg; The British Embassy in The Hague; and the Royal Netherlands Embassy in London. Special thanks for help and advice to Helen Rietveld (Relocation Services); Charles van Beuningen; and Karen Wolven. Many thanks also to Eileen Brown and Elisabeth Cox for agreeing to provide case histories of their own experiences of living and working in The Netherlands.

NOTE: While every effort has been made to ensure that the information contained in this book was correct at the time of going to press, details are bound to change and readers are invited to write to Vacation Work, 9 Park End Street, Oxford OX1 1HJ, with any comments or corrections.

CONVERSION CHART

LENGTH (N.B. 12 inches=1 foot, 10 mm=1 cm, 100 cm=1 metre)

inches	1	2	3	4	5	6	9	12		
cm	2.5	5	7.5	10	12.5	15.2	23	30		
cm	1	2	3	5	10	20	25	50	75	100
inches	0.4	0.8	1.2	2	4	8	10	20	30	39

WEIGHT (N.B. 14 lb=1 stone, 2240 lb=1 ton, 1,000 kg=1 metric tonne)

lb	1	2	3	5	10	14	44	100	2240
kg	0.45	0.9	1.4	2.3	4.5	6.4	20	45	1016
kg	1	2	3	5	10	25	50	100	1000
lb	2.2	4.4	6.6	11	22	55	110	220	2204

DISTANCE

mile	1	5	10	20	30	40	50	75	100	150
km	1.6	8	16	32	48	64	80	120	161	241
km	1	5	10	20	30	40	50	100	150	200
mile	0.6	3.1	6.2	12	19	25	31	62	93	124

VOLUME

gallon (UK)	1	2	3	4	5	10	12	15	20	25
litre	4.5	9	13.6	18	23	45	56	68	91	114
litre	1	2	3	5	10	20	40	50	75	100
gallon (UK)	0.2	0.4	0.7	1.1	2.2	4.4	8.8	11	16.5	22

CLOTHES

UK	8	10	12	14	16	18	20			
Europe	36	38	40	42	44	46	48			

SHOES

UK	3	4	5	6	7	8	9	10	11	12
Europe	36	37	38	39	40	41/42	43	44	45	46

Belgium

SECTION I

Living in Belgium

General Introduction
Residence and Entry Regulations
Setting Up Home
Daily Life
Retirement

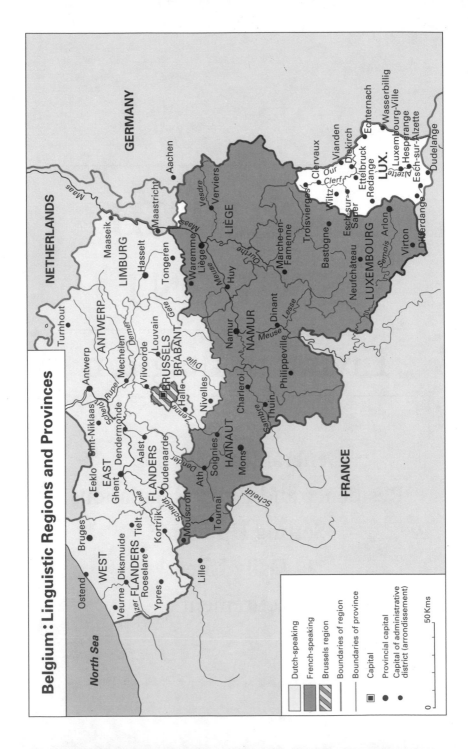

Belgium: Linguistic Regions and Provinces

General Introduction

Destination Belgium

Belgium is one of the UK's closest neighbours, both in terms of location (65 miles away), and its historical and economic links with this country, yet to most Britons it remains largely unknown. It is not one of our main tourist destinations, and most of us would be hard-pressed to name any important Belgian cultural figures.

Those who do take the trouble to look more closely at Belgium will find extraordinary linguistic and cultural diversity packed into an area about half as large again as Wales. Belgium is in many ways a rather fragmented country, where many institutions are divided into four — Dutch-speaking, French-speaking, Catholic, and secular. The two main communities — the Dutch-speaking Flemish and the French-speaking Walloons — are moving further apart just at the time that the European Community is moving ever closer towards federalism. Belgium only came into existence in approximately its present form in 1830, and there have always been those who felt that it should have remained unified with The Netherlands, or divided up in some other way. Even so, Belgium is definitely here to stay.

The Belgian people themselves, disregarding their linguistic quarrels, are exceptionally welcoming to those from other countries. The feelings of nationalism and cultural superiority prevalent in other European countries are generally absent. Having been variously occupied by the French, Spanish, Dutch, Austrians and Germans, the Belgians have learned to get along with other people, while maintaining a good-humoured cynicism towards all and sundry. Rather than blowing their own trumpets they would rather get on with enjoying the good things in life in their own down-to-earth way. Outsiders should always remember that Belgium has its own unique traditions and cultural identity, even if the locals do not make a great deal of fuss about these things.

Belgium is certainly a country which should not be overlooked, because it really is the Crossroads or Heart of Europe. If you are looking for a somewhat exotic and highly internationalized environment without going very far from home, then this could be the country for you.

Pros and Cons of Moving to Belgium

Those moving to Belgium will be able to enjoy a lifestyle as good as anywhere in Europe. Not surprisingly, Belgium is seen as an attractive country by immigrants, who now make up 9% (890,000) of the population. 23,000 British citizens actually reside in Belgium (1984 census), so the potential migrant will find a well-established expatriate community. British television stations are now easily obtainable, as are newspapers.

Belgians are still very favourably disposed to the British, with the exception of football hooligans, but one should remember that Brussels, in particular, is virtually saturated with foreigners, and you may feel that the locals are somewhat impersonal in their dealings with you. The Belgians are certainly not as outgoing as the French and other Latin peoples, and place more emphasis on family ties and long-term friendships than on casual acquaintances. On the other hand, with so many foreigners around, it is quite possible to have an exciting social life if you want one.

Working practices are becoming more relaxed than before, and Britons should not find too many problems here. The working week is fixed at $38\frac{1}{2}$ hours and minimum holidays at 4 weeks per year. Starting times may be earlier than in Britain, but this varies. Employees are afforded a large measure of protection by the law, but this has its disadvantages as well. One should not expect a lot of overtime work — your employer has to give you time off in lieu. The minimum weekly wage of a factory or clerical worker is now around BF12,000 (£180), while the cost of living is comparable to that in the UK. The most important consideration for those wanting to work in Belgium must be the high level of both direct and indirect taxation there. Many items carry 19.5% VAT, and someone on a moderate salary may be paying 48% tax. Those with a high income, or multiple sources of income, who can use tax advisers, may do much better than someone whose taxes are deducted at source. There is, for example, no capital gains tax in Belgium. Those working for the EC pay very little tax at all. Earnings often include a company car, and other benefits, as well as the so-called 'thirteenth month', all of which have to be taxed, of course (see *Taxation* section in Chapter Four *Daily Life*). On the plus side, once you are established in Belgium, you will be able to enjoy the benefits of its generous social security system.

Job opportunities for English-speakers are generally good and at a constant level, in spite of the overall weakness of the economy (unemployment stands at 8.8%, down from 13% in 1984). There are possibilities in most sections of the market. Temporary work is quite plentiful, although the trade unions tend to keep foreigners out of some jobs. On the other hand, all EC nationals have the right to use the services of the state employment offices to look for work, whether temporary or permanent. Trying to work without paying taxes/social security is not advisable, as the authorities are fairly zealous in seeking out illegal workers, and you will be competing with the latest influx of unemployed east Europeans.

There are always openings for language teachers, au pairs, secretaries, and so on, and these jobs are frequently advertised in the British press. Those with good language skills (any EC language is useful) are always in demand, and should consider going to job agencies and job fairs (see Chapter Six, *Employment*) in Belgium itself. Those with good qualifications will be able to make arrangements from Britain.

Rented accommodation is not hard to find, although becoming expensive in Brussels. Rental agreements tend to require a minimum 3-year commitment, with possibly expensive penalties if you move out. Accommodation is usually unfurnished. There is no housing shortage at all in Belgium — at any one time 3-4% of houses are empty — and prices are about a quarter of those in Britain. The property market in Belgium has been stagnant during 1991 and 1992. Further information on property is given in Chapter Three, *Setting Up Home*.

The physical environment is much more varied than one might think. The 40 mile North Sea coast has some of the best and safest beaches in Europe. In the south there are the unspoiled hills and forests of the Ardennes Plateau which offer skiing in the winter. Belgium is particularly rich in medieval architecture and art, and there are numerous châteaux and parks to visit. It has preserved a considerable amount of its folklore; Belgians love to hold carnivals and festivals where everyone can join in. The climate is similar to southern England's, but rather more consistent, with predictably warm summers and snow in winter.

The following is a summary of the main pros and cons of living in Belgium from the British point of view.

Pros.   Relatively healthy economy with good employment prospects.
Multinational organizations requiring English speakers.
Possibility of supplying services to other foreigners.
Multicultural environment.
Friendly and helpful locals.
Very favourable treatment of EC nationals.
Excellent job security and benefits.
Belgium is historically very interesting and has plenty to offer in most areas of culture. Belgian food is internationally highly regarded.

Cons.   Some sectors unlikely to employ foreigners.
Unfamiliar regulations in another language.
Rental agreements tend to be inflexible.
Taxes on the high side and hard to avoid.
Not the best place to save a lot of money in a hurry.

Political and Economic Structure

The key to understanding Belgium's political development lies in its long and complex history, which is characterized by frequent invasions and occupations. Those looking for more detail can consult *History of the Belgians* (Thames & Hudson, 1962) by de Meeüs.

Belgium takes its name from the Belgae, a Celtic tribe who moved here in prehistoric times. Julius Caesar conquered the area in 56 BC and made it into the Roman province of Gallia Belgica. The racial and linguistic division of what was to become Belgium started in the third century AD, as Germanic tribes moved into the north of the country, while the romanized Celts continued to occupy the south. As a result, there is an almost straight line across Belgium dividing the Dutch- and French-speakers, with Brussels a largely French island in the Dutch area. There are also 62,000 German-speakers in the east from the incorporation of the German areas of Eupen and Malmédy after World War I.

Dutch-speakers are often called 'Flemings' and their region Flanders, which includes the provinces of Limburg and Antwerpen, which were not part of medieval Flanders. The Flemings these days usually say that they speak Dutch (*Nederlands*), the standardized form of which is identical in most respects in Belgium and The Netherlands. The term 'Flemish' can be applied to the many dialects of Dutch spoken in Belgium, but not to the official language. The French-speaking area — Wallonia — has its own Walloon dialects, but the inhabitants would always claim to be speakers of French. The first thing to remember about Belgium is that the Dutch-speakers outnumber the French-speakers at a ratio of 3 to 2.

Contrary to widespread belief, French is not the only language spoken in Belgium. Medieval Flanders had close relations with England, while the rest of the country was ruled by an assortment of dukes, counts and prince-bishops. The major event of this period was the defeat of the French nobility at the Battle of the Golden Spurs in 1302 by the Flemish towns, which is still celebrated on 11 July in Flanders. Without this victory Belgium would probably not exist today. Nevertheless, Belgium gradually came under the domination of the Burgundians, the Habsburgs, and finally the King of Spain. Spanish efforts to suppress the Reformation in the Low Countries were entirely successful in Belgium, while The Netherlands managed to break free. As a result, Belgium's Christians are 95% Catholic and the Catholic church has enormous influence, another vital piece of information for the outsider.

Following the Battle of Waterloo (near Brussels) in 1815, Belgium and Holland were unified for 15 years under the King of the Netherlands. Many objected to unequal treatment by the Dutch, and finally Belgium gained its independence in 1830, with Queen Victoria's uncle installed as King Leopold I. While Leopold I's grandson, Albert, fought heroically in World War I, his son, Leopold III, was compelled to surrender to the Germans in World War II, and decided not to escape abroad. The king's credibility was severely diminished and he eventually abdicated in 1950, to be succeeded by his son Baudouin I, who has done much to restore the prestige of the monarchy.

Economy

Following independence the industrial revolution took off in Belgium in the 1840s, centred around coal, steel, textiles and other manufacturing industries. As it happened, most of the country's natural resources were to be found in the French-speaking south. Since education and government were conducted entirely in French, the Dutch-speakers became second-class citizens, tied to the land and denied any opportunities for advancement. Some Dutch-speakers looked to Germany for support, given that the Walloons (French-speakers) always looked to France, but after two German occupations their pro-German feelings largely disappeared. Other factors eventually tipped the balance towards the Dutch-speaking community, without eliminating their lasting feeling of bitterness towards the French-speaking élite.

Manufacturing industries suffered severely during the Depression, while at the same time agriculture in the north prospered, and the numbers of Flemings began to exceed the numbers of Walloons. Dutch was finally recognized as an official language in 1932, and could now be used in education and in the law-courts.

Belgium and Luxembourg entered into a pioneering economic union in 1921 — the BLEU (Belgo-Luxembourg Economic Union) — after Luxembourg decided it no longer wished to be tied to Germany. In 1948, a further free-trade area was created — the organization of the Benelux countries (Belgium, The Netherlands and Luxembourg), which anticipated the creation of the Common Market in 1957.

Belgium also benefited greatly from its acquisition of the Congo (now divided into Zaïre and the Congo), which was initially run by King Leopold II as his private property from 1885 until 1908, when it became a Belgian colony. The immense natural resources of the Congo were particularly important in Belgium's rapid recovery from World War II, and are still helping to support Belgian prosperity, even though the Congo became independent in 1961.

Following the war, Flanders became more and more prosperous, while the heavy industry of the south continued to decline. Relative political stability after the crisis over the monarchy had been resolved in 1950 helped to attract immense foreign investment, a lot going into developing the port of Antwerp and the surrounding area. In spite of its position 54 miles/85 km inland from the sea on the Scheldt estuary, Antwerp is now the second biggest port in Europe after Rotterdam and reputedly has the fastest ship turnaround time in the world. It is also the world's leading centre for the trading and polishing of diamonds. Belgium also has a number of other ports, some of them inland, thanks to its highly developed network of canals.

Investment in Belgium is largely concentrated in manufacturing industries, where regulations are liberal and a well-trained workforce already exists. The United States is the largest foreign investor — Ford and General Motors both have factories here — and you will find that some of the leading department stores are American-owned. Volvo has a car-factory outside Ghent, and has found the workers far more reliable than those in Sweden.

The traditional textile industries have, however, declined with competition from less developed countries, and the steel industry in Wallonia has contracted severely. On the other hand, chemicals, pharmaceuticals, electronics and other high-tech industries have all grown impressively, which has served to increase the prosperity of the Dutch-speaking areas of the north rather than of the south. Belgium now exports 60% of its GNP, one of the highest ratios in the world. In spite of its concentration of manufacturing, 47% of the land is still used for agriculture, but employs only 2.5% of the workforce.

International banks and financial institutions are also very active in Belgium although regulations are not very liberal. Because of the level of taxes and complex rules, tax evasion is rampant, and many Belgians put money into banks in The Netherlands and Luxembourg, or into Dutch shares.

After the boom of the 1960s and the oil shocks of the 1970s, the Belgian economy went into recession in 1979-1980. At a time of high unemployment and high inflation, the government had to grapple with a spiralling budget deficit. The country appeared to be on the verge of bankruptcy and the Belgian franc had to be devalued in 1982. Extraordinary economic austerity policies were eventually forced through by the centre-right government of Dr Wilfried Martens in the face of intense opposition and the economy showed a remarkable turnaround by 1985. The balance of trade is now in surplus, with 3% growth of GNP per annum projected for the next few years. Unemployment is expected to continue at the present level of about 8.8% for the foreseeable future. Although Belgium has weathered the 1991 recession far better than many other countries, growth in export earnings is not enough to cover the budget deficit, which still stood at 6% of GNP in 1990.

Government

Belgium has always been a fragmented country, and as a result its politics have largely revolved around working out a satisfactory balance between the interests of the different communities. The system of proportional representation used in Belgium is designed to ensure that no one group becomes completely dominant. Some of the issues which have caused Belgian governments to fall, which they do with astonishing regularity (there have been 37 changes of government since 1944), might appear quite trivial, but they certainly generate a great deal of passion amongst the participants.

Until recently, Belgium had three levels of government: national, provincial, and communal, with direct elections to all three. At the top level, there is the Chamber of Representatives, with 212 members divided between Dutch and French-speakers, and the Senate, with 183, some of them from provincial councils or co-opted. The government rules by decrees which must be countersigned by the King. The nine provinces also have their own councils, and then there are 589 communes with mayors and councillors elected every six years. The nine provinces are also divided up into 45 administrative units known as *arrondissements/arrondissementen* (see map) for which there is no electoral representation.

All Belgian governments since 1919 have been coalitions, with the Christian Social Party (Catholic Party) in alliance with the Socialists or Liberals. The only exception to this was the period 1950-54 when the Catholics had an absolute majority. The major trends of the 1960s were the decline of the Liberals (actually a secularist right-wing party) and the rise of the regionalist parties, the Volksunie, Rassemblement Wallon and FDF in Flanders, Wallonia and Brussels respectively. By the 1970s the three major parties had split along linguistic lines, and a further polarization had taken place, whereby the Christian party had become dominant in Flanders, and the traditionally anticlericalist Socialists' power base tended to shift to Wallonia. Henceforth the leader of the Flemish Christian party inevitably became the Prime Minister as well. The French-speakers were now threatened with permanent Flemish domination as well as the collapse of their economy. The Flemings, on the other hand, had no desire to bail out their former oppressors with their taxes.

The 1980s saw frequent changes of government, but some elements have remained stable. Dr Wilfried Martens (Flemish Christian Social Party) headed every government from 1981 to 1992, forming coalitions with either the Liberals or Socialists. The Heysel Stadium disaster actually led to the fall of the government in 1986, and there was a major crisis in 1989 when the King refused to sign a law legalizing abortion. Eventually he agreed to be suspended as monarch for a day, so the bill could go through without his signature. In May 1991 there was fighting between unemployed Moroccan youths and the police in Brussels which resulted in hasty measures to improve the status of immigrants. The Flemish ultra-rightist party, Vlaams Blok (Flemish Block), increased its representation in Parliament substantially in the election of November 1991. Belgium has traditionally been tolerant towards asylum-seekers, and is speeding up its asylum procedures. As a result of the end of the cold war in Europe, Belgium is also pulling its troops out of Germany almost entirely, and cutting its armed forces by 20%. In March 1992, a new coalition government was formed comprising Christian Democrats and Socialists, under a new Prime Minister, Jean-Luc De Haene, a Flemish Christian Democrat.

So that the regions and linguistic communities can realize their different aspirations, Belgium is now well on the way to becoming a devolved, federalist state. Some believe that Belgium may break up completely, but this is hardly possible in the present European context. The task of federalization has been addressed in three reforms of the constitution: in 1970, 1980 and 1988. The first revision fixed the boundaries of the language communities (Dutch, French and German), and created community cultural councils. It also stated that the Cabinet must have equal numbers of Dutch- and French-speaking ministers. Three regions were also created: Flanders, Wallonia and Brussels. By the revisions of 1980 and 1988, more and more of the power of the central government has been transferred to the Communities and Regions. It is envisaged that there will be direct elections to the Community/Regional Councils, although only the council of the German-speaking Community and of the Brussels Region are directly elected so far. The other councils are made up of members of parliament from both houses. The Flemish Community and Regional Councils are one body, whereas in the French area they are split into two.

The biggest problem has been to decide who is responsible for what amongst the five tiers of government: National, Regional, Community, Provincial and Communal; and complex institutions have been set up to arbitrate on disputes. At the moment, certain taxes are allocated to the Communities and Regions, and between them they now spend 40% of the national budget.

The distribution of government functions is roughly speaking as follows: the national level retains general control over policy-making and regulatory functions as well as defence, much of foreign relations, justice, social security, agriculture, the railways and the national airline (SABENA). The Regions have a large degree of power in deciding their own economic policies, and are responsible for public works, state-owned industries, employment, housing, traffic, harbours and water. The Communities deal with education, the media, scientific research, social services, the arts and the defence and promotion of their respective languages. Brussels has a Regional Council with much the same powers. The German-speaking area, on the other hand, falls under the control of the French-speaking Region of Wallonia. The Provinces also have certain powers, in particular in relation to public health and law and order, and are allocated some taxes.

It should be stressed that the whole system outlined above is in a process of transition, as the relationship between the different interest groups is worked out. Belgium is, then, in effect going back in time, from the centralized Napoleonic constitution of 1830, to the situation under the Dukes of Burgundy in the 14th and 15th century, where towns and counties had to be persuaded to work together as a common unit.

Political Parties

After the last election there were 13 political parties in the Chamber of Representatives, all but one also present in the Senate. Traditionally there were three main political parties: the Christian Social Party, the Liberals, and the Socialists. After dividing them into Dutch- and French-speaking wings, we now have: the CVP (Christelijke Volkspartij) and the PSC (Parti social-chrétien) who formed the 1987-1991 government together with the SP (Socialistische Partij) and PS (Parti socialiste). Between 1981 and 1987 the Christian parties were in coalition with the Liberal parties: the PVV (Partij voor Vrijheid en Vooruitgang — Party for Freedom and Progress) and the PRL (Parti réformateur libéral — Liberal Reformist Party). Parties promoting the interests of French-speaking Wallonia have been absorbed into the PRL. Some previous governments have also included the Flemish nationalist VU (Volksunie), but because of their pacifist stand they have found it difficult to go along with the stationing of nuclear weapons in Belgium. The only other party in the present Parliament which has ever been represented in government is the FDF (Front des francophones), which defends the interests of French-speakers in Brussels.

Other parties are the notorious anti-immigrant Vlaams Blok and its Walloon counterpart the Front National; the Dutch- and French-speaking Green parties, Agalev and Ecolo; and the anarchist party, known after its founder as Rossem.

Geographical Information

Area

Belgium occupies 11,781 sq miles/30,541 sq km, making it the second smallest country in the EC after Luxembourg. It is bounded to the north by The Netherlands, to the east by Germany and Luxembourg, and to the south by France; on the west it has a 40 mile/66 km coast on the English Channel/North Sea. At its closest Belgium is only 65 miles/104 km from the English coast. The longest distance from east to west is 175 miles/280 km and from north to south 140 miles/222 km. The land is cut into three by the two main rivers — the Scheldt (Dutch Schelde, French Escaut) and the Sambre/Meuse (Dutch Maas), which rise in France and enter the North Sea through The Netherlands. The Scheldt and Meuse are joined by a canal which runs roughly along the southern border of the Netherlands, so that Belgian shipping has access to the Rhine and other major river systems of Europe. West of the Sambre/Meuse line the country is mostly flat, fertile agricultural land; to the east it is hilly and forested, with its highest point reaching 2313 ft/694 m at the Signal de Botrange in the Hautes Fagnes region near Germany. Belgium does not have any foreign territories or offshore islands.

Regional Divisions and Main Towns

There are three official regions and nine provinces:
FLANDERS — West Vlaanderen, Oost Vlaanderen, Brabant (North), Antwerpen, Limburg
WALLONIA — Hainaut, Namur, Brabant (South), Liège, Luxembourg
BRUSSELS

Population

The current population of Belgium is just over 10 million, with a fairly negligible rate of increase of 0.2%. This makes the population the third smallest in the EC after Luxembourg and Denmark. Belgium is the second most densely populated country after the Netherlands, with 840 inhabitants per sq mile/323 per sq km. The Flemish region accounts for 57% of the population, Wallonia for 33%, and Brussels for 10%. There are also 62,000 German speakers in the eastern area of Eupen and Malmédy. Belgium is more urbanized than most European countries, with 30% of the inhabitants concentrated in the urban areas of Brussels (990,000), Antwerp (490,000), Ghent (234,000), Liège (203,000), and Charleroi (212,000). Even so, 47% of the land area is given over to agriculture, and 20% is wooded. Apart from the original division into Celtic French-speakers and Germanic Dutch-speakers, and various invaders who remained behind, Belgium has recently become a racially more and more diverse country. Of 900,000 foreigners living in Belgium, 521,000 come from the EC and most of these from Italy (50%), Spain and Greece. Of the rest many are Moroccans and Turks, some of whom are likely to remain in Belgium.

Climate

Belgium's climate is generally similar to that of England, with slightly hotter summers and slightly colder winters. The highest recorded temperature of the last ten years was 33.5°c and the lowest minus 26°c. Average annual rainfall in Brussels is 838 mm (33 inches), which is similar to the east of England. Rain falls on about

220 days per year. Temperatures in the east of the country tend to be slightly more extreme; snow on the Ardennes plateau makes it possible to ski in some years.

The following table (courtesy of the Belgian National Tourist Office) gives average temperatures for each month of the year.

Average Maximum Temperatures

Month	Brussels	Ostend
January	42°f/6°c	42°f/6°c
February	42°f/6°c	42°f/6°c
March	48°f/9°c	48°f/9°c
April	55°f/13°c	52°f/11°c
May	65°f/18°c	61°f/16°c
June	69°f/21°c	65°f/18°c
July	74°f/23°c	68°f/20°c
August	72°f/22°c	69°f/21°c
September	66°f/19°c	65°f/18°c
October	56°f/14°c	56°f/14°c
November	46°f/8°c	48°f/9°c
December	42°f/6°c	45°f/7°c

Regional Guide

Most English-speaking foreigners in Belgium will be found in and around Brussels and Mons (where SHAPE — Supreme Headquarters Allied Powers Europe is situated). Other large immigrant concentrations are to be found in the industrial areas of Antwerp, Brussels, Ghent, Charleroi and Liège.

Belgium is now divided up into the three regions of Flanders, Wallonia and Brussels, as well as the three language communities of Dutch, French and German-speakers, and the bilingual community of Brussels. Since 1980 Belgium has been moving towards a federal structure, with regional assemblies and executives, the status of Brussels remaining unresolved. The regions are already pursuing their own development policies and opening representative offices abroad. These moves all reflect the fact that most Belgians have little to do with members of the other linguistic community and would rather their taxes were spent on their own community. Everyone agrees that there is little sense of national identity. The most important entity is one's town or village rather than any larger unit, just as it was in medieval times. The visitor should at least try to be aware of the language spoken wherever they happen to be, which should not be difficult outside Brussels, given that the provinces reflect linguistic boundaries.

Information Facilities

A good starting point for information is the Belgian National Tourist Office (BNTO) in your home country for a supply of national maps, railway maps, and brochures on the main Belgian towns. In Belgium itself you will find tourist offices in most towns and they will usually have free maps of the town, information on places to visit and how to get there, etc. They will also be very willing to find and book a hotel room for you. You should not expect them to carry information on places outside their own region. Some railway stations have information offices which will book hotel rooms for you.

FLANDERS — THE DUTCH-SPEAKING REGION

West Vlaanderen (West Flanders)

Main tourist office: Burg 11, 8000 Brugge; tel 050 44 86 86.
Main towns: Brugge (Bruges), Oostende (Ostend), Ieper (Ypres), Kortrijk, Knokke, Zeebrugge.
West Flanders is the fifth largest province with over 10% of the land area and population. It has all of Belgium's seacoast and therefore many of its tourist/holiday resorts. These became fashionable in the last century with the French-speaking élite following royal patronage, and many French-speakers still spend their summer holidays there. Those with large families prefer to rent an entire apartment for a month. During the winter the coastal resorts are very quiet and many hotels close down. The Belgian seaside is no longer very fashionable and some may find the almost continuous hotels and apartments lacking in charm, but it offers excellent beaches, restaurants and sporting facilities. Ostend and Zeebrugge are both ferry ports, and there is a small airport near Ostend — Middelkerke — with flights to Southend in Essex. Zeebrugge is also a large container port. Perhaps the most interesting place to visit in Ostend is the house of the mystically-inclined Anglo-Belgian painter James Ensor, which is now a museum.

To many West Flanders is most memorable as the site of some of the fiercest battles of World War I; the area of Ypres is dotted with memorials to the dead of many nations. It is estimated that there are 400 million unexploded bombs and shells still waiting to be discovered. Ypres was largely destroyed in World War I and it took almost 50 years to rebuild the cathedral. East of Ypres is the town of Kortrijk, the centre of the flax and linen industry, just a few miles from the French industrial city of Lille-Roubaix. At one time Flanders extended into northern France, as one can see from the place names. Flemish was once widely spoken in the *départements* of Artois and Picardy, but has virtually died out during this century.

The capital of this province is Brugge (generally known by its French name of Bruges), more or less on the way from Ghent to Ostend, which has an unusually well-preserved medieval city centre and some world-famous art museums. Brugge became rich through selling cloth to England, but was eventually ruined when its outlet to the sea, the Zwin river, silted up.

West Flanders is now largely agricultural, one of the most typical features of the landscape being its pollarded willow trees. Towards the French border the landscape becomes more hilly in the area known as the West Vlaams Heuvelland.

East Flanders (Oost Vlaanderen)

Main tourist office: Stadhuis, Belfortstraat 9, 9000 Gent; tel 091 24 15 55.
Main cities: Ghent (Gent/Gand), St Niklaas, Dendermonde, Oudenaarde.
East Flanders comprises 10% of the land area of Belgium and 13% of the population. It has much the same topography as West Flanders — a fertile alluvial plain intersected by rivers — the Scheldt, Leie and Dender. During the Middle Ages it reached the height of its prosperity and power through importing wool

from England and then exporting it back as finished cloth. Religious wars and declining political fortunes eventually reduced the area to a backwater, and many of its citizens emigrated to The Netherlands and England.

Ghent still has many superb medieval buildings and is in some ways more attractive than Brugge, with wider streets and cleaner buildings. Ghent has regular festivals, in particular the Floralien, a five-yearly horticultural festival (last held in 1990) and the Festival van Vlaanderen or European Music Festival, a major music and cultural festival held over three weeks in August-September every year. In July there are the Gentse Feesten with traditional processions and carnivals.

Although Ghent is the capital of the Flemish area it was until recently a stronghold of middle-class French-speakers and the local dialect shows distinct French influences. The Nobel prize-winning writer Maurice Maeterlinck lived here, but as he wrote in French he is usually overlooked. Some of the 'high-class' shops still have French-speaking staff, but in general speaking French in shops here is inadvisable.

To the northeast of Ghent, on the way to Antwerp, there is the Waasland, originally marshland with poor soil which was drained and developed by religious communities in the Middle Ages and is now a quiet agricultural area popular with campers. The centre of the Waasland is St Niklaas where you can visit a museum dedicated to Mercator (of the well-known Projection) who was born in nearby Rupelmonde.

Antwerp

Main tourist office: Grote Markt 15, 2000 Antwerp; tel 03 232 22 84.
Main towns: Antwerp (Antwerpen/Anvers), Turnhout, Mechelen (Malines), Lier, Geel, Herentals.

The province of Antwerp includes Belgium's largest port of the same name, and covers 9% of the land area. Most of the population of 1,600,000 live in and around Antwerp, employed in the docks or in the numerous factories which have sprung up nearby. The name Antwerp was traditionally derived from the tale of a giant who threw sailors' hands (*handwerpen*) into the sea if they refused to pay their tolls. In truth it is a corruption of *aan 't werf* meaning 'at the wharf' in Dutch. From the early sixteenth century until 1648, when the Dutch closed the Scheldt to ships other than their own, Antwerp was Belgium's main port and commercial centre. The Protestant leanings of the inhabitants, however, brought down the wrath of the Spanish King Philip II, who eventually forced all Protestants to leave and incorporated it into the Spanish Netherlands. One of the worst Spanish excesses was the massacre of 8,000 citizens in 1576 after Philip's army mutinied over bad conditions. It took almost 200 years before the city began to recover its former status. During World War II it was heavily damaged by V1 and V2 rockets after it had already been liberated. Some 3,000 people were killed and 20,000 buildings destroyed.

Many new docks were built after the war and the port continues to expand relentlessly. In the case of Antwerp appearances are quite deceptive. To the outsider the city looks rather seedy and run-down like many ports; at the same time, its bohemian atmosphere and proximity to Holland make it a lively cultural centre. Antwerp has many fine museums, the most popular being the home of Rubens. The zoo also has an international reputation, although it is threatened with closure. Antwerp also has an international airport at Deurne 4 miles/6 km to the east of the city centre with daily flights to England.

Going east of Antwerp there is the area known as the Kempen/Campine, originally a desolate area of sandy heaths, marshes and forests considered almost worthless for agriculture until it was developed by religious communities in the Middle Ages. The Kempen still has considerable forest cover, but not many sites of great historical interest. The town of Geel, 15 miles/25 km east of Antwerp has had a worldwide reputation for innovation in the care of the mentally ill since the thirteenth century, when the church of St Dymphna became a centre of pilgrimage for those seeking relief from insanity. Dymphna was a sixth-century Irish princess who fled to Geel to escape her deranged incestuous father. Unfortunately her father caught up with her and beheaded her. The local community took mentally-ill pilgrims into their homes thus establishing the idea of community care when most mad people were outcasts. The people of Geel still look after the mentally ill within the national public health system. Towards the Dutch border, 6 miles/10 km east of Geel, is Mol, the home of Belgium's nuclear research programme.

On the southern edge of the province of Antwerp, halfway to Brussels, is the historical city of Mechelen (often known by its French name of Malines). Between 1473 and 1530 it was the administrative centre for the Holy Roman Empire's territories in the Netherlands. Margaret of Austria, the aunt of the future Emperor Charles V, built it up into a major religious and cultural centre. During the First World War its Cardinal-Archbishop, Cardinal Mercier, won worldwide respect for his resistance to the German occupiers. Along with Leuven, it is still the powerhouse of the Belgian Catholic faith. Most visitors will wish to visit the St Rombouts cathedral which dates in part to the thirteenth century. St Rombout was the eighth-century English missionary who first converted Mechelen to Christianity.

Limburg

Main tourist office: Lombardstraat 3, 3500 Hasselt; tel 011 22 22 35.
Main towns: Hasselt, St Truiden (St Trond), Tongeren, Genk, Heusden.
Limburg is Belgium's smallest province in surface area with 8% of the total and 7% of the population. Although it has some notable tourist attractions it is by far the least well known area of the country, a situation which the provincial government is trying hard to remedy. In earlier times the Duchy of Limburg was a major power in the Lowlands — hence the Dutch province of Limburg just across the border — but it was permanently partitioned after the 1830 revolt against the Dutch. The present province of Limburg roughly corresponds to the medieval County of Loon whose Count used to reside at Borgloon. The northern part of Belgian Limburg is a continuation of the Kempen, with sandy plains, moorlands and forests. The southern part, the Haspengouw (Hesbaye), is more fertile and undulating, with a large concentration of fruit-growing.

The provincial capital, Hasselt, is a modern town, notable as the centre of the Belgian *jenever* (gin) industry. To the northwest the racetrack at Zolder is sometimes the site of the Belgian Grand Prix and nearby is the holiday resort of Heusden. Southeast of Hasselt is the Roman town of Tongeren (Atuatuca Tongrorum), where the Romans were defeated in 54 BC during a brief revolt led by the Belgian chief Ambiorix. Tongeren was at different times destroyed by the Salian Franks, Norsemen, the Duke of Brabant and the French, but some parts of the fourth-century Roman wall and medieval fortifications can still be seen. West of Tongeren the town of St Truiden, founded in 655 by St Trudo, has substantial medieval remains and some significant late medieval frescoes.

Limburg is mostly Dutch-speaking but there are some French-speakers in the commune of Les Fourons/De Voeren, an enclave separated from the rest of Limburg by part of Liège. De Voeren has been the subject of bitter disputes since it elected a French-speaking mayor who refused to take an examination in Dutch. In 1986 this resulted in violent scenes in the national parliament and the fall of the government.

Brabant (North)

Main tourist office: Naamsestraat 1a, 3000 Leuven; tel 016 234 941.
Main towns: Leuven (Louvain), Tienen (Tirlemont), Halle (Hal), Vilvoorde.
Including the conurbation of Brussels, Brabant has 2.2 million inhabitants and covers 11% of the land area. It has now effectively split into three parts, with Brussels a separate region and the rest divided between the Flemish and Walloon executives. The provincial capital is still Brussels. North Brabant's most significant city is Leuven (often called Louvain by English-speakers) whose origins may well go back to Julius Caesar's time. It formed part of the Duchy of Brabant and was a prosperous cloth city in the thirteenth and fourteenth centuries. The university dating from 1425 became one of the leading institutions of learning in Europe in the early sixteenth century. Erasmus founded a college here in 1517 for the study of Latin, Greek and Hebrew but was driven out by religious intolerance. The university was closed down under Napoleon in 1797. The Dutch King Willem I refounded it as a secular college thus stirring up more unrest amongst the clerics, but it eventually re-emerged as a bilingual Catholic institution after independence. The university library was burnt out during both world wars and many unique volumes were lost. During the 1960s the Flemish community agitated for the university to become purely Dutch-speaking. In the end it split into two sections and a French-speaking university was established at Louvain-la-Neuve south of Brussels in 1970. The Koninklijke Universiteit Leuven is now a major centre for Flemish Catholic academics.

To the northeast of Leuven is the town of Aarschot, the centre of asparagus-growing in Belgium, and to the southeast Tienen (Tirlemont) where sugar is produced from locally-grown sugar-beet. West of Leuven, in the northern suburbs of Brussels, is the town of Vilvoorde, notorious for its prison where William Tyndale was burnt at the stake as a heretic in 1535 and where many other Protestants met their end. Nowadays it is more noted for its factories. West of Brussels is the agricultural region of the Pajottenland.

WALLONIA — THE FRENCH-SPEAKING REGION

Brabant — (South)

Main tourist office: Grande Place, 1400 Nivelles; tel 067 21 54 13.
Main towns: Nivelles, Wavre, Braine l'Alleud, Louvain-la-Neuve.
The south of Brabant shares much of the same history as the north. These days it is a fashionable area for wealthier locals and foreigners, with plenty of international schools. The landscape of rolling meadows dotted with small woods and châteaux makes it an attractive environment to live in.

Nivelles, on the way from Brussels to Charleroi was famous for its convent, founded in 650 AD by St Gertrude, daughter of the Merovingian king Pepin. Many of the city's medieval buildings were destroyed during World War II, including

St Gertrude's reliquary. One result of the bombing was to uncover the foundations of the earliest churches. Nivelles was also the birthplace of the sculptor Laurent Delvaux (1696-1778) whose pulpits adorn many Belgian churches.

For most foreigners the most important thing to see in this area is the site of the Battle of Waterloo. There are few actual physical remnants, and one would have to visit the museums and souvenir shops to understand much of what happened. The actual site is now just fields and farmhouses. The British contrived to build the biggest memorial, constructing an artificial hill with a lion on the top. In general, the Walloons took the side of Napoleon and the Flemings the British-Dutch-German side, and there is still some degree of rivalry between the souvenir shops. For Battle of Waterloo fanatics, there is a reconstruction of the battle once a year with a *son et lumière* show and fireworks.

Hainaut (Henegouwen)

Main tourist office: Grande Place 20, 7000 Mons; tel 065 33 55 80.
Main towns: Mons (Bergen), Charleroi, Tournai (Doornik), Mouscron, Ath (Aat).
The province of Hainaut, bordering France, makes up 12% of the land area and 13% of the population of Belgium. In early medieval times it was the County of Hainaut before becoming a Burgundian possession. One of the ruling family, Philippa of Hainaut (1314-69) married Edward III of England. Much of the province is still agricultural, while still having a heavy concentration of engineering industry. The coal-mining country of the Borinage near Mons inspired some of Vincent van Gogh's best early work. After unsuccessfully attempting missionary work amongst the miners in 1878-79 he decided to become a full-time painter.

The recorded history of the capital, Mons (population 90,000) goes back to the seventh century, although it may have been a staging post on a Roman road. It shared in the prosperity of other cloth-making towns as well as in their frequent wars. It was the site of one of the great opening battles of World War I, but then remained in German hands right up until Armistice Day. Nowadays it is well known as the command centre for NATO troops in Europe, which is actually located five miles away at Le Casteau. Several thousand Americans and other foreigners live in the area, and English is widely spoken.

For those looking for folklore, Binche, near Mons, is famous for its three-day Lenten festival, leading up to Ash Wednesday. For three days there are processions through the town, the last day being the most spectacular, when Gilles (clowns) dressed up in the national colours and huge white ostrich feather hats parade through the town throwing oranges at bystanders. You may also get hit with a pig's bladder if you fail to wear some kind of fancy dress.

Much the largest city in Hainaut is Charleroi (population 212,000), connected by motorway to Mons. Originally a mining village called Charnoy, it was made into a fortress by the Spanish in 1666 and named after King Charles II of Spain. It is significant as one of the centres of Belgium's traditional heavy industries. Along with mining and engineering, pottery and glass-making have always been important in Hainaut's prosperity and there is a glass museum here located in the Institut National du Verre. As a result of its smokestack pollution Charleroi is avoided by tourists. Because of the general decline of the local economy, houses are very cheap here.

Tournai (Doornik), on the way to Lille near the French border, is of exceptional historical interest, as the birthplace of Clovis, King of the Franks in AD 465. The tomb of King Childéric, who died in AD 481, was rediscovered untouched in 1653 with all its treasures. Tournai has always had a high reputation for its sculpture and metalwork, and was also important in early French literature.

Namur (Namen)

Main tourist office: Rue Notre Dame 3, 5000 Namur; tel 081 22 29 98.
Main towns: Namur, Dinant, Philippeville, Gembloux.
Namur province is relatively lightly populated, with 12% of the land area and 4% of the Belgian population. The Ardennes plateau begins here and extends through the provinces of Liège and Luxembourg, as well as through parts of France, Luxembourg and Germany. Namur is cut through by numerous rivers such as the Meuse, Sambre and Lesse and their tributaries, which have formed deep ravines amongst the forests, giving the region a wild, scenic beauty. Caves and grottos are another natural feature. Communications here are less developed than in neighbouring provinces and it is useful to have your own transport if you want to explore. Visitors are mostly attracted by the small towns perched on the sides of ravines and the numerous châteaux and churches. Restaurants and hotels are to be found here in abundance.

Chimay, near the French border, is famed for its dark beer brewed by Trappist monks. Otherwise the Meuse valley has always been famous for its metalwork, called Mosan. The north of the province is agricultural with sugar-refining carried on in Gembloux.

Namur, the provincial capital, lies at the confluence of the Sambre and the Meuse near the Brussels to Luxembourg motorway. Because of its fortified citadel it has suffered frequent damage from invaders. Although supposedly impregnable it fell to the Germans in three days in 1914, and was again bombed in World War II. The citadel is still very impressive, nevertheless. Many of the city's buildings are made from pink brick and date from the seventeenth and eighteenth centuries. In 1687 and 1708 edicts were issued forbidding the use of timber and thatch in building, so the town would not catch fire too easily.

17 miles/28 km south of Namur, built into a gorge on the river Meuse, is the tourist town of Dinant, which, like Namur, has a citadel and cable-car railway to the top. Dinant was also the scene of bitter fighting in both world wars. Apart from this it is notable as the birthplace of the inventor of the saxophone, Adolphe Sax. Gastronomes will find Dinant especially alluring. One local speciality is *couques*, a kind of gingerbread biscuit made in a fanciful wooden mould.

Liège (Luik)

Main tourist office: Féronstrée 92, 4000 Liège; tel 041 22 24 56.
Main towns: Liège, Verviers, Waremme, Huy, Spa.
The province of Liège, bordering on Holland and Germany, comprises 12.6% of the land-area and 10% of the population of Belgium. Surrounded by rich deposits of lead, zinc, iron and coal, the capital city, Liège, developed into a centre for steel and weapon making from the twelfth century onwards. While the steel industry is only a shadow of its former self, non-ferrous metals and mechanical engineering continue to prosper in the region. In the east of Liège the textile industry still lives on around Verviers.

Liège province was historically unique in Belgium, in that it remained independent under the Prince-Bishops of Liège until the time of Napoléon. The title Prince-Bishop was first bestowed on Bishop Notger in 980 by the German Emperor Otto I, in recognition of the military and economic power of Liège. The independence and neutrality of Liége were respected by the Burgundians and

Austrians but came to an end in 1794 when French revolutionaries expelled the Prince-Bishop and razed the great Gothic cathedral of St Lambert to the ground. The palace of the Prince-Bishops still stands; the nearby site of the cathedral is now being excavated for archaeological remains.

Liège still retains a great deal of original charm, with its wide boulevards and open-air cafés. It is also a major cultural centre. The composer César Franck, the writer Georges Simenon, and the painter René Magritte all came from here.

33 km/20 miles to the southwest is the historical town of Huy, built into a cliffside on the river Meuse. Huy's romantic past and picturesque streets make it one of Belgium's prime tourist spots. English visitors will be glad to know that William the Conqueror's, otherwise William the Bastard's mother, Arlette, was born here. The First Crusade was started from here by one Peter the Hermit.

The highest area of Belgium, the Hautes Fagnes (German Hohes Venn), the High Fens, is in the east of Liège province, on the German border. The German-speaking towns of Eupen and Malmédy are also in this province and are worth visiting. Nearby is the town of Spa, which gave its name to all the other towns named Spa, and the racing circuit of Spa-Francorchamps.

Luxembourg (Luxemburg)

Main tourist office: Place Leopold, 6700 Arlon; tel 063 21 63 60.
Main towns: Arlon, Bastogne, Libramont, Neufchâteau.
Luxembourg (not to be confused with the Grand Duchy) is by far the largest and also the most sparsely populated province of Belgium, with 14% of the land area and 2% of the population. The ancient Ardennes forest extends over the whole province, and has some of Belgium's scenic rivers, attracting campers and hikers. Many outsiders are also attracted by the province's historical associations. Although rail links are somewhat limited, there are good roads to most places. The far south of the province, known as La Gaume, or the Belgian Lorraine, is a tobacco-growing region. The Abbey of Orval, near the town of Bouillon on the French border, was the subject of a national effort to rebuild it in 1926, after it had been left devastated by the French Revolution for over a century. It is now well-known for its beer.

The provincial capital, Arlon is relatively small (22,000 inhabitants), but particularly significant as one of the major Roman settlements in Belgium. Remains dating back to the 2nd century A.D. can still be seen.

During the medieval period the Duchy of Luxembourg extended much further to the west and south than it does today, and was linked to the Holy Roman Empire. In 1443 Luxembourg was bought by Philip the Good of Burgundy and the region then shared much the same history as the rest of Belgium. After the Napoleonic wars Luxembourg lost all its territories to the east of the Mosel and Our rivers and was compensated with parts of the Duchy of Bouillon and the Prince-Bishopric of Liège in Belgium. Luxembourg was placed under the Dutch King Willem I, but was then split into two in 1839, with the French-speaking west becoming the present-day Belgian province of Luxembourg, and the more Germanic east staying under the Dutch crown until 1890.

40 km/25 miles north of Arlon, still right by the border of the Grand Duchy is the town of Bastogne, the site of the famous stand of the 101st Airborne Division against the encircling Germans during the Battle of the Bulge in December 1944. The area is popular with American tourists visiting memorials to the 76,000 Americans who died in the battle.

Brussels Region (Bruxelles/Brussel)

Main tourist office: Hôtel de Ville, Grande Place, 1000 Brussels; tel 02 513 89 40.
Brussels, with almost 1,000,000 inhabitants, is not only the capital of Belgium
and the administrative centre of both language communities, but also houses the
European Commission and the headquarters of NATO. As a result, many more
international organizations have set up offices in Brussels, bringing thousands of
expatriate workers along with them.

Brussels began as a small village on an island in the middle of the marshy river
Senne, hence its early name, Broekzele, the village in a marsh. In 979 a fortress
was built on the island, for which reason Brussels celebrated its millennium in
1979. Eventually the inhabitants drained the marsh and started to build their houses
up the hillside to where the Palace of Justice stands today.

At first a small staging post on the road from Ghent to Cologne, Brussels
developed into a town under the Dukes of Brabant, and eventually was made the
capital of the Spanish Netherlands in the sixteenth century. Louis XIV devastated
the city in 1695, but many new and magnificent buildings took the place of what
was lost. As the capital of Belgium, Brussels was beautified with parks and wide
boulevards, and the river Senne was filled in. In recent times a metro system has
been built. From an architectural point of view, Brussels is not especially attractive,
except for its justly famous Grande Place. Most new buildings have been put up
without much regard for their surroundings, resulting in an unaesthetic mess.
Brussels has a large number of art nouveau buildings, the most unfortunate example
being the national cathedral, the Koekelberg. A significant landmark is the
Berlaymont Building which houses the European Commission with its 10,500
employees. This remarkably undistinguished building is due to be torn down after
it was discovered to contain an excessive amount of asbestos. Until its replacement
is finished EC workers will be scattered in different offices around Brussels.

Apart from its national and international organizations, Brussels is also the
business capital of Belgium, with the Bourse (stock market) and the National Bank
located here. For the visitor there are many museums and restaurants. The real
heart and soul of Brussels, however, is very difficult to find. The old working
class areas, with their picturesque Flemish dialect, have been replaced by immigrant
ghettos, where you are more likely to find Spanish, Turkish or Arabic as the main
language. The French-speakers have also been displaced to some extent by an influx
of Dutch-speaking workers. At the present time, some 25% of the population are
foreigners, with the proportion rising to 35% in the central commune. EC nationals
make up 48% of the foreigners in the Brussels conurbation. Of the Belgian
inhabitants, about 20% are Dutch-speakers, and 80% French-speakers. The status
of Brussels has long been a bone of contention. It is now an autonomous region,
while the interests of its two language groups are looked after by their respective
communities.

For job-seekers, Brussels is an obvious place to consider, but it must be borne
in mind that Brussels is by far the most expensive place to live in Belgium. Unless
you are on a high income, a large part of your salary could go on your rent. The
charm of Brussels is less immediately apparent than that of many other Belgian
towns. It does have the advantage of being relatively small compared to other
European capitals, while being more cosmopolitan than any of them.

Residence and Entry Regulations

The Current Position

With the coming of the Single Market from 1993 and continuing moves towards a federal Europe, it might seem that this chapter could soon be irrelevant. The Single Market allows all EC nationals freedom of movement and residence in the EC, but of course this does not mean that there will be no regulations governing EC nationals who wish to live and work in another EC country.

In the case of Belgium, EC citizens receive the kind of favourable treatment that one would expect, even if there is still a degree of red tape to go through. The law states that no work permit is required. As regards residence, there is a graduated series of stages going from just being a temporary visitor, through permanent resident, right up to becoming a Belgian citizen. While the authorities would no doubt like to put off the destitute and the unemployable, the EC guarantees your basic right to live in Belgium. Those from EFTA countries (Austria, Finland, Iceland, Norway, Sweden and Switzerland) also receive favourable treatment. For most other non-EC citizens without very good reasons for being in Belgium the situation is more difficult. Since 1974 immigration from most countries has been officially 'suspended'.

EC Nationality

The right to live and work in Belgium is extended to all EC citizens, including Greece, Spain and Portugal, who are now full members. EFTA citizens have residence rights but no automatic right to work.

It is not sufficient to be the holder of a passport of an EC country: you must also possess right of abode in that country. This will be indicated in the passport, in the case of a UK national, by the wording 'British Citizen' or, for passports issued prior to 1983, 'holder has the right of abode in the UK'. Those who fulfil these criteria should follow the procedure for EC nationals shown below; those who fulfil the first but not the second requirement must follow the procedure for non-EC nationals described below. Anyone in any doubt about their status should check with the passport authorities in their own country or with the local Belgian Embassy's visa section.

Passports

In order to take up residence in Belgium a UK national must have a full valid passport. A visitor's passport or an excursion pass is sufficient when visiting

Belgium for up to three months, but not to work or to take up permanent residence, which is defined as a stay longer than three months. Nationals of The Netherlands, Luxembourg, Germany, Italy and France require only their national identity card. Note that a British visitor's passport is not an identity card as far as other EC countries are concerned.

Entry and Residence for EC Nationals

It is not necessary for EC nationals to apply for a visa or other permission before going to Belgium with a view to living or working there. Such persons can enter Belgium as tourists and then take the necessary steps to change their status to resident. If you wish to do voluntary work with a recognized institution for less than three months there is no need to register with the authorities.

EC nationals who know that they are going to stay in Belgium for more than three months for any purpose must register within eight days at the local town hall (*maison communale/stadhuis*). There are 589 communes in Belgium with their own maison communale: the names are listed at the beginning of the Yellow Pages for the relevant area. In the past there were over 2,000 communes, which were reduced to the present number in 1977. Large cities have generally absorbed many former communes, now renamed 'districts' or 'localities', with their former town halls still providing some services to local residents. Foreigners need to go to the main town hall, and ask for the 'Aliens' bureau' (*Bureau Administratif des Etrangers/Administratief Vreemdelingenbureau* or *Dienst Vreemdelingenzaken*).

When registering at the town hall, you should take your passport and three passport-sized photographs. At this point you will be placed on the Aliens' Register (*Registre des Etrangers/Vreemdelingenregister*) and issued with 'mauve card Model B' (*Attestation of Immatriculation*), which is valid for three months and can be renewed for a further period of three months. This card is to be used until one receives permanent resident status and applies to those staying between three months and a year who wish to work. You may be asked to produce an attestation of work signed by your employer to prove you can support yourself. There is a small charge to pay, and you may be asked to give fingerprints.

Once you have a fixed abode and a regular income, and if you decide that you would like to stay in Belgium for more than a year, you should then move on to apply for a blue card or 'EC Residence card' (*Carte de sejour de ressortissant d'un Etat-membre de la CEE/Verblijfskaart van onderdaan van een Lid-staat der EEG*) which is valid for five years. This confirms your right to stay in Belgium (which you always had in any case). If your employment is permanent, then one could apply for this card after three months. In any case, the law states that the card must be issued to you within six months of your application. It is then renewable indefinitely.

If you know in advance that you are going to spend a year or more working in Belgium you have to apply for a 'blue card' at the outset, taking along your employment contract or an attestation of work signed by your employer, or, if self-employed, documents and diplomas required for your profession. While you are waiting for your blue card, you will be issued with the mauve one mentioned above.

Acquiring the blue card means that you have been placed on the Population Register of the local commune and that you have permanent resident status (*Etablissement/Vestiging*). In general, you must continue to be gainfully employed and able to support yourself. The commune must always be informed if you move your place of residence and you will have to re-register with your new commune. If you decide to leave Belgium for more than a year, you must inform the commune how long you intend to be away for. Any doubts can be clarified by the immigration service offices shown below.

EC nationals who go to Belgium to study will be issued with a mauve card, which is then renewed for as long as they are in Belgium. EC citizens not intending to work or study in Belgium can remain in Belgium as long as they have some means of support. They can go on to the Population Register of the commune, and are given another type of identity card — the 'yellow card' — which is also issued to non-EC dependants of EC nationals working in Belgium.

Entry on a Self-employed Basis

EC citizens have the right to self-employed status in Belgium. If the area you wish to work in is one where trade unions are very active, for example building, then obstacles may be put in your way. Those in the professions will have to deal with the relevant professional body in order to become established in Belgium. In order to obtain a residence permit, a self-employed person must show that they are making social security payments. Where necessary they must also be registered on the Commercial Register and with the VAT authorities.

Those from outside the EC planning to be self-employed in Belgium need to obtain a Professional Card (*Carte professionnelle pour étrangers/Beroepskaart voor vreemdelingen*) from the Ministry of the Self-Employed (see below) via the Belgian Consulate in their country. This procedure can last up to a year. Applicants are only likely to be successful if they are planning to do work which could not be done by a Belgian or EC national.

Entry and Work Permits for Non-EC Nationals

Non-EC nationals may require a visa to enter Belgium as tourists. If they intend to stay in Belgium more than three months they will have to apply for an 'Authorization of Provisional Sojourn' or APS (*Autorisation de Sejour Provisoire/Machtiging tot Voorlopig Verblijf*) before entering Belgium. The applicant has to supply evidence that they do not have a criminal record, undergo a medical examination, and show that they can support themselves in Belgium. Once in Belgium, they can go on to the Register of Aliens and will obtain the provisional 'Orange card model A' (Attestation of Immatriculation) or the 'white card' known as the CIRE in French (*Certificat d'Inscription dans le Registre des Etrangers* or Certificate of Inscription in the Register of Aliens) or BIVR in Dutch, which is a 'Title of residence' valid for one year and renewable thereafter. Both these cards show that you have gone on to the Register of Aliens. Non-EC nationals working in Belgium, or residing in Belgium for a certain period of time can apply to go on to the Population Register and, if successful, will obtain the 'yellow card' mentioned before. Citizens of Norway, Sweden, Finland, Iceland, Switzerland, Liechtenstein and Monaco do not require an APS and can make arrangements within Belgium.

According to a law of 1985, which is still in force, the six central communes of Brussels (see below) and the City of Liège will only register Belgians and EC nationals. There may be exceptions.

It should be noted that it is difficult to sign a lease or to get public services without an identity card (blue, white or yellow card). It is also important to note that the Belgian authorities attach a great deal of importance to one's birth certificate, so it is essential to have this to hand. It is advisable to know the date and place of birth of one's parents and grandparents as well, something you are likely to be asked sooner or later. Whichever card you are issued with, it should be kept on your person at all times. If you fail to provide identification when asked by a police officer you may be detained at a police station until your identity has been established. Police officers are not allowed to take away your identity card.

Work Permits: There are three classes of work permit (*Permis de travail/Arbeidskaart*) in Belgium: Work Permits A, B and C. Work Permit A is the most favourable in that it permits the worker to work in any sector of the economy, change jobs, and is for an unlimited period, unless the worker leaves the country for more than one year. Work Permit A is granted to long-term residents from non-EC countries and to non-EC dependants of EC workers. Work Permit B applies to non-EC nationals, including the European countries mentioned above. Permit B is valid for only one employer and that employer must obtain an 'Authorization of Employment' (*Autorisation d'occupation/Arbeidsvergunning*) in advance. Workers from the six countries with bilateral labour agreements with Belgium — Algeria, Malta, Morocco, Tunisia, Turkey and Yugoslavia are given Work Permit B if they are offered a job. Work Permit C applies to non-EC nationals the nature of whose work involves multiple employers, such as musicians and film crews. The basic principle for foreigners is that you must have a work permit before you can get a residence permit. Journalists, seamen, flight crews and some other categories are exempted from the above restrictions.

If you believe that you need a work permit, the relevant application forms can be obtained from any Sub-regional Employment Office (see Chapter Six, *Employment*).

Nationality and Citizenship

Foreign nationals can, after at least five years, apply for Belgian citizenship, although this would serve little purpose for anyone from the EC. Children born of foreign parents in Belgium take the father's nationality. Foreign nationals with children born in Belgium should register the birth with their local embassy/consulate. A child with one Belgian parent can have dual nationality (as long as they apply for the nationality of the other country) but is treated as a Belgian citizen by the authorities, so that they become liable for military service between the ages of 18 and 33. The only way to avoid this is to go through the lengthy process of revoking one's Belgian nationality.

Although foreign residents do not have the vote, some Brussels communes have elected or appointed foreigners' councils which represent their interests with the local government, an idea first pioneered in Liège in the 1960s. These are known as *Conseils Communals Consultatifs des Immigrés* (Foreign Residents' Consultative Councils). In some places they run information services and assist immigrants who are in dispute with the immigration authorities. In the future it is also expected that foreign residents will be able to vote for commune councillors.

Summary

While the rules governing EC residents in Belgium are supposedly becoming more relaxed in the run-up to 1993 and the Single Market, their actual application can vary considerably between different Belgian communes and it is best to be prepared for this. Town halls in big cities are used to dealing with aliens and will certainly have some English-speaking staff. The Belgian Embassy can also provide you with their leaflet on living and working in Belgium.

Once resident in Belgium, it is essential to register with your local Embassy or Consulate. This enables UK authorities to keep you up to date with new information for overseas residents and to trace you in the event of an emergency. You also need to make sure that your passport remains valid while you are abroad. Consulates do not act as employment bureaux and are not a source of general help and advice.

Useful Addresses

Belgian Embassies
103 Eaton Square, London SW1W 9AB; tel 071-235 5422. Consular Section: tel 071-235 5144; fax 071-259 6213.
Shrewsbury House, 2 Shrewsbury Rd., Ballsbridge, Dublin 4, Eire; tel 01-69 20 82. 3330 Garfield St N.W., Washington D.C., 20008 USA; tel 202-333 6900.

Foreign Embassies in Belgium:
British Embassy: Rue d'Arlon 85, 1040 Brussels; tel 02 287 62 11; fax 02 287 63 60. Consular Section: tel 02 287 62 11 fax 02 287 63 20.
British Consulate: Korte Klarenstraat 7, 2000 Antwerpen; tel 03 232 69 40; fax 03 231 69 71.
British Consulate: Rue Beeckman 45, 4000 Liège; tel 041 23 58 32.
Irish Embassy: Rue du Luxembourg 19, 1040 Brussels; tel 02 513 66 33.
US Embassy: Bvd. du Régent 27, 1000 Brussels; tel 02 513 38 30.

Others:
City of Brussels Commune Administration Centre: Aliens' Bureau, Bvd. Anspach 6; tel 02 217 39 35 or 02 217 42 07.

Brussels communes only registering EC nationals, and the telephone numbers of their Aliens' Bureaux:
Anderlecht: Place du Conseil 1, 1070 Brussels; tel 02 523 62 80.
Forest/Vorst: Rue du Curé 2, 1190 Brussels; tel 02 370 22 11.
Molenbeek Saint Jean/Sint-Jans-Molenbeek: Rue du Comte de Flandre 20, 1080 Brussels; tel 02 423 26 72 or 02 423 26 73.
Saint Gilles/Saint Gillis: Place M. van Meenen, 1060 Brussels; tel 02 536 02 11.
Saint-Josse-Ten-Noode/Sint Joost-Ten-Noode: Av. de l'Astronomie 13, 1030 Brussels; tel 02 220 26 11.
Schaarbeek: Place Colignon, 1030 Brussels; tel 02 243 88 12.

For Professional Cards and information on self-employment:
Ministère des Classes Moyennes/Ministerie van Middenstand, World Trade Centre, Tower 2, Bvd. Emile Jacqmain 162, 1000 Brussels; tel 02 219 16 80.

Foreign Residents' Consultative Council:
Conseil Communal Consultatif des Immigrés, Bvd. Maurice Lemonnier 162, 1000 Brussels; tel 02 511 34 37.

Setting up Home

At the time of going to press, it seems that anti-European sentiment in the British government is as strong as ever. However, there is little sign of a corresponding antipathy on the part of British citizens, many of whom are voting with their feet by setting up home in another EC country, be it France, Italy, Spain, or the Benelux countries. Britons have been migrating to Belgium ever since the Battle of Waterloo, in far larger numbers than one might imagine. A significant group of British expatriates still in Belgium is made up of ex-servicemen and their dependants who moved there at the end of World War II. At present an estimated 23,000 Britons reside in Belgium, a substantial number in relation to Belgium's total population.

The areas where foreigners are mostly likely to buy property are those within easy commuting distance of major cities, which, given Belgium's small size, covers about half the country. Property in Belgium still looks cheap from the other side of the Channel, and could be a shrewd investment as long as the European Commission stays in Brussels, which seems likely. In the past few years, property prices in Brussels have soared to undreamt-of levels by Belgian standards. During 1991 prices remained stable, and the average property now costs about BF3,500,000 (£56,000). The average figure for apartments is BF2,434,000 (£42,000). In less fashionable locations within 30 miles of Brussels it is still possible to buy a flat or terrace house in good condition for less than £15,000. There is also an active market in properties on the Belgian coast for holidaymakers. For property prices in Belgium, see Tables 1 and 2 below.

While property prices may look cheap, potential buyers should be aware of the particular conditions of the market in Belgium. In the first place, estate agents in Britain do not deal with Belgian property, since the Belgian property market is generally buoyant and does not need to look for foreign buyers. The buyer is therefore obliged to go to Belgium and to deal with local estate agents and/or a notary (*notaire/notaris*). A notary is essential for the registration of the house purchase and for a mortgage agreement as well. In Belgium, estate agents are not regulated by the government and do not have to pass any kind of examination in order to conduct a business. If dealing with an estate agent it is advisable to check if they belong to the *Confédération Immobilière Belge (CIB)*, the association of Belgian real estate agents, who will mediate in a dispute.

In many cases you will find that the house sale is being handled by a notary on behalf of the seller. You should by all means engage your own notary to look after your interests. This will not add to your costs, since you would have to pay a notary's fees anyway. In any case, you will need professional advice; otherwise you could end up paying over the odds.

There are now a large number of British property companies in Brussels dealing with offices and investment property. Limiting your search to English-speaking estate agents or to the English press is a doubtful strategy, since you will not have a wide choice of properties to look at. The best source of properties, especially at the bottom end of the market, is the local press (see below).

If you intend to buy or invest in property in Belgium, it would be a good idea to obtain a copy of *A Practical Guide to Property Purchase and Arranging Mortgage Finance in Belgium*, published by Michael Kingshott & Associates, 22 rue de Hocaille, 1390 Archennes, Belgium (tel/fax (0)10 84 42 50), which can be paid for with a UK cheque for £14.00. The above company will provide assistance not only with house purchase and mortgages, but also with other investments in Belgium. Another possibility is to ask a reputable relocation company to handle matters.

When looking at property prices it is essential to take into account the costs of registration (12.5%) and a notary (a fixed fee of about 1-4%). Mortgages also attract legal fees and duties. If you buy at auction the notary's fees will be twice as high as with a normal sale, and you will be obliged to complete the purchase and arrange a mortgage within one month. Buying a new property entails paying 19.5% VAT. If you build a property yourself, labour and materials are also subject to 19.5% VAT, and there is the added complication of planning permission.

At the time of going to press the property market in Britain is in the doldrums, which means that anyone trying to sell their UK home in order to move to Belgium will be having a hard time. Most expatriates rent properties first, and as many of them are on fixed-term contracts in Belgium, the question of buying a property does not arise. If you are thinking of settling in Belgium permanently then paying rent could be money down the drain, and the difference between the price of your UK home and the one in Belgium could generate a substantial amount of capital as well.

How do the Belgians live?

The family unit is still very much in evidence in Belgium; stastically at least, the average Belgian lives in his or her own house — 61% of dwellings are owner-occupied and the number is still increasing. Houses are either detached or terraced — semi-detached houses are not all that common. Like the British, Belgians like a considerable amount of personal space, and houses are large by our standards. Almost 75% of houses are occupied by just one family, and the rest are mostly apartments.

The number of occupants per property at the moment stands at 2.6 and is tending downwards, largely because the divorce rate has gone up from 8% of marriages to 30% since 1970. There is generally no shortage of housing, and accommodation for single people is quite readily available. Unfurnished accommodation here means

unfurnished — you will probably have to buy your own cooker and fridge as well as everything else. Mobility is even further restricted by the strict nature of rental agreements. The average Belgian tends therefore to stay in one place, and to invest a considerable amount in equipping their flat or house.

Belgians are rather houseproud by our standards, as you will notice when you are invited to a Belgian home. A visit to a Belgian home has a certain formality which may surprise Britons. Dropping in on people unexpectedly is considered a bit eccentric. In apartment blocks people tend to keep themselves to themselves, with the result that single elderly people can be very isolated. On the plus side apartment blocks often have a live-in *concierge*, whose task is to keep an eye on things, as well as to deal with the dustbins and clean communal areas.

Second homes or holiday homes are a popular institution with the better-off; many Walloons own apartments on the coast. For others their second home may be ·a short drive away.

Useful Addresses

Estate Agents in Belgium:

Ageurop 92: Albert Biesmanslaan 24, 1560 Hoeilaart; tel 02 657 44 32. Property rental and purchase. Mortgages.

Centrale Informatique Immobilière: Grande Place 12A, 1000 Brussels; tel 02 512 16 24.

Delta Consultants: Av. de Bois de Satins, 1200 Brussels; tel 02 770 41 51; fax 02 770 31 57.

Rainbow Properties: Av. de Tervuren 37, 1040 Brussels; tel 02 732 37 24.

Useful Publications

De Gazet van Antwerpen: Antwerp daily.
De Nieuwe Gazet: Antwerp daily with property advertisements on Saturdays.
De Streekkrant: Free weekly in Flemish towns.
La Libre Belgique: French-language daily with property section on Thursdays.
Le Soir: French daily.
The Bulletin: English weekly available in Brussels newsagents.
Vlan: Free weekly published in Brussels and Wallonia.

Table 1 — House Prices in City Centres and Urban Areas (in Belgian Francs)

	65 sq m (1 bedroom)	130 sq m (2 bedrooms)	250 sq m (3 bedrooms)
Antwerp (centre)	1,233,000	2,030,000	2,809,000
Antwerp (urban area)	1,171,000	1,757,000	2,330,000
Brugge (centre)	1,357,000	2,207,000	2,699,000
Brugge (urban area)	1,300,000	1,876,000	2,475,000
Brussels-Anderlecht	2,170,000	2,681,000	3,178,000
Brussels-Schaarbeek	2,067,000	2,917,000	3,423,000
Brussels-Watermaal/Woluwe	2,800,000	3,565,000	4,000,000
Charleroi (centre)	615,000	885,000	1,050,000
Gent (centre)	635,000	1,337,000	1,967,000
Gent (urban area)	643,000	1,267,000	1,944,000
Liège (urban area)	795,000	1,170,000	1,425,000
Mons (centre)	837,000	957,000	1,661,000
Mons (urban area)	700,000	852,000	1,240,000
Oostende (centre/urban area)	1,353,000	1,856,000	2,469,000

Figures from *Waarde der onroerende goederen — April 1991* publ. An-Hyp Spaarbank.

Table 2 — Apartment Prices in Urban Areas

	Studios/1-bedroom	2-bedrooms
Antwerp	1,035,000	1,710,000
Brugge	1,309,000	2,713,000
Brussels-Anderlecht	1,700,000	2,700,000
Brussels-Schaarbeek	1,900,000	2,800,000
Brussels-Watermaal/Woluwe	3,000,000	4,000,000
Gent	1,305,000	1,780,000
Mons	1,125,000	2,205,000
Oostende	1,598,000	2,385,000

Figures from *Waarde der onroerende goederen — April 1991* publ. An-Hyp Spaarbank and from local press.

Finance

Mortgages with Belgian Banks

Taking out a mortgage (*hypothèque/hypotheek*) is just as common in Belgium as it is in Britain as a way to purchase property. At the time of writing Belgian mortgage interest rates are between 8.5% and 12%, rather lower than in Britain, but one should always bear in mind that currency fluctuations can affect the relative value of your house abroad and what you have to repay.

Mortgages in Belgium come in many shapes and sizes. Building societies, as such, do not exist in Belgium. Savings banks (*banque d'épargne/spaarbank*) are similar institutions and generally offer the best mortgage loan terms. If the savings bank you deal with is linked to an insurance company, however, they may try to impose expensive mortgage protection insurance on you. The best-known savings banks are An-Hyp, Ippa, Argenta and Spaarkrediet. You can also deal with ordinary high-street banks such as the BBL, Générale de Banque, Paribas and Kredietbank, but generally their interest rates are less competitive than those of savings banks.

It is also possible to take out a mortgage which is linked to an endowment or life insurance policy (known as a *vie mixte* policy in Belgium). This type of mortgage entails paying interest on what you borrow and life insurance premiums until you retire, whereupon the sum borrowed is repaid. The length of time you have to pay interest (even though the interest might seem low) and the high life insurance premiums in Belgium make this a poor option. Borrowing money from an insurance company for house purchase is not advisable in any event, as you will be obliged to buy house insurance and mortgage protection insurance at a high premium from the firm that is lending you the money to buy your property.

Useful addresses

Michael Kingshott & Associates: Rue de Hocaille 22, 1390 Archennes, Brabant; tel 010 84 42 50. Advice on mortgages, real estate and international investments.
Sohr & Son: Av. de l'Avenir 3, 1640 Rhode St Genèse, Brussels; tel 02 380 9360; fax 02 380 94 20. Specialize in arranging mortgages and house insurance for foreigners.

Registration and Mortgage Costs

Under Belgian law mortgages are registered for a 15-year term. If your mortgage runs for more than 15 years then a new registration fee will have to be paid. It is perfectly possible to negotiate a mortgage for a much shorter term, even as short as four years, but if you sell your house or want to pay in full before the mortgage term is up you will incur considerable 'withdrawal fees' (*frais mainlevée*) and a penalty of three to six months' interest on the remaining capital. You will therefore be saving money if you decide on the period of the mortgage (preferably less than 15 years) and then stick to it. If you expect to pay off your mortgage early, then it is best to negotiate a no-penalty clause if you can.

A mortgage agreement between a house buyer and a bank must be registered by a notary and this registration is subject to legal fees and taxes. Tax is levied at 1.3% of the amount borrowed while the notary's fees are on a sliding scale. On a loan of BF2,000,000 the registration tax and notary's fee will come to about 3% of the whole, but this amount decreases considerably for higher sums, down to about 1.8% on a loan of BF10,000,000. In addition a surveyor is often called in to value the property, thus adding at least BF3,500 to the cost of the mortgage. Some Belgian banks add on a negotiation fee of 0.5% payable when the sales agreement is signed. In some cases this fee may be deducted from the loan at the last minute, so that the customer ends up paying interest on money he or she has not received. Although this appears to be highly dishonest it is not illegal.

A major pitfall with Belgian mortgages concerns insurance. A condition of many Belgian mortgages is that you take out mortgage protection insurance with a Belgian insurance company. It is best to avoid paying high Belgian insurance premiums, either by taking out mortgage protection with a British life assurance company or finding a mortgage lender who does not demand insurance. These include An-Hyp, Spaarkrediet, Crédit Communal, CERA and the BBL.

Repayment Conditions

Most banks will now lend up to 100% of the value of the property, and some will go up to 125%. Properties are sometimes valued at the price they would fetch if sold privately (*valeur vénale*) within six months, and sometimes at what they would fetch at auction (*valeur vente publique*) which effectively reduces the value by about 10%. The advantage of borrowing more than 100% of the value of the house is that all sales costs will then be covered. The disadvantage is that you will be obliged to pay very heavy insurance premiums.

The rate of repayment depends on the net monthly income of the individual or husband and wife, including investment income and family allowance payments. Repayments cannot exceed one-third of this figure. It is a standard practice to fix the interest rate on the mortgage for five years at the outset, and then to raise or lower the interest rate if there has been a change of more than 1% in the prevailing rate. Very often the interest rate for the entire term of the mortgage is fixed at the outset, which involves paying a somewhat higher rate, but could be worth considering if you think that interest rates are going to rise.

UK and Offshore Mortgages

It is extremely unusual for a British building society to lend money for the purchase of a property abroad. A number of people have managed to buy homes abroad by remortgaging or taking out a second mortgage on their UK property in order to pay for a property in cash in another country. The property owner should be aware that he or she is liable to lose some UK tax relief if a UK property is remortgaged and if part of the original loan was used for home improvements or capital raising.

The principle of offshore mortgages involves turning a property into a company, the shares of which are held by an offshore bank based in a tax haven such as Gibraltar or the Channel Islands as collateral against a mortgage. It is then possible to sell your property by confidentially transferring the shares in the company to a new owner, thus avoiding Belgian transfer taxes. In practice there seems to be little to be gained from such a scheme in view of the high administrative costs and the efficiency of the Belgian tax authorities. A more workable scheme would be to form a company in Belgium itself to buy a property if you can show that you are working from home in some way. Further details of this type of scheme can be found in Michael Kingshott's *Practical Guide to Property Purchase and Arranging Mortgage Finance in Belgium* mentioned above.

Purchasing and Conveyancing Procedures

Finding a Property

A major consideration for many expatriates is finding a house close to their children's school. Apart from this you also need to decide how close you want to be to the centre of town, given the parking difficulties in many Belgian towns. The further you are prepared to commute, which does not have to be that far, the more likely you are to find a cheap property. The best way of finding a place is to look in the local free newspapers which carry thousands of advertisements from real estate agents (*agence immobilière/makelaar*) and notaries. Although there are some British estate agents operating in Belgium, they generally only deal with commercial property or high-priced investment property; hence they will not be able to help you. Many Belgian estate agents speak English and are used to dealing with expatriates.

Professional Assistance

Whichever way you go about buying a property in Belgium, the services of a notary are obligatory. Notaries are listed under 'Liberal professions' (*Professions libérales/Vrije beroepen*) in the Yellow Pages; someone who speaks and writes English is evidently going to be the most useful. There is also the regulatory body for notaries, the Fédération Royale des Notaires de Belgique (Rue de la Montagne 30-32, Brussels; tel 02 511 90 73). The notary's fees are fixed by law and are on a sliding scale depending on the value of the purchase. It is important to remember that the notary is also a kind of tax collector. During the property sale he will make a fiscal search, and if it becomes clear that either the buyer or the seller is liable for back taxes these sums will be seized by the notary at the moment of sale. If you are aware that you owe any taxes you should not buy or sell any property.

In addition to dealing with a notary you will also need to have the property surveyed. There are three organizations of quantity surveyors located in Brussels:

Union Belge des Géomètres des Immobilières: tel 02 218 07 13.
Association des Experts Belges: tel 02 520 7815.
Fédération Royale des Géomètres Experts Indépendants: tel 02 356 81 07.

Charges start at BF3,500, depending on the thoroughness of the survey.

The Compromis de Vente

The most common way to buy is through personal sale — *gré à gré/uit de hand.* It is also possible to buy a house at public auction, although this entails high costs at the outset.

House prices are negotiable. You can make an offer below the asking price and perhaps save a considerable amount of money. Once agreement is reached, the buyer and seller will sign the *compromis de vente* (sales agreement), which is then legally binding on both parties. The plus side of this is that the seller cannot then withdraw if they receive a higher offer: gazumping is impossible. On the down side, the buyer must be absolutely sure that they want the property before signing anything binding. If you change your mind you could be liable for 10 to 15% of the purchase price.

If you intend to apply for a mortgage it may be wise to append a clause to the sales agreement stating that the sale is conditional on obtaining mortgage finance. If you then fail to obtain a loan you may be able to withdraw from the sale without penalty. The agreement usually allows you up to four months to arrange finance. Normally, you will have to pay a ten per cent deposit to the seller, but this is not an inflexible rule.

If you have doubts about the purchase or the mortgage, it is possible, for a small fee, to purchase an option on the property at an agreed price. If you then pull out, you will only lose the fee for the option.

Registration Tax

The high level of registration tax (*droit d'enregistrement /registratierecht*) on house purchases is a major factor in discouraging property speculation in Belgium. Most property purchases are subject to a tax rate of 12.5%. New property is subject to VAT at 19.5%. If you build a property yourself, you pay 19.5% VAT on the labour and materials, as well as 12.5% on the land. Because of these taxes, the seller sometimes takes some of the purchase price under the counter, but this is a potentially dangerous procedure for foreigners. The Belgian authorities will levy tax on what they consider to be the real worth of the property if they suspect any irregularity, and any cash payment made to the seller could be lost for good.

If a foreign purchaser has reason to believe that they may sell the property again within five years, then it is possible to recover part of the registration tax. Doing this with a new property is far more difficult, however. Another possibility is to buy an older house and renovate it, in which case the registration tax is only 6% and VAT on the renovation, labour and materials 6% as well. For this to work, the property must be over 20 years old, and the *revenu cadastral* (a hypothetical annual rental value used to calculate property tax) below BF30,000 (£480).

Buying an Apartment

Apartments may be an attractive proposition, but it is important to be aware of the annual charges levied by the managers of the building. These can cover communal hot water, heating, cleaning of corridors and staircases, lift operating expenses, and maintenance of the building and gardens. Difficulties can arise with other owners of apartments in the same building. It is also necessary to have a third-party insurance policy which all the owners contribute to, in case of accidents occurring in the communal space.

The following table shows the registration tax and legal fees on the cost of property purchases:

Purchase Price BF Mill.	Registration Tax 12.5% BF	Notary's Fees BF	Total Tax and Legal Fees BF
1.0	125,000	31,920	166,000
1.5	187,500	41,610	239,500
2.0	250,000	49,163	309,500
2.5	312,500	54,863	377,500
3.0	375,000	58,140	443,500
4.0	500,000	63,840	574,500
5.0	625,000	69,540	705,500
6.0	750,000	75,240	836,500
7.0	875,000	80,940	967,000
8.0	1,000,000	86,640	1,098,000
9.0	1,125,000	92,910	1,241,500
10.0	1,250,000	98,040	1,359,500

Renting Property

Those who are employed by British or other foreign companies in Belgium will most probably have their accommodation arranged for them as part of their job package. In order to minimize the amount of time taken up with settling in, executives are often given the services of a relocation company. In the case of large companies there may be an in-house relocation department. If you are not in a position to use a relocator, you can easily find rented accommodation by looking in the newspapers mentioned for property purchases. English advertisements can be found in the weekly *The Bulletin*. Otherwise you can look for signs in windows saying *A Louer* (French) or *Te Huur* (Dutch), meaning 'To Rent', or notices in newsagents. The third possibility is to go to an estate agent (*agence immobilière/makelaar in onroerende goederen* or simply *makelaar*). In addition, there is now a computerized database of properties in Brussels which an estate agent may have access to. For a small fee your requirements can be fed in and a list of suitable properties will come out.

When looking at advertisements it is often difficult to understand the peculiar abbreviations in Belgium, which come in two languages of course. Firstly it is necessary to know if a property is furnished (*meublé/gemeubeld*) or not. Furnished property in Brussels is now becoming quite common. A further consideration is whether monthly 'charges' are included or not.

Useful Terms

French
appt/appartement: a flat with at least one bedroom.
bail loyer: rental agreement.
cave: cellar.
chf.maz./chauffage mazout: oil central heating.
ctre.chf./chff.centrale/chauffage centrale: central heating.
cuis.éq./cuisine équipé: kitchen with a sink and built-in cupboard.
cuis.sup.éq./cuisine super équipé: kitchen with cooker, fridge, dishwasher and
    more.
ent rén./entièrement rénové: completely renovated.
étg/étage: floor.
fermette: a house restored in a rustic style.
flat: flat with bed in living room and limited cooking facilities.
grenier: attic/loft.
pas de chgs/pas de charges: no monthly maintenance charges.
sdb/salle de bain: bathroom.
studio: very small studio flat; or a room to be hired by the hour, if there is a
    number after the word studio.
terr./terrace: terrace or balcony.
villa: a detached house in the countryside surrounded by a garden.

Dutch
bdk/badk/badkamer: bathroom.
cv/centraal verwarming: central heating.
cv mazout/centraal verwarming met mazout: oil central heating.
kamer: room.
kelder: cellar.
keuken: basic kitchen.
inger.keuken/ingeriefd keuken: kitchen equipped with cooker and fridge.
rijw./rijwoning: terraced house.
slk/slpk/slaapkamer: bedroom.
verdiep./verdieping: floor.
voll.vern./volledig vernieuwd: completely renovated.
zolder: attic.

Tenancy agreements

Finding a place to live is only the beginning of the intricate proce, a property. If you deal with estate agents you will probably find yours the same place several times. This is because the landlord does not use ι agent's services exclusively, but decides when an estate agent has found a .. You should on no account give any money to an estate agent — this is eι .ιrely the landlord's responsibility.

A landlord is legally obliged to provide you with habitable accommodation. Before a lease can be signed the parties must agree on the condition of the property, which requires an expert to perform an *état des lieux/staat van de huis* (state of the premises). This protects the tenant from having to pay for existing damage, but it also means that you may be forced to pay to bring the property back to its original condition. A lease with a clause requiring you to return the property to 'perfect' condition should be avoided.

The basic form of lease is now one of 9 years, or a so-called 3-6-9 year lease. According to the new law of 20 February 1991, a lease of indefinite duration is no longer permitted. The tenant pays a deposit of three months' rent. For expatriates it is important to have a so-called 'diplomatic clause' in the lease which allows you to break the rental agreement with three months' notice and the payment of an indemnity. If you give notice within a year, you lose three months' rent, in the second year, two months' rent, and in the third year, one month's rent. At the end of three years, it is possible to leave without paying any indemnity, if you give three months' notice. When you leave, damage will be paid for out of your deposit, and you will have to wait until all utilities and other outstanding bills are settled before your money is returned to you.

The owner can eject you with six months' notice if he can show that he needs the property for himself or his immediate family, or pays a large indemnity. Every three years the owner can undertake building work and ask you to leave with six months' notice. If the property passes to a new owner, that person is obliged to continue the lease in the same manner, as long as it is in a written form. The tenant or owner can have recourse to a court of law if there are repeated breaches of the rental agreement. In the first place, the tenant should send a registered letter (*recommandée*) to the owner detailing any complaints.

Any rental agreement of any complexity or duration should be in writing. The Belgian consumers' association supplies model leases as well as the booklet *Guide e la Location* telling you about clauses to watch out for (Union des Consommateurs, Rue de Hollande 13, 1060 Brussels; tel 02 536 64 11). This organization publishes invaluable monthlies such as *Test Achats* and *Budget et Droit* and will help non-members and members alike. Agreements in English are also valid if legally certified. Many rental agreements are far more informal, of course, and not of nine years' duration. If matters remain amicable, then owner and tenant can make whatever agreement they choose. The law states, however, that illegal clauses are null and void. It is in the tenant's own interest to be aware of what they are signing at all times.

In order to avoid the problems associated with long rental agreements, it may be easier to rent an apartment from a company specializing in short-term lets. One of these is Ixelinvest, which has a whole street of furnished apartments in the Rue Souveraine near Avenue Louise. They can be contacted in London on 071-724 8048 (fax 071-706 2698); or at Rue Souveraine 30, 1050 Brussels; tel 02 513 41 64 (fax 02 511 20 29).

Rental costs

In this respect Brussels is in a class of its own, for the obvious reason that there is intense competition for accommodation near the EC Commission and other major offices. Bargains are becoming hard to find, especially near English-language schools, but at least the rapid rise in rents is flattening out. Rents are index-linked and may be raised annually but the landlord must give written notice to the tenant. A one-room flat in a suburb will cost at least £60 per week. Three-bedroom flats in better areas (east and south of Brussels) exceed £150 per week. Well-appointed houses (known as 'villas') in the surrounding countryside cost £250 per week or more. In the case of apartments maintenance charges or share of facilities can add 10-20% to the rent and can be a source of dispute if they are not clearly stated at the outset. Apart from these charges, the tenant is responsible for the electricity, gas, telephone and cable TV.

Relocators

The purpose in using professional relocation firms is to minimize the cost, time and hassle for an executive or other employee to settle into Belgium. A good relocator will advise on education and spouse employment and know how to cope with the multitude of regulations and formalities. They advise on all local facilities and regulations, and — most important of all — are strong negotiators on the local property market. Once the relocator has the customer's requirements they can canvass owners and agents to produce an exhaustive list of likely properties and then invite the customer over to Belgium. They then accompany one around on a highly concentrated tour over several days and advise on fair rental prices. Unlike the new arrival, the relocator is experienced in property worth and will often negotiate a considerable reduction on the offered rental price. While relocation fees range from BF50,000 to BF90,000 for the complete process (some invoice their services by the hour) they generally save their customers many times more than that and make the expatriate's transfer far easier. There is also now a developing market in 'delocating', where the relocation firm handles all the formalities when

an employee moves out of Belgium, often at short notice and with consequent problems in applying the vital 'diplomatic clause' which allows you to break the rental lease agreement.

Unfortunately, not all relocation firms are totally independent of other interests. Some are little more than escort services that may show you around and provide a cultural tour but are neither experienced nor skilled enough to negotiate better deals on their customers' behalf. In the worst cases relocators function as estate agents on the side and collect commissions from the landlord (or agent) as well as the fee from the person whose interests they are supposedly defending. The problem is avoidable. Several reputable firms are members of the British Chamber of Commerce and others have voluntarily joined the Confédération Immobilière Belge (CIB). While this is not a government organization it does closely monitor the commercial practices of both estate agents and relocators as two separate professions. Several top relocators have even issued a deposition of ethical conduct with the CIB (particularly guaranteeing independence from estate agents and refusal of commissions). There is a clear line between residential and office relocators. The profile of a person moving to Belgium can be either 'cold', someone with no acquaintances there, or 'warm' if they are joining an established company. They are likely to use a relocator when looking to rent a property upwards of BF40,000 per month (£680) but some relocators who are members of the British Chamber of Commerce in Brussels have assisted incoming Britons at lower rental levels and at reduced relocation fees.

Relocation Firms

Brussels Relocation SC: Av. des Vallons 40, 1410 Waterloo; tel 02 353 21 01; fax 02 353 06 42. British/Belgian partnership. British Chamber of Commerce and CIB member.
Bussens Welcome Office: Av. de la Forêt de Soignes 334, 1640 Rhode St. Genèse; tel 02 358 17 72; fax 02 358 29 28. Established 1968.
Executive Relocation Service: Rue Bemel 6, 1150 Brussels; tel 02 772 20 40; fax 02 772 56 01.
Living Abroad: Kraaienheuvel 19, 2950 Kapellen; tel 03 665 42 39/40; fax 03 665 42 41.
Meeting Tops: Rue du Collège Saint-Michel 13, 1150 Brussels; tel 02 772 73 93 or 772 75 14; fax 02 772 73 22. British Chamber of Commerce member.
MIT: Av. Louise 207 box 10, 1050 Brussels; tel 02 645 18 02; fax 02 688 08 42.
Reloc SPRL: Av. de l'Université 96 bte 6, 1050 Brussels; tel 02 648 72 56; fax 02 647 73 67.
SMG Executive Relocation Services: Av. de la Couronne 154, 1050 Brussels; tel 02 649 01 36; fax 02 646 11 87.

Insurance and Wills

Belgium is notoriously expensive for insurance, which can cost 200% to 300% of UK rates. House and contents insurance is essential. Under Belgian law the tenant is liable for damage to leased property caused by fire, explosions, lightning, water and so on. House insurance is often called 'fire insurance', but there is in fact no separate category for fire. Insurance is calculated after an inspection by a surveyor, usually at the rate of 1% or 1.1% of the total value of house and contents per annum, plus 15.75% tax. Both rises in property prices and depreciation must be taken into account. The formula to obtain the value of a part of a house is 20 times the annual rental plus charges. A personal third-party liability policy is also necessary because of a person's high degree of responsibility under Belgian law for damage to other people and their property. The advantage of this type of policy is that you receive free legal assistance in the event of a claim against you. Those in communally owned apartment buildings will also have to contribute to a policy covering accidents in the communal space.

From July 1993 it will be possible to take out an insurance policy in the UK which is valid in other EC countries. While none of the Belgian insurance companies offers very good value, according to the consumers' magazine, *Budget et Droit* (October 1990), the following are the best: ASLK, ABB, OMOB, Unie der Assuradeuren and DVV. Assubel, Royale Belge, Groupe Victoire and Winterthur also offer better than average value. *Budget et Droit* is available from the Belgian Consumers Association at BF350 per issue (Rue d'Hollande 13, 1060 Brussels).

Wills

Belgian law subjects the value of an inheritance from a 'habitant' of Belgium to inheritance tax, and there is also a tax on change of ownership when real estate located in Belgium is inherited from a non-habitant of Belgium. If at the time of your death you administered your wealth or managed your business from somewhere in Belgium then you are a habitant, regardless of your nationality, legal domicile or place of death. This means in effect that any property or other assets in Belgium are subject to Belgian inheritance laws. In principle your property and half of your assets go to your spouse, and the rest is divided equally amongst your children. Legacies to other relatives or strangers are taxed very heavily indeed. If you die without leaving a will, then legal complications will ensue. It is therefore advisable to register a will with a notary and to appoint an executor to carry out your wishes. A will made under Anglo-Saxon or Scottish law can be taken into account by the Belgian authorities, but any unusual requests or conditions could be invalid if they affect assets in Belgium. Again, it is worth consulting back issues of the consumer association magazine *Budget et Droit*.

Utilities

If you are planning to move to Belgium, you should be aware of the potential delays and costs involved if gas, electricity and telephones are not already connected to your property. It is also legally necessary to be connected to the sewage system, even if you have your own well, unless you are in a remote location where cesspits are still in use.

Utility companies in Belgium issue estimated bills every two months; the meter is read once a year and a refund or extra bill is then issued. Bills must be paid promptly — generally within 10 days — otherwise the service will be cut off without warning. In the case of telephones you have to pay within five days. It is easiest to do this with a standing order (*domiciliation des paiements/domicilie*). If you are taking over from a previous occupant you should obtain forms from the company concerned and fill in the meter reading together with the previous occupant. The form is then sent to the company by the previous occupier with a copy of your identity card. A copy of your passport may be acceptable instead. If it is necessary to have a company representative to read your meter, they must be given adequate advance notice. When a property has been left uninhabited for some time, the power will have been disconnected, but reconnection can easily be arranged with two or three days' warning.

Electricity

The major power companies, Unerg, Intercom, and Ebes, produce the electricity, but local distribution is dealt with by the communes, who have formed various local electricity companies. The name of the company in your area can be found at the local town hall, or in the ordinary telephone book under *Electricité/Electriciteit*. If all else fails you can find out by calling 02 511 19 70.

Electricity in Belgium is 220 volts AC 50 cycles. British 240 volt appliances run quite satisfactorily, except for those with motors such as record turntables and washing machines, which run more slowly. American equipment needs a transformer to convert from 110 to 220 volts, but equipment meant to be run on 60 cycles AC will not work properly. In general two-pin round plugs are used in Belgium; you should make sure that your appliances are properly earthed. Most houses have a fuse-box (*coupe-circuit/zekering*) which you should become familiar with.

One problem which often arises is that the electrical capacity, or amperage, for your property is too small. It is then possible to have a larger meter installed by the utility company for a fee. A lot of Belgian houses do not have a hot water tank, but rather water is heated by a gas burner when you turn on the tap. In some houses the hot water supply can be virtually non-existent. A dishwasher or washing machine has the advantage of heating its own water, but you should first determine the power capacity of the socket if you want to use any high-amperage equipment and you may need heavy wiring. Connecting appliances to the mains must be done by a qualified electrician; the electricity company's responsibilities end at the meter.

In the event that you are moving into a brand-new house, the wiring will have to be checked by an inspector from the electricity company before you can have the power connected.

Gas

Natural gas is widely used in Belgium for cooking, central heating and heating water. Bottled propane and butane gas is also widely used — you can find a local distributor by looking under 'Gas — household' in the Yellow Pages. A gas bottle is a *bouteille de gaz* or *gasfles*. The name of the local gas company (of which there are many) can be found at the town hall, under *gaz/gas* in the ordinary phone book, or by calling (02) 519 41 11 as a last resort. The name may be on your central heating or other equipment. As with electricity, the utility company's responsibilities end with the meter, and you will need the services of a plumber (*plombier/loodgieter*) for the installation of appliances.

When renting accommodation, you must inform your landlord if you are planning to change the power supply or installing new appliances. You should also confirm that the landlord will pay for the repair of the central heating or the hot water heater when signing the lease.

Oil

Oil (*mazout/stookolie*) is widely used for central heating, and can be obtained from companies such as BP and Esso Belgium. You will find the fuel tank in the courtyard or garden, often under the grass with a metal lid, and there will also be a long metal ruler for measuring the fuel level to be found in your cellar or garage. The procedure for lighting oil heaters needs to be handled with some care. Mazout is cheaper than gas or electricity, but still attracts 19.5% VAT. The cost also varies depending on the world price of oil.

Water

Water is in plentiful supply in Belgium and entirely safe to drink, if not always very palatable. The name of your local water company is to be found under *Eaux/Water* in the white phone directory. In Brussels contact the Compagnie Intercommunale Bruxelloise des Eaux, Rue aux Laines 70, 1000 Brussels; tel (02) 518 81 11. The emergency number in Brussels is (02) 739 52 11. Cold water is charged for and the meters read once a year. The bill, which could amount to about BF6,000 for an average house is also issued annually, or in some areas quarterly. You may be asked to pay some of your bill in advance when moving in. Installations are again the domain of the plumber; for leaking mains contact the water company.

If you are lucky enough to have your own well (*puits/put*) you will enjoy much better-tasting water than that from the public supply. The water in Brussels has such a high calcium content that many apartment blocks have communal water softeners, which adds to your monthly charges. Not surprisingly, bottled water (especially Spa) is popular.

Telephones

Having a telephone installed can take from one to six months, depending on the availability of lines. Your first phone must be installed by the publicly-owned RTT (*Régie des Télégraphes et Téléphones/Regie van Telegrafie en Telefonie*). Subsequently you can buy or rent handsets from other sources as long as they conform to RTT standards. Telephone installation costs about BF5,000, including a refundable deposit which is adjusted to the average size of your two-month bill.

When moving into accommodation with an existing phone, the easiest solution is to go with the previous tenant to an RTT office and sign a transfer agreement for BF950 plus 19.5% VAT. Otherwise transfer of the line costs BF3,500 (plus VAT) and a deposit is payable. Your telephone bill includes BF500 rental per extension. Directories and Yellow Pages (*Guide d'or/Gouden Gids*) are provided free annually. Mobile telephones are available from the RTT or private companies at a price. Fax machines and telephone answering machines can be bought from the RTT or private companies.

The office which deals with telephone installations or transfers is your local RTT Commercial Centre (*Centre Commercial/Commerciëel Centrum*) which you can find by looking under Customer Services (*Service à la Clientèle/Klantendienst*) at the front of the white pages. Very often under the same number and address is a *Téléboutique* or *Telefoonwinkel* which deals with rental, handsets and some services. Initial enquiries are best addressed to the Centre Commercial.

As stated above, it is necessary to pay your phone bill within five days. This should not pose a problem since electronic transfer of money is instantaneous.

You should make arrangements to pay if going abroad, or inform the RTT well in advance.

Removals

While it could save money to take some of your possessions from home with you it is worth bearing in mind that electrical equipment may not function well in Belgium, and it is expensive to ship goods back and forth. With the implementation of the Single Market in 1993 the movement of goods should become much easier. The best course of action is to deal with an experienced and reputable international removals firm who can help you with the paperwork. The British Association of Removers can provide a list of international removers and other information in return for an SAE (BAR, 3 Churchill Court, 58 Station Road, North Harrow, Middlesex HA2 7SA; tel 081-861 3331). Removals can be done door-to-door or your possessions can be put into a warehouse in Belgium. Charges at the moment are around £40 per cubic metre, but the exact price depends very much on the total distance involved at both ends. Some removers dealing with Belgium include:

AFA Worldwide Shipping: 2-4 Kenway Road, Earls Court, London SW5 0RR; tel 071-244 7878.

Allied Pickfords: 490 Great Cambridge Road, Enfield, Middlesex BN1 3RZ; tel 081-366 6521.

Arthur Pierre: Tovil Green, Maidstone, Kent ME15 6RJ; tel 0622-691330. Brusselsesteenweg 344, 3090 Overijse, Belgium; tel 02 687 76 10; fax 02 687 3730.

Gauntlett International Ltd: Gauntlett House, Catteshall Road, Godalming, Surrey GU7 1NH; tel 0483-428982.

Scotpac International Moving: Security House, Abbey Wharf Industrial Estate, Kingsbridge Road, Barking Essex IG11 0BT; tel 081-591 3388; fax 081-594 4571.

Customs Regulations

Assuming that you have registered with your commune and are planning to move your residence to Belgium, you are entitled to import household goods, your car and tools needed for your work without paying import duty, as long as you can show that you have owned these items for over six months or if there is some wear and tear on them. This condition may be relaxed for EC citizens but not in the case of cars. Importation must take place within 12 months of your registration as resident in Belgium and can be in more than one consignment. Subsequently you are not allowed to sell or otherwise dispose of your goods for a period of six months, unless you have the permission of Belgian Customs. For EC citizens this condition applies mainly to cars.

Import Procedures

If you are already in Belgium you should write to the customs head office: Ministère des Finances, Direction Générale des Douanes, Bvd. du Jardin Botanique 50 bte 37, 1010 Brussels and obtain the leaflet entitled *Notice déménagements/Notitie verhuizingen.* General information is available on 02 210 30 11 or 02 210 30 29. You will then need to locate your nearest Customs and Excise Office (look for *Douane et accises/Douanen en accijnzen* under *Ministère des Finances/Ministerie van Financiën* in the white pages) where you submit the paperwork. You can save trouble by engaging the services of a Belgian 'customs broker' (*agence en douane/douane agentschap*).

You must then draw up a complete list of the goods in question with a declaration in French or Dutch that the list is accurate and enter five signed copies at the customs office, along with a copy of your residence registration card. Sometimes an English list is acceptable, or your removal firm will supply a standardized multilingual list. Insurance policies, invoices and proof of where you have been living are all useful documents.

If you have already arranged employment and/or an address in Belgium before leaving the UK your nearest Belgian embassy or consulate (see Residence and Entry section) will tell you how to import your effects. They will also legalize your signature on your inventory.

Importing a Car

Cars, motorcycles, caravans, mobile homes and even private boats and aeroplanes can be imported duty free as long as they are on your inventory, with the proviso that they are six months old and you do not resell them within six months. To import a car you need forms 133, 139B and three copies of form 48-ter from the customs office at Tour et Taxis, Rue Picard 1-3, 1020 Brussels (tel 02 427 27 20). Having returned these with copies of the invoice, registration and insurance you can drive for three months. Your car must then be converted to Belgian specifications and go through the *Contrôle Technique* (MOT). When insurance has been paid and new Belgian number plates put on you will have temporary permission to import the vehicle. Final permission to import a car without paying VAT and tax takes from nine months to two years and requires a further paper-chase.

Buying a Car

Belgium is well-known for its low car prices and dealers are used to foreign buyers. To find out current prices for new and second-hand cars look in the monthly *Moniteur de l'Automobile/Autogids* or look for special issues of the consumer magazine *Test Achats/Test Aankoop*. If you are not resident in Benelux it is possible to buy a vehicle 'in transit'. Dealers have their own 'transit departments' or a customs broker who knows all the formalities. If everything is in order you will be granted exemption from paying VAT for long enough to take your car home with Belgian transit documents and number plates. You can also escape VAT if you have been resident in Belgium and can show that you are about to leave. Further information about cars is given in Chapter Four *Daily Life*.

Insurance

Car insurance in Belgium is expensive and comprehensive. You cannot even get a licence plate without third-party insurance (*responsabilité civile/wettelijke aansprakelijkheidsverzekering*). You also need to be insured against fire and theft, and for legal costs in the event of court cases, which are frequent after accidents. From 1 January 1993 car insurance policies taken out with a UK company will be valid in other EC countries, but this could be very inconvenient in the event of a claim. The plan is to phase out the traditional Green Card for overseas

---

TRC MANAGEMENT SA
LET US HELP YOU WITH:

Insuring your vehicle, your home, household goods, your family liability, etc. . .

Buying your new or second hand vehicle.
Any make & type, tax free or tax paid.

Call TRC MANAGEMENT SA
— 32/2/346.24.95
— 32/2/646.77.83 (fax)

---

insurance but for the moment it is still necessary. You will have to inform your UK insurance company about your intention to go abroad in any case.

Useful Addresses

Automobile Association (AA): Information Service; tel 0345 500 600. Information on insurance and permanent importation of your vehicle will be supplied to AA members.

RAC Motoring Services: PO Box 700, Spectrum, Bond Street, Bristol BS99 1RB; tel 0272-232 340.

Royal Automobile Club de Belgique (RACB): Rue d'Arlon 53, 1040 Brussels; tel 02 287 09 11.

Sohr & Son: Av. de l'Avenir 3, 1640 Rhode St. Genèse; tel 02 380 9360; fax 02 380 9420. Insurance brokers.

TRC Management: Av. Ernestine 2, 1050 Brussels; tel 02 640 70 37; fax 02 646 77 83. Insurance brokers specializing in car insurance for foreigners.

Importing Pets

Many expatriates would like to have their four-legged friends with them abroad, and this should not be a difficult procedure. Dogs and cats being exported to Belgium must be vaccinated against rabies at least 30 days and not more than 12 months before export. In the case of dogs and cats vaccinated before the age of three months the validity of the rabies vaccination certificate is three months. After that the validity of the vaccination certificate is one year. Rabies is present in Belgium to the south of the Sambre and Meuse rivers, and annual inoculation will be needed if you are in this area. Remember that pets will not be able to return to the UK without undergoing a period of quarantine, even if they have been denied entry to Belgium.

With birds and other animals certificates of good health are needed. The UK Ministry of Agriculture, Fisheries and Food (Hook Rise South, Tolworth, Surbiton, Surrey KT6 7F; tel 081-330 4411) can provide forms for specific countries. If you are thinking of exporting a parrot or any rare or endangered species it is necessary to contact the Wildlife Conservation Section of the Department of the Environment on 0272-218017 for guidance.

Daily Life

When going to live in a foreign country, one will find straight away that there is a multitude of daily rituals, previously taken for granted, which now pose a seemingly insurmountable challenge. The intention of this chapter is to provide all of the practical information required to cope successfully with various aspects of life in Belgium. The key to dealing with daily life in Belgium lies to some extent in being able to speak French or Dutch reasonably well. The first section of this chapter covers this area, with subsequent sections dealing with all of those aspects of daily life, which, if handled successfully, can make living in another country an exciting rather than a daunting experience.

The Belgian Languages

Knowing which language to speak to whom is of considerable importance if you want to get on with the Belgians. There are three languages with official status: Dutch, French and German, and speakers usually occupy a well-defined region of the country. In Brussels Dutch and French have equal status. Brussels is entirely surrounded by Dutch-speaking communes, but in six of these there are French-speaking minorities with special status. Foreigners should always bear in mind that Dutch-speakers are in the majority in Belgium as a whole. Discounting immigrants, close to 60% of the population speak Dutch and 40% French. The number of German-speakers amounts to 62,000.

Dutch spoken in Belgium is largely the same as in Holland and this common language is called *Algemeen Beschaafd Nederlands (ABN)* or Common Civilized Dutch. If you speak Dutch you will become aware that almost every town in Belgium has its own dialect and some of these can sound like a foreign language to an untrained ear. Such dialects are generally not used when dealing with outsiders. Dutch in Belgium preserves certain archaic features in its spoken form not used in The Netherlands and also uses French and English loanwords in a different way, but such matters will remain quite academic unless you learn to speak Dutch well.

In spite of its very different pronunciation and appearance, Dutch is closely related to English. It is not a dialect of German although it shares the same basic vocabulary with German. The relationship between the spelling and pronunciation is very logical but the sounds of the language take some getting used to.

In the case of French, Belgians naturally aspire to speak and write standard French. Wallonia has its own dialects, and you will soon become aware of a Walloon accent and peculiarities in grammar and vocabulary in dealing with French-speakers. The words for 'seventy' and 'ninety' are invariably *septante* and *nonante* in Belgium, unlike in France. Belgian French-speakers also have a tendency to change the genders of nouns.

Language Manners

You cannot be expected to know automatically which language the person you are speaking to uses. In the case of Dutch-speakers, they will usually be very happy to speak English to you. In Brussels many Dutch-speakers do not mind using French. In Dutch-speaking areas French is best avoided. Using German may induce negative reactions as well. French-speakers are not as good at English as Dutch-speakers. It is important to remember that only 20% of Belgians are actually bilingual in Dutch and French. The Flemish are, statistically, the best linguists in Europe — speaking four or five languages is considered quite normal amongst educated people. Belgium is an ideal place to study any of the EC languages since there are plenty of teachers and people to practise on.

Language Study

Before paying a lot of money for a language course or lessons, it is a good idea to look at what your local library has to offer. You will probably be able to borrow a book and cassettes in the language you want to learn. In the case of Dutch it may be the only way to proceed until you arrive in Belgium. Dutch courses available in Britain are invariably from The Netherlands, but this makes no difference. The following beginners' books are recommended: *Praatpaal*, by Anne Schoenmakers (publ. Stanley Thornes at £8.95, including cassette); and *Levend Nederlands* (publ. Cambridge University Press at £16.40).

For French there is a wide choice of courses available. At the basic level there is the BBC Multimedia language course, *Get By In French* which includes a videotape, two cassettes and a book, at £29.95 from Exel DMS, 3 Sheldon Way, Larkfield, Aylesford, ME20 6SF (0622-882000). Another highly rated beginners course is *A Vous La France!* (book £7.99, or pack with two cassettes at £22.00). Further information is available from BBC Education Information (Room 202, Villiers House, The Broadway, Ealing, London W5 2PA; tel 081-746 1111).

Linguaphone (head office: St Giles House, 50 Poland Street, London W1V 4AX; tel 071-287 4050) also distribute self-study courses in the form of books, cassettes and compact discs. Boxed sets of cassettes for French are now available from W.H. Smith, AA Travel Shops and bookshops at £9.95 for the Travel Pack, and £29.95 for the Visa series.

Part-time Courses

Local colleges of further education often run day and evening classes in EC languages, which range in length from three months to a year. A-level courses, costing £50.00-£90.00, usually commence in October, so you need to register in September. The *Alliance Française* in your area will also run courses in French. There is no Belgian equivalent of the *Alliance Française*.

Courses in Belgium

In Belgium residential courses of varying length are conducted in rural surroundings. Céran hold courses in various languages in France and the Ardennes (Céran Ardennes, Av. du Château 133, 4900 Spa, Belgium; tel 087 77 41 64. In the UK call 0954-31956). For French, Dutch and German, Pro-Linguis, Place de l'Eglise 19, 6717 Thiaumont (tel 063 22 04 62) offer courses which include sport. You could also try Kasteel Van Velm, Halleweg 32, 3806 Velm (tel 011 68 82 60). There are also more official summer courses, such as four-week courses in French Language and Literature at the Free University of Brussels, Av. F.D. Roosevelt 50, 1050 Brussels; and two-week courses in Dutch Language and Culture held in Hasselt, Limburg (contact Ministerie van de Vlaamse Gemeenschap, Administratie voor Onderwijszaken en Internationale Samenwerking, Kunstlaan 43, 1040 Brussels; tel 02 513 74 64).

Apart from residential courses there are numerous language schools operating in Belgium of varying quality. You could just as well try to find a sympathetic conversation partner and arrange a 'language exchange' which costs nothing. In the case of formal lessons most language teaching specialists agree that a group lesson is just as good as learning one-to-one. It is also a great deal cheaper. Language courses are also organized by some local communes starting every September.

Useful Addresses

For French:
Alliance Française: Av. de l'Emeraude 59, 1040 Brussels; tel 02 732 15 92.
Amira: Av. Louise 251, 1060 Brussels; tel 02 640 68 50.
CLL, Université Catholique de Louvain: Place de l'Université 1, 1348 Ottignies Louvain-La-Neuve; tel 010 47 21 11.

For Dutch:
College of Europe: Dijver 11, 8000 Brugge; tel 050 33 65 62.
Nederlandse Academie: Verenigingsstraat 57, 1000 Brussels; tel 02 219 03 27.

For all nine EC languages:
Fondation Bruxelloise pour l'Apprentissage des Neuf Langues: Av. F.D. Roosevelt 41, Ixelles, 1050 Brussels; tel 02 640 21 92.

Schools and Education

The decision on how and where to educate one's children is something which has caused a quandary for parents wherever or however they live. Moving abroad with children of a young age is in some ways easier than moving with teenagers, as younger children are far more adept at picking up languages and fitting into new situations. As their education has not yet begun in earnest, the problem of juggling two different curricula does not arise. Switching over to a new and unfamiliar language can set a teenager back a year in their schooling. Belgium has an excellent education system and claims to be the only country in the western world that offers free schooling from the age of $2\frac{1}{2}$. This does not of course mean that a child being educated in the British system would immediately function well in a Belgian school. For this reason many parents choose to send their children to international schools in Belgium. Luckily, Belgium has a great concentration of international schools where children can enjoy the opportunity of mixing with many different nationalities, and of receiving part of their schooling in another language as well.

The Belgian state has always made education one of its top priorities, and spends 20% of its budget on this sector. School attendance is compulsory between the ages of 6 and 18. With the latest moves towards federalization, most of the responsibility for education has now moved from the central government to the Communities (the tier of government concerned with language and culture). General policy is still decided by the central state, but in other respects there are divergences between the regions.

There are two types of publicly-funded schools in Belgium: 'official' and 'free' (*libre/vrij*). In the French-speaking area a little over half of all secondary schools are 'free schools'; in the Flemish area almost three-quarters. In the official sector most schools come under the Community but some are run by the Provinces or Communes.

Most 'free' schools are linked to the Catholic church, but a few belong to other religious groupings or to none at all. A major difference between official and free schools is that parents have to pay for some equipment and activities at the latter.

The Structure of the Education System

Pre-school. This is divided into playschool ($2\frac{1}{2}$-4 years of age) and kindergartens ($2\frac{1}{2}$-5) which are often attached to a primary school. Playschools (*prégardienne/peuterschool*) are not usually free, whereas kindergartens (*jardin d'enfants/kleuterschool*) often are. The advantage of enrolling a child in a kindergarten, amongst other things, is that he/she will be better prepared in terms of reading and sociability than if he/she stayed at home. Kindergartens are not compulsory, but more than half of the children in primary school have been to one. Some international schools also have pre-school classes.

Primary. Children are usually six when they enter primary school (*école primaire/lagere school*), although they may be allowed to enter at five if the school thinks they are ready. Primary education lasts six years and concentrates on the mother tongue and mathematics. There are regular tests and students can be made to repeat an entire year if their performance is below standard. In the last year children are assessed by the 'psycho-medical-social centre' who will advise them on which type of secondary school is most suitable for them.

Secondary. Having obtained a primary school pass certificate, children then go on to the six-year secondary system (*école sécondaire/middelbare school*) where specialization begins in earnest. While there are some schools offering technical or vocational education at this level, called *institut/instituut*, most offer a wide range of options as well as vocational training. Secondary schools are generally known as *athénée/atheneum, lycée* or *collège* in the case of Catholic schools.

Since 1978 schools have been free to teach the revised system of education known as Type I. The traditional system (Type II) has virtually disappeared in Wallonia, but is still followed by 40% of Dutch-language schools. In the revised system students are continuously evaluated and specialization is introduced gradually. During the third year students go into a transitional period and can decide to take up technical and vocational studies which more or less excludes the possibility of going to university, or to select a curriculum chosen from up to 24 different options.

In the traditional system choice is considerably more limited and pupils must commit themselves to their specialization at the age of 12. There is again a choice between general and technical/vocational streams. In the general section there are options such as Latin and Greek, Latin maths, Latin sciences, scientific A (pure sciences), scientific B (science and modern languages), economics with modern languages and social sciences. After six years of secondary school students in the Flemish area receive a Diploma in Secondary Education (*Diploma van Secundair Onderwijs*). In the French area this is known as the Certificate in Secondary Education (*Certificat d'Etudes Secondaires*).

Universities

Belgian universities have a worldwide reputation for excellence in a number of scientific fields, in particular in biotechnology. The Koninklijke Universiteit Leuven (KUL) is the oldest and best-known, with 25,000 students of whom 10% are foreigners. The system is open to anyone who has gained a high school diploma and universities are to a large extent regulated by the State. As one might expect, institutions of higher learning are divided between French and Dutch, and the official and 'free' (Catholic) systems. About 26% of Belgians go on to higher education (compared with 19% in the UK) and of these about half pursue full-length university courses. These are divided into 'cycles' of two or three years each, with some institutions offering only one cycle. In a full (*complet/kompleet*) university course there is a preparatory cycle — the *candidature/kandidaatschap* followed by a second cycle leading to the equivalent of a bachelor's degree — the *licence/licentiaat*. In some fields a graduate will be awarded the title of medical doctor, civil engineer, and so on, after completing the second cycle. Beyond the level of 'licence' there is a third possible cycle conferring a master's degree or doctorate.

All instruction at Belgian universities is given free of charge, but there is an annual registration fee of about BF15,000 (£250). As far as living expenses are concerned, students receive grants according to the financial circumstances of their parents or they can take out loans from the state. EC citizens are legally entitled to attend EC universities and are also eligible for grants in another country if they qualify in their home country. Grants in Belgium are so low (£130 a month), however, that poorer students usually live at home and commute to university.

EC citizens can enter university courses if they have a secondary school leaving certificate and can pass a language test. All the six major universities offer courses in the medium of English, in particular at postgraduate level. For information on courses at secondary and university level contact the following institutions:

CSBO: Centrum voor Studies en Beroepsorientering: Maurice Lemonnierlaan 129, 1000 Brussels; tel 02 502 34 08.
CEDIEP: Centre de Documentation et d'Information sur les Etudes: Rue Philippe Baucq 18, 1040 Brussels; tel 02 649 14 18.
SIEP: Service d'Information sur les Etudes et les Professions: Chaussée de Wavre 205, 1040 Brussels; tel 02 640 18 32.
De Onderwijsgids/Guide de l'Enseignement: Rue de la Vignette 179, 1160 Brussels; tel 02 672 83 89.

International Universities

Belgium has an unusually high concentration of universities and colleges offering courses in management, law and politics with a European or international slant, in order to prepare students for possible careers in the EC Commission and other international organizations. For American-style university education there is Vesalius College, Brussels which works in cooperation with the Flemish Vrije

Universiteit Brussels. Boston University, Brussels, offers masters degrees in International Management, Information Systems Management and International Relations. A university with an excellent reputation for business studies is the European University, founded in 1973 in Antwerp. It now has programmes in most EC countries.

Useful Addresses

International Universities

Boston University Brussels: Av. Laarbeek 121, 1090 Brussels; tel 02 478 79 73.
College of Europe: Dijver 7, 8000 Brugge; tel 050 33 53 34.
European University — EEC College: Amerikalei 131, 2000 Antwerp; tel 03 238 10 82.
European University — EEC College: Rue de Livourne 116-120, 1050 Brussels; 02 648 67 81.
Vesalius College — VUB: Pleinlaan 2, 1050 Brussels; tel 02 641 28 21/641 28 22).

Business Schools

European Business School: Av. Molière 462, 1060 Brussels; tel 02 344 43 00.
European Institute for Advanced Studies in Management: Rue d'Egmont 11, 1050 Brussels; tel 02 511 91 16.
Management Centre Europe: Rue Caroly 15, 1040 Brussels; 02 516 19 11.

International Schools

Parents abroad have three main options for their children: to send them to local Belgian schools, to send them to boarding schools in Britain or elsewhere, or to use one of the many international schools in Belgium. These can offer British and American curricula, as well as the European and International Baccalaureate programmes. One major advantage of such a school is that your child can be prepared to enter university in their own country if they do not intend to go into higher education in Belgium. The following is a list of schools with English-speaking pupils and their annual fees. Unless otherwise stated there is some provision for British GCSE:

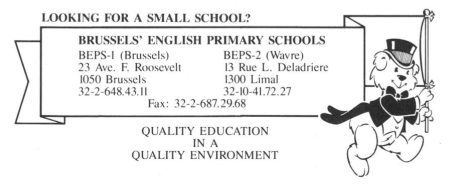

LOOKING FOR A SMALL SCHOOL?

BRUSSELS' ENGLISH PRIMARY SCHOOLS

BEPS-1 (Brussels)	BEPS-2 (Wavre)
23 Ave. F. Roosevelt	13 Rue L. Deladriere
1050 Brussels	1300 Limal
32-2-648.43.11	32-10-41.72.27
Fax: 32-2-687.29.68	

QUALITY EDUCATION
IN A
QUALITY ENVIRONMENT

Useful Addresses

Antwerp English School: Korte Altaarstraat 19, 2018 Antwerp (03 271 09 43) $2\frac{1}{2}$-16, BF74,000-246,000.

Antwerp International School: Veltwijcklaan 180, 2180 Ekeren, Antwerp (03 541 60 47) 3-18, 91,000-464,000.
British Primary School: Stationstraat 6, 1980 Tervuren (02 767 30 98) 3-8, BF30,000-60,0000.
British School of Brussels: Leuvensesteenweg 19, 3080 Tervuren (02 767 47 00) 3-18, BF95,000-527,000. Some assisted places.
Brussels American School: John F. Kennedylaan 12, 1960 Sterrebeek (02 731 56 26), 3-18. School for NATO and US personnel. US curriculum.
Brussels English Primary School (BEPS-1 Brussels): Av. Franklin Roosevelt 23, 1050 Brussels (02 648 43 11/fax 02 687 29 68) $2\frac{1}{2}$-$12\frac{1}{2}$, BF100,000-226,000.
Brussels English Primary School (BEPS-2 Wavre): Rue L. Deladrière 13, 1300 Limal (010 41 72 27) 3-8, BF120,000-256,000.
Ecole Internationale Le Verseau: Rue de Wavre 60, 1301 Bierges (010 22 61 35/36) 3-18, BF20,000-43,000.
EEC International School: Jacob Jordaen Straat 77, 2018 Antwerp (03 218 54 31) 1-18, BF120,000-320,000.
EEC International School: Bvd. Louis Schmidt 101-103, 1040 Brussels (02 734 44 13) 1-18, BF120,000-320,000.
European School — Brussels I: Av. du Vert Chasseur 46, 1180 Brussels (02 374 58 47) 3-18. Free to children of EC employees but takes others for small fee.
European School — Brussels II: Av. Oscar Jespers 75, 1200 Brussels (02 774 22 11). As above.

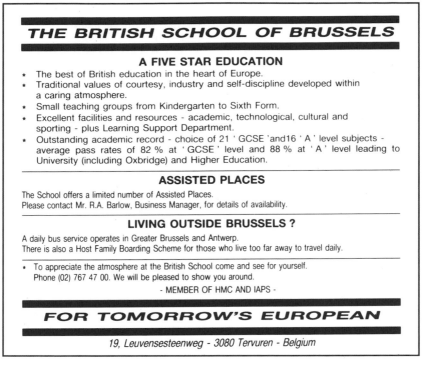

International School of Brussels: Kattenberg 19, 1170 Brussels (02 672 27 88) 3-18, 145,000-595,000. US curriculum.
Montessori School Brussels: Av. Eugène Demolder 113, 1030 Brussels (02 241 2094/242 4408/fax 03 231 5438) 2-6, BF150,000.
St John's International School: Drève Richelle 146, 1410 Waterloo (02 354 11 38/fax 02 353 04 95) 3-19, BF109,000-593,000. US curriculum, GCE 'O'-Level and International Baccalaureate.

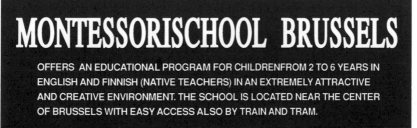

Further information from:
Council of British Independent Schools in the European Community (COBISEC):
c/o The British School of Brussels (see above).
European Council of International Schools: 18 Lavant Street, Petersfield, Hants
   GU32 3EW; tel 0730-68244.
Gabbitas, Truman and Thring (Counselling on British Education): 6-8 Sackville
   Street, London W1X 2BR; tel 071-734 0161.

Media & Communications

Newspapers

Belgian newspapers, as with everything else in Belgium, are divided by regions
and languages, and by their attitude towards the hegemony of the church and state.
In general French-speakers do not read Dutch language newspapers, while some
Flemings will read the French press. The Belgians are not great newspaper readers
in the British tradition — even the most widely read newspaper, the Dutch *Het
Laatste Nieuws*, has a circulation of less than 300,000. Newspapers are serious
and accurate in their reporting; consequently they do not have the appeal of the
British tabloid press. The popular press concentrates more on human interest stories
and sport, but is still rather sober by any standards.

Newspapers rely to a large extent on subscribers (*abonnés*) for their income
with a subscription (*abonnement*) generally costing about BF6,200 per year. Single
issues at the time of writing are BF25 for most papers. The most important edition
of the day is in the evening, with updates in the morning. Subscribers receive their
copies through the letterbox in the afternoon. The weekend edition is delivered
on Saturday morning.

National newspapers based in Brussels are *Le Soir, La Libre Belgique* (French),
Het Laatste Nieuws and *De Standaard* (Dutch). Newspapers published in Antwerp,
for example *De Gazet van Antwerpen*, are widely read in the Flemish area for
their financial reporting.

The state pays subsidies to the press which are mainly taken up by Catholic
newspapers. Most papers are pro-Christian or pro-Liberal (free-market secularist).
Those claiming to be 'neutral' or 'independent' combine respect for Christian values
with economic liberalism. Leftist papers such as *De Morgen* and *Le Peuple* have
very limited appeal.

Most British newspapers are available in Belgian cities during the morning of
publication at prices ranging from BF60 to BF150. The International Herald Tribune
costs BF55; subscriptions are dealt with from Paris (Av. Charles de Gaulle 181,
92521 Neuilly, Cedex Paris; tel 1-46 37 93 00). The Financial Times International
Edition costs BF60 or is obtainable by subscription from Financial Times Benelux,
Rue Ducale 39, 1000 Brussels; tel 02 513 28 16.

Major Newspapers

Dutch
Het Laatste Nieuws. Liberal. Colourful and middlebrow. Circulation 300,000.
Het Nieuwsblad. Christian/Liberal. Circulation 300,000.
De Gazet van Antwerpen. Partly Catholic-owned. Business-oriented. Circulation
   191,000.

Het Volk. Owned by Catholic trade union, De Algemeen Christelijk Vakverbond. Circulation 190,000.
De Standaard. Christian/Liberal. Owned by Flemish industrialist grouping. Circulation 80,000.
De Financieel Economische Tijd. Independent. Economic and news reporting. Circulation 38,000. Published from Antwerp.
Trends en Beleggen. Deals with financial trends and investments. Also French version *Trends et Tendances*. Circulation 60,000.
De Streekkrant. Dutch. Free weekly newspaper with various editions in different Flemish towns. Ghent edition has a circulation of 400,000.

French
Le Soir. Christian/Liberal. Serious news and comment. Owned by same company (La Régie Rossel) as *La Meuse-La Lanterne* in Liège and *La Nouvelle Gazette* in Charleroi. Circulation 155,000.
La Dernière Heure. Liberal. Colourful and middlebrow, with emphasis on sport. Same holding company as *La Libre Belgique* (SIPM). Circulation 97,000.
La Libre Belgique. Christian. Stodgy and serious. Heavy emphasis on culture. Useful economic pullout section on Saturdays *La Libre Entreprise*. Circulation 90,000.
L'Echo de la Bourse. French. Founded 1881. Independent stock market paper. Circulation 31,000.
Vlan. French. Main group of free weeklies in Wallonia. Brussels edition has a circulation of 400,000.

Magazines

Since 1970 there has been a huge increase in the number of weeklies and monthlies published in Belgium; the total is now around 8,000. The major evolution in the magazine market has been the decline of women's magazines, whose sales figures have fallen by half since the late seventies. The most popular magazines are now those that appeal to the whole family, such as the Dutch *Blik* (circulation 180,000) and the French *Le Soir Illustré* (120,000), and TV-listings magazines with interviews and articles, such as the Dutch *Humo* and the French *Télémoustique*. Sales of weeklies with political comment and international news, in particular *Knack* (Dutch) and *Le Vif-L'Express* (French) have increased considerably as young Belgians look for more and more sophisticated reading matter. In addition to purely Belgian magazines, glossy French colour weeklies, especially *Paris Match* and *Marie-France*, with their reports on European royal families are still immensely popular.

Books and Bookshops

The Belgian reading public benefits considerably from the large influx of books published in neighbouring Holland and France. Highbrow French literature is widely read, including by Dutch-speakers, and there is also a ready market for all kinds of translations from English into Dutch or French. Academic and scientific books in English are indispensable for university students and widely available, and you will also find a section of English novels and coffee-table books in any large bookshop. Naturally, English books in Belgium are expensive. The cheapest bookshops in Belgium are those run by De Slegte in Brussels, Ghent and Antwerp (main branch: Rue des Grands Carmes 17, 1000 Brussels). The French-owned

FNAC chain has an excellent range of books but no discounts. There are some specialist English bookshops in Brussels, including: W.H. Smith (Bvd. Adolphe Max 71-75, 1000 Brussels; tel 02 219 27 08) which has English magazines and newspapers; and The Strathmore Bookshop (Rue St Lambert 110, Woluwé, 1200 Brussels; tel 02 771 92 00). For a complete listing of bookshops look in the yellow pages under *Librairies/Boekhandels.*

Television

Belgium is ideally located to receive foreign TV broadcasts; with cable television it is now possible to receive up to 30 different channels, five of them emanating from Belgium. Because of the limited resources of Belgian TV companies, viewers have always preferred Dutch and French stations for more interesting programmes. Commercial television only started in Belgium in 1989. In the Flemish area, the commercial station VTM (Vlaamse Televisie Maatschappij) now has 35% of viewers, and the Flemish state channels TV1 and TV2 with 28%. The programme which attracts most viewers is the 7.30 evening news on TV1 with a maximum of 1,200,000 (20% of the whole Flemish population). TV1 mostly consists of general interest information programmes and homegrown drama along with the inevitable American films and series. TV2 covers sport and cultural programmes. VTM consists mostly of game shows and American imports. In Wallonia, RTBF 1 has similar programmes to the Flemish TV1, while RTBF Télé 21 is a more serious cultural channel. The French-language Luxembourg station, RTL TV1 has a mix of game shows and American and French-language imports.

Foreigners do not need to watch Belgian television — programmes from France, The Netherlands, Germany, Italy and Britain are readily available, as well as the American news channel CNN, the music channel MTV and Eurosport. To obtain this wealth of viewing, look under *Cable/Kabel* in the Yellow Pages for your local cable TV company. Apart from any cable fees, owners of TV and radios have to pay a licence fee. The office which collects licence fees can be found under *Radio et Television Redevances (RTR)* or *Kijk en Luistergeld (KLG)* in the Yellow Pages. A TV licence costs about BF4000 and a radio licence BF800.

Radio

Belgian radio has three channels for both languages. Radio 1 is mostly a news and cultural channel, and gives traffic information as well. Radio 2 is the most popular channel (58% of listeners in the Flemish area), and is much like British Radio 2 — light music and other bland entertainment. Radio 3 is a highbrow channel with a great deal of classical music and heavy academic discussions. The Brussels station *Studio Brussel/Bruxelles* offers continuous music and has considerable popularity. Besides the national stations there are numerous local stations which attract about 13% of total listeners.

Because of Belgium's geographical position it is easy to pick up British radio broadcasts, and those of many other countries.

Post

Postal services, together with telephones and telegraphs, are run by the national ministry known as the PTT. The Belgian postal service is more efficient than many of its EC counterparts: it aims to deliver letters in Belgium the following day. Most post offices are open from Monday to Friday from 9am to 12 noon and from

2pm to 5pm. Only main post offices open on Saturday mornings and stay open through the lunch break. One post office stays open 24 hours a day at the Gare du Midi/Zuidstation in Brussels. Service at post offices is usually infuriatingly slow because of the large number of financial and fiscal transactions which can be carried out there. You should first check that you are standing in the right queue. There is a board with window numbers — the correct window is the one with *Timbres postales/Postzegels* (stamps) next to it.

Internal letters cost BF10. Postcards and letters up to 20 grams to EC countries are BF14. Letters to the UK take anything from two days to a week; letters to the USA take about a week. The express surcharge is a flat rate BF100 for anywhere in or outside Belgium. It may or may not guarantee next-day delivery to the UK. A registered letter (*lettre recommandée*) which costs BF90 and is absolutely necessary if legal proof of postage is required. When addressing mail in Belgium the PTT requires addresses to be written in the form in which they are given in this book, namely street first, and house number second.

Small parcels in Belgium will be delivered the next day. An even faster service is offered by Taxipost, and for abroad by EMS Taxipost. For a complete list of courier services, look under *Courrier (service de)/Koerierdiensten* in the yellow pages.

If you want to send a telegram you can simply phone 1325 (for French) and 1225 (Dutch) and dictate your message, even from a public call box. Otherwise you can send your telegram from a post office or railway station. A ten-word telegram from Belgium to the UK costs BF419. Faxes can be sent from any one of 74 'Bureaufax' offices around the country.

Telephones

For installation and billing of telephones look under *Telephones* in Chapter Three, *Setting Up Home*. Call boxes are not as plentiful as in Britain, but they are at least in good working order. The minimum cost of a call is BF10 or two 5 franc coins. Telephone cards at BF200 for 20 units and BF1000 for 105 units can be bought at post offices, railway station ticket offices, and some kiosks and banks. Calls from private telephones cost BF5.95 a unit. A unit buys 3 minutes locally or 40 seconds over longer distances in Belgium. A 3-minute call to the UK costs BF56.4 (£1.00) at cheap rate (on Sundays and from 8pm to 8am) and BF76.5 (£1.30) at other times. A 3-minute call to the USA costs BF178.5 (£3.00) at any time.

Calls within Belgium are half-price between 6.30pm and 8.00am from Mondays to Fridays, and from 6.30pm on Friday to 8.00am on Monday. There are also reduced tariffs on calls to some foreign countries at these times.

Dialling in Belgium is not much different from dialling in the UK, except that you may notice that telephones work more slowly than at home. No area code is required within the same zone. Area codes within Belgium and some codes for abroad can be found at the front of the white pages, under *Indicatifs interurbains/netnummers*. Directory enquiries in Belgium are on 1307/1207 and in Europe on 1304/1204. Note that all telephone information services in French begin with 13 and in Dutch with 12. Reversed charge calls in Europe are on 1324/1224 and 1322/1222 outside Europe. For operator-assisted international calls, dial 1323/1224.

To make an international call from Belgium you dial the access code 00 followed by the country code followed by the subscriber's number minus the initial zero.

Note that Belgians are in the habit of quoting telephone numbers in pairs or even threes, thus a Brussels number such as that of the American Chamber of Commerce (02 513 67 70) comes over as *zero-deux cinq-cent-treize soixante-sept septante* in French and *nul-twee vijfhonderd-en-dertien zeven-en-zestig zeventig* in Dutch. Unless you are very good at numbers in Dutch and French you should therefore insist on numbers being quoted in single figures, or in English if necessary.

Cars and Motoring

Belgian drivers have a reputation for being dangerous and aggressive which is not altogether undeserved. Part of the problem stems from the fact that there was no driving test at all until 1967, and a hands-on test was not introduced until 1979. The Belgian driving test is now one of the stiffest in the world, and there are numerous rules and regulations drivers have to be aware of. The Belgian Road Safety Code has been translated into English as *The Illustrated Highway Code* and is available from English bookshops at BF500.

Belgium has an excellent system of motorways (*autosnelweg/autostrade*) which costs nothing to use. Within older towns there are still many cobbled streets which provide a somewhat hazardous driving surface. Road signs use the local language (except in Brussels where there are two) with the result that a place name may suddenly take on an unfamiliar form (e.g. Antwerpen becomes Anvers in French, Liège becomes Luik in Dutch).

The most important traffic convention is priority to the right (*priorité à droite/voorrang aan rechts*) which is a virtual obsession with Belgian drivers. When coming to any intersection, however minor, it is essential to slow down and give way to vehicles coming from the right. When coming to a main road you are likely to see one of two signs telling you to give way — a white triangle edged in red with a black arrow with a line through it, or a yellow diamond edged in white. You may also see a row of white shark's teeth painted on the road pointing towards you telling you to give way. At roundabouts entering traffic has right of way, unless indicated otherwise.

Another frequent cause of accidents involving foreigners is misunderstanding what is meant by flashing headlights at someone. This signifies 'Get out of my way' or 'I have priority' — not 'Please go ahead'. Trams are another unfamiliar hazard. Overtaking a tram on the inside when it is at a stop is illegal — you could hit passengers trying to get off — so watch out for tram stops. Trams have priority at all times in any case. While you cannot avoid parking near tramlines you should make sure that trams can get past.

Driving Regulations

There are two police forces in Belgium which deal with traffic violations: the local *Police/Politie* and the national *Gendarmerie/Rijkswacht*. The former deal with traffic accidents and parking; their vehicles have a blue stripe along the side. The *Gendarmerie* patrol the roads and also have the same functions as the *Police* when no local police are available. Their vehicles have a red stripe, as do their trousers.

Seat belts are compulsory in Belgium, front and back. Tyres should have a minimum tread of 1.6 millimetres. You are also legally obliged to carry the following: a fire extinguisher with the logo *Benor V*; a red triangular danger signal; a rear fog lamp; and an approved first-aid kit. You must also carry your identity card, car registration papers (*carte grise/grijze kaart*), driving licence and insurance papers.

Contrary to appearances, there are speed limits. Police radar traps are common and you can be fined on the spot if you are caught speeding. On motorways and four-lane highways there is a minimum speed limit of 70 kph (44 mph) and a maximum of 120 kph (75 mph). Other out-of-town roads usually have a 90 kph (56 mph) limit. In built-up areas the limit can vary between 40 and 80 kph (25-50 mph) but 60 kph (37.5 mph) is the norm.

Parking is regulated by meters, or by the display of a special disc if in a 'blue' zone in towns. Sometimes parking is on one side of the street 15 days of the month and on the other side the rest of the month. This will be shown by a sign with Roman numerals on it.

Drinking and Driving:
The permissible blood/alcohol level has now been fixed at 50 milligrams per 100 millilitres of blood, lower than the British level of 80 milligrams. Serious cases of drink driving can result in your licence being withdrawn and a jail sentence. Most breath tests take place at roadblocks where you can be tested at random. In 1990, of 164,647 tests administered 10.6% were positive.

Breakdowns and Accidents

Thanks to the introduction of driving tests and stricter police regulation the number of deaths and injuries on the roads has fallen somewhat since the 1970s, but there has recently been an upward trend in the number of accidents. In 1990 there were 1,978 deaths and 17,434 serious injuries on the roads, two of the worst figures in the EC. If you do have an accident it is only necessary to call the police (on 101) if someone is injured or there is a disagreement with the other driver about the circumstances. If there is no disagreement you can fill in a standard form supplied by your insurance company called a *Constat à l'aimable* — an 'amicable account of the accident' with details of car registration, type, and so on. Otherwise the police will have to draw up a written account of the accident. If a car cannot be moved or someone is injured, call 100, the number for both the fire brigade (*pompiers/brandweer*) and ambulances (*ambulance/ziekenwagen*).

Should you break down on a motorway you will find telephones every three kilometres by the side of the road from where you can call the *gendarmerie/rijkswacht* who will put you in touch with a breakdown service. There are three motoring organizations in Belgium which offer 24-hour-a-day breakdown services all over Benelux (Belgium, The Netherlands and Luxembourg). RAC and AA members get help from their sister organizations in Belgium — the RACB and TCB — provided that they have taken out extra insurance cover for Europe. If you are not covered at all you can join one of the Belgian organizations on the spot at a surcharge. These are (together with the name of the service they offer and emergency numbers):

Useful Addresses

Royal Automobile Club de Belgique/Koninklijke Automobiel Club van België (RACB/KACB): Rue d'Arlon 53, 1040 Brussels; tel 02 287 09 11. SOS Dépannage/Pechdienst — Antwerp 03 235 22 22; Brussels 02 736 59 59; Liège 041 86 22 88; Namur 081 22 50 00; Ghent 091 25 66 96.

Touring Club de Belgique/Touring Club van België (TCB): Rue de la Loi 44, 1040 Brussels; tel 02 233 22 11.
Touring Secours/Touring-Wegenhulp — Antwerp 03 353 88 88; Brussels 02 233 22 11; Liège 041 68 79 91; Namur 081 46 13 63; Ghent 091 62 65 65.

Vlaamse Toeristenbond/Vlaamse Automobilistenbond (VTB-VAB): St. Jacobsmarkt 45, 2000 Antwerpen; tel 03 252 62 70.
Wacht op de Weg (Road Watch) — All calls dealt with from HQ in Antwerp: 03 252 62 70.

Driving Licences

Anyone visiting Belgium can continue to use the driving licence of their home country. For Britons this means the traditional green licence or the new pink EC licence. If you intend to remain in Belgium, then you need to exchange your national licence for a Belgian one within a year of your arrival, even if you hold an EC licence. The EC directive making licences fully transferable will not be implemented until 1 July 1996. It is generally recommended to make this exchange as soon as is practical in case you lose your original licence. Your old licence will be held by the Belgian licensing authority until you need it again.

EC citizens and others with internationally recognized licences do not have to take any kind of test to obtain a Belgian licence. You simply hand in your licence, residence permit and two passport photos, and you will receive your Belgian licence within seven days.

Car Registration

If you are importing your own vehicle, you need to see that your car conforms to Belgian norms. You can check first with a dealer for your particular model if a change needs to be made. Your car must then be inspected at a Technical Inspection (TI) centre (look in the Yellow Pages under *Auto-inspection technique et centres d'examens/Automobielinspectie en rijbewijscentra*). If they are satisfied that your car is roadworthy, the TI centre will issue a 'Certificate of Inspection' and ask you to fill in a pink registration (*immatriculation/immatriculatie*) application form. You then take out an insurance policy with a Belgian company, with at least third-party protection. An insurance contract runs for a year and is automatically renewed. Notice of cancellation must be given three months before the renewal date. In the case of foreign residents it is possible to insert a clause into the contract making it possible to cancel before the usual date. Belgian car insurance is expensive and a comprehensive policy costs at least BF25,000.

Once you have an insurance policy the insurance company will pass on your application for registration to the relevant authority — the *Direction pour l'Immatriculation des Véhicules/Direktie voor Immatriculatie der Voertuigen (DIV)* (Cantersteen 12, 1000 Brussels; tel 02 517 06 11) — who will send you the rear registration plate and your registration card (*carte grise/grijze kaart*). You then have a copy made of the number plate at a car shop or Mister Minute shop and attach it to the front of your car. The DIV will also send a demand for payment of the road tax (*taxe de circulation/verkeersbelasting/*), which is calculated on the basis of the car's nominal horsepower. For an average-sized car this comes to about BF6,000 per year.

The procedure outlined above is much the same for buying a new or second-hand car in Belgium. If you require guidance the DIV have an information service on 02 517 07 45 (French) or 02 517 07 46 (Dutch).

Transport

Trains

Belgium has one of the densest railway networks in the world, noted for its punctuality and safety. Trains are coded according to the number of stations they stop at. Local trains (L) stop at every station, and peak-hour trains (P) at most stations. Inter-city and Inter-regional trains (IC and IR) miss out most small stops. Supplements (*supplément/toeslag*) have to be paid on international trains marked EC+. International trains marked INT do not require a supplement.

Tickets must be bought before getting on the train. Prices are calculated on the basis of total distance. A 100 km journey, for example, costs BF320. The price of a return ticket (*aller retour/heen en terug*) is double that of a single ticket (*aller simple/enkel*). Reduced rates on return tickets are generally only available at weekends. One very good deal, however, is the B-Tourrail Card which offers unlimited travel in Belgium on five out of 17 days for BF1,800. For those under 26 years of age this is reduced to BF1,350. Train times and prices are available on 02 219 26 40 (French) and 02 219 28 80 (Dutch).

City Transport

Urban transport systems are highly integrated, with metros in Brussels and Antwerp. A ticket is usually valid for one hour on the whole system in a particular city. A single ticket costs BF45 in Brussels, and a ten-ticket card (*carte reseau urbain/stadskaart*) BF275. In other towns single tickets are BF35 and BF175 for a strip of 10. It is preferable to buy your ticket in advance — they are sold in stations and bookshops — or to have the right change on you, as tram/bus drivers do not like wasting time. Once you get on, your ticket has to be 'invalidated' (*obliteré/ontwaardt*) so that the time is printed on it.

Air and Sea Travel

Belgium's main international airport (Brussels National) is at Zaventem, on the northwest side of Brussels. The national airline, Sabena, has made enormous losses in recent years, and has now entered into partnership with Air France to remain viable. Brussels is a frequent entry point for travellers from Zaïre and neighbouring African countries because of Belgium's earlier colonial links with the area. Flights from Britain to Brussels are becoming cheaper and more frequent. British Midland Airways offer a three-day return ticket for businessmen at £190. Tickets with restrictive conditions can be bought for as little as £105.

Most UK travellers still use the ferry, hovercraft or jetfoil to go to Belgium. The French port of Calais is very close to the Belgian border; ferry services to Ostend and Zeebrugge (closer to Holland) take rather longer. The opening of the Channel Tunnel will eventually make it possible to reach Brussels in $2\frac{1}{4}$ hours from London, but at the time of writing (1992) the high-speed rail link from Calais to Brussels has yet to be built.

Useful Addresses

Belgian Rail/Belgian Ferries: Premier House, 10 Greycoat Place, London SW1P 1SB; tel/fax 071-233 0360.
Belgian National Tourist Office: Premier House, 2 Gayton Road, Harrow HA1 2XU; tel 081-861 3300.

British Midland Airways: Donnington Hall, Castle Donnington, Derby DE7 2FB; tel 071-589 5599.
P&O European Ferries: Channel View Road, Dover CT16 3BR; tel 0304-203388.
Sealink: Park St., Ashford, Kent T24 8EX; tel 0233-47047.

Banks and Finance

If you have become used to the dismal service offered by UK high street banks, you will be in for a pleasant surprise if you settle in Belgium. Not only does it lead the world in the use of electronic banking, but it also has the largest number of bank branches per head in the world. The use of paper cheques has largely died out — 95% of transactions are carried out electronically. If you work in Belgium your employer will expect you to have a bank account so that your salary can be paid into it.

Bank accounts

Most people have accounts with one of the three major banks — Generale Bank/Générale de Banque, Bank Brussel Lambert/Banque Bruxelles Lambert, and Kredietbank — or a Post Office cheque account. Bank opening hours are 9.00am to 3.30pm, Monday to Friday, but there are variations, and some banks are open on Saturdays. If you bank with the post office, you will benefit from the longer opening hours (9 to 5). Anyone can open a current account (*compte à vue/zichtrekening*) by presenting their identity card or passport. You will receive a 12-figure bank account number which is unique in Belgium and identifies your bank and branch. If you can show sufficient funds, you will be given Eurocheques and a Eurocheque card. With these you can write cheques up to BF7,000 in any European country; but if your cheques are used by someone else you will be liable. Loss of cheques should be reported immediately to the police and the bank, preferably within two hours.

Your cheque guarantee card is also a debit and cash card. Not only can you make automatic electronic payments at over 20,000 terminals in retail outlets, but you also have access to the Bancontact and Mister Cash networks of cash dispensers, where you can withdraw cash 24 hours a day to a maximum of BF10,000 in one day. If you have a card you can run up an overdraft of between BF10,000 and BF50,000, depending on the bank. If you exceed the limit all transactions will be stopped until you resolve matters. Bank statements (*extraits de compte/rekeninguittreksels*) can be sent daily, weekly or monthly and cost very little.

Instead of using cheques, bills are usually paid by bank transfer (*virement/overschrijving*) using the red form attached to the bill or invoice. You can also use a direct debit (*domiciliation/domicilie*) or standing order (*ordre permanent/bestendige opdracht*).

In spite of the sophistication of electronic banking in Belgium, credit cards are also popular, in particular Visa, American Express, MasterCard and EuroCard.

Transferring Funds to and from Belgium

There are no foreign exchange controls in Belgium. When transferring amounts over BF10,000 ((£170) to another country Belgian residents are asked to inform the financial institution what the nature of the transaction is. This is for statistical purposes to help calculate Belgium's balance of payments and to stop tax evasion. Sending money from the UK should only take three days. It is worth checking if the bank uses the SWIFT system of electronic transfer of money.

Money

The Belgian Franc (French *Franc*/Dutch *Frank*) is made up of 100 centimes. 50-centime, 1, 2, 5 and 20-franc coins and 100, 500, 1000 and 5000-franc banknotes are in use. 10-franc coins and 50-franc banknotes are no longer legal tender.

Useful Addresses

BBL: Av. Marnix 24, 1050 Brussels; tel 02 517 21 11.
BBL (UK): 1 Appold Street, Broadgate, London EC2A 2BY; tel 071-247 5566.
Generale Bank: Bavaria House, 13/14 Appold Street, London EC2A 2DP; tel 071-247 5353.
Générale de Banque: Montagne du Parc 3, 1000 Brussels; tel 02 516 21 11.
Nationwide Overseas Ltd: P.O. Box 217, Market Street, Donglas, Isle of Man; fax 4 4 (0) 624 663495. Provides tax-free banking services for expatriates including a 90-day notice overseas Account.

Taxation

Belgians have long suffered from high levels of taxation, and therefore often try to hide some of their assets in neighbouring Holland and Luxembourg. In order to counteract this tendency, the Belgian state has lowered the withholding tax on savings accounts interest to 10%, while that on share dividends remains at 25%. For most foreigners the scope for tax evasion is limited, since most taxes are withheld at source.

Income Tax

The tax year is the same as the calendar year. By the beginning of April you should receive a tax return (*déclaration/aangifte*) for the previous year's income. Income tax (*impôt personnes physiques/belasting natuurlijke personen*) is deducted by your employer from your monthly salary, so this is an opportunity to adjust the total amount. The date by which the form has to be returned will be printed on the form. You have two months to pay any tax demand or face interest penalties. If you have not received a form by the beginning of June you are obliged to request one from the Finance Ministry (*Ministère des Finances/Ministerie van Financiën*). You are entitled to make a complaint if you believe the authorities have made an error. On the other hand, if you fill in the return incorrectly so that your liability appears to be higher than it really is, you have to pay up.

Foreigners working in Belgium can be treated as residents or non-residents. A resident is taxed on their worldwide income, whereas a non-resident is only taxed on income earned in Belgium. Foreign executives and researchers who are temporarily assigned to Belgium, benefit from a special tax regime, whereby they are treated as non-residents so that double taxation can be avoided. If you are in this category you will inevitably need the services of an accountant.

Professional expenses and social security payments are deducted from the gross salary in order to calculate taxable income. It should be noted that fringe benefits, bonuses and so on all count as taxable income. The basic single person's allowance (which is index-linked) in 1992 stood at BF176,000 (about £2,800) and for a married couple at BF139,000 for each partner. A number of allowances are applicable, including insurance payments, private pension schemes, mortgage repayments, and so on. There are also generous allowances for children — BF37,000 for the first child, BF59,000 for the second, and so on. It is important to understand that allowances take you into a higher tax bracket and rate of tax and so save you less tax than you might think.

Tax brackets for income earned in 1991 are as follows:

Bracket	Taxable Income (in BF)	% Tax	Amount of tax (in BF)
1	0-245,000	25%	61,250
2	245,000-325,000	30%	24,000
3	325,000-464,000	40%	55,600
4	464,000-1,067,000	45%	271,350
5	1,067,000-1,600,000	50%	266,500
6	1,600,000-2,347,000	52.5%	392,175
7	2,347,000	55%	

A single person with gross income of BF1,000,000 and no allowances pays BF297,754 (including 6% local tax) plus 12.07% social security. A married person earning a gross salary of BF2,000,000 with two children and claiming professional expenses pays about 30% of their total salary plus 12.07% social security, assuming the spouse does not work. A single person with a similar salary can expect to pay 35% of their income plus social security. Those with much higher salaries could well pay most of their tax at the top rate of 55%.

Self-employed workers usually arrange to pay income tax in advance at quarterly intervals on the basis of their predicted income, as there are substantial savings on interest to be made.

Local Tax

Quaintly called *centimes additionelles* or *opcentiemen* (additional centimes), this is paid to the commune and is calculated as a percentage of your income tax. The usual rate is between 6% and 10%, depending on how up-market the commune is.

Other Taxes

VAT: TVA (*Taxe Valeur Ajoutée*) or BTW (*Belasting Toegevoegde Waarde*) is levied at four different rates. These are: 1% on gold, 6% on basic foods, publications, medicines, coffins, hotels and transport; 12% on cigarettes, tobacco, coal and margarine; and 19.5% on new buildings, vehicles, petrol, clothes, services, beer, wines, spirits, televisions, audio equipment and cosmetics.

Précompte immobilière/Onroerende voorheffing: Withholding tax on non-movable assets. If you own any property or land you will be sent a demand for this in the first half of the year. This is a percentage of the nominal annual rental value of your property, the *revenu cadastral/kadastraal inkomen*, which is reviewed every fifteen years. This tax is distributed between the region, province and commune.

Droit de succession/Erfenisrecht: Inheritance tax. This is dealt with in the next chapter *Retirement*.

Plus values/Meerwaarde: Capital Gains. There is no Capital Gains Tax as such. If you happen to make a profit on the sale of private property, shares, goods, etc. and can argue you were not speculating in them you will not be taxed. Profit on the sale of land, however, is taxed at 33%. Any regular buying and selling is considered a business activity and comes under income tax.

Health Care, Insurance and Hospitals

Belgian medical services are some of the best in the western world. All doctors are trained for at least seven years, and specialists for 12. While you will not be refused medical treatment on the grounds of inability to pay, the financial implications of falling ill without proper cover are serious.

The E111

Until such time as you join a health insurance scheme in Belgium you will need to make provision for medical costs. It is possible to obtain refunds on treatment in Belgium, if you have a form E111 with you. You should ask for E111 from the DSS Overseas Branch, Venton Park Road, Newcastle upon Tyne NE98 1YX (tel 091-213 5000). Allow one month for the DSS to process your application. The form can be sent to you in Belgium. If you go to a doctor or dentist, check that they are *conventionné/gekonventioneerd*, i.e. linked to a sickness fund. Only 17% are not *conventionné*. The sickness funds (*mutualité/ziekenfonds*) keep lists. Show them your E111 and make sure you obtain a receipt for treatment (*Attestation de soins donnés/Getuigschrift voor verstrekte hulp*); if you buy medicines from a pharmacy, get a receipt and ask your pharmacist to stamp your copy of the prescription. You will then be able to obtain a refund of 75% of your treatment costs from the local sickness fund office (less for medicines). If you need hospital treatment, ask a sickness fund to recommend a hospital. They will then issue a certificate stating that they will pay part of your hospital costs. If you cannot contact a *mutualité* before entering hospital, show your E111 to the hospital and ask them to contact the *mutualité* for you. Ambulance costs are not refunded. As a rule of thumb, it is best to choose a university hospital (*hôpital/ziekenhuis*) which has a wide range of services, rather than a 'clinic' (*clinique/kliniek*) which has more limited services and is likely to be private.

An E111 is only valid for three months. It loses its validity once you are registered as resident in Belgium. Since the E111 is meant primarily to cover emergency medical care you would be well advised to take out private medical insurance for all eventualities (see below).

Emergencies

In the event of an emergency, dial 100 and ask for an ambulance (*ambulance/ziekenwagen*). If you are unable to speak, your call will be traced in five seconds if you leave the phone off the hook. If you think it is necessary, you can request a doctor to come with the ambulance. The ambulance will take you to the nearest hospital with an emergency service, which can lead to problems if you want to be transferred to a cheaper hospital. Most Belgian doctors understand

English. If you have a chronic illness, you could carry an account in English of the nature of your ailment. If you need to consult a doctor at the weekend or at night, you can go to the emergency section of any hospital. There are also pharmacists on duty 24 hours a day. The name is posted on every pharmacist's door. Needless to say, you should keep your E111 or *carnet de mutuelle* (sickness fund card) with you at all times.

Private Medical Insurance

If you hold a private health insurance policy in the UK, you will find that most companies will switch this for European cover when you are in Belgium. Private health insurance can be arranged through an organization such as BUPA, the British United Provident Association (head office: BUPA, 23 Essex Street, London WC2 8AX; tel 071-353 5212) or PPP, the Private Patients Plan (head office: PPP, Philips House, Crescent Road, Tunbridge Wells, Kent TN1 2PL; tel 0892-512345).

As a resident of Belgium, you will pay contributions into a Belgian sickness fund, but you need to pay six months' contributions before you can claim. Even then you still have to pay a part of your medical costs — 25% of treatment, and anything up to 100% of medicines. You could therefore consider paying your sickness fund for extra cover. If you work in Belgium as a non-resident, it is legal to continue using a private medical insurance scheme from your home country (e.g. BUPA's International Lifeline Scheme).

Useful Addresses

Recommended hospitals:
Academisch Ziekenhuis Jette: Av. de Laerbeek 101, 1090 Brussels; tel 02 477 41 11 emergencies 477 51 00.
Clinique Universitaire Saint Luc: Av. Hippocrate 10, 1200 Brussels; tel 02 764 11 11.
Hôpital Erasme: Route de Lennik 808, 1070 Brussels; tel 02 526 31 11 emergencies 526 34 02.
Institut Jules Bordet and Clinic Heger: Rue Heger-Bordet 1, 1000 Brussels; tel 02 535 31 11.
Sint-Vincentius Ziekenhuis: St Vincentiusstraat 20, 2018 Antwerpen; tel 03 218 6000.

24-hour helplines in Brussels:
Community Help Line: 02 648 40 14.
Dentists: 02 426 10 26.
General practitioners: 02 648 80 00 or 479 18 18.
Pharmacists: 02 479 18 18.
Veterinary surgeons: 02 538 16 99.

Social Security and Unemployment Benefit

Belgium aims to provide a high level of social security, and once you are established there you can be the beneficiary of this. The level of social security contributions is staggeringly high. As an employee you pay 12.07% of your salary for social security. Your employer, on the other hand, pays 32.46%-34.26%. Note that the latter figure is not included in the salary quoted in job advertisements.

You do not have to pay social security if you are a temporary worker in Belgium. This refers to high-level executives and researchers who pay social security in their home country. The time period covered by the word 'temporary' could extend to several years in practice. US citizens, for example, can be exempted from social security payments for up to five years.

Social Security Benefits
The minimum monthly wage for Belgian workers is BF38,857 (about £670). You are legally entitled to 20 days' paid holiday a year, plus an added holiday payment of 14.8% of your salary. If you are unable to work because of illness, the sickness fund pays 60% of your salary for a year; thereafter you receive a disability allowance of 45% of your salary. If you have dependants you will receive 65%. Pregnant women get 75% of their last wages for a period of up to 14 weeks plus a single payment per child. Note that there are minimum and maximum payments in all these cases.

The notice for terminating employment is generally a matter of mutual agreement between the employer and employee. For the low paid (under BF699,000 p.a.) it is legally fixed at three months, plus three months for every five years' service. You are usually entitled to severance pay related to length of service.

Unemployment
If you become unemployed against your free will, register at the local *Caisse Auxiliaire de Paiement des Allocations de Chômage/Hulpkas voor Werkloosheidsuitkeringen* (Unemployment Benefit Office), and you will be paid 60% of your former salary, or up to BF1,215 per day. There are a number of conditions attached to this. Firstly, you must have worked 300 days during the previous 18 months in Belgium or another EC state. Before making a claim you have to be registered at an employment office (see *Service de l'Emploi/Tewerkstellingsdienst* in the Yellow Pages) as seeking work. You will not receive any benefit for up to three months if you left of your own accord, or caused your own dismissal. Benefit is reduced after one year.

If you are thinking of going to Belgium to look for work, it is worth knowing that you can continue to receive UK unemployment benefit at UK rates for three months in Belgium. This is only applicable if you have already been unemployed for a month in the UK. You should contact your usual benefit office who will in turn contact the DSS Overseas Branch. They will issue a form E303, the document which is needed to claim benefit in Belgium.

Crime and the Police

Belgium has a low level of crime compared with neighbouring countries, but there has been an alarming rise in car thefts in Brussels recently. There are two police forces in Belgium — the local police (*police/politie*) and the national gendarmerie (*gendarmerie/rijkswacht*) — both of them armed. The latter deal with serious and interregional crime, while the local police deal with less serious offences and do a lot of administrative work. The police and gendarmerie have the same powers, but it is always advisable to contact the local police first. Both police forces have the same emergency number, 101; outside Brussels you are more likely to get the gendarmerie. The gendarmerie can be distinguished from the police by the red stripes on their trousers and red flashes on their lapels.

You must keep your identity card with you at all times; otherwise you could be arrested and held until you can prove who you are. The police have the right to hold anyone without arresting them for up to 24 hours. If you are arrested, you should inform the Consul of your country immediately. You also have the right to free legal representation — the so-called *Pro Deo* lawyer. The police can only search your home between 05.00 and 21.00, and then only with a search warrant. You can refuse entry to the police between 21.00 and 05.00 even if they have a search warrant.

Social Life

The key to understanding the Belgians undoubtedly lies in their strong respect for the Catholic church. Even when dealing with avowed atheists, as an outsider you should not criticize the church or the Pope. It is also just as well not to comment on politics, which are inextricably linked with religion. Belgium's colonial past is another area to avoid. On the other hand, it is always safe to talk about one's family or about sport.

The Belgian view of life may well seem serious and austere to the average Briton — frivolity and eccentricity are not greatly appreciated or understood. Work in particular is taken very seriously. Tea-breaks are unheard of. A more positive side of the Belgians' Catholic piety is a strong sense of social justice, which has led them to create an all-embracing welfare state, and a less materialistic attitude towards life than in some neighbouring countries. The attempt to create social justice has, however, also led to excessive bureaucracy and regimentation.

Manners and Customs

On a personal level, Belgians are friendly and accommodating, but you should be warned that some petty officials can be very rude. If you have to deal with the authorities a respectful attitude is still expected. When addressing people you do not know well, it is usual to use their titles — Mr and Mrs are *Monsieur/Madame* in French and *Meneer/Mevrouw* in Dutch — on the end of greetings and questions. With superiors at work, you are not likely to get on to first name terms. In spite of this formality, Belgium is not a class-ridden society in the British sense. Modesty and realism are the archetypal Belgian virtues. Social status is largely related to one's profession and reputation as a respectable member of society.

If you go to work in Belgium the first thing you will notice is a great deal of hand-shaking in the office and anywhere else when people meet and part. Between men and women, or women and women, the *trois bises* or three pecks on the cheeks, are still customary when meeting socially.

In their own homes, the Belgians tend towards formality. They prefer to be told in advance if you are planning a visit, so that they can be sure to have sufficient food and drink available. Since they are hearty eaters, you should be prepared for a big meal if you are invited to dinner. Even on informal occasions it is a good idea to offer flowers (but not chrysanthemums or carnations which are unlucky) or chocolates to the hostess. It is not usual to take wine or spirits. If you cannot invite someone round to your home, then taking them to a restaurant is always greatly appreciated.

Making Friends

Outsiders, especially Americans, will have the impression that friendships take a long time to develop in Belgium. Because of their close involvement with their families and long-established family friends, Belgians feel less need for a large circle of more casual acquaintances. They are also reluctant to invade other people's privacy, which might mean that you do not get to know your neighbours very well. On the other hand, when you have made friends with someone, you will find them to be very loyal and supportive when needed.

In a place like Brussels there are great numbers of foreigners who form their own groups and clubs. It is very easy to locate groups of compatriots if you feel the need to meet people from back home. *Living in the Heart of Europe* (publ. Pelckmans; available from W.H.Smith, Bvd. Adolphe Max 71-75, Brussels) has a long list of expatriate clubs, and *The Bulletin* (from main newsagents in Brussels) publicizes their meetings.

Food and Drink

Eating and drinking assume an importance in Belgian life which is difficult for many Britons to comprehend. Fresh produce is cheap and of a very high quality. The multiplicity of local delicacies and beers is well covered in publications such as *Living in Belgium* and in tourist handouts. A lot of Belgian food is fried in butter or lard, so it might be a good idea to avoid high-cholesterol food in between going out for meals.

Public Holidays

On the following days banks, offices, schools, etc. are closed.

1 January — New Year's Day (*Nouvel An/Nieuwjaar*)
Easter Monday (*Pâques/Pasen*)
1 May — (*Jour du Travail/Dag van de Arbeid*)
Ascension Day (*Ascension du Seigneur/Hemelvaart*)
Whit Monday (*Pentecôte/Pinksteren*)
21 July — National Day (*Jour National/Nationale Dag*)
15 August — Assumption (*Ascension de la Vierge/Maria Hemelvaart*)
1 November — All Saints' Day (*Toussaint/Allerheiligen*)
11 November — Armistice Day (*Armistice/Wapenstilstand*)
15 November — King's Name Day (*Jour de la Dynastie/Dag van de Dynastie*)
25 December — Christmas (*Noël/Kerstmis*)
26 December — Boxing Day (*Deuxième Jour de Noël/Tweede Kerstdag*)

11 July is a holiday in Flanders commemorating the defeat of the French at the Battle of the Golden Spurs in 1302. The anniversary of the defeat of the Dutch in the 1830 Revolution — 27 September — is celebrated by the Walloons.

Retirement

Background Information

Belgium is not an obvious place to retire to unless you have some prior connections there. You would not be short of company, however, as there is a well-established community of retired Britons who have spent some part of their working life in Belgium and put down roots there. One obvious attraction of being retired in Belgium is the high level of amenities provided for senior citizens and the convenience of never being far away from essential services. Retirement properties are still cheap and plentiful. If you are looking for good food and culture this is the place to be. The climate, on the other hand, is much like that of England — the number of days you can sit on the beach in a deckchair is limited.

The Decision to Leave the UK

Moving to another country when you retire requires energy and enthusiasm. One must have a clear idea of the compensations for leaving behind home, friends and family. Many people who move do so on the basis of a love of the country discovered through past holidays. Living permanently in a country is not the same as spending holidays there, and it may be a good idea to stay for a longer time in the area one is interested in. If you can buy a second home in Belgium and spend part of the year there you can form some idea of what it would be like to live there outside the holiday season. It is of course crucial to have adequate financial arrangements, and probably of equal importance, a prior knowledge of or commitment to learning the local language. A good knowledge of French would not necessarily help you very much in a Flemish-speaking area. It is worth considering how your social life might be affected by your language capabilities.

Financially you would not be at a disadvantage living in Belgium as both company and state pensions are honoured in Belgium at the UK rate (further details later in this chapter). As a Belgian resident, you will be taxed on any pension you receive from abroad.

Residence and Entry

Since 1 January 1992 EC countries have allowed pensioners who can support themselves to settle anywhere in the EC without asking them to make prior arrangements before leaving their own country. This directive has applied in Belgium for some time in any case. If you know that you are going to stay in Belgium for over three months, then you should register at the commune within eight days of your arrival. You are then issued with the mauve card mentioned in Chapter Two, *Residence and Entry*, and placed on the Register of Aliens. The first three months of your stay are a sort of trial period, during which you have to show that you are receiving a pension or have some other kind of income. While the State does not prescribe a standard figure, it is usually reckoned that you need £12,000 per year to live comfortably in Belgium. Arranging health insurance is an absolute necessity. Since Belgian sickness funds (*mutualités*) are very reluctant to take on clients who are over 65 when they first apply for sickness cover, this means continuing your own private health care plan from the UK.

Assuming that you are able to show sufficient funds, you will be able to exchange your mauve card for the yellow card of a non-working EC citizen which is valid for five years. If you intend to engage in any kind of work other than voluntary, then you are entitled to a blue card for EC workers, also valid for five years. Should you not be able to show sufficient funds after three months, you can expect to be asked to leave the country even as an EC citizen.

The Right to Remain

If an EC national resides in Belgium for three years and reaches the age of retirement they can then stay on permanently, provided they worked during the year just before retirement. The same right to remain is extended to the spouse and family of an EC worker if the worker dies after two years of residence.

Non-EC Nationals

Entry for non-EC nationals is heavily restricted, as stated in Chapter Two, *Residence and Entry*. The first step in this case is to contact the Belgian Embassy or nearest Consulate in your home country. To obtain permission to enter Belgium as a non-worker, you have to show, at the very least, that you are financially completely independent and covered by health insurance, as well as being able to prove that you have no criminal record. A medical examination by a doctor appointed by the Embassy is obligatory. It is also necessary to give convincing reasons for wanting to live in Belgium with documentary evidence. If your application is approved you then receive the APS (Authorization of Provisional Sojourn) and can go to live in Belgium.

Possible Retirement Areas

Those who already know Belgium may have some idea of where they would like to retire to, and those who do not should try to find out something about the way of life as well as looking at different regions. There is no particular area with a large number of British retired people. A major consideration concerns the proximity of services. The only area of Belgium which could be described as remote from public services is the southeastern province of Luxembourg; even here the distances involved are not that great compared with larger European countries.

The Coast: This is a popular area in the summer for tourists. The advantages are excellent sports facilities, such as golf courses and tennis courts, a concentration of convalescent homes and medical facilities, and superb restaurants. In winter the area is quiet, but most facilities remain open all the year round. Property prices vary greatly depending on how fashionable a resort is. At the top end, a three-bedroom apartment in Knokke, near the Dutch border, costs about BF8,000,000 (£137,000) while a similar apartment in De Panne, near France, is only BF4,700,000 (£81,000). In less fashionable areas, three-bedroom apartments can be found for under BF3,000,000 (£50,000). The cheapest prices of all are in unfashionable

Ostend, which is nevertheless the most conveniently located and most interesting of all the seaside towns. A further attraction of Ostend is its closeness to England, and the large numbers of foreigners who pass through here.

The Ardennes: Undoubtedly the most scenic part of Belgium, the area around Bastogne and St Vith is strongly associated in American minds with the Battle of the Bulge of World War II. The most popular retirement home in this area is the so-called *fermette*, a converted farmhouse or farm cottage. One could also consider a chalet or villa (often a large bungalow). The drawback to the Ardennes is the relative isolation and lack of public transport. Unless you have a car, living out in the sticks here would be out of the question. If you are energetic and enjoy horse-riding or similar pursuits, this would be a good area to look at.

Flanders: In this case referring to Flanders proper, i.e. the provinces of East and West Flanders, rather than the whole Dutch-speaking region. This area has traditionally had close links with England going back to the early Middle Ages. Bruges and Ghent have great artistic heritages; if you enjoy painting or drawing you might find one of the artists' communities close to these cities a congenial place to live. Although this is not a region with wide open spaces, there are plenty of retirement villas and bungalows with large gardens where you can be at a reasonable distance from your neighbours.

Brussels: The area to the south of Brussels is very much favoured by wealthy expatriates. The landscape is more hilly than in Flanders; the best houses have woods and artificial lakes attached. If you are in this league you can enjoy a very good social life indeed with other émigrés living all around you. A further advantage of this area is that you will be able to use French all the time if you are not inclined to try speaking Dutch.

Pensions

There is no reason why a move to Belgium should affect the provision or rate of state pension for the vast majority of people. The main point to remember is that if a pension is sourced from the UK it will always be pegged at UK levels. At one time this was a major problem for expatriates, as the rate of exchange between the pound (sterling) and the franc could severely affect the amount of pension they received. Now that the UK has joined the European Monetary System (EMS) the possibility of a severe devaluation has been reduced.

Some time before you retire abroad, you need to find out how many different pensions you are going to receive. For many people this can be a complex combination of state pensions, occupational pensions and private pension plans. If you find that the total sum is short of expectations, it is possible to pay additional voluntary contributions (AVCs) into your company pension during your last few years of work. If you are going to live in an EC country such as Belgium, there should be no problem about having your pension paid abroad.

Taxation

The DSS will, in principle, pay your gross pension direct into a Belgian bank account without any deductions, as long as you have a declaration from the Belgian tax authorities that you are paying taxes in Belgium. It would be advisable to inform the Inland Revenue office with which you last dealt about your plans, or to contact the Inland Revenue's information office (Citygate House, 39-45 Finsbury Park, London EC2A 1HH; tel 071-588 4226).

If you are quite certain that you are going to become a Belgian resident, then the situation should be straightforward in that you will only be liable for Belgian income tax. At the present time pensions up to BF370,000 (£6,380) are tax free in Belgium and most pensioners are exempt from property taxes. A more complex situation arises if one intends to divide one's time between the UK and Belgium. In this case specialist advice is essential. In particular you cannot totally escape UK taxes if more than 183 days are spent in the UK in the first year of possessing a residence abroad. It should also be remembered that the Belgian tax year runs from January to December, whereas the UK tax year runs from April to April. The date of moving could then have an effect on your tax liability.

Belgian Pensions and Health Insurance

If you have worked in Belgium for any time, you will be entitled to Belgian pension payments in proportion to the years worked. The general procedure is that your social security records will be exchanged by the British and Belgian authorities, and the amount of pension payable by each country worked out. You are entitled to receive all your pension at the rate payable in Belgium, which is higher than the UK rate. The Belgian pension equals 60% (for single people) and 75% (for those with dependants) of the average annual gross salary multiplied by the number of years worked, and then divided by the maximum number of possible years worked. The maximum total of years worked is reckoned to be 45 years for men and 40 years for women. The minimum pension for someone who has worked a full 45 years now stands at BF25,000 a month (approximately £430) for a single person. A single pensioner is guaranteed an income of BF18,000 a month (£310) in any case, and this provision is extended to foreigners who have been in Belgium for more than five years before retirement. Pensions are index-linked.

A potential problem could arise in that Belgian *mutualités* (sickness funds) do not generally take on clients who are already retired. You are expected to remain with the same *mutualité* you dealt with when you were working, and they cannot refuse to insure you once you are established with them. There are special sickness insurance plans for the over-50s — the price depends on the level of benefits and can vary from BF4,000 to BF12,000 (£69-£206) per year. The *mutualité* is likely to place a limit on the maximum weekly amount it will pay out and this is rarely enough to cover your costs. For retired British people the only option could be to continue with a private health plan from the UK.

Wills and Legal Considerations

Most people of retirement age have either already made, or are intending to make a will. This step assumes even greater importance if one intends to move abroad. If a will has not been made then take the advice of a UK solicitor with knowledge of Belgian law. If a will has been made it must be reviewed before any move takes place.

In Belgium itself, it is vital to draw up a will with the help of a *notaire* (notary). Writing down your wishes without consulting a notary is hazardous, as your intentions could well be overridden by Belgian inheritance laws. Once you have drawn up your will, the notary is obliged to register it with the Central Register of Testaments (CRT, Rue de la Montagne 30 bte 2, 1000 Brussels; tel 02 511 90 73).

A major consideration affecting inheritance tax is the domicile of the deceased. It is possible (but difficult) to convince the British Inland Revenue that you are domiciled in Belgium; if you have no property in Britain, apply for Belgian citizenship, arrange to be buried in Belgium, and never try to vote in British elections, you can escape British death duties. Inheritance taxes are much heavier in Belgium than in Britain, however, so this would not be financially beneficial for your heirs. The greatest difficulty lies in the fact that the Belgian fiscal authorities could try to tax you on property and assets held outside Belgium if you were domiciled in Belgium at the time of death. Domiciled here means that you were a Belgian resident and administered your affairs from Belgium. By the same token the British Inland Revenue can tax British citizens on their worldwide assets, unless it is agreed that they are not domiciled in the UK.

If you have interests in both the UK and Belgium, you will evidently need a will for both countries. In Belgium, a notary acts as a trustee after your decease and draws up lists of creditors, claimants and heirs. The heirs are required to file an inheritance tax return within five months of death and to pay the tax within two months thereafter. Taxes are on a sliding scale with a tax-free allowance of BF500,000 (£8,620). They are quite modest for the spouse and children (no more than 30%) but very heavy for more distant relatives and unrelated persons (anything up to 80%). Taxes can be partly avoided by transferring assets to your children at least three years before you die. The way in which this is done is crucial, and you will have to go to a notary who specializes in such matters.

There are strict laws concerning the way inheritances are divided up between family members. The spouse is entitled to half your assets, including the family home. A single child also has a right to half your assets; if there are two children, each receives at least a third; three children receive a quarter each, and so on. If your will is unclear or there is a conflict between your heirs, the result is that your heirs will have to argue their case before a judge resulting in extra legal costs. The moral therefore is to know what the laws are when drawing up your will.

Death

This is an eventuality which affects everyone and which should be planned for. The fact that one's close relations may not be at hand complicates matters, and makes it all the more important that one's wishes are known in advance. It is as well to realize that having one's body shipped home for burial is very expensive, and there may be no alternative but to make arrangements in Belgium itself.

Deaths must be certified by a doctor and registered within 24 hours at the commune, with the death certificate and identity papers. In the case of foreigners the main consulate also issues a death certificate. A funeral director will help with formalities concerning the commune. Funerals (whether burials or cremations) cost from £500 upwards. Because Belgium is virtually entirely Catholic, those of other Christian denominations are likely to be buried in a Catholic cemetery. Cremations are also quite common now. There should be no difficulty in having a Protestant church service if you want one. Some names of churches are given below.

Churches

Apart from being indispensable for births, marriages and deaths, going to church services is a very good way of meeting expatriates. Sunday services in English are held in the churches given below (Anglican unless otherwise stated).

St Boniface: Grétrystraat 39, 2018 Antwerp; tel 03 329 33 39.
St Peter's Chapel: Keersstraat, Bruges; tel 059 70 28 59.
Pro-Cathedral of the Holy Trinity: Rue C. Crespel 29, 1050 Brussels; tel 02 511 71 83.
St Andrew's Church of Scotland: Chaussée de Vleurgat 181, 1050 Brussels; tel 02 649 02 19.
St Anthony's Roman Catholic Parish: Av. des Anciens Combattants 23-25, Kraainem, Brussels; 02 720 19 70.
St John's: Edmond Boonenstraat 4, 9000 Ghent; tel 091 22 36 59.
Synagoge de Bruxelles: Rue de la Régence 32, 1000 Brussels; tel 02 512 43 34.
International Chapel Centre: SHAPE, 7000 Mons; tel 065 36 04 26. Anglican and Episcopalian.
The English Church: Langestraat 101, 8400 Ostend; tel 059 70 28 59.
Notre Dame d'Argenteuil: Chaussée de Louvain 563, Ohain, Waterloo; tel 02 354 33 28. Episcopalian.
St Anne's Church: Av. du Feu, Waterloo; tel 02 354 53 43. Catholic.
St George's Memorial Church: Elverdingsestraat 1, 8900 Ypres; tel 091 22 36 59. Sunday evening service only.

Hobbies and Interests

Retirement is the ideal time to pursue old and new interests. Finding some part-time work is also a possibility, although the present level of unemployment in much of Belgium may work against this. There is also considerable scope for doing charity work, another excellent way of meeting new friends; look under the list of charities given in *Living in the Heart of Europe* (publ. Pelckmans). Homesickness should be less of a problem in Belgium than elsewhere in Europe. All the British TV channels are available, and British newspapers are delivered on the morning of publication. The *Wall Street Journal* and the *International Herald Tribune* have European editions and can be ordered by subscription (see section on Newspapers, *Employment* Chapter. Unless you have a very good radio the only British radio channel you are likely to get is the World Service.

Many Belgian pensioners join clubs of one kind or another. Playing cards is a popular pursuit, and is a good way to increase one's circle of friends. The following are just a few clubs for English-speaking expats:

Antwerp
American Women's Club of Antwerp: PO Box 20, 2930 Brasschaat; tel 03 384 23 69.
Antwerp British Community Association: tel 03 237 84 99.
Royal British Legion: tel 016 56 68 91.

Brussels
American Women's Club of Brussels: Av. des Erables 1, 1640 Rhode St-Genèse; tel 02 358 47 53.
British and Commonwealth Women's Club: Rue au Bois 509, 1050 Brussels; tel 02 772 53 13.
The Irish Club: Rue de Spa 28, 1040 Brussels; tel 02 687 55 30.
Royal British Legion: Rue des Cerisiers 1, 1390 Grez-Doiceau; tel 010 84 19 92. Women's section: tel 02 345 61 56.

Liège
Association Belgo-Britannique: Place Cockerill 3, Liège; tel 041 66 54 37.
Liège Rencontre: Palais des Congrès, Esplanade de l'Europe, Liège.

SECTION II

Working in Belgium

Employment
Business and Industry Report
Temporary Work
Starting a Business

Employment

The Employment Scene

As with all industrialized countries, Belgium has suffered from the global recession of 1991-92. The effects have been fairly mild compared with the UK; the balance of payments has remained in surplus and GNP is expected to grow by 3% annually for the next few years. Belgium's greatest problem is that it has one of the highest per capita national debts in the world — more than a quarter of the budget is eaten up by interest payments. Unemployment in Belgium is quite high, at 8.8% in 1992, and not expected to diminish perceptibly in the near future, but much of this unemployment is in the declining manufacturing sector where English-speaking foreigners are not likely to want to work.

Present economic conditions in Belgium have no effect on the number of workers employed by the EC Commission in Brussels (about 10,500), and it is well-known that Britain is under-represented as regards numbers of EC employees. As more countries join the EC, and more governmental functions are transferred to the EC, the number of EC-related staff is bound to rise. Along with posts for translators and administrators, numerous posts for clerical and technical support staff could be filled by British workers, even those who are not very good linguists. A similar situation exists with NATO and its affiliated organizations, such as the North Atlantic Assembly and the Supreme Headquarters of Allied Powers in Europe (SHAPE). NATO does not employ as many foreign workers as the EC, but there are opportunities which tend to be overlooked by the insular British.

Belgium is an excellent place to look for work, provided that what you have to offer is what Belgian employers are looking for. In the main this means relevant training and qualifications, and a commitment to acquiring French or Dutch. A desire to work hard is also indispensable. If you go to Belgium without arranging employment beforehand you can benefit from the numerous temporary employment agencies in every Belgian town. Because of the sky-high social security contributions payable by employers, and the difficulties involved in dismissing workers from their jobs, many employers would prefer to employ you on a trial basis for six months to see if you are the kind of worker they want to commit themselves to. This creates the ideal opportunity for anyone who wants to prove that they can do a good job. This does not mean that Belgium is a land of temporary workers: 95% of employment contracts are permanent. If you are prepared to stay in Belgium for some time, you will profit from the exceptionally generous social security and pension payments, as well as a high degree of job security.

Residence and Entry

The Belgian authorities try hard to apply EC directives in full, not only because Brussels is at the centre of the EC, but also because they believe it to be in Belgium's

"I can fly business class at an economy fare?

Are you serious?"

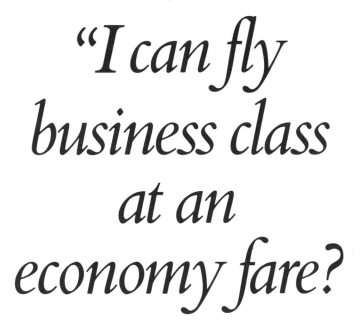

Sometimes it is possible to have the best of both worlds.

On all British Midland's major routes, domestic and international, our unique Diamond Service delivers a true business class service.

And since Diamond Service means business class travel at economy class fares, you can make serious savings every time you fly between Amsterdam or Brussels and London Heathrow.

In short, British Midland's award-winning service and value for money fares make an unbeatable combination that's worth considering. Seriously.

Diamond Service
BM British Midland
THE SERIOUS ALTERNATIVE

long-term interest to do so. Of all EC countries Belgium is probably the most strongly committed to internationalism — it is very much dependent on attracting multinational businesses and organizations in order to remain economically viable.

What few formalities there are for EC citizens going to Belgium to look for work are detailed in Chapter Two, *Residence and Entry*. If you hold an EC passport it should be entirely unnecessary to go to the Belgian Embassy in the UK or Ireland before you leave home.

Skills and Qualifications

Many EC directives have appeared over the years concerning mutual recognition of professional qualifications, for instance those of doctors, veterinarians and nurses, in all EC countries. Recent EC directives have now extended this mutual recognition to 92 different professions. This means in practice that if your profession is included within the 92 listed, you are eligible to join the counterpart professional association in Belgium without having to take a test or go through a training programme. The basic directive on training and qualifications (89/48/EEC) which recognized three-year training courses, has recently been expanded so that qualifications gained through any post-secondary course of more than one year, as well as work experience, must be recognized or taken into account where entry to a job is regulated in some way on the basis of specific national qualifications. This means that National and Scottish Vocational Qualifications (NVQs/SVQs) and their equivalents are now recognized by the EC.

If you have experience but no formal qualifications in a job, it is now possible to obtain a European Community Certificate of Experience. For EC citizens in the UK this is issued by the Department of Trade and Industry (DTI). Since the Certificate costs £45 to process, you should first make sure that your type of work experience is covered by an EC directive by asking your trade union or professional organization. If you are in doubt the DTI will send you a copy of the relevant directive if you write to them at: Department of Trade and Industry, European Division, Ashdown House, 6th Floor, 123 Victoria Street, London SW1E 6RB; tel 071-215 5354. The DTI also supplies the application form for a Certificate of Experience — form EC2 — with explanations attached.

The EC directive for your profession will tell you what you need to qualify for a Certificate. Usually you require either several years' managerial or self-employed experience in your profession, or a reasonable level of training and work experience. When you fill in the form you have to give all your work history, and supply two references. After receiving your Certificate of Experience it has to be registered with the competent authority in Belgium. It is also possible that you will be asked to declare on oath that you have no criminal record and have never been made bankrupt.

Professional associations in Britain are usually able to put you in touch with their counterparts in Belgium and may have some knowledge of EC directives. A list of associations is to be found in *Trade Associations and Professional Bodies of the UK*, available at most reference libraries.

Regulated Professions

Apart from the professions regulated by professional bodies, there are a considerable
number of non-salaried or independent trades which are subject to statutory
conditions in Belgium. To become self-employed in one of these areas you will
be expected to show managerial as well as work experience, and to register your
qualifications with one of the Chambers of Crafts and Trades (*Chambre des Métiers
et Négoces/Kamer van Ambachten en Neringen*) whose address can be found in
the Yellow Pages.
Some of the jobs concerned are the following:

English	French	Dutch
Bicycle mechanic	Mécanicien de cycles	Fietsmecanicien
Bricklaying contractor	Entrepreneur en maçonnerie et béton	Metselwerkondernemer
Carpenter/joiner	Menuisier-charpentier	Schrijnwerker-timmerman
Electrician	Electricien-installateur	Elektricien
Glazing contractor	Entrepreneur de vitrage	Glazenmaker
Hairdresser	Coiffeur	Kapper
Insurance broker	Courtier d'assurances	Verzekeringmakelaar
Optician	Opticien-lunetier	Opticien
Painter and decorator	Peintre	Schilder
Photographer	Photographe	Fotograaf
Plasterer	Plafonneur-cimentier	Stukadoor
Plumber	Plombier	Loodgieter
Restaurant-owner	Restaurateur	Uitbater
Secondhand car dealer	Négociant en véhicules d'occasion	Okkazieautohandelaar
Stonemason	Tailleur de pierres	Steenhouwer
Upholsterer	Tapissier	Stoffeerder
Watch-repairer	Horloger-réparateur	Uurwerkmaker

Sources of Jobs

Depending on your profession, it may or may not be advantageous to go to Belgium
to look for work on the spot. Someone who wants to work for the EC Commission,
for example, can make their application from the UK. There is no advantage in
going over to Brussels first. If you are going to go to Belgium without arranging

work in advance, it is important to have enough money to support yourself for a few weeks. You should also make sure you have copies of all your diplomas and degrees with you. The British Embassy in Brussels is at pains to point out that British consulates have only limited resources to help British citizens. They cannot help you to find a job or give you legal advice. Belgian Embassies and consulates do not give help with finding work either.

Newspapers

National Newspapers

Vacancies at the European Commission in Brussels, and in Belgium generally, are often advertised in the British press. *The Guardian*, for example, has a European Appointments page on Fridays. If you are looking for English-teaching work, then the *Guardian's Education* section on Tuesdays is essential reading. *The Independent* and *The Times* also advertise jobs in Belgium. Apart from EC jobs, dealt with under the section Working for the EC (see below), many of the advertisements are for secretaries and personal assistants to Brussels-based executives. Advertisements for lawyers and financial analysts also appear from time to time.

International Newspapers

International Newspapers are a fairly new development in newspaper publishing. These publications circulate editions across several national boundaries and carry a number of job advertisements for different countries. The following are the names and addresses of the four newspapers in this category:

The European: Orbit House, 5 New Fetter Lane, Holborn Circus, London EC4 1AP; tel 071-822 2002.
Financial Times: 1 Southwark Bridge, London SE1 9HL; 071-873 3000.
International Herald Tribune: 103 Kingsway, London WC2; 071-242 6593.
Wall Street Journal: The International Press Centre, 76 Shoe Lane, London EC4; 071-334 0008.

Magazines, Journals and Directories

Financial weeklies like *The Economist* often carry advertisements for jobs in Brussels. If you want to teach in Belgium you can sometimes find advertisements in the *Times Educational Supplement* published on Fridays. The specialist fortnightly publication, *Overseas Jobs Express* (available only by subscription from PO Box 22, Brighton B1 6HX) boasts, in addition to many wide-ranging, well-researched articles by working travellers, a substantial *Jobs* section, covering a weird and wonderful range of jobs abroad: accountancy, banking, EFL teaching, management consultancy, hotels and catering, agriculture, agribusiness, equestrian work, secretarial work, nannies, au pairs, and so on *ad infinitum*.

You do not have to be a member of a professional association in order to have access to their professional journal. Many of these journals are available at public libraries where they can be consulted free of charge. Examples include *The Architects' Journal* and *The Bookseller*. Some journals are not actually tied to one specific organization but are read by everybody in the trade, such as *Farmers' Weekly*, *Caterer and Hotel Keeper*, or *Flight International* for the airline industry. You can find valuable leads in these publications, even if there are no jobs advertised for the country you want to work in.

Some journals and trade magazines are more obscure, so it is worth looking through a media directory, such as *Benn's Media*, to see what is available. One journal which is essential to English teachers is the monthly *EFL Gazette*, which not only carries advertisements for jobs and training courses, but also has a lot to say about working conditions in foreign countries for English teachers. The *EFL Gazette* can be found at specialist English teaching bookshops, or can be ordered direct from: EFL Gazette, 10 Wrights Lane, London W8 6TA; tel 071-938 1819.

A further source of jobs is directories. A wide range of casual jobs, including secretarial, agricultural, tourism and domestic work, are advertised in the directory *Summer Jobs Abroad*; the directory *Teaching English Abroad* lists schools all over the world which employ English language teachers. Both publications are available from Vacation Work Publications, 9 Park End Street, Oxford OX1 1HJ; tel 0865-241978; fax 0865-790885.

Belgian Newspapers and Magazines
Numerous job advertisements appear in the newspapers and magazines mentioned in the Media section of Chapter 4, *Daily Life*. Obtaining copies of Belgian newspapers is difficult in the UK outside central London. The French-language newspaper *Le Soir* carries most job advertisements on Tuesdays and Saturdays. The main weekly English-language publication for job advertisements is *The Bulletin*, which also has a Situations Wanted section. Advertisements can be placed in *Le Soir* and the Dutch-language *Het Laatste Nieuws* through their British representative: Publicitas Ltd, 525/527 Fulham Road, London SW6 1HF; 071-385 7723; fax 071-381 8884.

Useful Addresses
Le Soir: Rossel & Cie SA, Rue Royale 112, 1000 Brussels; tel 02 217 77 50.
The Bulletin: Ackroyd Publications, Av. Molière 329, 1060 Brussels; tel 02 343 99 09. English-language weekly for foreigners.

Professional Associations
Many professional associations do not provide any official information on working overseas as such. However, most of them will have had contact with their counterpart association in other EC countries during negotiations over the question of EC recognition of qualifications, as required by the EC directives. Such associations should provide individual help if asked.

Details of all professional associations are to be found in the directory, *Trade Associations and Professional Bodies of the UK*, available at most reference libraries. It is also worth trying to contact the Belgian equivalent of UK professional associations. In addition, some trade unions have links with their counterparts in Belgium and may be able to supply addresses.

Specialist Job Publications
There are a few specialist publications, in both the UK and Belgium, which contain only job vacancies and articles aimed at helping the unemployed. In the UK, *Executive Post* handles some foreign vacancies. This is available from the Professional and Executive Recruitment (PER) agency (the local address is in the telephone directory). In Belgium a similar publication has recently started up called

De Werkzoeker in Dutch and *Offre d'Emploi* in French which is available twice a month at BF30. A Situations Wanted section is also included.

The UK Employment Service

The employment services of most EC countries, including those of the UK and Belgium, are members of various schemes, including International Circulation of Vacancies (ICV) and the European System for the International Clearing of Vacancies (SEDOC), by which information on specialist vacancies notified to the employment service in one EC country can be made available to the employment services in the others.

The British branch of SEDOC is based at the Overseas Placing Unit (OPU) of the Employment Service in Sheffield (Steel City House, Moorfoot, Sheffield S1 4PQ; tel 0742-596051/2). Most UK Employment Service offices have computer access to the vacancy details held at Sheffield. However inspired the idea behind SEDOC, the reality is that it is a slow and under-exploited system that falls far short of even modest expectations. There are usually fewer than 50 vacancies held on the Sheffield database at any time. The majority of vacancies are those for skilled craftspersons. Others include TEFL teachers, secretarial staff and occasionally, hotel and catering staff. A list of the vacancies available through the OPU is published in the fortnightly newspaper *Overseas Jobs Express* (see above).

At the time of writing the SEDOC system is under review. According to the Department of Employment, a long-term project is under consideration which will involve the UK employment service in general. Eventually, according to the thinking behind this project, job-seekers will be able to go into any UK Employment Service office and access on a computer a whole range of information regarding working in other EC countries from the level of benefit payments available to actual jobs. It is intended that SEDOC (which will probably be renamed EURES) will be an integral part of such a project.

From mid-1992, a series of booklets on working conditions in each of the twelve Community states will be available from Employment Service offices nationwide.

UK Recruitment Agencies

There are some agencies in the UK which specialize in finding overseas jobs for clients. In general, these agencies deal with a specific sector such as electronics, computers, secretarial, medical, English teaching, etc. and can only place people with suitable qualifications. As a rule, agencies are retained and paid by employers to fill specific vacancies and do not search on behalf of prospective workers, but there are also firms which maintain databases of jobs and will try to match you with the ones you are qualified for. The pioneer in this area is CV Database which puts UK final-year students in contact with graduate recruiters, and is likely to expand its operations to Europe by the end of 1992. University careers services can help to put students onto CV Database, or you can make contact with them yourself from the address below.

The Federation of Recruitment and Employment Services (FRES) issues a list of employment agencies who are members (see below). As an alternative, some 550 recruitment agencies can be located through the *CEPEC Employment Guide* which is available at reference libraries or from the Centre for Professional Employment Counselling (67 Jermyn Street, London SW1Y 6NY; tel 071-930 0322) at £21.50 including postage and packing. The *Recruitment Directory* lists agencies which arrange jobs, primarily for graduates and professionals, in the UK and sometimes abroad. CEPEC also publishes a useful guide entitled *The Job Search: for Executive and Professional Staff* (price £10.95 including p&p) which deals with job application procedures, from researching the job market, CV's and letters of application, to the all-important interview technique, as well as providing notes on self-employment and personal finance.

Useful Addresses

Cavell Bilingual Recruitment: 26 Goodge Street, London W1P 1FG. Managers and executives.
Computing Professionals: 16 Red Lion Square, London WC1R 4QS; tel 071-405 1006.
CV Database Ltd: World Trade Centre, International House, St Katherine's Way, London E1 9UN.
Eagle Recruitment: Eagle Place, 210-212 Piccadilly, London W1V 9LD; tel 071-823 9233. Secretarial and middle management.
Federation of Recruitment and Employment Services: 10 Belgrave Square, London SE1X 8PH.
James Duncan & Associates: 8 St John's Road, Tunbridge Wells, Kent T4 9NP; tel 0892-544757. Computer and administrative personnel.
Manpower: UK International House, 66 Chiltern Street, London W1M 9PB; tel 071-224 6688. Can supply a list of Manpower branches in Belgium.
Merrow Employment Agency: 73 New Bond Street, London W1Y 9DD; tel 071-499 3939. Specializes in multilingual secretaries.
Michael Page Group: 39-41 Parker Street, London WC2B 5LH. Finance and accountancy.
Neville John Associates: 9 The Quad, Chester West Employment Park, Sealand Road, Chester CH1 4PH. Recruits Information Technology staff for clients in UK, Germany and the Benelux countries.
PA Consulting Group: 123 Buckingham Palace Road, London SW1W 9SR; tel 071-730 9000. Managerial and professional recruitment on behalf of companies and individuals.

Belgian State Employment Offices

Employment offices come under the national Ministry of Employment and Labour (Ministère d'Emploi et Travail/Ministerie van Tewerkstelling en Arbeid, Rue Belliard 51-53, 1040 Brussels; tel 02 233 41 11). If you need information about workers' rights in Belgium, you can ask the Administration of Employment Regulation (*Administration de la Réglementation/Administratie van de Reglementering*) at the same Ministry.

The main employment office in Brussels is known as the ORBEM (*Office Régional Bruxellois de l'Emploi*) or BGDA (*Brusselse Gewestelijke Dienst voor Arbeidsbemiddeling*). In addition there are 11 sub-regional employment offices in Wallonia — the *Services Subrégionaux de l'Emploi* (SSE); and 18 in Flanders — the *Subregionale Tewerkstellingsdiensten* (STD), which can be found in the local Yellow Pages. Employment offices used to be known as *Offices Nationals de l'Emploi* (ONEM), but this term is now no longer used. A list of sub-regional employment offices can be obtained from: ORBEM/BGDA, Boulevard Anspach 65, 1000 Brussels; tel 02 513 78 90.

Private Employment Agencies

Brussels has become a mecca for recruitment agencies and executive search companies who all want to be in the best possible position to take advantage of the Single Market. There has also been an explosion in the number of firms offering human resource management, career evaluation, psychographology and other exotic-sounding services. Personnel recruitment companies can be found in the Yellow Pages under *Personnel (Recrutement et Sélection de)* or *Personeelsrecrutering en -selectie*. A few recruitment companies are given below.

Useful Addresses

ACT Careers: Av. des Arts 50 bte 3, 1040 Brussels; tel 02 511 94 57.

Bosman EC Management Consultants: Av. de Tervueren 114a, 1040 Brussels; tel 02 732 25 10. Computer and DP professionals.

Career Secretaries: Av. des Arts 50 bte 3, 1040 Brussels; tel 02 513 77 19; fax 02 513 29 42.

Fontaine Archer Van De Voorde: Av. Louise 382, 1050 Brussels; tel 02 647 63 50. Finance, accountancy and banking.

Michael Page International: Av. Molière 262, 1060 Brussels; tel 02 347 02 10. Finance, accountancy and banking.

PA Consulting Group: Av. Louise 390, 1050 Brussels; tel 02 648 65 55.

Personnel Management Services: Av. des Croix du Feu 231, 1020 Brussels; tel 02 268 66 71. Secretaries, clerical and low/middle management.

Profile Group (The): Av. de la Toison d'Or 10 bte 2, 1060 Brussels; tel 02 512 73 42. Secretarial and administrative staff.

Rainbow Careers: Av. de Tervuren 37, 1040 Brussels; tel 02 735 41 54. Specializes in multilingual secretaries.

Recruitment Partners (Computer Related Recruitment): Sq. Vergote 32, 1040 Brussels; 02 736 00 53.

Secretary Search: Av. Brugmann 32, 1060 Brussels; tel 02 344 07 72.

Specialist Recruiters International (Europe): Bvd. de ι.   ` 33-39, 1050 Brussels. Managerial and executive.

Outplacement Bureaux

Outplacement bureaux assist those who are being made redundant to find new careers, by analysing the candidate's potential, advising on interview techniques, providing secretarial services, and so on. They are paid by the companies who are releasing their staff, not by the employee. Outplacement bureaux deal with groups as well as individuals. They sometimes advise blue-collar workers.

Useful Addresses

Coutts Outplacement International Ltd: Av. de Beaulieu 25, 1160 Brussels; tel 02 672 60 00.

Vlaamse Vennootschap voor Outplacement (V.V.O.): Antwerpsesteenweg 124, 2630 Aartselaar; tel 03 887 2077; fax 03 887 1016. Will also advise on spouse-employment and pre-retirement.

V.V.O. Outplacement International: Leuvensesteenweg 613, 1930 Zaventem; tel 02 759 4424; fax 02 759 8061.

Temporary Employment Agencies

There are a truly astonishing number of temporary work agencies in Belgium. Often they are all to be found in one street in a city, which makes life convenient for the job-seeker. It is important to note that temping agencies usually have separate offices for manual and office workers. Some also have separate sections for computer personnel, nurses, and so on. Office workers should look under *Intérimaires — travail intellectuel* or *Uitzendkrachten — hoofdarbeid* in the Yellow Pages. For manual workers the heading is *Intérimaires — travail manuel* or *Uitzendkrachten — handenarbeid*. Agencies can offer not only daytime work, but also evening and weekend work. There is, however, a strict separation between agencies offering temporary and permanent work.

A temping agency receives the equivalent of up to a month's salary when it places a worker, so good workers are a very valuable commodity. If a worker should decide to accept a full-time job with a company, the temping agency is not allowed to charge the customer anything. A temporary worker has the same rights as a permanent worker, even as far as receiving holiday pay and compensation if he/she is dismissed without good reason. In many cases, temporary work can lead to a full-time job, so this is an excellent way to begin your career in Belgium.

The Belgian Ministry of Employment also runs a network of temporary work offices in 12 major towns, known as the 'T-Service'. T-Service offices are usually in a separate building from the permanent employment office and have a different telephone number. They can be found in the Yellow Pages under T-Service, or you can ask for a list from the Brussels office: Boulevard Anspach 69, 1000 Brussels; tel 02 511 23 85. T-Service has another Brussels office at Avenue des Arts 46, 1040 Brussels; tel 02 513 77 39.

Useful Addresses

Antwerp

Creyf's Interim: Leysstraat 27-29, 2000 Antwerp; tel 03 231 66 88.

Gregg Interim: Frankrijklei 40, 2000 Antwerp; tel 03 233 94 75. Office staff.

Gregg Interim: Frankrijklei 53-55, 2000 Antwerp; tel 03 232 34 75. Managerial, technical, computer staff.

Manpower: Frankrijklei 27, 2000 Antwerp; tel 03 231 77 75.

Brussels

Creyf's Avenue Louise: Av. Louise 473, 1050 Brussels; tel 02 646 34 34.

Creyf's Engineering: address as above; tel 02 646 43 70.

Creyf's: Schildknaapstraat 21-23, 1000 Brussels; tel 02 218 83 70. Call 02 218 82 85 for industrial section.

Express Interim: Centre Rogier bte 66, 1210 Brussels; tel 02 218 83 83 (nurses) tel 02 218 20 40 (secretaries).

Gregg Executive Secretaries: Place de l'Albertine 2/3, 1000 Brussels; tel 02 511 18 36.
Manpower: Rue de Luxembourg 13, 1040 Brussels; tel 02 512 38 23.
Select Interim: 1/5 Av. de la Joyeuse Entrée, 1040 Brussels; tel 02 231 0333; fax 02 230 1210. Secretarial temps.

Liège
Creyf's Interim: Bvd. de la Sauvenière 56, 4000 Liège; tel 041 22 39 22.
Gregg Interim: Bvd. de la Sauvenière 70, 4000 Liège; tel 041 23 58 10.

Chambers of Commerce

Chambers of commerce exist to promote the interests of companies trading in Belgium and the UK; they do not offer help in looking for work. However, they can be a useful source of information on companies operating in their geographical area and they will usually sell you a copy of their directory of members. Once you have a list of companies you can then make applications for current or prospective vacancies even if they are not being advertised in the press. The British Chamber of Commerce for Belgium and Luxembourg's Directory of Members costs BF1,000 including postage (see address below). The American Chamber of Commerce's Directory, which has information on 1,600 companies operating in Belgium, costs BF3,050 from within Benelux.

Anyone who is setting up a business in Belgium must be sure to register with the local chamber of commerce (*Chambre de Commerce/Handelskamer*) on arrival. A list of regional chambers of commerce is given in the section *Regional Employment Guide,* at the end of this chapter.

Useful Addresses

American Chamber of Commerce in Belgium: Av. des Arts 50 bte 5, 1040 Brussels; tel 02 513 67 70.
British Chamber of Commerce of Belgium and Luxembourg: Britannia House, Rue Joseph II 30, 1040 Brussels; tel 02 219 07 88.

Letters of Application

Whether you are applying speculatively, or in answer to a job advertisement, in most cases it will be necessary to write a letter, and very often your curriculum vitae will be attached. Needless to say, the way your letter is presented can greatly influence your chances of success.

If you are making a speculative job application, your letter should be typed rather than handwritten. Belgian companies set a great deal of store by graphology, but at the initial stage it is more important to make your letter legible. Try to be brief, polite and to the point. Rather than a lengthy life history, a statement of your qualifications and professional interests is the most important thing. A photocopied letter is not likely to make a good impression; a word-processed letter is just as convenient and will receive a much more positive response.

If you are dealing with a Belgian company, it is vital to know which language to use. In central Brussels it is generally safe to use French or English, but if you are dealing with a Dutch-speaking company always use English. Letters to companies in Wallonia will probably be more successful if they are in French, as long as you remember not to give the impression that your French is much better than it really is. There are a number of books on how to write business letters in French, for example, *How to Address Overseas Business Letters* by Derek Allen (Foulsham). If necessary, have the letter professionally translated into French. The Institute of Translation and Interpreting (318a Finchley Road, London NW1; tel 071-794 9931) charges from £70 for one thousand words. It is also worth contacting a college of further education for this purpose.

The letter of application can be written in much the same way as a letter in the UK, with the proviso that it is best to avoid using abbreviations, or, even worse, trying to be humorous. If your letter is speculative, the company in question may be surprised to hear from you. At the same time, the fact that you had the initiative to contact them gives a good impression. Belgian companies are very good about replying to letters. However, they do not like to feel that their time is being wasted, so it is best to be very clear about your purpose in writing. On the whole, Belgians prefer to communicate by telephone or fax machine, since they feel that time is at a premium. If you do establish a positive contact with a firm or agency in Belgium, you could well be asked to fax a copy of your CV or diplomas.

Transfers

The alternative to finding work directly in Belgium is to do this through the longer-term procedure of finding a position within a company in the UK which offers the eventual prospect of being transferred to Belgium. Few companies recruit staff with a guarantee that they will be posted to a specific country afer a certain period. With the coming of the Single Market there will undoubtedly be a much greater mobility of labour in the EC. While English will certainly remain the most widely spoken European language, the ability to speak French or another EC language will assume a crucial importance for those who seriously want to work abroad, so now is the time start learning.

The following types of company offer the option of transfer abroad:

Belgian Companies Operating in the UK: Belgian companies have quite a low profile in the UK, but there are far more of them than you might suspect. Two of the most significant are Solvay, the giant chemicals multinational, and Agfa-Gevaert, one of the world's leading photographic products suppliers. Belgian food producers are also expanding their UK presence, the biggest being Vandemoortele. Subsidiaries of Belgian companies are also to be found in the engineering, glass and transport sectors. The Belgian Embassy can supply a list of Belgian companies with subsidiaries in the UK.

British Companies Operating in Belgium: Most major UK-based multinationals already have subsidiaries or branches in Belgium. ICI has its European headquarters in Everberg, near Brussels. Pilkington Glass have also recently moved their European head office to Brussels. British banks, estate agents, accountants and management consultants are all heavily represented in Brussels. Numerous British law firms are opening offices in Brussels to offer advice on EC law to companies wanting to set up in Europe, and this will continue to be a growth area. A list of major British employers in Belgium is given at the end of this chapter.

International Companies: Belgium attracts multinationals in large numbers, not only because it is the centre of the EC, but also because of its liberal investment climate. American firms have been particularly drawn to Belgium, so that the USA is now the largest foreign investor with 40% of the total. Companies which set up 'co-ordination centres' in line with certain criteria benefit from generous tax-breaks, as well as exemptions from the rules governing work permits for their employees. A company setting up a co-ordination centre must have sales of more than BF10 billion (£170 million) a year.

It is not always easy to know the extent of a company's involvement in Belgium. Addresses can be found in the directories of Chambers of Commerce. If you can contact a subsidiary directly in Belgium you may well be able to obtain a brochure on their activities from them. While not many companies recruit with a transfer in mind, you can always discuss your long-term aims at interview.

International Organizations: More than 1,000 international, non-governmental organizations and associations are located in Brussels, including the Union of International Associations (UIA) which has been in Brussels since its foundation in 1910. Many of them are in Brussels to lobby or take part in the work of the EC Economic and Social Committee. A list of some of the major international organizations can be found in *Living in the Heart of Europe* (publ. Pelckmans).

The Curriculum Vitæ

A typical application would comprise a letter of application and a curriculum vitae (CV). If you do not have one, then now is the time to prepare one. There are agencies which will prepare your CV; some advertise in newspapers or you can look under 'Employment Agencies' in the Yellow Pages. A one-page graduate CV will cost £20 upwards. You can also have it done by a word-processing agency. If you have access to a word-processor and can find a suitable model CV, then you can save yourself some money by producing your own CV and updating it every time you have something new to add to it. This is also a good way of learning how to use a word-processor. Advice on how to lay out your CV is contained in *The Right Way to Write Your Own CV*, John Clarke (Paper Fronts) and *CV's and Written Applications*, Judy Skeats (Ward Lock).

A CV should be printed on A4 paper and can be photocopied if necessary. Be careful to remove any abbreviations that could confuse a foreign employer. Most employers prefer to see a one-page CV in the first place. If they are interested you can send them more details later on. Note that American CVs list education and work experience in the opposite order from British CVs, that is, the most recent job or qualification is placed first and the earliest one at the end.

It is expensive to send copies of certificates or photographs with an enquiry, as these will not usually be returned. It is best to wait until you are asked to send further documentation.

Interview Procedure

If a company asks you to attend an interview in Belgium, then this should be taken as a sign that they are seriously interested in hiring you. Since Belgian companies operate on the philosophy that time is money, they are not keen to interview everyone whose application seems to be in order. Unfortunately you can expect to have to pay your own travel costs.

As stated earlier under Manners and Customs (*Daily Life* chapter) it is important to use the correct terms of address (*Monsieur/Madame* in French and *Meneer/Mevrouw* in Dutch). You can also expect to shake hands on arrival and departure. The degree of formality of an interview can vary between the language communities. Dutch-speakers tend to favour a more informal approach than French-speakers. If your interview is conducted in French, be prepared for a close scrutiny of your language abilities. Sounding polite will help your cause considerably.

One way to make a favourable impression is to find out something about Belgium and show some interest in the country. Belgians do not expect foreigners to know anything about their country, so they will be pleasantly surprised if you do. You should, however, avoid commenting on controversial matters such as the language question or Belgian politics. Remember also that modesty is the key virtue in Belgium and exaggeration a cardinal sin.

Aspects of Employment

Salaries

Belgian salaries compare well with those of other EC countries. Most people moving from Britain can expect a salary increase, whatever level they happen to be working at. The difference in salary levels is greatest at managerial and executive level. In general terms it is reckoned that salaries in Belgium exceed those in the UK by about 30 to 40%, but it must be remembered that taxes are anything up to 30% higher, with the result that take-home pay is not much better than at home. The cost of living is considered to be higher than in the UK; on the other hand, Brussels is cheaper to live in than London according to some surveys. The following table gives an idea of salary levels in industrialized countries compared with the UK:

	Salaries	Living costs
Belgium	30%-35% more	5% more
France	30%-50% more	5%-10% less
Germany	50%-60% more	10%-15% more
Italy	50% more	20%-25% more

Japan	80%-100% more	35%-50% more
Scandinavia	40%-55% more	up to 50% more
USA	80%-250% more	20%-30% less

While Belgian salaries are attractive to those from the UK, they are less so to people from other major industrial countries. As far as executive and professional jobs are concerned this cuts down on some of the competition from other foreigners.

The statutory minimum wage for workers over 21 years old is BF38,857 (£670) per month. Employees are divided into blue-collar (*ouvriers/arbeiders*), white-collar (*employés/bedienden*) workers and managers (*gérants/beheerders*). Wages are standardized in most industries by collective bargaining through Labour and Management Committees (*commissions paritaires/paritaire komitees*). They are usually index-linked, but at times of economic crisis, such as 1981-1986, indexation may be suspended. Minimum wages for clerical workers, for instance, depend on age and qualifications, and range from BF420,000 (£7,200) p.a. to BF700,000 (£12,000). The average wage outside Brussels for clerks and factory workers is about BF600,000 (£10,300). Highly skilled workers in industry earn at least 50% more than this. In Brussels junior managers can expect to earn at least BF1,200,000 (£20,000), middle-ranking executives BF2,500,000 (£43,000) and the managing director of a medium-sized firm BF5,000,000 (£86,000).

Benefits and Perks

Salaries are paid at the end of the month. Manual workers are usually paid every week, or every two weeks. It is a general practice to grant a 13th month (*treizième mois/dertiende maand*) and sometimes half of a 14th month, at the end of the year. This is also sometimes known as a yearly bonus (*prime de fin d'année/jaarpremie*). It is also common practice to pay a profit-related bonus (*participation aux bénéfices/aandeel in de winst*), which also sometimes goes under the name of a productivity bonus (*prime de productivité/productiviteitspremie*).

Managers and executives also have the added attraction of company cars, enhanced sickness insurance and extra pension schemes. For low-paid workers the employer is obliged to subsidize their travel costs to and from work. Companies who reimburse their employees' commuting costs can claim tax rebates, on the grounds that the environment benefits from fewer cars on the road.

Working Hours, Overtime and Holidays

Working hours are limited by law to 40 hours a week in most cases, and 8 hours a day. In some industries the unions and employers have negotiated a longer working week or shift system. In a typical office the worker is contracted to do 38 hours a week, but in practice works 39 hours and receives one extra day's holiday a month. The working day lasts from 8.30am to 5.00pm, with a half-hour lunch-break. Work ends at 4.00pm on Fridays in many offices. As far as the statistics go, the average Belgian works 38½ hours a week, about two hours less than in the UK.

Employees are not obliged to work overtime. If overtime is worked, this has to be paid at an additional 50%. Overtime on Sundays and public holidays is paid at double time. In addition to extra pay, workers are entitled to take time off.

All workers are entitled to 20 days' paid holiday, as well as public holidays. Those working a six-day week receive 24 days' holiday. Not only is salary paid during the holiday period, but a further 85% of a month's salary is paid at the time of the annual holiday.

Trade Unions

Belgium is one of the most heavily unionized countries in the Western world; 50% to 90% of workers are likely to be members of unions in any given industry. The percentage for the workforce as a whole is 65%. There is no such thing as a closed shop, however, and the unions generally co-operate with employers to ensure peaceful industrial relations. Strikes have been rare in recent years. Unions are organized by industry, and affiliated to one of three trade union federations, which are split up on linguistic and political/religious lines. The federations are:

CSC/ACV: *Confédération des Syndicats Chrétiens de Belgique/Algemeen Christelijk Vakverbond:* The most powerful confederation (especially in Flanders), with 1,388,462 members. Affiliated with the Christian Social parties.
FGTB/ABVV: *Fédération Générale des Travailleurs de Belgique/Algemene Belgische Vakverbond:* Has 1,190,462 members and is linked to the Belgian Socialist parties.
CGSLB/ACLVB: *Confédération Générale des Syndicats Libéraux de Belgique/Algemeen centrale van de Liberale Vakbonden van België:* Has only 211,114 members. Affiliated with the Belgian Liberal parties.

Every business with over 50 workers must have a Workers' Council (*Conseil d'entreprise/Ondernemingsraad*) made up of both management and workers, with elections held every four years. The workers' council mainly functions as a channel of communication between managers and personnel. Businesses with more than 50 personnel must also institute a health and safety committee.

Wages and salaries are determined by Labour Management Commissions (*commissions paritaires/paritaire komitees*) for entire industries. Pay levels are then made compulsory by royal decree.

Employment Contracts

A written employment contract is not obligatory, but is usually desirable, given the complexity of the labour laws. A contract is only valid if it is in French or Dutch. There is usually a trial period of employment, not exceeding a year, during which an employee can be dismissed with one week's notice. After the trial period, a typical contract runs for an indefinite duration, and at least three months' notice has to be given. Length of notice increases with seniority; in some cases this goes up to three years. Employees are generally expected to give at least six weeks' notice if they intend to leave.

Work Practices

Belgians like to work fixed hours and keep their work and home life strictly separate. It is considered bad form to telephone people about work matters during their free time, or to discuss work in front of outsiders. If you are in the habit of being unpunctual you could soon be out of a job. In general, taking tea-breaks or chatting on the office phone are frowned upon. This does not mean that Belgian firms are super-efficient, but it is important to be seen to be working hard. The Dutch do not have a high opinion of the Belgians' organizational capabilities, to the extent that chaotic or disorganized situations are called *Belgische toestanden* (Belgian conditions) in Holland.

Working with Walloons has something in common with working with the French themselves. The Flemish are in many ways more entrepreneurial and open to change than the Walloons. They are also more likely to be aware of what is happening in other countries because of their better language abilities.

Women in Work

Equality of opportunity for women is guaranteed by law in Belgium. Barriers to professional advancement have largely been eliminated. Women are, however, at a disadvantage in some sectors since it is illegal for them to work at night (with the exception of nurses and barmaids). Women are being employed more and more in technical fields, but they are less likely to be given opportunities for heavy physical work. Taking the workforce as a whole, women earn 25% less than men.

Permanent Work

Executive Recruitment Prospects

According to a survey conducted by the American Chamber of Commerce in Belgium and the executive recruitment firm Management Resources, published in December 1991, the best job prospects are in marketing, finance, general management and data processing. Law firms and consultancies on government affairs are also seen to be expanding rapidly. The worst areas to be in are personnel and administration. Of 128 organizations surveyed only 25% expected to increase executive recruitment during 1992; 39% said that they had increased executive staffing in 1990 and 1991. A summary of the survey mentioned above is available from: Management Resources, Av. Louise 148, 1050 Brussels; fax 02 647 11 22.

As far as the country of origin goes, the European headquarters of US companies are looked on as the best sector for recruitment. Virtually any foreign company is looked on as a good job prospect. Belgian companies are not highly favoured, either because they do not have many openings for foreigners, or because prospects for advancement are not as good. Many Belgians prefer the security of working for a Belgian company to the perceived uncertainty of working for a foreign company. As a result, those employed by Belgian and foreign companies usually follow separate career paths.

If you do want to make your career in a Belgian-owned company, it is as well to be aware of the fact that in family-owned companies, promotion tends to go automatically to family members, rather than to the best-qualified people. This type of nepotism has been heavily criticized in Belgium recently and may eventually change.

Working for the European Commission

The European Commission, the central administrative body for the Common Market, employs about 11,000 foreign staff in Brussels. Because nine languages are used in the Commission's work, there is an immense demand for translators and interpreters. Over 1,000 are employed by the Commission in Brussels alone. There is also a great demand for economists and lawyers with more than one EC language. In practice, day-to-day work at the Commission is conducted in English and French; training in languages is offered where necessary. Perhaps because of the language requirements, British workers are under-represented in EC institutions relative to the British population and measures are being taken to raise their numbers.

EC workers enjoy very good salaries and working conditions. They pay taxes directly to the EC at a lower rate than in any of the EC countries. Those who work outside their own country receive a 16% expatriate allowance. Children of EC workers can have free schooling at one of the EC schools in Belgium.

Careers Structure

The Commission is divided into 23 Directorates-General administering different areas of policy. There are also various other units such as the Secretariat General, Translation Service, Joint Interpreting and Conference Service, and so on. The EC Commissioners also have their own offices or 'cabinets'. The great majority of EC Commission personnel are located in Brussels, but some work in Luxembourg and other EC member countries.

There are four grades of workers in EC institutions, classified A, B, C and D. Each grade is further divided into levels eight to one. In order to apply for a post at the EC you must be an EC citizen, under 35 years of age (in most cases), and know one EC language at native speaker level and have a conversational knowledge of at least one other.

Grade A: This grade is reserved for university graduates and includes administrators, scientists and advisory personnel. When there is sufficient demand for staff, open competitive examinations are held in member countries. Successful entrants are then invited for interview in Brussels, and if they pass this hurdle, are placed on a reserve list of available staff. It can then take a further year before a post is actually offered. Even then, only two-thirds of candidates on the reserve list are offered a post. Candidates without work experience enter at Grade A8, while those with experience can enter at between A7 and A5. Contracts are all labelled 'temporary', but some are of indefinite duration and others renewable fixed-term contracts. The starting salary for Grade A8 workers stood at about £26,000 in 1992.

Grade A and B posts are advertised in national newspapers such as *The Times*, *The Independent* and *The Guardian*. Details of competitions and application procedures appear regularly in the Official Journal of the European Commission, available from the Commission's Information Offices (see below).

Grade LA: Linguists are classified as Translators or Interpreters. Because of the shortage of interpreters, the Commission offers a six-month training scheme for those who already speak two EC languages fluently as well as their own mother tongue. The entrance requirements for this training scheme are extremely rigorous, and only 2% of applicants are accepted for it. If you have a degree in one of the more unusual EC languages, such as Greek or Danish, your chances of being accepted are much higher. Further information about translating and interpreting is given below.

Grade B: Education up to A-level standard is required for this grade, which covers various levels of managers. EC institutions other than the Commission do not accept university graduates for Grade B posts. Once you are in Grade B it is difficult to move to Grade A, except by going through the entire procedure of competitive examinations and interviews along with other candidates. Workers with a background in computers are particularly in demand for this grade.

Grade C: This is the grade for secretaries and clerical staff. It is rare for graduates to be recruited to secretarial posts. Education to O-level and some work experience are sufficient qualifications. Languages are important at this level as well. Grade C and D posts are advertised in The *Daily Mail* and *The Mirror* in the UK.

Grade D: Workers in this category are manual and support service staff, for example, drivers, printers and messengers.

Entry via the Civil Service

The British Civil Service operates a scheme whereby every year 30 graduates with a second or first class degree are selected to work in Civil Service departments with a strong European connection, and given help and preparation to enter EC competitive examinations. Details of this scheme are given in the booklet *European Fast Stream* published by the Civil Service Commission whose address is given below.

Stagiaires

The EC gives a limited number of graduates the chance to follow a six-month training course (*stage*) in one of its institutions where they can learn about the workings of the EC. While the course does not guarantee a post, trainees (*stagiaires*) have a better chance of passing the selection procedures than others. Recruitment for courses takes place at the beginning of February and September. Enquiries should be addressed to: Bureau des Stages, Commission of the European Communities, Rue de la Loi 200, 1049 Brussels.

One further possible entry route to an EC post is to take a one-year postgraduate course in European Studies at the College of Europe in Bruges (see Education section in *Daily Life*). Subject areas include Advanced European Economics, Administration and Law. Graduates whose qualifications are considered relevant to the Commission's requirements have a good chance of being recruited. The British government has 30 bursaries on offer each year for such courses.

Useful Publications and Addresses

A Career in the Commission of the European Communities. Published by the EC
  Directorate General for Personnel and Administration. Available from:
  Recruitment Division, European Commission, Rue de la Loi 200, 1049 Brussels,
  Belgium; or from Press and Information Offices of the European Commission.
The European Fast Stream. Civil Service Commission, Alencon Link, Basingstoke,
  Hants.
Opportunities to Work in the European Community's Institutions, by J.A. Goodman
  and C. Tobin. Association of Graduate Careers Advisory Services, c/o Peter
  Rankin, Lancashire Polytechnic, Preston, Lancs PR1 2TQ.

Press and Information Offices of the European Commission

8 Storey's Gate, London SW1P 3AT.
Windsor House, 9/15 Bedford Street, Belfast BT2 7EG.
4 Cathedral Road, Cardiff CF1 9SG.
7 Alva Street, Edinburgh EH2 4PH.
39 Molesworth Street, Dublin 2.

Translating and Interpreting

Translators convert written documents into their own mother tongue, and have usually mastered two foreign languages. They tend to specialize in certain subject areas, such as technical or legal translation. Some translators have worked in scientific or other fields before training as translators. A degree in languages is not enough to become a translator — further training at an institute for professional linguists or university is needed.

Interpreters have an even more difficult job than translators, in that they have to interpret while someone is actually speaking (simultaneous interpreting) or during pauses left by the speaker (consecutive interpreting). Sometimes the interpreter translates from and into two languages as people speak to each other. Full-time jobs as an interpreter are hard to find outside the EC Commission, so most interpreters are freelances who do translating and other work as well. Conference interpreters usually belong to either the *Association Internationale des Interprètes de Conférence (AIIC)* or the *Institute of Translation and Interpreting (ITI)*.

Further information on careers in interpreting and translating is available from:

Institute of Linguistics: 24a Highbury Grove, London N5 2EA.
Institute of Translation and Interpreting: 318a Finchley Road, London NW3 5HT.

Working for NATO
The North Atlantic Treaty Organization (NATO) moved its headquarters to Brussels in 1967 after France withdrew from the military command structure. Its policy-making body is the North Atlantic Council of Ministers, and its parliamentary body the North Atlantic Assembly. NATO headquarters employs 3,000 workers from 16 different member countries; several thousand more are employed at Supreme Headquarters Allied Powers in Europe (SHAPE) at Le Casteau, near Mons. Workers at NATO are classified according to Grades A, B, C and L, in a similar way to EC workers (see above). Applications are made through the delegation of one's home country. In the case of British people, the address is: British Delegation NATO, Boulevard Leopold III, 1110 NATO, Brussels; tel 02 728 41 11.

Teaching
There are regular opportunities for school and university teachers in Belgium. Names and addresses of potential employers can be found in the Schools and Education section in the *Daily Life* chapter. Some names of organizations in the UK and the USA which can place schoolteachers are given below.

UK:
Central Bureau for Educational Visits and Exchanges: Seymour Mews House, Seymour Mews, London W1H 9PE; tel 071-486 5101.
3 Bruntsfield Crescent, Edinburgh EH10 4HD; tel 031-447 8024.
16 Malone Road, Belfast BT9 5BN; tel 0232-664418.
Council of British Independent Schools in the European Communities: COBISEC: c/o the British School of Brussels, Chaussée de Louvain 19, 1980 Tervuren, Belgium; tel 02 767 47 00.
European Council of International Schools: 18 Lavant Street, Petersfield, Hants GU32 3EW; tel 0730-68244.
Service Children's Education Authority: Court Road, Eltham, London SE9 5NR.

USA:
Council for International Exchange of Scholars: 3400 International Drive, NW, Suite M500, Washington 20008; tel 202-686-4000.
Department of Defense Dependent Schools: Teacher Recruitment Section, Hoffman Building I, 2461 Eisenhower Ave., Alexandria, VA 22331.
International Schools Services: PO Box 5910, Princeton NJ 08540; tel 609-452-0990.

Short-term Employment

Teaching English

The demand for English language teachers remains high, not only because most Belgians consider English indispensable but also because of the presence of large numbers of EC citizens with the time and money to pursue language studies. Belgians are well aware that native speakers are the best teachers. They are themselves ideal language students: eager to 'have a go' and communicate with other people with whatever linguistic resources they have at their disposal.

It is quite feasible to put up notices in one of the large university towns (Brussels, Antwerp, Ghent, Liège, Mons) offering 'conversation lessons' and make enough money to get by on. Most prospective teachers look in the Yellow Pages and go round the language schools. Many language schools will be eager to give you work even if you have no TEFL qualifications. What they will not do, however, is deal with your tax and social security affairs. They would rather not have the added burden of paying 34-36% of your salary in social security contributions. Many English teachers therefore take their gross salary and never declare any of it. They should actually become self-employed *indépendants* and pay their taxes but, in practice, after about six months they move on elsewhere, thus accounting for the easy availability of jobs. Both the employer and the employee take the risk of being fined; nevertheless the practice seems to be tolerated by the authorities. Once you have worked *en noir/in het zwart* ('in black' — without paying taxes) for a while it is difficult to become legal, as you would have to declare everything you had earned up until then, so it is important to decide whether you want to be legal or not, which largely depends on how long you want to stay in Belgium.

The best way to approach English teaching is to obtain an English teaching qualification in the UK first and then try to get a contract with a school in Belgium. The minimum useful qualification is the RSA Certificate, a one-month course which costs up to £800. It is also possible to do this course in Belgium once you have managed to find work. Prospective employers tend to look not only for qualifications and experience, but also for an enthusiastic and outgoing personality. For further information on English-teaching, the publication, *Teaching English Abroad* (Vacation Work, £7.95) is an invaluable source of references. Also try the *Education* section of *The Guardian* on Tuesdays, the *Times Educational Supplement* on Fridays and the fortnightly *Overseas Jobs Express*, all of which provide an unfailing source of TEFL jobs. If you are already in Belgium, the British Council will supply a list of language schools in Brussels (Rue Joseph II 30, 1040 Brussels; tel 02 219 36 00). The British Council does not run language courses or employ teachers.

Useful Addresses

Language schools in Belgium:
Berlitz Language Centre: Rue St. Michel 28, 1000 Brussels; tel 02 219 02 74.

The English Institute: Rue Lesbroussart 77, 1050 Brussels; tel 02 647 89 83.
inlingua School of Languages: Limburgstraat 62, 9000 Gent; tel 091 25 11 04.
May International: Rue Lesbroussart 40, 1050 Brussels; tel 02 640 87 03.
The Mitchell School of English: Rue Louis Hap 156, 1040 Brussels; tel 02 734 80 73.
School voor Europese Talen: Charlottalei 28, 2018 Antwerp; tel 03 218 73 70.

TEFL recruitment agencies in the UK:
Bell Educational Trust: Overseas Department, The Lodge, Redcross Lane, Cambridge CB2 2QX; tel 0223-246644; fax 0223-410282.
Berlitz: Wells House, 79 Wells Street, London W1A 3BZ; tel 071-580 6482.
ELT Banbury: 49 Oxford Road, Banbury, Oxon OX6 9AH; tel 0295-263480; fax 0295-271658.
inlingua Teacher Service: Essex House, Temple Street, Birmingham B2 5DB; tel 021-643 3472.
ILC Recruitment (International Language Centres): 1 Riding House, London W1A 3AS; tel 071-580 4351; fax 071-631 0741.

Au Pair Work

Au pairs are very much in demand among wealthier expatriate and Belgian families. In exchange for board, lodging and pocket money (at a minimum of £110 per month), au pairs are expected to devote a certain amount of time to their hosts' offspring, to attend a part-time language course at a local school and generally to promote cultural exchange. If you are lucky, the family you stay with will rent an apartment on the coast during the summer and take you along.

The status of au pairs is regulated by Belgian laws and Council of Europe regulations. Although there are no legal obstacles to male au pairs, they are certainly very rare in Belgium. General rules are that the au pair should have her own bedroom and cannot be asked to do more than four hours of housework a day, in addition to one or two hours looking after the children. Au pairs are entitled to one free day a week. Employers are legally bound to pay pension contributions, sickness insurance and accident insurance for au pairs, whichever country they are from. British au pairs should take Form E111 (see Section on E111 in *Daily Life* chapter) to cover them for health insurance in the first three months.

Non-EC au pairs must obtain Work Permit B (see *Residence and Entry* chapter) from a Belgian Embassy before leaving. To qualify they must submit a document proving that they have a working knowledge of Dutch or French or that they are registered at an approved language school for at least 10 hours a week. EC au pairs only have to register at the local commune when they arrive in Belgium. They will then be given the mauve card model B (see *Residence and Entry*) which can be renewed every three months. Strictly speaking, no one can be an au pair for more than one year.

A good source of au pair jobs is *The Lady* magazine published weekly in the UK. It is possible to find an au pair position for the summer only, but you will have to start looking several months beforehand. Another way to find an au pair position is to go over to Belgium and look at notice boards or in the classified sections of newspapers and magazines, especially the English-language weekly *The Bulletin*. Meeting a family in advance helps to minimize the risks of exploitation or a personality clash. There are organizations in Belgium which can help you find a position as well (see below). Many UK agencies arrange au pair posts abroad and the better-known ones are listed in the *Useful Addresses* section below.

Remember that it is illegal for any agency to charge a registration fee to the prospective au pair, who is liable to pay only a reasonable charge to cover administration fees (about £40), once a job has been organized and the contract actually signed. The publication, *The Au Pair and Nanny's Guide to Working Abroad* is an invaluable source for those looking for au pair work abroad and is available at £7.95 (plus £1 p&p) from Vacation Work in Oxford.

Useful Addresses

Anglia Au Pair and Domestic Agency: 70 Southsea Avenue, Leigh-on-Sea Essex SS9 2BJ; tel 0702-471648.

Anglo Pair Agency: 40 Wavertree Road, Streatham Hill, London SW2 3SP; tel 081-674 3605.

At Your Service Agency: 163a Gwent Sreet, London NW4 4DH; tel 081-203 6885/6862.

Cotswold Nannies: Stonecroft, High Street, Bisley, nr Stroud, Glos GL6 7BS; tel 0452 770076.

De Bond van Jonge en Grote Gezinnen (Association of Large and Young Families): Rue du Trône 125, 1050 Brussels; tel 02 507 88 11.

De Windrose: Av. des Quatres Vents 9, 1810 Wemmel, Brussels; tel 02 460 34 59.

Interlingua Centre: Torquay Road, Foxrock, Dublin 18, Ireland; tel 01-893876.

La Petite Maison: 11 The Green, Newick, Lewes, East Sussex BN8 4LA; tel 0825 72 26 09.

Ligue des Familles: Rue du Trône 127, 1050 Brussels; tel 02 507 22 11.

Service de la Jeunesse Féminine: Rue Faider 29, 1050 Brussels; tel 02 539 35 14.

Secretarial Work

There are numerous opportunities for well-qualified bilingual secretaries in Brussels and other parts of Belgium. Bilingual here means that you are able to write letters and take shorthand or dictation in another EC language. The languages most in demand are French and Dutch, but there are good openings for other languages as well. The best way to obtain work is to go over to Belgium in person. At the time of writing (1992) many overseas companies in Brussels have frozen their recruitment because of the recession, thus depressing the demand for secretaries. The main growth area at the moment is for legal secretaries. Salaries range from BF50,000 to BF90,000 per month (£860-£1,550). Secretarial temps can expect to earn from £7 to £10 per hour. A good source of jobs is the weekly *The Bulletin*. Names and addresses of agencies have been given under UK and Belgian Employment Agencies above.

Tourism

One way of working in Belgium is to join a tour firm in the UK which sends coach drivers, couriers and tour guides over there. Knowledge of French and/or Dutch is often required. You can expect to work very long hours and have a lot of fun at the same time.

Useful Addresses

British tour companies operating in Belgium:

Belgian Travel Service: Tour Operator, Bridge House, Ware SG12 9DG.

Cotswold Travel: Bearland House, Longsmith Street, Gloucester GL1 2HL; tel 0452-524151.

Eurocamp: Edmundson House, Tatton Street, Knutsford WA16 6BG.

Thomsons Tour Operations: Greater London House, Hampstead Road, London NW1 7SD; tel 071-387 9321.

Hotels:
Hotels and catering come under the rather oddly named *Horeca* sector (*Ho*tels, *Re*staurants and *Ca*fés). Work in hotels is seasonal and not necessarily well-paid. The likely areas for hotel work in Belgium are West Flanders, mainly on the coast, and in the provinces of Namur and Luxembourg, in the Ardennes. Lists of hotels can be obtained from Belgian Tourist Offices. Alternatively, local employment agencies will be able to put you in touch with prospective employers.

Agricultural and Industrial
Belgian agricultural is highly mechanized and employs only 2-3% of the total workforce; there is not much scope for casual work here. Temporary jobs in industry are easily available through the regional employment offices.

Voluntary Work
Belgium has a long of tradition of voluntary work, some of it under the auspices of the Catholic church. The International Building Companions (*Internationale Bouworde* in Dutch) have their headquarters in Brussels and send volunteers to construction work camps for the underprivileged in different European countries including Belgium. Camps last from two to four weeks in the summer. Free board and lodging are provided, but you are responsible for your own travel costs. The *Service Protestant de la Jeunesse* (Protestant Youth Office) can place volunteers aged between 18 and 26 in Christian or other institutions in Belgium for nine to 12 months. Volunteers receive pocket money and free board and lodging. Placements begin in September.

Other kinds of voluntary work can be for much shorter periods and without any provision of accommodation. You may be asked to pay towards board and lodging where they are provided.

Useful Addresses
Année Diaconale Belge: Service Protestant de la Jeunesse, Rue de Champ de Mars 5, 1050 Brussels; tel 02 513 24 01.

Archeolo-J: Av. Paul Terlinden 23, 1330 Rixensart; tel 02 653 8268. Archaeological workcamps.

ATD Quart Monde: Av. Victor Jacobs 12, 1040 Brussels; tel 02 647 99 00.

Belgian Evangelical Mission: 60 Main St., Lubenham, Market Harborough, Leicester LE16 9TF; tel 0858-434627. Evangelical campaigns in Belgium.

Bouworde: Tiensesteenweg 145, 3200 Kessel-Lo. Flemish branch of Internationale Bouworde.

Caritas Catholica Belge: Rue du Commerce 1, 1040 Brussels; tel 02 511 42 55.

Compagnons Bâtisseurs: Rue Notre-Dame des Graces 63, 5400 Marche. Walloon branch of Internationale Bouworde.

Entraide et Amitié ASBL: Rue du Boulet 9, 1000 Brussels; tel 02 512 36 32. Helping elderly patients in hospitals.

Internationale Bouworde: Rue Amédée Lynen 8, 1030 Brussels.

Mouvement des Jeunes pour la Paix: Bvd. de l'Empereur 15, 1000 Brussels.

Business and Industry Report

Belgium has few natural resources, apart from some small coal and iron deposits, and is highly dependent on the export of goods and services. The golden era of the Belgian economy was undoubtedly the 1960s, when strong economic growth brought a high level of prosperity to the whole country. The first oil crisis of 1973 brought this period of expansion to a sudden end and Belgian industry became less and less able to compete with its neighbours. The traditional heavy industries of Wallonia went into a steep decline. Industrial productivity and investment failed to keep up with levels in other EC countries, and the second oil price shock of 1979-80 made matters even worse. Current account and budget deficits became a major problem, and unemployment rose to almost 15% at one point in 1984.

As a result of extraordinary fiscal measures, including the devaluation of the franc by 8.5%, the situation rapidly improved and by 1986 the balance of trade was in the black for the first time since 1973. Unit labour costs declined significantly in the 1980s and this helped to restore Belgium's international competitiveness and credibility. Fiscal measures were also taken to encourage private individuals to invest more in Belgian companies, rather than send their money abroad. The years 1988 to 1990 saw investment increase at over 10% annually, far above the EC average. Because of large-scale new foreign investment the effects of the 1990-1992 recession have not been as severe in Belgium as elsewhere, although there has been a noticeable slow-down in economic growth. While exports rose by a remarkable 8% in 1989, they only rose 3% in 1990, and 2% in 1991. Exports to Germany increased by 14% in 1991 thanks to reunification.

The budget deficit has been reduced to some extent as a result of recent economic growth to about 6% of GNP, but the total national debt is still astronomical at 108% of GNP. This means that painful measures will have to be taken to reduce social security benefits as well as other government expenditures. Another deep-seated problem is the lack of labour mobility. There are large disparities between the regions in terms of investment and training. The traditionally industrial south is finding it hard to attract high-tech industries, which strongly favour the Dutch-speaking north.

There are only a few state-owned industries in Belgium. These are mainly public services such as the post office, telephones, the railways and the national airline, Sabena. The Belgian National Bank is half owned by the state and half by private individuals. In recent years, the state has become increasingly involved in providing venture capital for private investment through its various credit institutions. The regional governments are now taking on more of the state's role in this respect as Belgium becomes more decentralized.

Belgium's major trading partners are its neighbours, Germany, The Netherlands and France. In 1990 these three countries alone accounted for 60% of imports and 55% of exports. The United Kingdom is Belgium's fourth largest trading partner with 8.3% of imports and 8.7% of exports. After the UK come Italy, the United States, Spain and Japan.

Out of the total population of 10 million, 4,180,000 are considered to be economically active. Men make up 59% of the workforce and women 41%. The employment rate of women is somewhat lower than the EC average. Industry now accounts for only 20% of the workforce, while the service sector employs 70%. Employment in industry is expected to contract further in the future with increasing automation. There are 672,000 self-employed (*indépendants/zelfstandigen*) workers and 966,000 in the public sector.

Automotive

Car manufacturing has always played a major role in Belgium's industrial success. From 1895 Belgian makers produced their own models, but the indigenous industry was all but obliterated by American competition during the 1930s. Except for coaches and buses there are no Belgian-owned car makers left. Car assembly is, however, still thriving. Belgium is a net exporter of cars — 98% of car production goes abroad. Numerous foreign-owned and local companies specialize in supplying the car industry with components, to the extent that cars could be manufactured entirely from Belgian-made parts. Three-quarters of car-related manufacturers are located in Flanders and the Brussels area, and only a quarter in Wallonia, which does not have a single car assembly plant as such. In Brussels the Volkswagen assembly plant employs 6,200 workers. Major firms operating in this area are: Ford, GM-Opel, Volvo, Volkswagen, Renault (passenger cars) and Van Hool, Jonckheere, Eos (coaches and buses). In addition Solvay, Du Pont De Nemours, Akzo, Monsanto, Cockerill Sambre, Sekurit Saint Gobain, Uniroyal, Bell Telephone produce components.

Banking and Finance

The central bank is the National Bank of Belgium (Banque Nationale de Belgique/Nationale Bank van België), which is 50% owned by the state and 50% owned by the public. Its functions include issuing currency and controlling banks and financial institutions where necessary. There are about 85 commercial banks offering a full range of services, of which 63 are wholly or mainly foreign-owned. Of these 37 are European banks, most of them French. In recent years there has been a tendency for American banks to close down in Brussels and for Japanese banks to move into their place.

As Belgium is the world leader in electronic banking, it is not surprising that two major bank clearing systems have established their headquarters in Brussels — SWIFT and Euroclear. As well as commercial banks, there are banks specializing in savings and loans to individuals, in particular mortgages (see Mortgages section in *Setting Up Home*).

The third sector of Belgian banks are the semi-public credit institutions which channel investment funds to industry and other businesses. Other banks under this heading are the General Savings and Pensions Fund (Caisse Générale d'Epargne et de Retraite/Algemene Spaar en Lijfrentekas) which deals with pensions and mortgages; and the Credit Communal/Gemeentekrediet, the bank used by the local and provincial governments. More information about banks is given in the following chapter *Starting a Business*.

There are four stock exchanges in Belgium — in Liège, Antwerp, Ghent and Brussels. The Brussels stock exchange (La Bourse/De Beurs) conducts 85% of business, but is still relatively small compared with some EC stock markets. There is still considerable scope for expansion for banking and financial services in Belgium — only 1.25% of workers are engaged in this sector. Given that the Belgian government is strongly committed to internationalizing banking and finance, more job opportunities for English-speakers should result. The following are major commercial banks in Belgium: Générale de Banque, Banque Bruxelles Lambert, Kredietbank, Crédit Lyonnais, Banque Nationale de Paris, Banque Paribas, Algemene Bank Nederland, Nationale Middenstands Bank, Citibank, Indosuez Bank, Mitsubishi Bank.

Chemicals

Belgium has had a significant chemicals industry since the end of the eighteenth century. Mass production of photographic paper and plates was pioneered by Lieven Gevaert in 1890, and Agfa-Gevaert is still the largest chemicals company in Belgium. The forerunner of plastics — Bakelite — was invented by a native of Ghent, Léo Baekeland in 1908. Belgian firms have also been innovators in pharmaceuticals, fertilizers and paints. During the 1980s the chemicals industry expanded rapidly and now accounts for some 15% of total industrial production. Investment has risen rapidly in recent years, reaching a peak of BF70 billion (£1.2 billion) in 1989. Belgium now has a significant foreign surplus in chemical products, amounting to BF115.7 billion (£2 billion) in 1989.

In recent years the focus of the chemicals industry has shifted decisively towards Flanders, most of it based in or around Antwerp. Here it benefits from the proximity of refineries and seaports. Many chemical companies have sales or registered offices in Brussels, but 80% of production is located in the Flemish region. Of the large number of foreign chemical companies established in Belgium, many are American and British household names. French, German and Swiss pharmaceuticals companies also have a large presence and include the following:

Chemicals: Solvay, Solvic, UCB, BASF, ICI, Union Carbide, Dow Corning, Fisons, Rhône-Poulenc, Akzo, 3M, Exxon.
Pharmaceuticals: Janssen, UCB, Boots, Bayer, Glaxo, Du Pont de Nemours, Monsanto, Sandoz, Schering, Squibb, Beecham.

Food and Agriculture

Employment in agriculture has diminished far more rapidly in Belgium than in other EC countries over the last few decades, yet thanks to better training and the application of science and technology, agricultural production has grown continuously. One agricultural worker is now reckoned to feed 80 consumers. Arable land takes up 25% of the total surface area of the country, the most important crops being potatoes, grains and sugar beet. The Belgians' fondness for potatoes and potato chips (*frieten/frites*) has led to them being given the nickname *patattekes* (little potatoes) by the Dutch. Belgian agriculture has suffered somewhat from recent low prices for basic agricultural products such as sugar, but the country is still a net exporter of food.

The food industry was one of Belgium's greatest success stories in the 1980s, with production and exports rising at a 10% higher rate than in industry as a whole. It is now the second largest industrial employer in the country with 90,000 workers. There has been a determined drive towards finding new markets for well-known Belgian products such as chocolates, beers, soft drinks and waffles. Belgian food and drink have a well-deserved reputation for their excellent quality, and exports will no doubt continue to grow. The largest importer of Belgian food in 1990 was France with BF59.7 billion (£1 billion). The Netherlands and Germany were next, followed by the UK and other EC countries. Some of the major food producers are: United Belgian Mills, Kathy, Vandemoortele, Corman, Nutricia, Mabidic, Amylum, Delhaize-Le Lion, Jacobs-Suchard-Côte d'Or, Belcolade, Nestlé, Spadel, Soubry.

Petrochemicals

Belgium has no oil reserves of its own, and is therefore entirely dependent on imports of crude oil from abroad. Since the oil shock of 1973 Belgium has moved away from dependence on Libya and Saudi Arabia for its oil, and spread its sources of supply far more widely. The largest suppliers are now Iran, Great Britain, Norway and Russia. Belgium's refining capacity fell considerably after the second oil shock of 1979, from 55.5 million tons per year in 1979 to 35 million tons in 1984, where it remains today. Belgium still has a refining capacity in excess of its own domestic needs and exports marginally more petroleum products than it actually uses. While it runs a large deficit with The Netherlands in this sector, it maintains a healthy surplus with the USA, Germany, France and Luxembourg. The largest surpluses are in car fuel (*essence/benzine*), fuel oils, lubricants and bitumens.

As a result of the Gulf War and political instability in Algeria, Belgium is trying hard to diversify its sources of energy. In the future it plans to rely more heavily on gas supplies by linking up to the trans-Siberian pipeline which ends in Germany at the moment, and also by building a gas pipeline to Norway. The Netherlands is also likely to become a major source of natural gas supplies.

The Fédération Petrolière Belge (Belgian Petroleum Federation) has some 21 member companies, but only five of them are involved in refining, notably Fina Raffinaderij, Esso Belgium and the Belgian Refining Corporation. Major retailers in Belgium include: Aral, BP, Castrol, Elf Belgique, Mobil Oil, Texaco, Belgian Shell and Total.

Retailing

The retail sector in Belgium is rather different from that in the UK. There are still traditional shopping streets in every Belgian town; it has been difficult to build shopping centres because land tends to be in the hands of many small owners and local governments have no wish to expropriate their land. While there are hypermarkets and other specialized retailers on the edges of most towns, they are rarely very large as it is virtually impossible to obtain permission to build shops with a sales area of over 750 sq. metres outside town centres. Most retailing is still in the hands of small independent family-owned firms rather than chain-stores; department stores and other large sites are usually owned by foreign (often Dutch) multiples. The major Belgian group of supermarkets is GIB (short for Grand Bazar-Innovation-Bon Marché). An important development in the 1980s has been the increase in the number of supermarkets selling food, led by the German chain Aldi. In most respects small- and medium-sized retailers have maintained or even improved their position. Some department stores have even been divided up into smaller units owned by specialist retailers. Belgian consumers are well-known for their insistence on quality products and have more faith in specialized outlets than chain-stores. Chain stores in Belgium include: Delhaize, Innovation, GB, Sarma, Marks & Spencers, Fnac, C&A, Mothercare, Witteveen, Hunkemöller, Blokker, Eram, 3 Suisses, Bally, Benetton.

Steel and Non-ferrous Metals

Belgium has traditionally been a world leader in metallurgy and still maintains this position today. Employment in the steel sector has fallen by half since 1979 to about 26,000, while production has gone up considerably in recent years. Over half of steel products are destined for the Belgian railways. The situation in non-ferrous metals is even healthier than in the steel sector, but both industries found the going difficult during 1991, with lower prices worldwide for most metals and a drop in demand for exports. In 1989 a giant new non-ferrous metals company was formed when ACEC-Union Minière took over Vielle-Montagne and Métallurgie Hoboken Overpelt. This new combine is now reckoned to be the world leader in the metallurgy of zinc, cadmium, germanium and cobalt, and the European leader in the metallurgy of copper and lead.

Main steel and metallurgical companies:
Steel: Cockerill Sambre, Forges de Clabecq, Sidmar, Gustave Boël, ALZ, New Tubemeuse.
Metallurgy: ACEC-Union Minière, Hoogovens Aluminium, UCA, Remi Claeys.
Aluminium: Johnson Matthey, Boliden Cuivre et Zinc.

Textiles

The traditionally healthy textiles sector went through a major crisis in the late 1970s and contracted substantially in the 1980s. The decline in clothing and knitwear manufacturing has proved to be irreversible and Belgium now imports a lot of finished goods from Asia. On the other hand, Belgium is now the world leader in synthetic floor coverings through such companies as Lano, Beaulieu and De Poortere and also exports large amounts of upholstery coverings, specialized industrial textiles and carpets. In 1990 textile exports exceeded imports by BF29 billion (£500 million). 1991, however, proved to be a very bad year for the textile industry, with production likely to diminish by 4% or more over the whole year.

Textile and clothing companies:
Textiles: De Witte-Lietaer, Louis De Poortere, Balta, De Praetere, Santens, UCO.
Clothing: Levi-Strauss, Lee Europe, Deltex, Van Overdijk, Staels Borco, Alcico.

Regional Employment Guide

In Chapter One, *Introduction*, the main cities and provinces of Belgium were discussed with a view to residence. In this section the same cities and provinces are covered, but this time with a view to the employment prospects available.

The information provided will give some idea of the dominant industries and which types of jobs are available in each area. In each case, further sources of information are given. The press listing is for the major newspaper in the area where job advertisements are most likely to be found. There is usually more than one chamber of commerce in each province. Many of these also have a Euro-Info Centre attached. All of these offices publish brochures and journals which they will supply on request.

ANTWERPEN

Major City: Antwerp.
Regional Newspaper: *De Gazet van Antwerpen*.
Chambers of Commerce: Markgravestraat 12, 2000 Antwerpen 1; tel 03 232 22 19/20; fax 02 233 64 42.
Industry/Other Comments: Antwerp is by far the wealthiest area of Belgium. Industries favour the Antwerp area because of the port facilities and transport connections. Major activities: automotive, diamonds, chemicals, oil refineries, shipping, electronics, engineering, nuclear power, furniture-making, agricultural.

BRABANT (NORTH)

Major City: Leuven.
Regional Newspaper: see Brussels.
Chamber of Commerce: Brucargo, Gebouw 706 — Lokaal 7123, 1930 Zaventem; tel 02 751 91 26.
Industry/Other Comments: Dutch-speaking Brabant includes Vilvoorde and other industrial suburbs of Brussels, the national airport at Zaventem, and the university city of Leuven. The town of Tienen (Tirlemont) is the centre of the sugar industry. There is a high concentration of chemical factories around Brussels, in particular battery-makers. Major activities: chemicals, pharmaceuticals, telecommunications, distribution, agriculture, sugar-refining.

BRABANT (SOUTH)

Major City: Nivelles.
Regional Newspaper: see Brussels.
Chamber of Commerce: Rue St André 1, box 108, 1400 Nivelles; tel 067 21 08 08; fax 067 21 08 00.
Industry/Other Comments: French-speaking Brabant, known locally as Brabant-Wallon, is a small but prosperous area with a large range of industries. Banking and finance are also important sectors. Major activities: steel, paper, pharmaceuticals, electronics, finance.

BRUSSELS

Major Newspaper: see Media section in *Daily Life* chapter.
Chamber of Commerce: Av. Louise 500, 1050 Brussels; tel 02 648 50 02; fax 02 640 93 28.
Industry/Other Comments: Brussels has 10% of the Belgian population but employs 20% of the workforce, and generates 15% of GNP. Brussels is the third autonomous region of Belgium and has its own ministries, development board and so on. At the same time it functions as the capital of the Belgian state, of the Dutch- and French-speaking regions and of the province of Brabant. Most workers are employed in administration, finance and other services, but there are also 15 industrial parks and 4 science parks dedicated to keeping Brussels in the forefront of industrial development. While there are hundreds of representative offices of foreign companies, their production facilities are usually in other countries or other parts of Belgium. Major activities: finance, insurance, distribution, chemicals, car-assembly, aerospace, engineering, printing, publishing, furniture, food, tobacco.

EAST FLANDERS

Major City: Ghent.
Major Newspaper: *De Gentenaar.*
Chamber of Commerce: Building Lieven Bauwens, Martelaarslaan 41, 9000 Ghent; tel 091 25 33 07.
Industry/other comments: East Flanders continues to be one of the most prosperous regions of Belgium, thanks to high levels of investment in automation and high technology. Some of its prosperity is a result of overspill from the Antwerp area. The province benefits from having Belgium's second largest port in Ghent, connected to the Scheldt estuary by the Ghent-Terneuzen canal, as well as the new port on the left bank of the Scheldt, the Waaslandhaven. The automotive

industry is represented by the Volvo car factory on the outskirts of Ghent, which may soon be producing a new range of models in co-operation with Mitsubishi of Japan. The steel-producer Sidmar in Ghent is now one of the most efficient in the world. The textile industry has contracted but is still significant. Some household names in the chemicals and plastics industry are to be found here, such as Rhône-Poulenc, Bayer and Samsonite. A great deal of investment has recently gone into the area of electronics and computers. East Flanders also has one of the world's leading biotechnology centres in Plant Genetic Systems. Major activities: metal-working, automotive, textiles, chemicals, agriculture, horticulture, biotechnology.

HAINAUT
Major City: Charleroi.
Major Newspaper: *La Nouvelle Gazette.*
Chamber of Commerce: Av. Général Michel 1A, 6000 Charleroi; tel 071 32 11 60; fax 071 33 42 18.
Industry/Other Comments: The traditional industrial heartland of Wallonia, Hainaut is in the process of restructuring its entire economy. Mining has closed down completely in the province and the steel industry has shrunk considerably. Hainaut hopes to attract new high-tech industries but is finding it difficult to do so in the face of competition from the Flemish north. Major activities: steel, metallurgy, engineering, glass, plastics, rubber, cement, quarrying.

LIÈGE
Major City: Liège.
Major Newspaper: *La Meuse.*
Chamber of Commerce: Rue des Mineurs 16, 4000 Liège; tel 041 23 62 11; fax 041 23 30 62.
Industry/Other Comments: The city of Liège was a world leader in heavy engineering and weapons manufacturing during the nineteenth century. The weapons industry is still healthy (the most famous manufacturer is F.N. Herstal) but other sections of the steel and metal-working industries have had to be rationalized in order to survive. The workforce in these sectors has fallen by more than half since 1974. Verviers has traditionally been a major textile-producing city, but has been adversely affected by competition from the Far East. The province of Liège includes the German-speaking area of Eupen, Malmédy and St Vith, whose foremost employer is Kabelwerk Eupen, a leading manufacturer of electrical cables. Major activities: steel, weapons, machine tools, textiles, cables, telecommunications.

LIMBURG
Major City: Hasselt.
Major Newspaper: *Het Belang van Limburg.*
Chamber of Commerce: Kunstlaan 20, 3500 Hasselt; tel 011 22 18 00.
Industry/Other Comments: The province of Limburg, although historically an agricultural area, benefited along with Antwerp from the huge foreign investment of the 1950s and 1960s. The existing coal-mining industry expanded rapidly along with steel and car production. While other industries continue to thrive in Limburg, the local coal-mines became uneconomical and had to close down, thus spelling the end of the Belgian coal-mining industry for the time-being. Car-production

is concentrated in Hasselt and Genk; Tessenderlo and its surrounding area has the largest concentration of chemicals factories. Major activities: automotive, chemicals, rubber, steel, engineering, electronics, fruit-growing, distilling.

LUXEMBOURG

Major City: Arlon.
Major Newspaper: *L'Avenir du Luxembourg.*
Chamber of Commerce: Place Communale 2bis, 6800 Libramont; tel 016 22 26 80.
Industry/Other Comments: Although thinly populated and better known for its scenic beauty than for its industries, Luxembourg has attracted its fair share of investment from abroad. As well as the traditional industries such as agriculture and forestry, chemicals and car components are represented here. The American firm Champion manufactures spark-plugs and windshield-wipers in Libramont. Major activities: paper, plastics, car-components, chemicals, packaging, agriculture, cosmetics, forestry, chocolates.

NAMUR

Major City: Namur.
Major Newspaper: see Brussels.
Chamber of Commerce: Av. Sergent Vrithoff 2, 5000 Namur; tel 081 73 52 09; fax 081 23 09 45.
Industry/Other Comments: The province of Namur was never heavily industrialized and was therefore shielded to some extent from the worst of the economic crises of the 1970s and 1980s. The work environment is more attractive than in neighbouring Hainaut and Liège. Tourism is a major industry here and half the surface area is devoted to agriculture. Namur is especially known for its beers, jams and cheeses. Since 1980 there has been a strong shift away from basic industries into the service sector which now employs 75% of the workforce. Another important feature of the local economy is the fact that 96% of firms employ less than 50 people; only six firms employ over 1000 people. The largest growth has been in finance and insurance. A number of foreign firms have established themselves in Namur, including some household names such as Rank Xerox and Tandy (electronics), Siemens (software) and Gestetner (printing). Major activities: agriculture, food-processing, tourism, electronics, chemicals, computers, finance, glass, quarrying, furniture.

WEST FLANDERS

Major City: Bruges.
Major Newspaper: *De Gazet van Antwerpen* (West Flanders edition).
Chamber of Commerce: Ezelstraat 25, 8000 Brugge; tel 050 33 36 96.
Industry/Other Comments: In earlier times this was a mainly agricultural area without much heavy industry. Fishing and tourism are also important activities, although they have declined somewhat in the last few decades. The container port of Zeebrugge is an important employer, along with the coach-assembly plants Mol and De Jonckheere in Roeselare. New industries are coming into the area, in particular chemicals and biotechnology. Major activities: tourism, agriculture, automotive, chemicals, food-processing, fishing.

Directory of Major Employers

Accountancy
Arthur Andersen & Co: Av. des Arts 56, 1040 Brussels; tel 02 510 42 11.
Coopers & Lybrand: Av. Marcel Thiry 216, 1200 Brussels; tel 02 774 42 11.
Ernst & Young SC: Av. Marcel Thiry 204, 1200 Brussels; tel 02 774 91 11.
Fiduciaire Moores Rowland SA: Place Rouppe 16, 1000 Brussels; tel 02 510 32 11.
Grant Thornton EC Office SC: Rue de la Loi 227, 1040 Brussels; tel 02 231 05 80.
KPMG Peat Marwick Belgium SC: Rue Neerveld 101, 1200 Brussels; tel 02 773 36 11.
Price Waterhouse SA: Bvd. de Woluwe 62, 1200 Brussels; tel 02 773 14 11.

Banks
Allied Irish Banks: Sq. de Meeûs 30 bte 1, 1040 Brussels; tel 02 513 84 64.
Associated Banks of Europe ABECOR SA: Av. Louise 326 bte 26, 1050 Brussels; tel 02 649 97 05.
Bank of Ireland: Rue de la Loi 15 bte 11, 1040 Brussels; tel 02 231 12 10.
Banque Indosuez Belgique: Rue des Colonies 40, 1000 Brussels; tel 02 515 91 11.
Barclays Bank plc: Av. Louise 65, 1050 Brussels; tel 02 535 52 11.
Citibank NA: Av. de Tervueren 249, 1150 Brussels; tel 02 761 12 11.
Lloyds Bank (Belgium) SA: Av. de Tervueren 2, 1040 Brussels; tel 02 739 58 11.
Mitsubishi Bank (Europe) SA: Av. des Arts 39, 1040 Brussels; tel 02 513 97 70.
Morgan Guaranty Trust: Av. des Arts 35, 1040 Brussels; tel 02 508 82 11.
NatWest Bank: Treurenberg 2-4, 1000 Brussels; tel 02 219 25 70.
The Sumitomo Bank: Av. des Arts 21-22, 1040 Brussels; tel 02 230 49 00.

Chemical and Pharmaceutical Companies
3M Belgium: Nieuwe Nijverheidslaan 7, 1920 Machelen (Diegem); tel 02 722 51 11.
Agfa-Gevaert NV: Septestraat 27, 2640 Mortsel; tel 03 444 21 11.
BASF Belgium: Av. Ramoir 14, 1180 Brussels; tel 02 373 21 11.
Beecham Pharma NV: Rue Intendant 59, 1210 Brussels; tel 02 423 09 11.
Belgian Shell: Cantersteen 47, 1000 Brussels; tel 02 512 31 60.
BOC Gases NV: Excelsiorlaan 41, 1930 Zaventem; tel 02 719 71 11.
BP Belgium NV: Nieuwe Weg 1, 2070 Zwijndrecht; tel 03 252 21 11.
Deceuninck Plastics NV: Ieperstraat 287, 8800 Roeselare; tel 051 20 03 68.
Dow Corning Europe: Rue Gen. de Gaulle 62, 1310 La Hulpe; tel 02 655 22 10.
Du Pont de Nemours: Antoon Spinoystraat 6, 2800 Mechelen; tel 015 40 14 11.
Exxon Chemical International Inc: Vorstlaan 280, 1160 Brussels; tel 02 674 41 11.
Floridienne SA: Av. Louise 479, 1050 Brussels; tel 02 649 01 73.
Gechem SA: Av. de Broqueville 12, 1150 Brussels; tel 02 762 16 72.
Glaxo Belgium NV: Rue Blanche 15, 1050 Brussels; tel 02 734 01 08.
Hydro Agri Europe SA: Rue Neerveld 107, 1200 Brussels; tel 02 773 52 11.
ICI Belgium NV/ICI Europe Headquarters: Everslaan 45, 3078 Everberg; tel 02 758 92 11.
Janssen Pharmaceutica NV: Turnhoutseweg 30, 2340 Beerse; tel 014 60 21 11.
Johnson Matthey SA: Av. de Schiphol 6, 1140 Brussels; tel 02 729 07 11.
Monsanto Europe SA: Av. de Tervueren 270-272, 1150 Brussels; tel 02 761 41 11.
Petrofina SA: Rue de l'Industrie 52, 1040 Brussels; tel 02 233 91 11.
Smithkline Beecham SA: Rue du Tilleul 9, 1332 Genval; tel 02 656 28 11.
Socomer NV: Nieuwbrugstraat 73, 1830 Machelen; tel 02 254 46 11.

Solvay & Cie SA: Rue du Prince Albert 33, 1050 Brussels; tel 02 509 61 11.
UCB SA: Av. Louise 326 bte 7, 1050 Brussels; tel 02 641 14 11.
Unilever Belgique: Rue Montoyer 51, 1040 Brussels; tel 02 516 75 11.
Upjohn: Lichterstraat, 2670 Puurs; tel 03 890 92 11.
Wellcome NV: Industriezone III, 9320 Erembodegem, Aalst; tel 053 85 25 11.

Computers
Barco NV: Theodoor Sevenslaan 106, 8500 Kortrijk; tel 056 23 32 11.
Honeywell: Av. du Bourget 1, 1140 Brussels; tel 02 243 12 11.
IBM Belgium SA: Sq. Victoria Regina 1, 1210 Brussels; tel 02 214 21 11..
Nixdorf Computers: Rue Colonel Bourg 105. 1040 Brussels; tel 02 739 42 11.
Rank Xerox SA: Bvd. Woluwe 38, 1020 Brussels; tel 02 761 16 11.
Siemens: Chaussée de Charleroi 116, 1060 Brussels; tel 02 536 21 11.

EC Consultants
Adamson Associates SC: Rue de Toulouse 28, 1040 Brussels; tel 02 230 07 75.
Belmont European Community Office: Bvd. Charlemagne 42, 1040 Brussels; tel
  02 231 03 40.
Berkley Associates SC: Rue de la Presse 4, 1000 Brussels; tel 02 219 05 32.
Charles Baker: Rue Montoyer 31 bte 2, 1050 Brussels; tel 02 511 06 45.
Community Trade Advisers EPPA SA: Rue van Campenhoute 22, 1040 Brussels;
  tel 02 735 82 30.
DRT European Services: Av. des Arts 27, 1040 Brussels; tel 02 230 59 80.
Gentraco Ltd: Place du Roi Vainqueur 15 bte 10, 1040 Brussels; tel 02 735 60 58.
Market Access Europe SA: Rue de la Loi 99 bte 5, 1040 Brussels; tel 02 230 05 45.
McIntyre Owen Associates Ltd: Rue de Trèves 45, 1040 Brussels; tel 02 238 78 72.
Nicholas Phillips Associates SA: Rue Joseph II 36 bte 6, 1040 Brussels; tel 02
  218 25 58.
Randall Berendt Europe Ltd: Av. de Mai 67, 1200 Brussels; tel 02 762 50 32.
Single Market Ventures SPRL: Rue de la Presse 4, 1000 Brussels; tel 02 479 12 00.

Food and Drink
Chocolaterie Callebaut NV: Aaltersestraat 124, 9280 Lebbeke; tel 053 71 43 33.
CPC Europe Consumer Foods Ltd: Av. de Tervueren 300 bte 7, 1150 Brussels;
  tel 02 761 09 11.
Jacobs-Suchard-Côte d'Or NV: Bilkensveld 1, 1500 Halle; tel 02 356 38 25.
Nestlé Benelux SA: Rue Birmingham 221 bte 7, 1070 Brussels; tel 02 523 00 40.
Schweppes Belgium SA: Rue du Cerf 117, 1332 Genval; tel 02 656 52 11.
Spadel SA: Rue de Molenbeek 113, 1020 Brussels; tel 02 426 48 00.
United Distillers Belgium NV: Doornveld 1 bte 19, 1731 Zellik; tel 02 466 70 00.
Vandemoortele NV: Kuhlmannlaan 36, 9020 Gent; tel 091 44 88 21.

Insurance
Commercial Union Assurance (Belgium) Ltd: Av. Hermann Debroux 54, 1160
  Brussels; tel 02 676 61 11.
Compagnie de Bruxelles SA: Rue de la Loi 62, 1040 Brussels; tel 02 237 12 11.
General Accident Plc: Meir 14, 2000 Antwerpen; tel 03 221 57 11.
Guardian Royal Exchange Assurance Plc: Bvd. de l'Impératrice 66 bte 5, 1000
  Brussels; tel 02 512 30 64.
Sun Alliance NV: Bvd. de Woluwe 64 bte 1; 1200 Brussels; tel 02 773 03 11.

Willis Faber Boels & Begault SA: Rue des Chevaliers 13, 1050 Brussels; tel 02 511 59 88.

Legal

Ashurst Morris Crisp: Av. Louise 65, 1050 Brussels; tel 02 537 68 95.
Berwin S J & Co: Sq. de Meeûs 19 bte 3, 1040 Brussels; tel 02 511 53 40.
Cleary Gottlieb Steen & Hamilton: Rue de la Loi 23, 1040 Brussels; tel 02 287 20 20.
Clifford Chance: Av. des Gaulois 9, 1040 Brussels; tel 02 739 39 11.
Davies Arnold Cooper: Rue Marie de Bourgogne 52, 1040 Brussels; tel 02 230 60 01.
Denton Hall Burghin & Warrens: Rue de la Loi 38, 1040 Brussels; tel 02 231 19 15.
Forrester Norall & Sutton: Rue Joseph II 36 bte 2, 1040 Brussels; tel 02 219 16 20.
Frere Cholmeley: Rue Guimard 15, 1040 Brussels; tel 02 513 86 04.
Freshfields: Rue de la Loi 15, 1040 Brussels; tel 02 230 08 20.
Hammond Suddards: Av. des Arts 41, 1040 Brussels; tel 02 511 16 20.
Herbert Smith Partners: Rue Guimard 15, 1040 Brussels; tel 02 511 74 50.
Leboeuf Lamb Leiby & MacRae: Sq. de Meeûs 30 bte 2, 1040 Brussels; tel 02 514 56 50.
Linklaters & Paines: Rue du Luxembourg 47, 1040 Brussels; tel 02 513 78 00.
Lovell White Durrant: Av. Louise 489 bte 24, 1050 Brussels; tel 02 647 06 60.
Norton Rose: Rue Montoyer 40, 1040 Brussels; tel 02 237 61 11.
Price & Associates: Bvd. Brand Whitlock 114, 1200 Brussels; tel 02 735 45 11.
Richards Butler: Av. de la Renaissance 1 bte 11, 1040 Brussels; tel 02 732 20 55.
Slaughter & May: Rue d'Arlon 69, 1040 Brussels; tel 02 230 56 31.
Squire Sanders & Dempsey: Av. Louise 165 bte 15, 1050 Brussels; tel 02 648 17 17.
Stanbrook & Hooper: Rue du Taciturne 42, 1040 Brussels; tel 02 230 50 59.
Stephenson Harwood: Av. du Diamant 139, 1040 Brussels; tel 02 735 91 90.
Taylor Johnson Garrett: Sq. de Meeûs 30 bte 2, 1040 Brussels; tel 02 514 46 72.
Turner Kenneth Brown: Av. des Arts 19, 1040 Brussels; tel 02 218 21 88.
Wollastons: Rue Stevin 65, 1040 Brussels; tel 02 230 62 94.

Management Consultants

Berkley Associates SC: Rue de la Presse 4, 1000 Brussels; tel 02 219 05 32.
Deloitte Haskins Sells: Av. Louise 287, 1050 Brussels; tel 02 645 04 11.
Egon Zehnder International SA: Av. F.D. Roosevelt 41, 1050 Brussels; tel 02 648 00 83.
European Business Advisory Group: Rue du Moniteur 9, 1000 Brussels; tel 02 219 18 52.
Management Networking Systems Associates MNSA: Frankrijklei 101 bte 4, 2000 Antwerpen; tel 03 231 64 36.
Taylor & Co.: Kalenbergstraat 2, 1700 Dilbeek; tel 02 567 00 29.

Property Management

Brixton Zaventem SA: Av. Louise 250 bte 1, 1050 Brussels; tel 02 649 52 07.
Debenham Tewson Winssinger SA: Rue du Monastère 10, 1050 Brussels; tel 02 647 98 58.
Healey & Baker: Rue Montoyer 14, 1040 Brussels; tel 02 514 40 00.
Jones Lang Wootton SA: Av. des Arts 36 bte 1, 1040 Brussels; tel 02 511 91 70.
Ketteridge St Quintin Belgium NV: Gramayestraat 4 bte 1, 2000 Antwerpen; tel 03 231 46 30.

King & Co: Rue de la Loi 26, 1040 Brussels; tel 02 230 79 00.
Knight Frank & Rutley: Av. des Arts 4, 1040 Brussels; tel 02 218 54 85.
Richard Ellis: Bvd. du Régent 45-46, 1000 Brussels; tel 02 511 25 05.

Steel and Metallurgy
ACEC-Union Minière: Av. Lloyd George 7, 1050 Brussels; tel 02 536 21 11.
ALZ NV: Industrieterrein, Genk-Zuid Rechteroever, Klein Langerlo, PB7, 3600 Genk; tel 011 30 21 11.
Bekaert NV: Bekaertstraat 2, 8550 Zwevegem; tel 056 76 61 11.
Boliden Cuivre et Zinc: Rue du Fourneau 43, 4030 Liège; tel 041 41 17 80.
Cockerill Sambre SA: Chaussée de la Hulpe 187, 1170 Brussels; tel 02 674 02 11.
Sidmar NV: John Kennedylaan 51, 9042 Gent; tel 091 42 31 11.
Usines Gustave Boël: Rue des Rivaux 2, 7100 La Louvière; tel 064 27 27 11.

Miscellaneous
Alcatel Bell Telephone: Francis Wellerplein 1, 2018 Antwerpen; tel 03 237 17 17.
Belgian Shell SA: Cantersteen 47, 1000 Brussels; tel 02 508 91 11.
British Aerospace: Rue de la Loi 227, 1040 Brussels; tel 230 60 04.
DAF (Trucks): Montoyerstraat 17-19, 1040 Brussels; tel 02 511 43 41.
Ford Motor Company (Belgium) SA: Kanaaldok 200-204, 2030 Antwerpen; tel 03 541 00 80.
General Motors Continental NV: Noorderlaan 75, 2030 Antwerpen; tel 03 543 51 11.
Jonckheere BVBA: Schoolstraat 50, 6800 Roeselare; tel 051 23 26 11.
Michelin SA: Quai Willebroek 33, 1210 Brussels; tel 02 218 61 00.
Pirelli Tyres Benelux SA: Av. Louise 225, 1050 Brussels; tel 02 648 31 40.
Van Hool NV: Berard Van Hoolstraat 58, 2578 Lier; tel 03 482 15 00.
Volvo Cars Europe Industry NV: Kennedylaan 25, 9042 Gent; tel 091 50 21 11.
Wiggins Teape Belgium SA: Av. Ducpétiaux 72, 1060 Brussels; tel 02 537 83 55.

American companies

The American Chamber of Commerce in Brussels publishes a yearly list of its 1,600 members and all American firms operating in Belgium at BF3,300 (surface mail in Europe) or BF3,600 (air mail to the USA). From: American Chamber of Commerce, Av. des Arts 50 bte 5, 1040 Brussels; tel 02 513 67 70. A complete list of businesses in Belgium can be found in the Kompass Register Belgium/Luxembourg at public libraries in the UK.

Further information

The Belgian Employers' Federation issues a free list of member organizations. Obtainable from: Verbond van Belgische Ondernemingen, Ravensteinstraat 4, 1000 Brussels; tel 02 515 08 11. Each member organization publishes yearly reports and statistics.

Starting a Business

With the inauguration of the EC Single Market on 1 January 1993, Europeans from the EC are becoming more aware than ever that starting a business in another Community country can be a rewarding experience both professionally and financially for those who have the skills and energy for such a move. In the case of Belgium, support in the form of advice and business loans is readily available. While the bureaucracy may appear more formidable than in one's own country, much of this is due to unfamiliarity, and it becomes less daunting if one is able to speak Dutch or French. Belgium has always gone to great lengths to make foreign investors and businessmen feel welcome. For a foreigner starting a business or becoming self-employed, the barriers to be overcome are much the same as those for a native Belgian. Only those who have properly understood the market and have a product or service that customers want can expect to succeed. Managerial ability of some kind or another is also crucial. A business is more likely to fail because of bad management rather than adverse economic circumstances.

Many Britons who move to Belgium start out by working for someone else and then use the knowledge they have gained to become independent. Those who plan to run their own business there will most probably already have a successful business or professional career in the UK and hope to take advantage of greater access to the European market or of a perceived gap in the market in Belgium itself. In certain professions, the target market is other expatriates or foreign companies in Belgium. Having English as one's first language then gives one an advantage over Belgian competitors. Once you have been through the whole process of settling down yourself, your knowledge of local conditions then becomes a major selling point.

The prospective entrepreneur in Belgium should be aware of the major differences between Belgium and its neighbours, The Netherlands and France. The Belgians are more cautious about new business ideas than the French and Dutch and you may feel that you are up against excessive red tape (known as *chasse-papier* in French and *rompslomp* in Dutch). As long as you have a well worked-out plan, however, and know whom to address your questions to, there should not be any insurmountable problems. As with any bureaucracy, a great deal of time can be wasted in talking to the wrong people. In a country with half a dozen levels of government this problem is particularly acute. Much of the headache can be removed by employing one of the well-established Brussels business relocation agencies. There are also British-trained lawyers and accountants on hand to ease the process of settling in.

Procedures Involved in Starting a New Business

One question which arises is whether one should take over an existing business or start entirely from scratch. Although it could be argued that taking over an existing business avoids a great deal of bureaucracy, the other side of the coin is that it is difficult to know the exact financial state of the package that one is acquiring. If the package includes employing staff, then Belgium's strict labour laws can make a shake-up or dismissal of staff very costly.

Preparation from Scratch

Exhaustive research is essential before launching oneself into the actual process of setting up a business in Belgium. Information about Belgium is more plentiful than one might suppose, but it tends not to come in the form of off-the-shelf books.

Because of Belgium's size and lack of highly developed institutions there are definite gaps in the market to be exploited. Lawyers, chartered accountants and property companies from the UK are moving into Belgium in considerable numbers because there is a demand for their services which is not being filled by their Belgian counterparts.

Preparation is not only about spotting a gap in the market. You also need to know how you would relate to the Belgians on a daily basis. The best way to find out is to spend as much time in Belgium as possible, building up a network of advisers and allies who can support you when you finally take the plunge. Many successful newcomers say that, initially, the advice of the British Chamber of Commerce in Brussels and the Trade Section of the British Consulate has been invaluable.

Other sources of information in Belgium are the numerous Euro-Info centres, usually at the same address as the Chambers of Commerce (see Regional Guide, *Employment* chapter), the regional and provincial investment bodies and the Ministry of Economics library. The National Institute of Statistics has a vast amount of information on the BLEU (Belgian-Luxembourg Economic Union). The documentation centres of the Banque Générale and Banque Bruxelles Lambert in Brussels keep data bases on foreign and Belgian companies which can be consulted by prior appointment.

The Brussels Chamber of Commerce will, for a small fee, go through your business plan with you and explain the procedures for setting up a company. The national Federation of Small & Medium Industries of Belgium (Fédération des PME's/Verbond van KMO's) can also help in this regard.

For those who are already in Brussels there is Focus, a self-help group originally set up for the spouses of expatriates who want to develop their careers or start a business. Membership costs BF2,200 (£38) or BF3,300 for couples (£57) and is open to both male and female, single and married people. Members help each other by exchanging their professional expertise. Focus plans to publish a book *Setting up a Business and Becoming Self-Employed* by the end of 1992, which will only be available from Focus's office in Brussels.

Useful Addresses

American Chamber of Commerce in Belgium: Av. des Arts 50 bte 5, 1040 Brussels; tel 02 513 67 70/79.

Banque Bruxelles Lambert Documentation Centre: Av. Marnix 23, 1050 Brussels; tel 02 517 39 12.
Belgian-American Chamber of Commerce: Empire State Building, 350 Fifth Avenue, Suite 703, New York, N.Y. 10118; tel (212) 967-9898.
Belgo-Luxembourg Chamber of Commerce in Great Britain: 6 John Street, London WC1N 2ES; tel 071-831 3508.
British Chamber of Commerce of Belgium and Luxembourg: Rue Joseph II, 1040 Brussels; tel 02 219 07 88.
Brussels Chamber of Commerce: Av. Louise 500, 1050 Brussels; tel 02 648 58 73.
Commercial Section — British Embassy: Rue d'Arlon 85, 1040 Brussels; tel 02 287 62 11.
Commercial Section — Embassy of the United States in Belgium: Bvd. du Régent 27, 1000 Brussels; tel 02 513 38 30.
Confederation of British Industry: Rue Joseph II 40 bte 14, 1040 Brussels; tel 02 231 04 65.
Direction Générale des Etudes et de la Documentation: Ministry of Economic Affairs, Rue de l'Industrie 6, 1040 Brussels; tel 02 506 51 11.
Fédération des PME's: Rue de Stalle 90, 1180 Brussels; tel 02 376 85 57.
Focus: The Metairie, Kattenberg 19, 1170 Brussels; tel 02 672 34 08.
Générale de Banque Business Information Services: Montagne du Parc 3, 1000 Brussels; tel 02 516 31 01.
Institut National de Statistique/Nationaal Instituut voor de Statistiek: Rue de Louvain 44, 1000 Brussels; tel 02 513 96 50.

Accountants
Anyone planning to set up a business in Belgium would be well advised to talk a British accountancy firm with a branch in Belgium. Ernst & Young publish a range of books on Belgium, including *Doing Business in Belgium* (1991). These are available from their Belgian offices (see advertisement above), or from Ernst & Young Publications Department, Melrose House, 42 Dingwall Road, Croydon, Surrey CR0 2NE; tel 071-928 2000. A list of international accountants can be found in the section *Major Employers.* Further names of accountants can be found in the Directory of the British Chamber of Commerce in Brussels.

Choosing an Area
The area you decide to live and work in will depend to a large degree on what

kind of business you want to carry out. If other expatriates or foreign companies are your intended market, then you are almost inevitably going to work in Brussels or Antwerp. Incentives to foreign businesses do not vary greatly throughout Belgium. There are certain special employment or development zones ('T-zones') which offer additional incentives if you are thinking of employing Belgian workers. Apart from this it is generally true to say that Dutch-speaking Flanders is more prosperous than French-speaking Wallonia, although unemployment blackspots are not restricted to the latter by any means. Whether you prefer Wallonia to Flanders may also depend on how you feel about French culture and business style, or vice versa.

Useful Publications

Books and Information Packs:

A Businessman's Guide to Belgium: 1986. Free from the Banque Bruxelles Lambert.

Business Briefing for Belgium: Published by the British Chamber of Commerce in Brussels in 1986. Very useful but needs to be updated. Price BF480.

Doing Business in Belgium: Essential book published by the American Chamber of Commerce in Brussels, revised up to 1990; next edition in November 1992. Price BF1,200 to non-members.

Doing Business in Belgium: Price Waterhouse, 32 London Bridge Street, London SE1 9SY; tel 071-939 3000.

Flanders Investment Guide: 1990. Free from Flanders Investment Opportunities Council (FIOC), Markiesstraat 1, 1000 Brussels; tel 02 507 38 70.

Setting Up In Belgium: 1988. 210-page information pack from Générale de Banque, at BF2,500 (address above).

Tax & Investment Profile — Belgium: From Touche Ross International, Hill House, 1 Little New Street, London EC4A 3TR; or Tinnemans Van der Steen & Co, Bvd. Saint-Michel 27, 1040 Brussels.

Your Investment Guide to Belgium: 1991. Free information pack from the Ministry of Economic Affairs, Sq. De Meeûs 23, 1040 Brussels; tel 02 506 54 14.

Periodicals:

AmCham: A monthly magazine from the American Chamber of Commerce. Former name was *Commerce in Belgium.* Subscription cost BF4,200, or BF100 for a single issue.

Business Journal: Monthly magazine of the British Chamber of Commerce. BF90 per issue.

Entreprendre: (French). Brussels Chamber of Commerce monthly. Free of charge. Dutch version called *Dynamiek.*

Le Marché/De Markt: Weekly magazine for managers. Costs BF130 per copy.

Trends-Tendances: (French). Weekly business magazine. Costs BF130. Dutch version *Trends.*

Raising Finance

Those contemplating starting a business in Belgium should be aware that UK banks will not be able to provide start-up loans where the prospective proprietor intends to be resident abroad. Belgian credit institutions are willing to finance foreign investment to a considerable extent. Smaller entrepreneurs will need to rely on their own resources in the beginning, but once they are established in Belgium the whole range of credit facilities will be open to them. The obvious way to raise money is by selling one's UK home. If this proves insufficient it should be possible to raise a mortgage on a Belgian property. Mortgages are available in Belgium on up to 125% of the value of the property.

An unemployed person in Belgium can apply for a loan of up to BF500,000 (£8,500) known as a *prêt subordonné chômeur* in French, with only interest payable for the first five years, in order to start up a new business. Such a loan is in principle available to any EC national who is established in Belgium if they can convince the authorities that their business is likely to succeed.

As an alternative it is well worth looking at regional investment schemes in Belgium.

Investment Incentives

Generous incentives and subsidies are available to foreign investors in Belgium. Some of the tax-breaks offered are so generous that they have prompted complaints from the Dutch government that too much foreign investment is going into Belgium at the expense of her neighbours.

In general, the amount of investment incentives depends very much on the size of the company, its location, the nature of its activities, and its proposed sources of finance. For example, within EC-recognized development regions there are eight so-called Tax-free zones (T-zones) where a high-technology enterprise is exempt from income tax and many other taxes for 10 years if it employs between 10 and 200 workers within two years of start-up. T-zones are to be found in the Kempen (the eastern part of the province of Antwerp), the Westhoek (in the south of West Flanders) and in the provinces of Liège, Namur and Hainaut (the industrialized parts of Wallonia).

Capital grants and/or interest rebates are available up to a maximum of 18% of investment in most of Belgium, and up to 21% in development regions. As well as the regions mentioned in the previous paragraph, Limburg in Flanders, and parts of the province of Luxembourg in Wallonia, are also official EC development regions. The regional government will pay up to half the interest on a loan from a Belgian credit institution for up to five years. Where the enterprise is self-financing, capital grants will be paid out at six-monthly intervals over a five-year period. These and other incentives are usually dependent on a certain number of new jobs being created over a specified period of time. The government will not subsidize any enterprise whose production processes involve the release of hazardous substances such as cadmium, lead, and so on into the environment.

Small and Medium Enterprises (SMEs)

Belgium is very much a land of SMEs, known as KMOs (*Kleine en Middelgrote Ondernemingen*) in Dutch, and PMEs (*Petites et Moyennes Entreprises*) in French. A business is (roughly speaking) considered to be an SME if it employs fewer than 50 workers and has a turnover of less than BF170 million per year (£2.9 million). The definition of an SME varies somewhat in different sectors of the economy and between the three regions. Only 2% of industrial and 0.5% of non-industrial enterprises employ more than 50 workers; over half of Belgian businesses are one-person operations.

Precise details of support offered to SMEs are available in the publications given below. It should be noted that support for small businesses is now the responsibility of the regional governments and not of the central government.

Useful Publications

Les Aides aux PME: Obtainable from Ministère de la Région Wallonne, Division de l'Expansion Economique des PME, Av. Prince de Liège 7, 5100 Jambes; tel 081 32 12 11.

Vade Mecum du Créateur d'Entreprise (Région Wallonne): Latest edition 1991. 164 pages. BF190. From: Office des Créations d'Entreprises, Bvd. de la Sauvenière 136C, 4000 Liège; tel 041 22 10 11.

Expansiesteun voor KMO's en Zelfstandigen: (Dutch). From: Ministerie van de Vlaamse Gemeenschap, Administratie voor Economie en Werkgelegenheid, Dienst Economische Expansie Middenstand, Markiesstraat 1, 1000 Brussel; tel 02 507 31 11.

Regional Investment Offices

As well as the three regional investment offices given below, there are provincial investment offices, whose addresses can be obtained from Chambers of Commerce or Euro Info Centres. Investment offices are usually a good source of documentation.

Regional Investment Company for Brussels (SRIB/GIMB): Av. Marnix 13 bte 5, 1050 Brussels; tel 02 511 64 83.

Gewestelijke Investering Maatschappij Vlaanderen (GIMV): Karel Oomsstraat 37, 2018 Antwerpen; tel 03 248 23 21.

Société Régionale d'Investissement Wallonne (SRIW): Place Josephine Charlotte 19 bte 1, 5100 Jambes; tel 081 32 22 11.

Relocation Agencies and Business Services

Newcomers who are deterred by the practical difficulties involved in setting up a new business can turn to a business relocation agency for assistance. These are always separate from relocation offices for individuals moving to Belgium. Relocation agencies are particularly useful in helping to find office space and equipment at a reasonable price. Other services, such as lawyers, accountants, translators and interpreters can be found in the Directory of the British Chamber of Commerce and the Yellow Pages.

Useful Addresses

Analysts International SPRL: Abstraat 39, 3090 Overijse; tel 02 687 31 76. Consultants in multinational/Belgian financial management accounting. Provide temporary financial management, accounting and word processing staff.

DB Associates SA: Rue Belliard 203 bte 8, 1040 Brussels; tel 02 231 04 30. Business relocation. Plant and office location.

Ernst & Young: Marcel Thirylaan 204, 1200 Brussels; tel 02 774 9111; fax 02 774 9090. International accountants.

Horwath Tax Holland: Weerdestein 117, 1083 GH Amsterdam; tel 010 31 20 646 2746/661 2777; fax 646 1248. Tax advice for migrants to Belgium, The Netherlands and other EC countries. Advice on investment and exporting to the Benelux countries.

Jordan & Sons Ltd: 21 St. Thomas Street, Bristol, Avon BS1 6JS, UK; tel 0272-230600; fax 0272-230063. Specializes in company formation in the EC, and offshore company formation. Conducts searches on existing companies in Belgium. Established 1863.

Meeting Time SA/NV: Av. E. de Béco, 1050 Brussels; tel 02 648 63 30. Business relocation services. Conference management.

Wood Appleton Oliver & Co Ltd: Av. Louise 207 bte 8, 1050 Brussels; tel 02 640 07 96; fax 02 640 53 43. Accounting and financial services. Company formation.

Business Structures

In order to operate commercially in Belgium, an individual or company must have a recognized Belgian business structure. It is quite possible to start one's business as a self-employed person and then change to one of the forms of company given below. The procedures involved in changing over from self-employed to limited company status are explained in *La Transformation d'une Entreprise Personelle*

en Société, by E. Bours (publ. Editions du Jeune Barreau de Liège, Palais de Justice, 4000 Liège).

Most foreigners choose a limited liability company: either an SA/NV (*Société Anonyme/Naamloze Vennootschap*) or the simpler SPRL/BVBA (*Société Privée à Responsabilité Limitée/Besloten Vennootschap met Beperkte Aansprakelijkheid*). Partnerships and co-operatives are also sometimes used by foreigners.

The formalities of setting up a company are usually entrusted to a fiscal or legal adviser. The British Chamber of Commerce in Brussels will be happy to suggest suitable advisers.

The different business entities and the steps required to form them are as follows:

SA/NV. An SA/NV must have at least two shareholders, and three directors. The subscribed capital must be seen to be sufficient for the planned activity and cannot be less than BFl,250,000. At least one quarter of subscribed capital, with a minimum of BFl,250,000, must be paid into a bank in Belgium at the time of incorporation. The statutes of the company are drawn up by a notary and signed in his/her presence. The statutes are then filed with the Commercial Court (Greffe du Tribunal de Commerce/Griffie van de Handelsrechtbank) and an application made to be put on the Register of Commerce (Registre de Commerce/Handelsregister). Extracts of the statutes will appear in the Belgian Official Gazette (*Moniteur Belge/Belgisch Staatsblad*). If the business involves the sale of goods or services under the VAT Code, then the company must obtain a VAT number from the VAT administration. The fee for setting up an SA/NV with the minimum capital requirement of BFl,250,000 is likely to come to BF55,000, including capital duty at 0.5%, notarial fees, stamp duty and publication costs.

The SA is the favoured form for large enterprises which need to raise capital.

SPRL. The SPRL is a private limited liability company and is the preferred form for family enterprises. There are at least two shareholders, and one director. The running of the company is entrusted to one or more managers (*gérants/zaakvoerders*), who need not be shareholders. The subscribed capital requirement is BF750,000. At least 20% of the subscribed capital, with a minimum of BF250,000, must be paid up at the time of incorporation. There is also a form of SPRL with only one shareholder — an SPRLU/EBVBA (*SPRL Unipersonelle/Eenpersoons BVBA*).

The formalities for incorporating an SPRL are similar to those for an SA, but the fees can be as little as BF20,000. Publication requirements for balance sheets and articles of incorporation are not as strict as for an SA.

SC/CV. This is a co-operative known as a *Société Cooperative/Cooperatieve Vennootschap* and is favoured by groups of professionals, such as lawyers, accountants, and so on, who want a loose business association. The Belgian government has recently imposed a minimum capital requirement of BF650,000 on SCs, all of which must be lodged in a bank.

Partnerships: The only type of limited partnership much used by foreigners is the SCA/CVA (*Société en Commandite par Actions/Commanditaire Vennootschap op Aandelen*), a company with share capital, where liability is limited to the amount of shares subscribed.

Non profit association: Another business entity one frequently comes across is the ASBL/VZW (*Association Sans But Lucratif/Vereniging Zonder Winstoogmerk*), a non-profit making association.

Branch: It is also possible to set up a branch (*succursale/bijhuis*) of an existing foreign company. The main requirement for this is the publication of the articles of association of the parent company in the state gazette. The company then operates under the same name as in its home country. Total costs for translation of documents, registration etc. are likely to come to at least BF100,000.

All companies must prepare accounts and file them with the Commercial Court within 30 days of their approval by the shareholders. An audit must be carried out by a statutory auditor (*réviseur d'entreprises/bedrijfsrevisor*) if two of three conditions apply: the turnover exceeds BF170 million, the balance sheet exceeds BF85 million or there are more than 50 employees. An auditor can be chosen from the members of the Institute of Auditors (*Institut des Réviseurs d'Entreprises/Instituut der Bedrijfsrevisoren*). Where an auditor is not required, the services of a member of the Institute of Accountants (*Institut des Experts-Comptables/Instituut der Accountants*) may be used.

Ideas for New Businesses

English-speaking expatriates in Belgium are largely concentrated in cities such as Brussels, Antwerp, Ghent and Mons, and, to some extent, on the coast. It is quite feasible to start up a bar, restaurant or shop which relies on expatriate customers. At the same time one must be aware of the high expectations of Belgian consumers with respect to quality, and think about how one can compete with local enterprises. For this reason newcomers may feel happier about taking over an established and profitable business, through which new products can be introduced on a trial-run basis. Small businesses for sale are frequently advertised in the Belgian press.

Chartered Accountants

Belgian accountants do not have the same high profile or prestige as British chartered accountants. Their services are in many cases limited to checking the company books at the end of the year rather than giving advice on financial management. There is therefore a need for cost and management accountants who have some knowledge of business in other EC countries to advise foreign companies and expatriates setting up businesses in Belgium.

Estate Agents

At the moment a number of British commercial property agents have established themselves in Belgium, but the residential property market is still wide open to newcomers. While Belgian estate agents are not an endangered species, it should be noted that anyone can become an estate agent. The profession is more or less unregulated and there is no special training required. British estate agents are better trained than their Belgian counterparts and could sell not only to expatriates but also to Belgians.

Food

Belgium is rightly famous for its food, and standards are high even in fast food restaurants. While Belgian food is very good, it tends to be high in cholesterol.

Interest in health foods is growing and there are opportunities in setting up restaurants or retail outlets for this kind of product. Health food is usually overpriced in Belgium, and there is certainly scope for more efficient operators in this field.

Graphic and Industrial Design
These are areas where Belgium has traditionally lagged behind its neighbours, partly because of a lack of specialized training. Good designers can make their mark here without having to deal with the same level of competition as in Britain.

Publishing
There are considerable opportunities for journalists and writers who can write reports, advertising copy, in-house newsletters and so on for multinationals and local companies. With the use of DTP (Desk-Top Publishing) equipment, it is possible for individuals to design publicity materials and even entire books to a high standard. DTP equipment can also be used for word-processing for which there is always a big demand. Another possibility could be running a newspaper for the expatriate community.

Other
Other foreign professionals who have found a demand for their services include lawyers, public relations consultants, architects and landscape gardeners.

Exporters
The Belgium desk of the Exports to Europe Branch of the Department of Trade and Industry in London (DTI, 1-19 Victoria Street, London SW1H 0ET; tel 071-215 5103; fax 071-215 5611) and the regional offices provide help and information for exporters in a number of ways. They can provide basic market information, commission status reports on specific companies and find suitable representatives for UK firms, as well as giving current information on tariff rates and import procedures. Fees are charged for most of these services. The DTI also publishes the booklet, *Doing Business in Belgium, The Netherlands and Luxembourg* as well as booklets focusing on the Single Market, such as *Financial Services, Company Law Harmonisation* and *Starting Up a Small Business*, which are potentially useful to anybody considering setting up a business abroad. In addition, the free quarterly magazine, *Single Market News* is a good source of business news and regulations concerning the Single Market. All of these publications are available free of charge from the DTI hotline on 081-200 1992. The DTI's Export and Market Information Centre Library (Room 150, 1st Floor, Ashdown House, 123 Victoria Street, London SW1; tel 071-215 5444) is also worth a visit. The library has a wealth of statistical information and all the Belgian Yellow Pages. The reference book *Country Profile of Belgium* can be consulted there or purchased for £10. It can also be ordered by telephone on 0789-296212. The library is open from 9.30 am to 5.30 pm Monday to Friday. You will be asked to sign in with a business address. Otherwise you need to make an appointment in advance.

Running a Business

Employing Staff
Employer and employee relations in Belgium are controlled by a mass of social and labour legislation, parts of which vary according to the type of industry involved

and the status of the employee. The three main categories of staff are managers (*gérants/beheerders*), white-collar staff (*employés/bedienden*) and workmen/women (*ouvriers/arbeiders*). The level of social security payments, holiday allowance, notice of dismissal and so on will vary depending on the category of worker.

Over the years Belgian labour legislation has aimed to increase job security for workers, but employers still have the absolute right to dismiss workers if they respect the terms of notice. Where a worker is dismissed without good reason, the employer can be made to pay an indemnity by a labour court equivalent to at least six months' salary, or the amount of salary that the worker would have earned during the statutory period of notice. There is no such thing as obligatory reinstatement in Belgium.

Belgian employment law is clearly explained in English in the *Industrial Encyclopaedia for Labour Law and Industrial Relations*, volume II, edited by R. Blanpain (Kluwer Law and Taxation Publishers, Deventer, The Netherlands: 1991).

Trade Unions
Apart from the three major trade union federations (see Chapter Six, *Employment*) which are based on the three main political parties, there are trade unions in specific work sectors almost all of which belong to one of the three federations. Although trade unions have considerable power in Belgium, strikes are not very frequent, because of the well-established procedures for consultation between management and workers. Companies which employ more than 100 workers must institute a company council (*conseil d'entreprise/ondernemingsraad*), where representatives of employers and employees meet once a month to discuss work practices and other matters. Workers have the right to detailed information about the company's affairs and can appoint their own accountant to look at the books. There is no requirement for workers to be represented on the board of directors.

Employers' Organizations
The main employers' organization is the Fédération des Entreprises Belges (FEB)/Verbond van Belgische Ondernemingen (VBO), Rue Ravenstein 4, 1000 Brussels; tel 02 515 08 11. There are also three regional federations of employers whose addresses are given below.

Union des Entreprises de Bruxelles/Verbond van Ondernemingen te Brussel: Rue Botanique 75, 1210 Brussels; tel 02 219 32 23.
Union Wallonne des Entreprises: Rue Capitain Crespel 42, 1050 Brussels; tel 02 513 45 34.
Vlaams Economisch Verbond: Brouwersvliet 5, 2000 Antwerpen; tel 03 231 16 60.

Categories of Underemployment
There is no shortage of well-trained workers in Belgium, many of whom speak English. Unemployment tends to be concentrated in the declining industrial regions of Flanders and Wallonia, so that there are considerable numbers of former miners, metal-workers, textile-workers and so on. One area where workers are hard to find is in computer programming. It is also hard to find workers who have completely mastered several languages. Part-time work is not as popular as it is in Britain, at around the EC average of 11% of employment.

Employee Training
Employers pay 0.04% of gross salary towards 'educational leave', as part of their social security contributions. Employees can take up to 240 hours leave a year

for professional training, or 180 hours for general education. The employer pays their salary up to BF62,000 a month during the period of leave, which is then reimbursed to the employer by the employment ministry. Employers have the right to stop too many employees taking educational leave at the same time.

Staff Agencies

In some cases it is possible to acquire specially trained staff through a recruitment agency: Rainbow Careers (37 Avenue de Tervuren — 1040 Brussels; tel 02 735 41 54) specialize in providing multi lingual secretaries.

Wages and Salaries

For each Belgian industry there is a national minimum wage and salary scale. Further details of pay levels and bonuses are given in Chapter Six, *Employment.*

Social Security

Employers and employees are obliged to pay social security contributions, which cover health insurance, unemployment benefit, pensions, family allowances, holidays, industrial accidents, and so on. The employer's contribution in the case of white-collar workers stands at between 32.46% and 34.26% of gross salary, and in the case of manual workers at 38.46% to 40.26%. The employee's contribution is always 12.07% of gross salary. The precise amounts of social security payments and taxes are normally computed on the employer's behalf by the local social security institution, the Secretariat Social or Sociaal Secretariat. A self-employed person pays about 22% of their gross income in social security contributions and receives smaller benefits than employees. In the case of a limited company such as an SPRL, social security contributions are only payable on the director's salary, not on the company's income. It is therefore highly advantageous to form an SPRL if you become successful as a self-employed person.

Paid Holidays

The subject of holidays is dealt with in the Aspects of Employment section of Chapter Six, *Employment.*

Taxation

Belgians and foreigners alike find Belgian taxation laws difficult to understand. For this reason companies have their tax returns prepared by tax accountants (*experts-comptable*). The status of the self-employed and small companies has recently become somewhat similar in that taxes have to be paid in advance based on an estimate of projected income in both cases. Above a certain income level trading as an SPRL becomes fiscally advantageous. However, many self-employed Belgians prefer to work in the black economy or to do several jobs at once, thus making the formation of a company irrelevant.

The starting point for determining corporation tax is gross income reported in the financial statements of the company. The reporting period may be either a financial year, or a fiscal year ending any day except 31 December.

Impôt des sociétés/Vennootschapsbelasting: Corporate income tax. This has been decreasing over the last several years. Corporate income tax will be levied at the following rates from fiscal year 1992:

Gross Income in Belgian Francs	Corporate tax
0-1,000,000	28%
1,000,000-3,600,000	36%
3,600,000-13,000,000	39%

Where income exceeds BF13,000,000 the total income is taxed at 39%. Corporate taxes are payable in advance on April 10, July 10, October 10 and December 20. If payment is not made in advance, a 24% surcharge is added to the tax bill at the end of the year. Self-employed people and companies frequently borrow money from their banks in order to make these advance payments (*versements anticipés/voorafbetalingen*). The interest on these loans is tax-deductible.

Précompte immobilier/Onroerende voorheffing: Real estate tax. The basic rate of this tax is 1.25% of a hypothetical rental value, the *revenu cadastral/kadastraal inkomen*, but the effective rate is 18% to 40% after municipal surcharges.

Précompte mobilier/Roerende voorheffing: Withholding tax. Levied on dividends and interests at 25% and 10% respectively.

Plus values/Meerwaarde: Capital gains. These are in many cases exempt from taxation, in particular where they are reinvested in Belgium. Otherwise they are taxed at half the standard corporation tax rate, i.e. 19.5%.

TVA/BTW: VAT is charged at four different rates in Belgium (before 1 April 1992 there were six rates). The standard rate is now 19.5%. For businesses, each month's VAT is payable on the 15th of the following month, and is calculated on the basis of one-third of the previous quarter's payment. Adjustments are made every quarter in case of under- or over-payment. VAT is administered by the TVA Enregistrement et Domaines/BTW Registratie en Domeinen, (Tour des Finances, Bvd. du Jardin Botanique 50 bte 37, 1010 Brussels; tel 02 210 26 11.)

The Netherlands
SECTION I

Living in The Netherlands

General Introduction

Residence and Entry Regulations

Setting Up Home

Daily Life

Retirement

The Netherlands: Provinces, Main Towns and Water Barriers

Noordzee

Éemshaven

GRONINGEN
Delfzijl

Waddenzee Leeuwarden

Harlingen FRIESLAND Groningen

Sneek Drachten

Den Helder Heerenveen Stadskanaal

Assen

DRENTHE

IJsselmeer Steenwijk Emmen

Emmeloord Hoogeveen

Alkmaar Enkhuizen Meppel

Hoorn Coevorden

NOORD- Kampen

HOLLAND Lelystad Zwolle

Zaanstad OVERIJSSEL

Haarlem FLEVOLAND Nijverdal Almelo

Almere

Amstelveen Amsterdam Harderwijk Deventer Hengelo

Hilversum Bussum Apeldoorn Enschede

Leiden Nijkerk

Den Haag Utrecht Amersfoort Zutphen

ZUID- Zeist GELDERLAND

HOLLAND Gouda UTRECHT Doetinchem

Delft Rotterdam Nieuwegein Rijn Arnhem

Europoort Culemborg Wageningen Winterswijk

Schiedam Tiel Waal

Görinchem Nijmegen

Dordrecht Maas

Waalwijk 's-Hertogenbosch GERMANY

Veerse Oosterschelde Breda NOORD-BRABANT

Gat Roosendaal Tilburg Veghel

Middelburg Bergen op Eindhoven Helmond

Vlissingen Zoom Veldhoven Geldrop

ZEELAND Valkenswaard LIMBURG Venlo

Terneuzen Weert

BELGIUM

———	International borders
┃┃┃┃┃	Provincial boundaries
▨	Randstad conurbation
▤	Areas flooded in February 1953
ZEELAND	Province
Haarlem	Provincial capitals
═══	Dam
======	Storm surge barrier
+++++	Secondary dyke

Kerkrade

Maastricht

0 _____ 50 Miles

0 _____ 50 Kms

General Introduction

Destination The Netherlands

Now that the last barriers to the free movement of people and goods are falling within the Common Market, more and more British and Irish citizens are looking to the Continent for professional and business opportunities, in the knowledge that success is just as likely, or even more likely, abroad as it is in their own countries. Professional and entrepreneurial skills are greatly respected and highly rewarded by the Dutch, and there has in the past been something of a brain drain in the direction of The Netherlands from other European countries. Because of the close cultural and linguistic links with the English-speaking world (most Dutch people born after 1945 speak good English), adjusting to life in The Netherlands could not be easier.

Many outsiders have a somewhat romantic image of The Netherlands as a land of windmills and tulips, whose inhabitants wear clogs and make cheese when they are not fighting off the encroaching North Sea. This kind of image is useful in promoting tourism but does not give us much insight into the country. A closer look at The Netherlands reveals a highly organized, ultra-modern industrialized society, which has been able to overcome its internal divisions in the pursuit of physical survival and a high standard of living. Anyone who spends more than a short holiday in The Netherlands will also become aware of the peculiar combination of deep-seated conservatism and apparently extreme liberalism which characterizes the people.

The main forces that have moulded the Dutch character are undoubtedly the immense national effort needed to prevent a large part of the country from being flooded by the North Sea, and the desire for freedom of thought and religion, which almost led to the annihilation of the country by the Spanish in the sixteenth century. The Dutch have had to be tough and self-disciplined in order to create a prosperous country out of a very unpromising physical environment. Without many natural resources of their own, they were obliged to become traders and middlemen, thus accounting for their highly-developed commercial sense.

The Dutch are self-confident people, and they expect others to be self-confident as well. They do not like to waste time when there is work to be done and they expect to be able to rely on their fellow workers. The Protestant work ethic rules everyone, be they Calvinists, Catholics or atheists. The influence of Protestantism is also apparent in an almost religious reverence for reason and tolerance.

Pros and Cons of Moving to The Netherlands

For several hundred years the Dutch have enjoyed one of Europe's highest standards of living, thanks to their commercial abilities and dedication to hard work. The

Netherlands has traditionally welcomed immigrants with useful skills, as well as absorbing large numbers of citizens of its former colonies. Nevertheless, only 5% of its population hold foreign passports, a much smaller proportion than in neighbouring Belgium and Germany. The Dutch authorities do not encourage asylum-seekers or economic refugees, which is understandable given that The Netherlands is already densely populated and the population is growing faster than in many of its EC neighbours.

Because of the relative absence of a language barrier and the constant demand for highly skilled workers, there has been a steady stream of British and Irish citizens to The Netherlands in the last 20 years, and this trend is likely to continue, given the favourable prospects for the Dutch economy in the 1990s.

During the 1960s and 1970s, The Netherlands acquired the reputation of being a haven for anarchists and hippies, and it still has a lively counterculture. Unfortunately, the liberalization of the 1960s has brought a serious drugs and vice problem in its wake, which in turn has given Amsterdam one of the highest crime-rates in the EC. Amsterdam is not at all typical, however, and most of the Dutch are still basically conservative and middle class in their outlook.

The Dutch are hard workers. Business people start work at 8.30am or even 8.00am in some offices, and may carry on after 5.00pm. It would be reasonable to expect to work more hours than are stipulated by your contract. Lunch-breaks are short and the main meal of the day is in the early evening between six and seven. The Dutch prefer an informal atmosphere at work. Clothing is casual but smart, and colleagues use each other's first names. The emphasis is on efficiency and getting things done quickly.

Initial contacts with the Dutch can be unnerving, since they can seem very direct and even brusque with strangers. It is just as well to stand one's ground and try to be equally direct, or at the very least not to take offence. If you live in The Netherlands, you will come to appreciate the advantages of speaking your mind and knowing where you stand with other people. It is also worth noting that the Dutch, by their own admission, are given to impatience and this is something which one has to get used to. Once initial communication problems have been overcome, however, you will find the Dutch helpful and good-natured, and even sentimental at times.

English-speakers usually have a good social life in The Netherlands, and ample opportunities to pursue the same interests as at home. English-language books, films, music and newspapers all have a wide distribution, and the local people are very aware of what is happening in the English-speaking world.

Dutch people enjoy outdoor pursuits and there are excellent sports facilities of every kind. Except during the summer, however, the climate does not encourage sitting around outdoors. The Dutch spend a lot of time in their homes, which are tidy and comfortable. As a result, Dutch towns can have a strangely deserted feeling about them in the evenings.

Pros: Strong economy with constant employment prospects.
English widely used in business and elsewhere.
Favourable treatment of EC citizens.
High standard of living.
Excellent social security system.
Dutch people are receptive to foreigners.
Lively cultural scene.

Cons: Good-quality rented accommodation is expensive.
Often wet and windy.
Flat landscape.
Higher taxes than in Britain.
Densely populated.

Political and Economic Structure

The earliest known inhabitants of The Netherlands were a mixture of Germanic tribes and others, who built mounds known as *terpen* linked by causeways to escape from the sea. These are still visible today in the provinces of Groningen and Friesland. The area south of the Rhine delta, corresponding to the modern provinces of Zeeland, North Brabant and Limburg, was part of the Roman provinces of Gallia Belgica and Germania Inferior from 55 BC, while the north remained unsubdued.

The Dutch are not purely Germanic people, even though many of them are tall and blond. The national language, Dutch, is closely related to English. In the north-east, there are also about 250,000 speakers of another Germanic language, Frisian, a language which is even more closely related to English than Dutch itself. This connection is accounted for by the fact that the Anglo-Saxons remained in the area of Friesland for some time prior to their invasion of England in the fifth century AD.

In order not to offend the Dutch, it is best to call their country The Netherlands, rather than Holland, even though they often use the word Holland themselves. Holland (meaning 'wooded land') refers to the modern provinces of South and North Holland, the historical centre of the independent Netherlands. The Dutch term for the indigenous language is Nederlands; the word Dutch originally meant any Germanic-sounding language spoken in Germany, Flanders or The Netherlands.

During the Middle Ages, The Netherlands was an assortment of duchies and principalities which acknowledged their allegiance to the Holy Roman Empire. The two major powers were the Counts of Holland and the Bishops of Utrecht. The northern provinces of Groningen and Friesland did not even have dukes or counts, but rather councils of leading merchants who dealt with the all-important problem of organizing the coastal defences. Even at the dawn of the Middle Ages, the Dutch had already built up a great deal of expertise in draining low-lying land and were much in demand in northern France and Flanders for this type of work. They also established an intermediary role in the trade between the Baltic and the rest of Europe, thus laying the basis for their future commercial success.

Centralized authority was weak at this time. The national decision-making body, the States General, was made up of representatives of the state councils, and could only make decisions with the unanimous support of all the Dutch states. One or other of the local rulers was appointed as the *stadhouder* or 'ruler by proxy', as a nominal representative of the Holy Roman Emperor.

During the fifteenth century, The Netherlands (a term which at this time included the future kingdom of Belgium) came under Burgundian control, and then under the Habsburgs, with the result that it found itself ruled by the fiercely Catholic King Philip II of Spain from 1555. The Reformation had already taken a strong hold in The Netherlands and a confrontation was inevitable. The struggle for independence lasted from 1568 to 1648 (the Eighty Years' War). The future shape of The Netherlands was more or less determined in 1579, when the six southern provinces of the Spanish Netherlands (corresponding to what was to become Belgium) reconciled themselves to Spanish domination, while the more Protestant-minded north continued to fight for independence. The great hero of the day was William the Silent, Prince of Orange (1533-1582). It should be noted that the Princes of Orange were not rulers of The Netherlands, but rather continued to be *stadhouders* appointed by the States General who could be dismissed if necessary.

Once the Spanish threat had receded, The Netherlands entered its Golden Age. Thanks to their sea power, the Dutch were able to acquire a number of former Spanish and Portuguese colonies in the East and West Indies, and thus establish a solid base for future economic expansion. At home, the arts and sciences flourished as never before. Dutch painters such as Rembrandt, Vermeer, Frans Hals and others built up an unrivalled reputation which continues to the present day. During the seventeenth century, the Dutch became powerful enough to challenge the British for commercial supremacy in many parts of the world. The relationship was not always antagonistic, however, and one of the Princes of Orange, Willem III, even became King of England as William III (from 1688 to 1702). During the Napoleonic Wars the Dutch found themselves in the French camp, and consequently lost many of their most valuable colonies to the British, in particular South Africa and much of Guyana. Their only North American colony, New Amsterdam (now New York), had been exchanged for Surinam (Dutch Guyana) in 1667 after a similarly unsuccessful war against the British.

The Dutch aversion to centralized government continued up until the time of Napoleon, who appointed his brother Louis, King of The Netherlands. Louis Bonaparte's success and popularity persuaded the Dutch to go over to a hereditary monarchy, and thus Prince Willem VI of Orange became King Willem I of The Netherlands in 1815. From 1815 until 1830, Belgium and Luxembourg also came under the Dutch crown. The Belgians felt dissatisfied with Dutch rule, however, and set up their own Catholic state in 1831. Luxembourg continued to owe some allegiance to the Dutch crown until 1890, when it became an independent Grand Duchy.

During the twentieth century, The Netherlands remained neutral during World War I. In spite of its declared neutrality, it was invaded and brutally occupied by the Germans during the Second World War. As a result of its inability to react quickly to the post-war independence movement in Indonesia, The Netherlands lost all its East Indies possessions in 1949, except for New Guinea, which was taken over by Indonesia in 1963. Dutch Guyana also became independent under the name of Surinam in 1975. About 250,000 Surinamese then emigrated to The Netherlands, leading to considerable social problems. The only colonies left to the Dutch now are some West Indian islands, the Antilles, which have an equal status to The Netherlands itself in a loose commonwealth.

Economy

The Industrial Revolution began late in The Netherlands. The Dutch were used to living from trade rather than from agriculture and industry, so that when the industrialized provinces of Belgium seceded in 1830 it took some time for them to catch up. In the beginning Dutch industry centred on shipbuilding and the processing of imports from the East Indies, in particular cotton. In 1866, the coal-mining region of Limburg became a full member of the Dutch State, and in the 1880s large quantities of oil were discovered in Sumatra, laying the foundation for the present-day petroleum industry. Dairy product exports and the commercialization of margarine also became major activities, still carried on by the Anglo-Dutch multinational Unilever. In the wake of plentiful electricity supplies becoming available in 1886, the Philips brothers were able to start the mass manufacture of light bulbs in Eindhoven. Philips Gloeilampen is now one of the largest electronics and telecommunications companies in the world. The Dutch also took care to develop their own steel and chemicals industry, lest they should become entirely dependent on Germany for these products. Aviation developed early in The Netherlands, and the present-day Fokker company still maintains its share of the world market for civil airliners. After 1945, the Dutch also developed their own car industry in the form of the DAF company (Doorne Auto Fabrieken).

Huge harbour-building and land-reclamation projects gave a constant impetus to the Dutch economy in the early years of the twentieth century, as well as helping to develop new technologies. In 1932 the Zuiderzee was sealed off by the 19-mile long Afsluitdijk which joined North Holland to the formerly remote province of Friesland. Plans were also made to reclaim large areas of land from the former Zuiderzee (now called the IJsselmeer). These were interrupted by World War II, but eventually the new province of Flevoland was created almost entirely from reclaimed land (known as *polders*). Plans to reclaim a further area of the IJsselmeer, to be known as Markerwaard, have been shelved, because of the prohibitive financial cost. After the catastrophic floods of 1953, huge sums of money had to be invested in building dykes and sea-defences in Zeeland (the Delta Project).

The Dutch economy emerged from World War II in an impoverished state, and many economists predicted disaster would follow the loss of the East Indies. The Dutch now had to look to their European trading partners. The Netherlands, Belgium and Luxembourg established a free trade area in 1948, the Benelux Economic Union. The Netherlands was also a founder member of the EC at its inauguration in 1957. The Dutch economy entered a period of rapid expansion in the 1950s, along with its partners, which was only brought to a halt in 1973 by the first oil shock. In spite of periods of high unemployment in the 1980s, the Dutch economy is still considered to be one of the most stable in the world, with consistently low inflation and healthy trade surpluses. In recent years, it has been buoyed up by the discovery of vast natural gas reserves as well as oil. The Netherlands is now the world's second largest exporter of natural gas, after Russia. In 1991 there was a marked slowdown in the Dutch economy, with only 2% growth in GNP, as against 4% in 1990. Unemployment stood at 6% at the end of 1991, and should decrease, assuming that the world economy comes out of recession during 1992.

As with most North European countries, The Netherlands is grappling with the twin evils of mounting social security payments and a shrinking number of young people, but given their past successes in overcoming threats to their national survival, the Dutch should be able to maintain their current prosperity.

Government

The tradition of finding a consensus between different parties before taking action is deeply engrained in the Dutch. Different groupings in The Netherlands are traditionally labelled *zuilen*, or pillars of the state. Since the last century the four main pillars of Dutch society have been seen as the Catholics, Protestants, Socialists and the 'neutral' pillar, and the state has attempted to ensure that they have equal representation in national institutions.

Estimates of the numbers of Christians in The Netherlands vary considerably, but it is evident that their numbers are declining. At the moment about 35% of the people are Catholics, 19% belong to the Calvinist Dutch Reform Church (Nederlandse Hervormde Kerk), 7% to other Protestant groupings, and 39% profess no religion or are non-Christians. Catholics are largely concentrated in the provinces of North Brabant and Limburg. Dutch Catholics have a reputation for being very liberal, and have often found themselves in conflict with papal authority.

The present system of government was to some extent modelled on the British one. The Parliament (Staten Generaal) has an Upper House (Eerste Kamer — First Chamber) and a Lower House (Tweede Kamer — Second Chamber). Only the Lower House can propose or amend bills. The Upper House, like the British House of Lords, debates bills and can delay them, but has very limited powers otherwise. The Lower House has 150 members, who are directly elected every four years. The voting system is based on proportional representation and takes the whole country as one electoral unit. The number of votes is divided by the number of seats, and parties are then allotted seats on the basis of their national vote. The 75 members of the Upper House are elected indirectly by the provincial assemblies. Although Members of Parliament are paid, they are also expected to continue to practise an outside profession.

The Netherlands is divided into 850 municipalities (*gemeenten*), which are governed by councils (*gemeenteraden*) whose members are elected every four years, except for the mayor (*burgemeester*) who is appointed by the Crown. Between the local and national government are the provincial assemblies (*Provinciale Staten*), whose members are also elected every four years.

Until World War II, Dutch governments were formed either by the Protestant Anti-Revolutionary Party and Christian Historical Union, or by the Liberals, with the Catholic People's Party more often in coalition with the Liberals than with the Protestants. During the 1950s, the socialist Willem Drees was the dominant political figure and did much to establish the Dutch welfare state. Most Dutch governments since the war have been coalitions between the Christian parties, who joined together as the Christian Democrat Appeal in 1977, and the Partij van de Arbeid (Labour Party).

In the 1960s there were frequent riots over inadequate housing and other issues. Some rioters were classified as *nozems* (rowdies) and others as *provocateurs* or *provos* (political activists). Eventually the *provos* formed a political party, the Kabouters (Gnomes) and managed to exert some influence on the Amsterdam City Council in the early 1970s, for example by instituting a free bicycle scheme in the city. Squatters (*krakers*) had some success in preventing the demolition of cheap inner-city housing, but eventually the youth movement degenerated into aimless violence and drug-taking.

An obscure group of Indonesians, the South Moluccans, made international headlines in 1975 and 1977, when they attempted to publicize their grievances by taking hostages on trains and in a school, resulting in several deaths. The South Moluccans had been promised their own state independent of Indonesia by the Dutch in 1948 but this never materialized. The Moluccan question has never been resolved but has not led to any violence recently.

Since 1982, the country has been led by Ruud Lubbers, a Christian Democrat, who has had to deal with such contentious issues as the stationing of Cruise missiles on Dutch territory and cutting back the welfare state. The 1989 elections centred around Lubbers' plan to reduce environmental pollution by 70% at a projected cost of 15 billion guilders (£4.5 billion) by the year 2010. This found widespread support in most sections of society. The Christian Democrats' coalition partners since 1982, the pro-business VVD (Liberal Party), opposed the plan, and as a result lost a number of seats and had to make way for the Partij van de Arbeid (Labour Party), who now hold half the seats in the Cabinet.

Political Parties

In the elections of 1989, nine political parties, or groupings, gained representation in the Lower House. In some cases smaller parties which would have no hope of representation in the national Parliament band together under one name in order to obtain a large enough percentage of the vote to gain seats. Parties (especially left-wing parties) tend to split and regroup quite frequently in The Netherlands. At the present time the largest party is the Christen Democraten 'Appel (CDA — Christian Democratic Appeal), which is actually made up of three older Christian parties, the Katholieke Volkspartij (Catholic People's Party), the Anti-Revolutionaire Partij (Anti-Revolutionary Party — a right-wing Protestant anti-secular party), and the Christelijk-Historische Unie (Christian Historical Union — a more moderate Protestant party). The CDA's coalition partner, the Partij van de Arbeid (PvdA), was formed out of several socialist, Christian and liberal groupings in 1946. The Volkspartij voor Vrijheid en Democratie (Liberal Party) was formed at the same time and is now a right-wing pro-business party. The only other major party in Parliament is Democrats '66, usually known as D'66, a more radical offshoot of the PvdA, formed in 1966, which is mainly famous for its advocacy of legalized euthanasia. Apart from these parties there is the so-called Groen Links grouping (Green Left), made up of four left-wing environmentalist parties. There are also three small Calvinist fundamentalist parties represented in Parliament, the SGP, GPV and RPF. The neo-Fascist Centrum Democraten (CD) have one seat.

Geographical Information

Area

The Netherlands takes up 15,770 sq miles/40,844 sq km, more or less comparable to the American state of Maryland or half the size of Scotland. It is bounded to the east by Germany and to the south by Belgium. The average distance from north to south is about 188 miles/300 km and from east to west about 125 miles/200 km. The River Rhine flows through the centre of the country where it divides into the Waal, Lek, IJssel and Neder Rijn and is joined by the Maas before it reaches the sea. In the southwest much of the Scheldt delta has been reclaimed from the sea. Over half of the country is below sea level and is protected from inundation by 1,500 miles/2,400 km of dykes. The threat of flooding from rivers is equally serious, and a vast system of canals and drainage ditches has also been constructed. There are 3,100 miles/5,000 km of navigable rivers and canals, which provide a useful means of transport and link up with the waterways of neighbouring countries.

The Netherlands is mostly flat, except for the hilly area of Limburg in the southeast. The highest point is the Vaalserberg near Maastricht at 1,035 ft/310 m. The Netherlands is the least wooded country in the EC with only 8% forests; 54% of the land is used for agriculture.

Regional divisions and main towns

There are 12 provinces:
Zeeland, North Brabant, Limburg, South Holland, North Holland, Utrecht, Gelderland, Flevoland, Overijssel, Drenthe, Friesland and Groningen.

Population

The present population of The Netherlands is approximately 15,100,000, with an annual rate of increase of about 0.8%. Half of this is made up of the surplus of immigration over emigration. The Netherlands has the highest population density in Europe at 434 per sq km (compared to 232 per sq km in the UK). Almost half of the population is concentrated in the Randstad (rim city) area, a circle of towns which includes Amsterdam, Haarlem, Leiden, The Hague, Rotterdam, Dordrecht and Utrecht.

Out of a total foreign population of 740,000, most are guest workers from Turkey and Morocco. Large numbers of Indonesians and Surinamese have also settled in The Netherlands and most have Dutch citizenship. During the 1950s more than 500,000 Dutch citizens emigrated, with the encouragement of the Dutch government, mainly to English-speaking countries such as New Zealand, Australia, Canada and the United States.

Climate

The Netherlands has a temperate maritime climate with mainly southerly and westerly winds. The weather is unsettled much of the time because of the collision of high and low pressure systems coming from the south and north. It is frequently wet and windy; it is estimated that there are only 25 days in the year when the sky is free of clouds. Summers can be pleasantly warm, but sudden squalls are always possible. In 1991 649 mm/26 inches of rain fell, there were 65 days of frost and 26 days where the temperature reached 25°C.

Average maximum temperatures in Amsterdam

Jan	Feb	Mar	Apr	May	June
5°c/41°f	5°c/41°f	8°c/46°f	11°c/52°f	16°c/60°f	18°c/65°f

July	Aug	Sept	Oct	Nov	Dec
21°c/69°f	20°c/68°f	18°c/64°f	13°c/56°f	8°c/46°f	5°c/41°f

Regional Guide

English-speaking foreigners looking for an exciting social and cultural life are generally attracted towards the Randstad cities, and most of all towards Amsterdam. Every city in The Netherlands has something to offer, however, and there are few areas of the country which could be described as remote, except perhaps for the north. In any case, distances between towns are short and the public transport system is superb, so one will never feel isolated from civilization.

Information Facilities

One first source of information is The Netherlands Board of Tourism Office in your home country, where you can find maps and brochures on different areas of the country. In The Netherlands itself, all tourist offices go under the name VVV (Vereniging Vreemdelingen Verkeer) and they will usually have brochures, for which there is a small charge, and information on places to visit and how to get around. The VVV will also book a hotel room for you for a small fee and can usually supply information on neighbouring towns.

ZEELAND

VVV: Markt 56a, Middelburg; tel 01180-16851.
Main towns: Middelburg, Goes, Terneuzen, Oost-Souburg, Vlissingen (Flushing), Zierikzee.
Zeeland (Land of the Sea), with a population of only 365,000, is one of The Netherlands' smaller provinces. The main activities are farming, fishing and tourism. The provincial capital, Middelburg, is one of the most picturesque and best-preserved medieval towns in The Netherlands, and is well worth a visit. The town of Zierikzee on the island of Schouwen Duiveland is also particularly well-preserved.

The landscape of Zeeland has changed constantly over the centuries because of the activity of the sea and the shifting delta of the River Scheldt originating in neighbouring Belgium. In 1953 the area was inundated by a combined storm and tidal surge which killed 2,000 people. As a result, the Delta Project was started, and by 1986 a vast system of movable barriers was in place between the islands of Noord Beveland and Schouwen Duiveland. The entire project cost some Df 10 billion (£3 billion).

The islands and peninsula are now joined by bridges and motorways to the rest of the country. The southern part of Zeeland, Zeeuws Vlaanderen, is only accessible by ferries from the peninsula of Zuid Beveland or via Belgium. This was historically part of Belgian Flanders, but was incorporated into the Dutch kingdom by Willem I in 1815.

NORTH BRABANT (Noord-Brabant)

VVV: De Moorian, Markt 77, s'Hertogenbosch; tel 073-123071.
Main towns: s'Hertogenbosch, Eindhoven, Breda, Tilburg, Bergen-op-Zoom.
North Brabant is the second largest province in The Netherlands in land area, stretching from the North Sea to the border with Germany, and has 2.2 million inhabitants. Until the Eighty Years' War against the Spanish, the area was part of the Duchy of Brabant. It became part of The Netherlands in 1648, while South Brabant remained in the Spanish Netherlands, which eventually became Belgium.

The countryside of North Brabant consists of a variety of moorlands, fens, creeks and woods which attract large numbers of birds. There are several nature reserves which cater for bird-watchers.

The provincial capital, s'Hertogenbosch ('Dukes' Wood') is known colloquially as s'Bos or sometimes Seskebos or Settekebos. It has a renowned Gothic cathedral built between 1380 and 1530, the St Janskathedraal and was the home of the painter Hieronymus Bosch (1450-1516), but only a few of his prints can be seen here.

The other towns of North Brabant are mostly industrial. Breda is the most attractive and was the home of Charles II for a while during his exile from England. Eindhoven is famous as the headquarters of the multinational Philips. Without Philips it would probably be no more than a village. Philips also sponsor the local football team, PSV Eindhoven, who have dominated Dutch football in recent years.

LIMBURG

VVV: Dinghuis, Grote Straat, Maastricht; tel 043-252121.
Main towns: Maastricht, Kerkrade, Sittard, Roermond, Venlo.
The province of Limburg is a long wedge of land between Belgium and Germany in the southeast of The Netherlands. It was captured in 1839 by King Willem I in a last-ditch attempt to profit from the weakness of newly independent Belgium. Dutch Limburg continued to have close ties with the German Confederation until 1866, when it finally became a full province of The Netherlands. Historically it had always been part of the Duchy of Limburg, the southern part of which became the Belgian province of Limburg.

Limburg is rather different from the rest of The Netherlands, both because of the hilly landscape and as the most strongly Catholic part of the country. The towns bear more resemblance to Belgian and German towns than to the squeeky-clean, chocolate-box image of most Dutch tourist towns.

The capital, Maastricht, derives its name from the Latin Mosae Trajectum, meaning 'Meuse crossing'. It gained new fame as the setting of the EC's Maastricht Conference in December 1991. The area of Valkenburg east of Maastricht is famed for its ancient castles, some of them dating back to the tenth century. The hills around here, which reach the dizzying height of 300 metres in places, are humorously referred to as the Dutch Alps.

SOUTH HOLLAND (Zuid-Holland)

VVV: Den Haag Centraal Spoor (Central Station), The Hague; tel 070-354 6200.
Main towns: The Hague (Den Haag/s'Gravenhage), Rotterdam, Leiden, Dordrecht, Delft.
South and North Holland constitute the historical centre of The Netherlands, and continue to lead the country politically and economically. The capital of The Netherlands is Amsterdam, but the Parliament and administration are based in The Hague. The official name of The Hague is s'Gravenhage (Counts' Hedge). It was originally a village called Haag, until one of the Counts of Holland built a hunting lodge there in the early thirteenth century thus giving it its present name. In conversation Dutch people refer to it simply as Den Haag.

The Hague is now a very expensive city, full of foreign embassies and multinational company headquarters, and houses the International Court of Justice. Its architecture is solid and demure in comparison to Amsterdam's. Although it is not a place to stay for most tourists, the city's art museums are essential viewing. The annual North Sea Jazz Festival also brings in large numbers of foreigners.

Just south of The Hague is Rotterdam, whose port — the Europoort — is the largest in the world. The entire conurbation of Rotterdam has a population of 1,044,000, virtually the same as Amsterdam's. Parts of Rotterdam are sleazier than Amsterdam and best avoided. Between Rotterdam and The Hague there is the town of Delft, which gave its name to the blue and white Delftware pottery (originally an imitation of Chinese pottery found on captured Portuguese merchant vessels). Delft has now become an obligatory stopping-off point for package tourists and has lost much of its charm. The old university town of Leiden a few miles to the north is more peaceful and more interesting.

NORTH HOLLAND (Noord-Holland)

VVV: Centraal Station, Amsterdam; tel 020-266444.

Main towns: Amsterdam, Haarlem, Alkmaar, Amstelveen, Hilversum. Amsterdam is the official capital of The Netherlands, but only in name. It attracts large numbers of foreign tourists, drawn by its world-class museums and reputation as one of the world's liveliest cities.

The rest of North Holland is rather more sedate than Amsterdam. To the north there are the tourist towns of Volendam and Alkmaar, with their carefully preserved traditions. On the eastern edge of North Holland is Hilversum, the home of Dutch TV and radio. To the west of Amsterdam is the ancient town of Haarlem with its superb Frans Hals Museum. To the south of Haarlem lie the vast bulb fields of Heemstede and Haarlemmermeer. Nearby is Aalsmeer, the site of the world's largest flower auction house, which is itself a stone's throw from The Netherlands' main international airport, Schiphol. It is estimated that over half of the world's cut flowers are distributed from here.

UTRECHT
VVV: Vredenburg 90, Utrecht; tel 030-314142.
Main towns: Utrecht, Zeist, Amersfoort, Soest, Veenendaal.
Utrecht is The Netherlands' smallest province in land area, but is one of the most densely populated with 965,000 inhabitants. Of these about 250,000 live in the provincial capital, Utrecht, one of the most significant historical cities in the country. The Treaty of Utrecht was signed here in 1579, whereby the seven United Provinces (Holland, Utrecht, Gelderland, Zeeland, Overijssel, Friesland and Groningen) finally constituted themselves into a Protestant republic free from Spanish domination. The Romans constructed a fort here and later the Bishops of Utrecht exercised both spiritual and temporal power on behalf of the Holy Roman Empire and the Pope. Utrecht has a 365-foot cathedral tower, the Dom. The rest of the cathedral fell down in a storm in 1674.

The other major medieval city in the province is Amersfoort, a mere 10 miles/17 km to the northeast of Utrecht. To the north of Utrecht is the region of lakes and woods known as Het Gooi, part of which is in North Holland.

GELDERLAND
VVV: Stationsplein 45, Arnhem; tel 085-420330.
Main towns: Arnhem, Nijmegen, Apeldoorn, Doetinchem, Zutphen.
Gelderland is the largest Dutch province in land area. In terms of population, it is ranked fourth, with 1,784,000 inhabitants. During the Middle Ages, Gelderland enjoyed a large degree of independence under the Dukes of Gelre until the sixteenth century, when it was first taken over by the Habsburgs and then incorporated into the new Dutch Republic. The province is divided into four by the Rhine, the Waal, the Nederrijn and the IJssel. The River Maas (or Meuse) forms the southern border. The northern half of the province is known as the Veluwe, an area of heathland and woods. Between the IJssel and the German border is the Achterhoek (back corner), a region of farmland and castles.

The provincial capital of Arnhem is famed as the furthest bridgehead of 'Operation Market Garden', the failed Allied attempt to invade Germany via Holland in September 1944. The strategic bridge at Arnhem over the Nederrijn lent its name to the film '*A Bridge Too Far*'. The other city associated with the campaign, Nijmegen, suffered considerable damage to its old buildings, although many have been restored. The city was founded on the River Waal by the Roman Emperor Trajan in 105 AD as a frontier town, under the name Noviomagus (new market).

The Emperor Charlemagne built a castle here, the Valkhof, and used it as an administrative centre between 800 and 814 AD. Unfortunately it was thoroughly obliterated in the eighteenth century.

As one would expect, Gelderland has its fair share of museums. The Rijksmuseum Kröller-Müller, at Otterlo in the Hoge Veluwe National Park, has one of the best art collections in The Netherlands. As well as 110 works by Van Gogh, there are paintings by Cranach, Mondriaan, Braque and Picasso, to name but a few. The museum also features sculptures by Henry Moore, Rodin and others.

FLEVOLAND

VVV: Wijk 2, No.2, Urk; tel 05277-4040.
Main towns: Lelystad, Almere, Urk, Emmeloord.
Flevoland is made up entirely of land reclaimed from the sea since World War I. The land is completely flat and mostly given over to agriculture and new housing estates. Flevoland is a popular area for recreation and is gaining the reputation for offering some of the finest water sports facilities in The Netherlands. The population of the new towns like Lelystad is expanding rapidly as they are now within commuting distance of Amsterdam.

OVERIJSSEL

VVV: Grote Kerkplein 14, Zwolle; tel 038-213900.
Main towns: Zwolle, Deventer, Almelo, Hengelo, Enschede.
Overijssel, north of Gelderland on the German border, did not play a major role in Dutch history and is not much frequented by tourists. The province has its fair share of interesting medieval towns, in particular the capital, Zwolle, where the medieval writer Thomas à Kempis made his home for a few years from 1399. The town of Elburg is popular with local Dutch day-trippers.

As one moves into the eastern part of Overijssel, the landscape becomes more wooded and hilly. Close by the German border is the region known as Twente, which at one time had a flourishing textile industry. The main town, Enschede, was burnt to the ground in 1862, but is worth a visit for its art galleries and festivals.

DRENTHE

VVV: Brink 42, Assen; tel 05920-14324.
Main towns: Assen, Hoogeveen, Emmen, Meppel, Coevorden.
Drenthe was another backwater in medieval times because of its poor agricultural land. The province was ruled by the Bishops of Utrecht until it came into the Habsburg Empire in 1538 and it then joined the Revolt against the Spanish in 1568. The marshlands and peat-bogs of the area were reclaimed for agriculture in the nineteenth century. The most famous feature of the landscape are the *hunebeds*, megalithic tombs dating from 5,000 BC. These days the province is attracting more and more industry looking for greenfield sites close to the German border (Drenthe is exactly equidistant between Brussels and Hamburg). Coevorden and Schoonebeek, in the southeast corner of the province produce enough oil to supply about 7% of The Netherlands' needs.

FRIESLAND

VVV: Spoor Station, Leeuwarden; tel 058-132224.
Main towns: Leeuwarden, Sneek, Heerenveen, Drachten, Dokkum.
Friesland is one of The Netherlands' least heavily populated provinces with about

600,000 souls, and is third largest in size. It includes all the West Frisian islands, apart from the largest island, Texel, which is part of North Holland, and a few small islands close to Germany which are part of Groningen province. At some future time, assuming there is enough money, the Dutch plan to build dykes between the West Frisian islands, in order to make the Afsluitdijk joining North Holland to Friesland less vulnerable.

In medieval times, the Frisians maintained their independence against all-comers until they joined the United Provinces at the Treaty of Utrecht in 1578. Even now the Frisians like to think of themselves as different from other Dutch people, and try hard to keep up their own language, Frisian. In 1955, the Dutch government introduced Frisian classes in schools, as it was found that younger children had difficulty understanding Dutch.

The capital, Leeuwarden was built on three *terpen* (mounds) when the surrounding area was under water. Apart from its medieval buildings, it is also famous as the birthplace of Mata Hari, spy and *femme fatale*. Friesland's other native of international renown, Pieter Stuyvesant, founded New York.

Friesland is generally known for ice-skating, in particular the Elfstedentocht, a notoriously difficult annual circuit of 11 Frisian towns (weather permitting). Friesland has also produced a number of champion ice-skaters, notably Sjoukje Dijkstra. Another Frisian tradition is *wadlopen*, walking across mud-flats at low tide, something only to be attempted with a trained guide.

GRONINGEN
VVV: Naberpassage 3, Groningen; tel 050-139700.
Main towns: Groningen, Veendam, Winschoten, Sappemeer, Delfzijl.
Groningen, the so-called 'top of Holland', first developed as a trading post on the way from the Baltic to the rest of Europe. Nowadays its prosperity is based on its large reserves of natural gas, first discovered at Slochteren in the 1960s. Groningen used to have 1,400 windmills, of which only 80 remain in working order.

The most famous native of Groningen is undoubtedly Abel Tasman, who was the first white man to discover New Zealand and gave his name to Tasmania and the Tasman Sea. In general, the province of Groningen is not all that rich in historical monuments. It does have special appeal to sailing and wind-surfing enthusiasts, although it is by no means unique in this respect, since nowhere in The Netherlands is far from water.

Residence and Entry Regulations

The Current Position

The Dutch have two good reasons for wanting to restrict entry and residence into The Netherlands. Firstly, the country has one of the highest population densities in the world, 1,040 persons per square mile (or 434 per sq km), and is in danger of quite literally bursting at the seams. Secondly, the benevolent social security system, on which the Dutch pride themselves, has been subject to abuse by visitors who, having obtained a residence permit contrive to live off the state. As a consequence permanent settlement is extremely difficult in The Netherlands and this fact is spelled out in bold print in a circular from the Royal Netherlands Embassy — 'in view of considerable unemployment, a housing problem and an increasing density of population permanent residence is only rarely granted.' However, The Netherlands is a member of the European Community and as such UK citizens have the right to live and work there for as long as they wish. A visa is not required for visits of up to three months but to remain longer it is necessary to obtain a residence permit (*verblijfsvergunning*). To qualify for this it is up to you to prove your stay is bona fide. If the Dutch immigration authority is not satisfied it has the right to refuse entry to anyone. So you have been warned!

Residence Permit

British nationals wishing to stay in The Netherlands for longer than three months need a residence permit (*verblijfsvergunning*). To apply for one you must contact the local aliens police (*vreemdelingenpolitie*) within eight days of arriving in The Netherlands. The Dutch authorities will require proof of identity, half a dozen passport photographs and most importantly a reason to allow you to remain in the country. The police will turn down applications for residence if a job has not been secured (for either you or your spouse) or you cannot show adequate funds to support your stay. A *verblijfsvergunning* can also be refused on the grounds of public security or public health. Residence permits are normally granted for the duration of an employment contract. All Dutch municipalities maintain a register in which inhabitants are listed (*bevolkingsregister*); anyone taking up residence in The Netherlands must sign on at the local town hall (*gemeentehuis*).

A special foreigners' helpline has been set up by the Dutch Ministry of Justice to answer queries concerning the red tape involved in applying for residence in The Netherlands. English-speaking enquirers should call 070-3703533 or 3703544.

Entering to Work

The prospects for work in The Netherlands are reasonable: the country has an unemployment rate of 4.4% (May 1992) of the total labour force and should you enter into correspondence with the Dutch authorities they are quick to point this out. However, European Community regulations do allow for the free movement of labour within the EC and UK citizens do not require a work permit. British nationals looking for employment can enter The Netherlands on a valid passport but must apply for a residence permit (*verblijfsvergunning*) if intending to stay and work for more than three months. The application must include a letter from your prospective employer stating the terms of the contract, salary level and proof that the company will pay your health insurance contributions. The translation of all documents into either English or Dutch is not essential but it will help to speed up the application process. Foreign firms are able to employ their own specialist staff as long as the work performed by foreigners is deemed to be of economic interest to The Netherlands. In practice this means firms can employ whoever they wish, provided that he or she passes the entry requirements.

Entering to Start a Business

UK nationals considering setting up a business are free to enter The Netherlands on a valid passport and carry out the necessary groundwork. The Dutch authorities are always willing to help new enterprises and The Netherlands Foreign Investment Agency part of the Ministry of Economic Affairs provides free and confidential help with immigration red tape. Business promotional activities which are usually carried out by embassies have largely become the responsibility of the Netherlands-British Chamber of Commerce. This group can provide help and information for prospective entrepreneurs planning to go Dutch. The procedures for officially establishing a business are detailed in the Chapter Seven *Starting a Business*.

Many employment contracts in The Netherlands, especially in the construction industry, are issued on a self-employed basis. A prospective employee must complete form E101, issued by the Overseas Branch of the Department of Social Security (DSS) (see Chapter Six, *Employment*). He or she must also complete form CF11 declaring the intention to become self-employed. This can be done at any DSS office in the UK. A Dutch employer may insist on seeing this document before the work contract is signed.

Useful Addresses:

Ministry of Economic Affairs (Ministerie van Economische Zaken): Bezuidenhoutseweg 6, PO Box 20101, 2500 EC Den Haag; tel 070-3798911.
Association of the Dutch Chambers of Commerce: Watermolenlaan 1, PO Box 265, 3440 AC Woerden; tel 03480-26911.
The Netherlands-British Chamber of Commerce: The Dutch House, 307-308 High Holborn, London, WC1V 7LS; tel 071-405 1358, fax 071-405 1689.

Entering with Retirement Status

In theory since 1 January 1992 pensioners from EC Member States have been able to live wherever they choose in the new boundaryless European Community.

In practice the Dutch do not encourage additions to an already dense population and costly social services system. Anyone who intends to retire to The Netherlands will have to obtain a residence permit for pensioners. The application must be made to the aliens police. It will have to provide pension details, prove adequate health insurance and supply proof that individuals have 'sufficient' funds with which to support themselves without working.

Dutch Residency

The Dutch are very reluctant to grant permanent residence but the residence permit (*verblijfsvergunning*) is renewable every five years, and provided you can give a satisfactory reason for staying, residence in The Netherlands on such a permit can be indefinite. Once a UK citizen has obtained the *verblijfsvergunning* he or she is entitled to the same rights as a Dutch national, with the exception of voting in Dutch elections. British nationals still retain the right to vote in UK elections even though they are resident in a foreign country. Should you decide to leave The Netherlands on a permanent basis you must notify the local police before leaving.

Non-EC nationals

US, Canadian, Australian and New Zealand nationals can enter The Netherlands for up to three months without a visa. Other non-EC citizens require permission to enter and must apply for an *Authorization for Provisional Sojourn* from the Dutch Consulate General in their country of residence. An application must include five completed forms, three passport photographs and details of means of support and accommodation. Non-EC nationals entering The Netherlands on a visitor's visa are not permitted to seek or accept work. All non-EC nationals intending to take up employment in The Netherlands must complete a *Machtiging voor voorlopig verblijf (MVV)*; this is a request for permission to live and work in The Netherlands. Applications should be made to a Dutch embassy at least three months before departure and the request must be accompanied by a letter confirming that a job has been secured. The authorities will require proof of medical insurance and evidence of no criminal record. They will sometimes also request a medical check. The prospective employer must apply to the local Ministerie van Arbeid for permission to employ a foreign national (*terwerkstellingsvergunning*). Both applications must be granted before the work permit (*werkvergunning*) is issued and the applicant can travel to The Netherlands. It is necessary to report to the aliens police (*vreemdelingenpolitie*) on arrival. The police will check the work permit and stamp the passport to allow residence for one year (this is renewable annually).

Useful Addresses

Royal Netherlands Embassy: 38 Hyde Park Gate, London SW7 5DP; tel 071-584 5040.
Netherlands Consulate: 102 Hope Street, Glasgow G2; tel 041-221 0605.
Netherlands Vice Consulate: Kings Court, 12 King Street, Leeds; tel 0532-340795.
British Embassy: Lange Voorhout 10, 2514 ED Den Haag; tel 070-3645800.
British Consulate-General: Koningslaan 44, Postbus 5488, 1007 AL Amsterdam; tel 020-6764343.
US Embassy: Lange Voorhout 102, Den Haag; tel 070-3624911.

US Consulate: Museumplein 19, 1017 DJ Amsterdam; tel 020-6645661.
Royal Netherlands Embassy: 4200 Linnean Avenue, NW Washington DC 20008-3896, the United States of America; tel 202-244 5300.

Honorary Consulates:

The Royal Netherlands Embassy represents and promotes Dutch interests in the UK from its London base. However, The Netherlands is further represented by a number of honorary consulates throughout the UK. These include:

Consul for The Netherlands: P.E. Richardson, Devonshire House, 40 Great Charles Street, Queensway, Birmingham.

Consul for The Netherlands: M.H. Hazzard, c/o Hodder Whitwill Ltd, Avonmouth Dock, Avonmouth, Bristol.

Consul for The Netherlands: S.P. Green, 41 Spring Gardens, Manchester.

Consul for The Netherlands: N. Thom, c/o Williamson & Co, Williamson House, 63 High Bridge, Newcastle.

Consul for The Netherlands: J.M. Souness, 10 George Street, Edinburgh.

Consul for The Netherlands: D.I. Williams, Idwal Williams & Company Ltd, 113-116 Bute Street, Cardiff.

Setting Up Home

The golden rule to remember when renting or buying property in The Netherlands is if you are in doubt keep quiet. An oral agreement is legally binding under Dutch law. Do not even say that you think the house looks nice as this simple statement can be interpreted as an acceptance of the contract being discussed at the time. It is easier and safer to sit back and let your representative do the talking. With that in mind this chapter aims to unravel some of the ins and outs of the Dutch property market. There are no restrictions on foreign nationals owning property in The Netherlands but it is an expensive business, especially in the more fashionable areas of Amsterdam and The Hague. The majority of UK citizens have traditionally settled in and around the major cities. However, increasingly British expats are opting to move out to smaller towns, especially those in the east of the country. Deciding where to stay has often had as much to do with the education of one's children as it has to do with the environment. The choice of schools is dealt with in Chapter Four, *Daily Life*. But it might be prudent to base your choice of area on the proximity of schools as commuting is relatively easy in The Netherlands; getting the kids to class could be a different matter.

How do the Dutch Live?

Dutch families are independent so extended groups of relatives do not tend to live under the same roof, but the family still plays an important part in life in The Netherlands and relatives are usually never far away. The Dutch are a polite and considerate people and they expect the same courtesy in return. If you are a noisy neighbour they will say so. However, they will also be more than happy to help out with any problems you may encounter (and practise their English into the bargain). The home is the place for socializing with family and close friends and parties can be memorable affairs. Restaurants and bars are the more usual place for business and formal meetings.

The standard of living and quality of accommodation in The Netherlands is high. The Dutch are very houseproud and their homes are kept immaculately clean and tidy. Nearly three-quarters of the population live in one-family houses and a further 20% live in apartments. Property ownership is relatively high with 54% of the adult Dutch population owning their own home. The Netherlands is a highly urbanized country; just 2% of the population lives in villages with less than 5,000 inhabitants. The high density of the population has resulted in high concentrations of residential buildings. This proximity of housing does not always lend itself to neighbourly harmony, and a recent survey by the Netherlands Central Bureau of

Statistics revealed one-fifth of the population would like to move house. But do not let that worry you unduly as the Dutch in general make good neighbours, love their homes and enjoy their living environment.

Estate Agents

In The Netherlands the majority of reputable estate agents (*makelaars*) belong to the national association: the Nederlandse Vereniging van Makelaars in Onroerende Goederen (NVM). The association has more than 2,000 members, and choosing to use the services of an NVM member has a number of benefits. Each member has passed rigorous examinations in subjects such as property valuation, law, finance and insurance (in fact, the three-year training course is so tough that two-thirds of applicants drop out in the first year of study); the fees the NVM charges are uniform and all members adhere to a strict code of conduct. However, probably the most useful service the NVM operates is a national multi-listing register in which members have at their fingertips all properties offered by both themselves and colleagues via a constantly updated computer network. This reduces much of the legwork associated with buying a home in the UK when clients often have to trudge from one estate agent's office to another. The association also publishes the useful booklet *You and Your NVM broker, Conditions and Rates*.

Dutch law prevents a conflict of interests by stipulating that a *makelaar* can act only for one client: either the seller (or lessor) or the buyer (or lessee). The commission from the lessor and lessee is 8% of the first year's lease, plus 18.5% VAT. The commission from the buyer and seller is approximately 1.85% of the house price, plus VAT. The NVM will provide help in finding an estate agent and publishes a list of its members. There is no UK-based estate agent (affiliated with the National Association of Estate Agents) that deals specifically with The Netherlands. However, the NAEA is one of six members of the Confederation Européenne d'Immobiliers (which includes the NVM) and it can offer advice to individuals planning to move to The Netherlands.

Useful Addresses:

Estata Makelaars: Badhuisweg 199, 2597 JP Den Haag; tel 070-3515269, fax 070-3503121.
Renthouse International BV: Nederhoven 19, 1083 AM Amsterdam; tel 020-6448751, fax 020-6465909.
Nederlandse Vereniging van Makelaars in Onroerende Goederen (NVM): Fakkelstede 1, PO Box 2222, 3430 DC, Nieuwegein; tel 03402-33494, fax 03402-34003.
National Association of Estate Agents (NAEA): Arbon House, 21 Jury Street, Warwick, CV34 4EH; tel 0926-496800, fax 0926-400953.
Huub van Leeuwen: Stevinstraat 157, 2587 ED Scheveningen; tel 070-3502304.
Makelaars Associatie BV: Steinstraat 201, 2587 EG Den Haag; tel 070-3526800.

Where to look for Accommodation

Dutch newspapers carry property listings which can provide a useful source of information. The two largest circulation newspapers, the Amsterdam-based *De Telegraaf* and *Algemeen Dagblad* in Rotterdam, carry daily listings. Further details of these are given in Chapter Four *Daily Life*. In The Netherlands it is also common practice to advertise properties in shop windows and on supermarket notice boards.

Relocation Agencies

An increasing number of relocation agencies are being set up in The Netherlands to take the hassle out of moving. These companies will do practically everything for new residents, from finding accommodation to securing a place at a local school. Clients are asked to answer a questionnaire about themselves and how they want to live in The Netherlands. The agency will then draw up a tailor-made moving schedule which will usually require just one fact-finding trip to The Netherlands.

A client will be shown ten to 15 properties suitable for his or her needs (i.e. size, location, price) and given guidance on the practical and legal procedures involved in buying or renting accommodation. Additional services relocation agencies offer can seem endless. They include: helping with the general problems of setting up a new home such as buying furniture, discovering the nearest supermarket and connecting up the telephone, outlining the procedures for registering a car or opening a bank account, and even introducing you to the neighbours! The services of the relocator do not come cheap but they are comprehensive and for people with tight moving schedules the time saved can more than make up for the cost. This can be especially true for companies paying for staff to move. Formula Two Relocations and Relocation Services assist companies and their expatriate staff with the planning and management of a move, and offer full support and practical assistance to individuals in The Netherlands.

Useful Addresses

Relocation Services: (Van Hamellaan 40, 2252 BN Voorschoten; tel 071-614643, fax 071-615934) provides a service throughout The Netherlands.

Formula Two Relocations: Vondelstraat 120A, 1054 GS Amsterdam; tel 020-6129121, fax 020-6124646, and Kwartellaan 25, 2566 DS The Hague; tel 070-3623686.

Finance

Dutch Mortages

In The Netherlands there are no UK-style building societies and all mortgages (*hypotheek*) are taken out through banks. The conditions relating to Dutch mortgages differ to some degree from those in Britain. One of the important factors favouring guilder mortgages at the moment is that the Dutch interest rate is currently up to 2% below the UK rate. Banks in The Netherlands offer home loans of up to 125% of the value of the property and the repayment period is fixed by agreement for between five and 30 years. It is common practice that lenders send a future borrower a letter outlining the conditions of the loan. The borrower has the right to cancel a loan agreement before it is signed. However, once the contract has been signed it may be cancelled only after the loan has been redeemed in full. According to Dutch law the lender is entitled to compensation of up to 3% of the loan.

A mortgage will only be given to UK citizens resident in The Netherlands. To assess an applicant's suitability for a home loan the bank will require proof of salary and it may also contact the applicant's current employer for a personal reference. A mortgage arrangement fee of 1% is charged by the bank.

Useful Address

The Netherlands Association of Mortgage Banks: (De Nederlandse Vereniging van Hypotheekbanken) Adelheidsstraat 8, 2595 ED Den Haag; tel 070-3814861, will provide a list of Dutch banks that offer mortgages.

UK Mortgages

Until the European Community has a common currency there will always be some fluctuation in exchange rates. It is useful to bear in mind that if the value of the Dutch guilder rises against sterling, the mortgage repayments for a purchaser financing his or her loan with a UK bank or building society will increase correspondingly. The majority of mortgages for Dutch properties are taken out with Dutch banks but it is possible to use a UK mortgage. The method of calculating the amount that may be borrowed is worked out at between two and a half to three and a half times your primary income. However, one must be aware that a property owner is liable to lose some UK tax relief if his or her UK property is re-mortgaged. A variety of costs will be involved. These will include revaluation of your UK property, arrangement fees for the bank or building society, and legal costs for registering the mortgage. A final word of warning is to ensure that the details of a UK loan are included in the Dutch property contract.

Mortgage Comparison Table

	UK Mortgage	Dutch Mortgage
Types available:	Repayment, endowment, pension mortgages etc.	Mostly repayment
Maximum % of value:	95%	up to 125%
Maximum compared to income:	2.5 x joint, or 3.5 x 1.	up to 4 x 1, related to property value
Interest rate:	approx 11%	9 to 9.8%
Repayments made:	monthly	monthly

Offshore Mortgages

The principle of offshore mortgages involves turning a property into a company, the shares of which are held in a tax haven such as the Channel Islands, as collateral against a mortgage of up to 75% for the repayment term of up to 20 years. The property owner's name is strictly confidential and the company is administered on his or her behalf by the offshore trustee. The advantage in the past of using an offshore loan was that it reduced tax liability in the country of purchase, and when the property was resold it merely became a question of transferring the shares to a new owner. However, the Dutch authorities take a very dim view of tax evasion and it is strongly recommended that anyone considering taking out an offshore mortgage should take professional advice.

Useful Address

Abbey National: 237 Main Street, Gibraltar; tel 010-351-450 76090.

The Purchasing and Ownership of Property

To buy a property in The Netherlands a UK citizen requires: a residence permit, the deposit and a *Gemeentelijke Dienst Volkshuisvesting* (Department of Housing Authority approval).

Your *makelaar* will guide you through the Department of Housing Authority approval, which basically requires proof of one's upstanding character and adequate finances. The sticking point is likely to be the down payment which can be anything between 30% to 40% of the house price. In addition, the buyer will have to pay 10% of the property value in fees; 2% to the estate agent, an appraisal charge, loan initiation fee, a 0.15% recording fee and a 6% registration tax (*overdrachtsbelasting*). All legal transactions go through a solicitor specializing in property (*notaris*) who will charge an additional 2% of the cost of the house for drawing up the agreement. A mortgage can be obtained from any reputable bank and the contract will include a get-out clause, should a mortgage application be unsuccessful. If you should later decide to move house you must obtain permission from the Department of Housing Authority and notify the Town Hall (*Gemeentehuis*). Also, to build an extension a special permit is required from the same authority.

The Koop

Buying property in The Netherlands is divided into two parts: the purchase (*koop*) and the transfer of property ownership (*transport*). In The Netherlands the price of a property is usually negotiable. The agent will estimate what he believes is a fair price and the first bid can go in (as with most types of haggling it is expected that you bid lower than the amount you are prepared to spend). After bidding and counter-bidding the price is verbally agreed. This deal is legally binding and if the agreement is broken the prospective buyer can be held liable. The contract is subsequently put into writing and signed by both the buyer and seller. The buyer is expected to immediately deposit a down payment at the notaris' office and within. three weeks pay the outstanding amount. This completes the purchase part (*koop*) of buying a Dutch property, but you are not yet the legal owner.

The Notaris and the Transport

The transfer of the property into the buyer's name (*transport)* can be completed only by a notary public. Both the buyer and the seller must attend a meeting in which the notary will examine the property deeds to determine whether the house is free of claims. If all sides are satisfied the transfer of ownership will take place and the buyer's name will be placed on the public register (*kadaster*). It is strongly recommended that your representative attends the meeting to ensure the process is handled correctly.

Property-Related Tax

A transfer tax (*overdrachtsbelasting)* amounting to 6% of the property value is levied when a house is sold. The purchaser is legally responsible for this charge but contracts are increasingly specifying that the transfer tax is shared between the vendor and the purchaser. A municipal tax is charged at a percentage of the market value of, or income derived from, a property. Inheritance tax is calculated at a rate between five to 68% of the inheritance depending on the value of the property and the relationship between the donor and recipient.

Useful Addresses

Broederschap der Notarissen: 't Hoenstraat 5, 2596 HX Den Haag; tel 070-3307111, fax 070-3453226.
Ministerie van Volkshuisvesting: Ruimtelijke Ordening en Milieubeheer, PO Box 20951, 2500 EZ Den Haag; tel 070-3353535.

Renting Property

The cost of rented accommodation is generally high, and as a foreigner you can expect to pay the highest rates. More than nine out of ten British citizens moving to The Netherlands rent property. An assortment of Dutch homes are listed by rental departments of estate agents and rental agencies (*woningbureau*). The Dutch government keeps a tight rein on the fees of unfurnished living quarters (*ongemeubileerd*) and rents are annually indexed. Landlords, however, are known to bypass these strict controls by partly or fully furnishing properties.

Rental costs can be divided into two residential areas: the Randstad (the urban area including Amsterdam, The Hague, Rotterdam and Utrecht) and, the less urbanized area to the east. The following table gives an indication of monthly rental prices for partly-furnished properties (*gestoffeerd*) at the start of 1992.

Property	Randstad	Eastern region
1 bed apartment	Dfl 1,500 (£470) to Dfl 5,000 (£1,560)	generally do not exist
rowhouse (2/3 bed) (terraced)	Dfl 3,500 (£1,090)	Dfl 1,700 (£530)
detached house (2/3 bed)	Dfl 4,500 (£1,400) to Dfl 10,000 (£3,125)	Dfl 2,500 (£780)

Expect an unfurnished house to be just that. Such properties do not have furniture, light fittings, curtains, water heaters or floor coverings. *Gestoffeerd*, or partly furnished properties, will have light fittings, and floor and window coverings but furniture and appliances may disappear after viewing so make sure that what you see is what you get. *Gemeubileerd*, furnished homes, will have just about the lot, including furniture, fixtures and fittings, pots and pans, linen, cutlery and crockery, but perhaps rather surprisingly not always an oven. A deposit will be charged which can be anything from one to three months rent.

Electricity and gas bills are usually charged separately from the rent. It is advisable to keep receipts for utility payments to enable your rental agency to accurately calculate your bills. An extra service charge is often necessary for apartments. This covers maintenance and sometimes the central heating bill. Heating costs in The Netherlands tend to be high as insulation and double glazing are not common. To keep out the cold the Dutch traditionally hang heavy curtains in front of doors and windows.

The Rental Contract

The final written contract simply puts down onto paper the verbally agreed deal. The standard terms of the majority of contracts are as follows:

— rent is payable on the first day of every month.
— a deposit, or bank guarantee, is required.
— minor repairs are the responsibility of the lessee; major repairs are the responsibility of the lessor.
— rent is reassessed annually (by the Dutch government).
— utilities are excluded from the rent.

If you are likely to have to move out at short notice it is strongly advisable to ensure the contract has at least a two months' notice clause. Before agreeing to anything make sure an inventory lists all items in the property to your satisfaction.

Also, make a record of the condition of walls and doors in the presence of the owner or representative.

Renting Out Property

An estate agent can handle all the processes involved in renting out your property, from putting the house on the market to supervising maintenance and collecting rent. The cost of this management can be anything up to 6% of the yearly rent and comes out of the agent's commission.

Useful Addresses

Estata Makelaars: Badhuisweg 199, 2597 JP Den Haag; tel 070-3515269, fax 070-3503121.

Renthouse International BV: Nederhoven 19, 1083 AM Amsterdam; tel 020-6448751, fax 020-6465909.

Nassauhuis BV: Jan Van Nassaustraat 14, Postbus 85503, 2508 CE Den Haag; tel 070-3241141.

Holland Home Service BV: van Alkemadelaan 1, 2597 AA Den Haag; tel 070-3245360.

Unique Housing Service: Keizergracht 520, 1017 EK Amsterdam; tel 020-6259095/6208797.

GIS Apartments: Keizergracht 33, Amsterdam; tel 020-6250071, fax 020-6380475.

I.D.A. Housing Services: den Texstraat 30, 1017 ZB Amsterdam (PO Box 843, 1000 AV Amsterdam); tel 020-6248301, fax 020-6233844.

Eigen Haard: Rental Department, Geversstraat 63, 2341 GC Oegstgeest; tel 071-175151, fax 071-175634

Useful Dutch words

Kosten Koper or *k.k.*	Registration and legal fees paid by the buyer
Vraagprijs	Registration and legal fees negotiable
Te Koop	for sale
Te Huur	for rent
Voorlopig Koopcontract	offer to buy
Makelaar Onroerend Goed	estate agent
Hypotheek	mortgage
Vrijstaand	detached
Villa	large detached house with garden
Halfvrijstaand	semi-detached
Hoekhuis	end terraced house
Gestoffeerd	partly furnished
Gemeubileerd	fully furnished
Onderhouden	well-maintained, in good repair
Inbouwapparatuur	built-in appliances
Centrale Verwarming	central heating
Kamer	room
Badkamer	bathroom
Woonkamer	living room
Slaapkamer	bedroom
Keuken	kitchen

Utilities

The Gemeente Energiebedrijf supplies both gas and electricity in The Netherlands, and usually charges both together on one bill. The invoices are sent out ten times a year and charges are estimated. The meters are read once a year, usually in December, and any discrepancies in the account are then corrected. Reading times are unlikely to coincide with your date of entry to a property, but on request an interim reading can be made prior to the day you move in. The Gemeente Energiebedrijf will also carry out a free check on pipes and wiring and the cost of any repairs must be met by the owner of the property. The domestic electricity supply is 220 volts. Fifty-cycle appliances must be fitted with two-pin round plugs and light fittings are screw-type.

The local municipality charges a separate, monthly utility bill, which includes: refuse removal, sewerage, water, an environmental tax and in some areas cable television charges. The levy is fairly uniform throughout The Netherlands and charged according to the size of the house; an apartment costs Dfl 150 (£47) per month, a rowhouse Dfl 220 (£69) monthly, and a detached house is charged at Dfl 450 (£140) per month.

Insurance and Wills

Insurance

Any responsible homeowner will want to arrange appropriate insurance cover for his or her property in The Netherlands. Dutch law requires a minimum of third party insurance, and it is advisable to have at least a multi-risk policy that covers theft and damage by fire. Insurance is widely available but it is strongly recommended that you seek the help of an insurance adviser (*verzekeringsadviseur*). The Netherlands Organisation of Insurance Advisers (*Nederlandse Vereniging van Assurantie Adviseurs, NVA*) can offer help and advice.

Useful Addresses

Lobbes Insurance: Concertgebouwplein 13, 1071 LL Amsterdam; tel 020-6791336.
Bekouw Mendes Insurance Brokers: Mr. Treublaan 7, 1079 DP Amsterdam; tel 020-5607436.

Wills

One of the first tasks to carry out after the completion of a property purchase is to draw up a Dutch will. This has to be done by a notary public (*notaris*) and can either cover just property and belongings in The Netherlands, or also include possessions in the UK and elsewhere. The drawing up of a new will automatically renders all previous wills void under international law. However, the *notaris* can state in the new document whether parts of the old will still apply. Death duties are payable where the deceased is deemed to have had his or her principal place of residence (see the section on Taxation in Chapter Four *Daily Life*).

Removals

Moving home is not easy at the best of times — moving overseas can present even more obstacles. In general, for a longer stay people will want to take a number

of personal possessions, but because the cost of transportation is high it is advisable to reduce the mountain of items by packing only what is essential. When choosing a removals company contact an experienced international remover. All items need to be cleared through customs and charges are calculated on their value, so to save time make an inventory, and to save money list the lowest estimated values. The cost of moving to The Netherlands is likely to run into several hundred pounds. Scotpac International charge a £220 minimum fee (for 150 cubic feet), plus a £95 customs clearance charge. Gauntlett International have a minimum fee of £200, and charge £42 per cubic metre for the first 5.71 cubic metres, and £40.95 per each additional cubic metre.

Useful Addresses

Arthur Pierre Removals: Tovil Green, Maidstone, Kent ME15 6RJ; tel 0622-691330, or Brusselssesteenweg 344, Overijse, 3090 Brussels, Belgium; tel 02-6877610, fax 02-6873730.

Scotpac International Moving: Security House, Abbey Wharf Industrial Estate, Kingsbridge Road, Barking, Essex IG11 0BT; tel 081-591 3388, fax 081-594 4571.

Scotpac International Moving: Kilsyth Road, Kirkintilloch, Glasgow G66 1TJ; tel 041-776 7191, fax 041-777 7746.

Steens International Moving: Gildenweg 18, 3334 KC Zwijndrecht-noord; tel 078-100011, fax 078-103346.

The British Association of Removers: (3 Churchill Court, 58 Station Road, North Harrow, Middlesex HA2 7SA; tel 081-861 3331) produces a leaflet of handy hints for anyone contemplating removals overseas. Send a stamped addressed envelope.

Gauntlett International: Gauntlett House, Cattershall Road, Godalming GU7 1NH; tel 04834-28982.

Pickfords Ltd: 492 Great Cambridge Road, Enfield, Middlesex EN1 3SA; tel 081-367 0045, fax 081-367 8445.

General Import Conditions

The conditions for importing personal effects into The Netherlands are very much in line with EC regulations. In the simplest terms British nationals can apply to the Dutch authorities to take any household goods and effects duty free, provided their principal place of residence is transferred from the UK to The Netherlands. It is also a requirement that the items will not be disposed of or sold for at least six months. This exemption does not apply to new items, food, or goods which are temporarily left behind and used by others. The rules do change and it is recommended that before travelling you contact the Dutch Embassy for the latest regulations.

The Import Procedure

To apply to import personal effects into The Netherlands one should contact the Royal Netherlands Embassy in London. The Dutch authorities will require the following documents:

1. Proof that your principal place of residence is being transferred to The Netherlands; a residence permit or an employment contract are sufficient.
2. Three signed inventories of the goods to be imported.
3. A Single Administrative Document (SAD) — this is required if the move is arranged through a professional company. It is issued by the UK Customs and Excise Department.

Useful Addresses

HM Customs and Excise: New King's Beam House, 22 Upper Ground, London, SE1 9PJ; tel 071-620 1313, fax 071-865 5565.

Inspecteur der Invoerrechten en Accijnzen: (Dutch Customs and Excise), Steenvoordelaan 370, 2284 EH Rijswijk; tel 070-3725911.

Importing a Car

The Dutch authorities do not charge duty on cars (and motorbikes) imported into The Netherlands provided the person importing the vehicle is moving his or her principal place of residence to The Netherlands and, the car has been registered in his or her name for at least six months prior to the date of entry. A residence permit or employment contract and the car's registration document are sufficient proof. A vehicle must be registered and issued with Dutch registration plates as soon as possible after arrival in The Netherlands; road tax also becomes payable. (For details see the section entitled Car Registration in Chapter Four, *Daily Life*.)

A complex levy is charged on the importation of cars and motorbikes that have been in the owner's possession for less than six months. A comprehensive guide to the charges is available from the Royal Netherlands Embassy in London and the Dutch Customs and Excise Department.

Buying a Car

There are no restrictions on EC nationals buying a car in The Netherlands. Dutch car prices are lower than in the UK but unlike the British motor trade special offers and finance deals are not generally available. It must also be remembered that a car bought in The Netherlands is subject to UK import restrictions if the purchaser returns it to Britain.

Importing Pets

Dogs and cats will be admitted to The Netherlands only if the animal has a certificate of inoculation against rabies. The certificate, which is acceptable in English, must state the description of the animal, the owner's name, the date of inoculation (at least 30 days, but not more than 12 months, before importation) and the type of vaccine. The certificate is valid for one year — except for animals aged less than three months, in which case it must be renewed after three months. Pets such as horses and birds, which do not need to be vaccinated against rabies, must obtain an import permit prior to export. The permit is issued by the Dutch Ministry of Agriculture and applications should include the following details;
— age, breed, colour, sex and name of the animal.
— the country of export and place of import.
— intended address in The Netherlands and date of arrival.
The use of the rabies vaccine is restricted in the UK and special arrangements will need to be made to make it available. The Ministry of Agriculture will provide details of the vaccination procedures.

The Dutch veterinary authorities do not require a health certificate but some airlines may insist one is issued to ensure an animal is healthy enough to travel. To issue the certificate a veterinary surgeon will need to examine the animal seven days before it travels to The Netherlands. All dogs and cats brought back into the UK require an import licence and must undergo six months' quarantine (although this is currently under review). The animal's owner is liable for transportation and quarantine expenses.

Useful Addresses

Ministry of Agriculture, Fisheries and Food: Animal Health (International Trade) Division, Hook Rise South, Tolworth, Surbiton, Surrey KT6 7NF; tel 081-330 4411.

Dutch Ministry of Agriculture: RVV, PO Box 30724, 2500 GS The Hague, The Netherlands.

Daily Life

Certain aspects of life which often constitute the more mundane side of existence in the UK can take on a nightmarish quality when encountered in conjunction with a new home and a different culture. Opening a bank account, going to the doctor and using public transport can cause panic attacks. This chapter deals with all such dilemmas and will serve to smoothe your way into Dutch society.

The Language

The Dutch have an amazing facility for foreign languages and in all but the most inaccessible parts of The Netherlands, English, as well as German and French, is understood. However, if you intend to stay in The Netherlands for a long period of time it is essential to try to learn the language. Dutch is not easy to master, although it is closely linked to English and words such as deck, landscape, hops, brandy, mannikin and sketch all have their origins in Dutch. German speakers will also find some similarities in terms of vocabulary. There are a number of schools that specialize in teaching Dutch to foreigners and if you have the opportunity to learn a little it will undoubtedly pay dividends. The Dutch do not expect foreigners to speak their language and a few pleasantries will therefore make a good first impression.

The standard Dutch language of today, General Refined Dutch (*Algemeen Beschaafd Nederlands*), came into being in the seventeenth century. It developed, along with English and German, over a period of about two thousand years from an original Germanic form, *theod*. This later spawned High Dutch (now German) and Low Dutch (now modern Dutch). The Dutch language followed its seafarers around the world. Most notably it provided the basis for Afrikaans — the language spoken today by the former Dutch colonists in South Africa. Modern Afrikaans is recognizable to the Dutch, especially speakers of the Zeeland dialect. Dutch also survives in Surinam and the Dutch Antilles, in a pidgin form, however, it has died out in the former colonies of Indonesia and Sri Lanka.

Language Courses

A number of colleges and educational establishments in Britain offer Dutch language courses. The Berlitz School of Languages (79 Wells Street, London W1A 3BZ; tel 071-580 6482), inlingua School of Languages (Buckingham House, Wellington Street, Cheltenham; tel 0242-250493) and Linguarama (New Oxford

House, 16 Waterloo Street, Birmingham B2 5UG; tel 021-632 5925) all offer courses, taught by native speakers, catering for a wide range of standards and abilities. For those who are unable to attend formal classes a number of self-study courses and texts are also available. Linguaphone (head office: St Giles House, 50 Poland Street, London W1V 4AX; tel 071-287 4050) provides self-study courses in the form of books, cassettes and compact discs.

Courses in The Netherlands: Direct Dutch (Anna Paulownastraat 27, 2518 BA Den Haag; tel 070-3654677) and Talencentrum Den Haag (Prinsessegracht 31, 2514 AP Den Haag; tel 070-3654936) specifically aim to help foreigners living and working in The Netherlands to learn Dutch. These schools offer beginners, intermediate and advanced courses, both in the classroom or at home. The Foreign Student Service (Orange Nassaulaan 5, 1075 AH Amsterdam; tel 020-6715915) provides a comprehensive list of further names and addresses of schools and institutions which organise Dutch language courses for foreigners.

Schools and Education

The Ministry of Education and Science spends more than 29.6 billion guilders (£9 billion) a year on education. This sum is 17% of the national budget — the highest single budget of any Dutch ministry — and means education is for the most part free. (Some schools do ask parents for a small contribution, usually for classroom materials.) In 1848 a 'Freedom of Education' clause was written into the Dutch constitution which passed the running of schools from the government to the municipal authorities. Nearly 80 years later the government also voted to grant state and private schools equal rights. Three-quarters of schools in The Netherlands were originally private institutions, the majority of which were religious (Protestant or Catholic).

The decision as to whether to educate children within the Dutch or British/American systems of education (see *International Schools* below) is one which must include such considerations as the age of the child and the length of one's stay. Remember, also, that while Dutch schools will require pupils to have some ability in spoken Dutch is it much easier for younger children to master a new language.

The Structure of the Education System

Primary Schools: Primary education caters for children aged four to 12 years old. It is compulsory from the age of five and the curriculum includes reading,

writing, history, science, English language and social studies. In the last year pupils sit a state exam and their placement into secondary education is based upon these results and a teacher's report.

Secondary Education: Secondary schools are divided into three different types and pupils are able to change from one to another. General secondary schools consist of junior (MAVO) and senior (HAVO) establishments, which administer four and five-year courses respectively. Vocational education covers more practical subjects and has the same junior (LBO) and senior (MBO) levels. The *atheneum* and the *gymnasium* are regarded as pre-university schools and both offer six-year courses. All secondary education culminates in written state examinations. Pupils who leave school at the age of 16 are required by Dutch law to attend a one-year course of continued training for one or two days a week.

Special Schools: Special education centres cater for physically, mentally and socially handicapped children from the age of three to 21. The aim of the schools is to enable individuals to participate in as normal primary and secondary education as possible.

Higher Education: There are two higher education streams in The Netherlands: the universities (*universiteiten*), and the HBO Institutes (*hogescholen*). University education is divided into four-year *doctoraal* (undergraduate) courses and *doctorate* (postgraduate) research or study. Higher vocational courses cover subjects such as social work, agriculture, health care and teacher training. All higher education establishments are financed entirely from government funds. There are also seven theological colleges which are partly funded by the state.

Useful Addresses

The Netherlands Ministry of Education and Science: PO Box 25000, 2700 LZ, Zoetermeer; tel 079-533379.
International School Association (Stichting Internationale Scholen): Burgemeester de Monchyplein 14, 2585 BD Den Haag; tel 070-3122659.

International Education

A considerable number of English-speaking schools and classes exist to cater for children whose parents have moved temporarily to The Netherlands. All British schools provide the GCSE curriculum and international schools tend to follow a broadly American-based education. Some Dutch schools run an English stream (ES) which is taught along the lines of the European International Baccalaureate curriculum. International schools overcome any language or cultural problems and do offer qualifications better known to British and American universities or employers. However, this advantage must be balanced against the possible disadvantage of isolating children from the community in which they live thus accentuating cross-cultural divisions. International schools are also fee paying. A number of higher education establishments provide courses for UK graduates. They are in special subject areas and mostly conducted in English. A university degree is usually required for admission to these courses.

Useful Addresses for Primary Education

The European Council of International Schools: 21B Lavant Street, Petersfield, Hants GU32 3EL; tel 0730-68244.

AMERICAN INTERNATIONAL SCHOOL OF ROTTERDAM Elementary & Middle School	Hillegondastraat 21 Rotterdam Tel. 010-422 5351 Fax 010-422 4075	Excellence Personal Attention Multi-national Student Enrollment English as a Second Language

Den Haag
The British School in the Netherlands: (nursery and infants) Granaathorst 2-4, 2592 TD Den Haag; tel 070-3477256, fax 070-3479777.
The British School in the Netherlands: (junior) Tapijtweg 10, 2597 HK Den Haag; tel 070-3548911, fax 070-3541206.
Haagsche Schoolvereeniging: (International) Nassaulaan 26, 2514 JT Den Haag; tel 070-3638531.
The American School of The Hague: Rijksstraatweg 200, 2241 BX Wassenaar; tel 01751-40113, fax 01751-12400.

Amsterdam
The British School of Amsterdam: Jan van Eijckstraat 21, 1077 LG Amsterdam; tel 020-6797840, fax 020-6758396.
The International School of Amsterdam: A.J.Ernstastraat 875, 1081 HL Amsterdam; tel 020-6422227, fax 020-6428928.

Rotterdam
Basisschool De Blijberg: (ES) Gordelweg 216-217, 3039 GA Rotterdam; tel 010-4669629.
American International School of Rotterdam: Hillegondastraat 21, 3051 PA Rotterdam; tel 010-4225351, fax 010-4224075.

Other
Groningse Schoolvereeniging: (ES) Sweelincklaan 4, 9722 JV Groningen.
British School in the Netherlands: Mozartplaats 4, 9402 VM Assen; tel 05920-44590.

International School: Huize Vilsteren, Vilsterseweg 16, 7734 PD Vilsteren; tel 05291-58283.
Dr Aletta Jacobsschool: Slochterenweg 27, 6835 CD Arnhem; tel 085-230729.
Regional International School: Humperdincklaan 4, 5654 PA Eindhoven; tel 040-519437.
Basisschool Joppenhof: Kelvinstraat 3, 6227 VA Maastricht; tel 043-613242.
Violenschool: (ES) Violenstraat 3, 1214 CJ Hilversum; tel 035-216053.

Secondary Education
Den Haag
British School in The Netherlands: Jan van Hooflaan 3, 2252 BG Voorschoten; tel 071-616966, fax 071-617144.

American School of The Hague: (see address above).
International Music, School: de Sillestraat 127, 2593 TV Den Haag; tel 070-3834350, fax 070-3476508.
The International School of The Hague: (ES) Bouwmeesterlaan 75, 2597 GV Den Haag; tel 070-3281450, fax 070-3282049.

Amsterdam
British School of Amsterdam: Jan van Eijckstraat 21, 1077 LG Amsterdam; tel 020-6797840, fax 020-6758396.
International School of Amsterdam: AJ Ernststraat 875, 1081 HL Amsterdam; tel 020-6422227, fax 020-6428928 (PO Box 7983, 1008 AD Amsterdam).

Rotterdam
American International School of Rotterdam: Hillegondastraat 21, 3051 PA Rotterdam; tel 010-4225351, fax 010-4224075.
Wolfert v. Borselen: (ES) Bentincklaan 280, 3039 KK Rotterdam; tel 010-4660322.

Other
Alberdingk Thijm College: Emmastraat 58, 1213 AL Hilversum; tel 035-214944, fax 035-218504.
European School: Molenweidtje 5, 1862 BC Bergen; tel 02208-96641.
International School: Kasteel Beverweerd, Beverweerdseweg 60, 3985 RE Werkhoven; tel 03437-1341/1597, fax 03437-2079.
International School Eerde: Kasteellaan 1, 7731 PJ Ommen; tel 05291-51452, fax 05291-56377.
Jeanne d'Arc College: Oude Molenweg 130, 6228 XW Maastricht; tel 043-612200.
Lorentz Scholengemeenschap: Groningensingel 1245, 6835 HZ Arnhem; tel 085-231435.
Prince Willem Alexander College: Gravenallee 11, 7591 PE Denekamp; tel 05413-3485.
Het Rijnlands Lyceum Oegstgeest: (ES) Apollolaan 1, 2341 BA Oegstgeest; tel 071-155640, fax 071-153872.
Sint Maartens College: Rijksstraatweg 24, Postbus 6105 AE Haren; tel 050-30084.

Media and Communications

Newspapers and Magazines

The Dutch are avid consumers of newsprint and there is a choice of several national newspapers, as well as many regional papers that concentrate on events of local interest. The majority of newspaper readers appear to be interested in the more serious aspects of news coverage. This is reflected in the high circulations of the quality newspapers; *De Telegraaf* sells 725,000 copies daily, the *Algemeen Dagblad* nearly 500,000 a day, and *De Volkskrant* 400,000 daily. (The top circulation broadsheet in Britain is the *Daily Telegraph* which sells just less than one million copies a day to a population four times the size!) The Dutch tabloid press is more serious in nature than its UK counterparts and much of the gossip news is covered by magazines. The *NRC/Handelsblad* carries business news and has a daily circulation of 241,000.

The majority of national British newspapers appear on the day of publication on news-stands in the main cities.

Useful Addresses

Algemeen Dagblad: Marten Meesweg 35, Postbus 241, 3000 DB Rotterdam; tel 010-4066077/7211, fax 010-4066969.

Amsterdam This Week: c/o VVV, PO Box 3901, 1001 AS Amsterdam; tel 020-266444.

Amsterdam Times: Van Hallstraat 685, 1051 HG Amsterdam; tel 020-6843804, fax 020-6845847.

Dagblad Trouw: Wibautstraat 131, Postbus 859, 1000 AW Amsterdam; tel 020-5629444, fax 020-6680389

De Telegraaf: Basisweg 30, Postbus 376, 1000 EB Amsterdam; tel 020-5859111, fax 020-5852113/216.

De Volkskrant: Wibautstraat 148-150, Postbus 1002, 1000 BA Amsterdam; tel 020-5629222, fax 020-5626289.

NRC/Handelsblad: Marten Meesweg 35, Postbus 824, 3000 DL Rotterdam; tel 010-4066077/7211, fax 010-4066969.

Roundabout Magazine: c/o Axioma Communicatie, Hettenheuvelweg 37-39, 1101 BM Amsterdam; tel 020-6913141.

Television and Radio

The Dutch can tune into enough channels to suit even the most fanatical TV addict. There are three national television stations, Nederlands 1,2 and 3, as well as regional and local broadcasts. The programmes range from news and documentaries to quiz shows and soaps, but should you get bored with Dutch programmes, virtually all households are linked to cable television. This enables viewers to choose from BBC1 and BBC2, BSkyB, MTV, Germany 1,2 and 3, BRT 1 and 2, and RTBF 1 (Belgian), TV5 (French) and Raiuno (Italian). Radio Nederland broadcasts daily in seven languages including English. The Dutch are required to buy a yearly TV and radio licence *Kijk en Luister Geld*. The licence is available from post offices and the cost depends upon the number of televisions and radios in a household. TV listings are carried in weekly television guides and newspapers.

The Postal System

The postal service is operated efficiently by the Dutch PTT, with letters to addresses in The Netherlands almost always arriving the following day. Stamps can be purchased from post offices (*postkantoren*), vending machines and sub-post offices in the larger department stores and some petrol stations. The main post offices are open 8.30am to 6pm on weekdays, and 9am to 12 noon on Saturdays. Letters can be dispatched at post offices or from post boxes, which are red, rectangular, and found on street corners. Groningen City Council is pioneering an anti-junk mail scheme. It is issuing yellow stickers to households that do not want to receive unsolicited post. Firms that ignore the sign face fines of up to Dfl 5,000 (£1,550).

Telephones

The Dutch telephone system is cheaper to use than that in the UK and most phone boxes are in working order. A daytime call to a number in the same dialling code area costs 15 cents (4.5p) for five minutes; cheap rate calls (after 6pm and at weekends) are charged 15 cents for 10 minutes. When you move into new accommodation make sure the previous occupant notifies the PTT to change the user name and not disconnect the line. Also, make sure it has a telephone in the first place as it can take several weeks to get a private phone installed. Bills are issued bi-monthly and it is advisable to pay up quickly as lines are disconnected after just one reminder. The majority of payphones have instructions in English. The minimum call charge is 25c (about 8p) for two minutes. It is useful to remember that unless the phone has a credit counter there is no advance warning when your money runs out.

To telephone the UK from The Netherlands dial 09, wait for the continuous tone and then dial 44 followed by the area code, omitting the first zero, and the person's own telephone number. To call The Netherlands from the UK dial 010-31 and the Dutch number, again omitting the first number of the provincial code. To make an internal call in The Netherlands dial the area code (*netnummer*), wait for the dialling tone, then dial the subscriber's number (*abonneenummer*). Each town or area has its own commercial directory (*Gouden Gids* — Yellow Pages) and the country is covered by nine personal directories (*Telefoon Gids*). In directories the diphthong IJ is treated as one letter and comes between Y and Z in the alphabet. The following is a list of provincial codes which one is most likely to use within The Netherlands:

Amsterdam 020	Leiden 071
Arnhem 085	Maastricht 043
Eindhoven 040	Nijmegen 080
Groningen 050	Rotterdam 010
Den Haag 070	Utrecht 030
Haarlem 023	Zwolle 038

Useful Numbers

Directory Enquiries	06-8008 (8am to 10pm)
	06-8991133 (after 10pm)
Emergency	06-11
Customer Services	06-0402
Telephone Repairs	06-0407
Telegrams	06-0409
International Directory Enquiries	06-0418
Operator Assisted calls	06-0410

Cars & Motoring

Roads

The Netherlands has an excellent network of roads and toll-free motorways which link all the main cities and towns. Dutch roads are among the safest in the EC and the number of road deaths is falling each year (in 1980 there were 1,997 fatalities, in 1990 1,400). In the cities the biggest hazard is likely to be bicycles rather than other cars. Cyclists appear to go anywhere they please, although cycle paths are usually well-defined.

Breakdowns and Accidents

Members of British motoring organizations will receive a free accident and breakdown service if they pay for extra cover in Europe. The RAC operates Reflex and the AA runs Five Star Service. In The Netherlands two motoring organizations, the ANWB and the Koninklijke Nederlandse Automobile Club (KNAC), operate 24-hour breakdown services on main roads and motorways. They will give free assistance to AA and RAC members with the appropriate cover. Temporary membership of the Dutch organizations can be paid for at a breakdown and costs about Dfl 75 (£23).

Useful Addresses

ANWB: Wassenaarseweg 220, The Hague; tel 070-3141440.
Koninklijke Nederlandse Automobile Club: Westvlietweg 118, Leidschendam; tel 070-3997451.
RAC Motoring Services: Reflex, PO Box 700, Spectrum, Bond Street, Bristol, BS99 1RB; tel 0272-232340.

Driving Regulations

Dutch motorists are limited to a speed of 30kph (18mph) or 50kph (31mph) in built-up areas, 80kph (50mph) on single and dual carriageways and 100kph (62mph) or 120kph (75mph) on motorways. Road signs in a red warning triangle are obligatory and through routes are indicated by the sign *Doorgaand Verkeer*, or by rectangular blue signs with a slender white arrow. In a built-up area a blue sign bearing a white house means traffic must proceed at walking pace (10kph). The practice of flashing car headlights does not mean 'please go ahead' but rather 'get out of my way'. Military convoys, funerals and trams have absolute priority on Dutch roads and it is necessary also to give way to police cars, ambulances and fire engines. Seat belts must be worn at all times by drivers and front seat passengers (also in the back where fitted); children under 12 are banned from the front seat. A word of warning: ignorance of the Dutch traffic laws is not considered an acceptable excuse by the police.

Drink-Driving: The Dutch drink-driving limit is lower than in the UK and strictly enforced. It is currently 54 milligrams of alcohol per 100 millilitres of blood; or less than one pint of beer. (The UK limit is 80 milligrams of alcohol per 100 millilitres of blood.) The Dutch police carry out spot checks and by law drivers are required to take a breath test if asked. The penalties for drink driving are tough and the higher the alcohol level the higher the penalty. Drivers showing an alcohol level between 54 and 80 milligrams of alcohol per 100 millilitres of blood are fined Dfl 400 (£124). A level of more than 131 milligrams of alcohol means an automatic court appearance, a fine of between Dfl 1,250 and Dfl 2,000 and the loss of a driving licence for between six and 12 months. A drink-driver who registers an alcohol level above 211 milligrams will receive an automatic prison sentence.

Driving Licences

British citizens who hold the pink UK driving licence can drive in The Netherlands with no alteration to it at all. However, holders of the old green licences must either exchange it for the pink licence or obtain an international driving licence. Drivers intending to stay in The Netherlands must exchange their national licence for a Dutch one within one year of arrival, even if they hold an EC licence. EC citizens and people with internationally recognized licences are not required to take a driving test. It is necessary to provide only proof of residency, two passport photos and the old licence, which will be held by the Dutch authorities until it is needed again. The EC directive making licences fully transferable will not come into force until 1 July 1996. In The Netherlands no one under the age of 18 is allowed to drive a car or a motorcycle, even if you hold a valid UK licence.

Car Registration

To register an imported car it must conform to Dutch standards. The *Rijksdienst Wegverkeer* will inspect the car and issue a 'certificate of conformity'. At the same time they will ask you to fill out a registration application form. The registration documents will be sent to the owner within seven days of a satisfactory inspection. The registration papers consist of three parts: *Deel I* (the title and description of the car), *Deel II* (details of the owner) and *Deel III* (registration disc). The first two parts, or copies of them, must be kept in the car for inspection and *Deel III* must be displayed in the car's windscreen. The annual car tax (*Wegen Belasting*) can be obtained from any post office, on production of the registration documents and insurance details. The car tax is proportional to the size of the vehicle.

Insurance

Both third party liability and fully comprehensive insurance policies are available

in The Netherlands. Insurance cover is expensive and it is necessary to take out
at least third party cover. Insurance contracts run for one year and are automatically
renewed. Dutch insurance companies will usually accept up to 70% of no claims
bonuses accrued in the UK.

Transport

Waterways

The Dutch were among the pioneers of waterway travel and established an extensive
inland waterway system long before a road network was developed. A reliance
on waterways still remains and an intricate web of rivers, canals and lakes plays
an important role in both domestic and commercial activity. Amsterdam is the
city of a thousand and one bridges and famous for its miles of canals. The IJsselmeer
is the largest man-made lake in the world and the *Afsluitdijk* (the 32km dam
separating the IJsselmeer from the sea) is the only man-made object on earth,
besides the Great Wall of China, visible to the naked eye from outer space. These
are impressive achievements, but the jewel in the crown of the entire Dutch
transport system is Europoort, near Rotterdam. It is arguably the world's largest
seaport and stands on the Golden Delta at the head of three great rivers: the Maas
(Meuse), the Rijn (Rhine) and the Scheldt. Europoort handles nearly 250,000 ships
and an estimated 292 million tons of cargo annually. The Dutch dominance of
water transport is further highlighted by the fact that throughout the European
Community Dutch-owned carriers handle about half the international cargo.

Rail

The state-owned NV Nederlandse Spoorwegen (NS) operates one of the most
efficient railway systems in the European Community and an estimated 700,000
customers use rail travel everyday. As in the UK there are two classes of travel
and first class seating costs 50% more than second. Fares are uniform throughout
the country and slightly cheaper than in Britain. For example a single to The Hague
from Amsterdam (64km) costs Dfl 14 (about £4.30); a return ticket costs Dfl 24.
Children under four years old can travel free and children aged four to 11 receive
a 40% discount. Timetables (*spoorboekje*) are updated annually in May and are
on sale at stations, bookshops and some post offices.

Useful Address

NV Nederlandse Spoorwegen: (Netherlands Railways) 25/28 Buckingham Gate,
    London, SW1E 6LD; tel 071-630 1735, fax 071-233 5832.

Air

The Dutch do not rely a great deal upon internal air travel due to the relative
proximity of their major cities. Domestic flights are expensive and the principal
services link Amsterdam with Enschede and Groningen in the north, and with
Eindhoven and Maastricht in the south. Schiphol airport is the nearest to
Amsterdam and acts as the hub of all Dutch air travel: in 1990 it handled 16.6
million passengers. Sixty airlines operate from it including the national carrier
KLM (Royal Dutch Airlines), which has services to 119 cities in 75 countries.
Two Dutch charter companies, Martinair Holland and Transavia, also carry
international passenger traffic. Schiphol is situated 19km from Amsterdam and
is easily accessible from all over the country. Trains operate every 15 minutes

to Amsterdam and Leiden/Rotterdam. Buses run regular services to The Hague, Utrecht, Delft and Eindhoven.

Useful Address
KLM: G.Metsusstraat 2-6, Museumplein; tel 06-8747747.
British Airways: Stadhouderskade 4, Amsterdam; tel 020-6852211.
British Midland Airways Ltd: Strawinskylaan 1535; tel 060-222426, or Donington Hall, Castle Donington, DE7; tel 071-589 5599.

Public Transport
The Dutch public transport system (excluding trains) carries an estimated three-quarters of a billion passengers every year. Buses and trams operate an ultra-modern network of regional and municipal services and reach virtually every town and village in the country. Villages with less than 2,000 inhabitants are normally served by a community minibus service manned by volunteer drivers and financed by the state. The bus and tram services have a unified fare system which divides The Netherlands into zones. The price per zone is the same nationwide and the same tickets can be used on both urban and regional transport. The cities of Amsterdam and Rotterdam also have their own metro systems.

Bicycle
Eleven million bicycles and one and a half million regular cyclists make The Netherlands the two-wheeled land of Europe. The Dutch have built an extensive network (6,200 miles/9,920 km) of cycle paths, which are marked by a round blue sign with a white bicycle superimposed. Hiring bicycles is popular among the Dutch and they are available from cycle dealers and railway stations. Renting a bicycle costs around Dfl 8 (£2.50) for a day or Dfl 30 per week. It is strongly advisable to lock cycles as an estimated 500,000 are stolen every year.

Banks and Finance

Opening an Account
There are no legal restrictions for UK nationals who wish to bank in The Netherlands and it is a relatively simple process to open a Dutch bank account. The bank will only require to see some form of identification (a passport will suffice) and an initial deposit to open an account. However, should you wish to borrow money, either in the form of an overdraft or a loan, the bank will want evidence of adequate financial support. This can take the form of either a letter from your employer or your bank in the UK. It is very difficult to open an account in The Netherlands from the UK as the majority of Dutch banks insist on a personal visit to finalize the details.

Choosing a Bank
The banking system is dominated by the big four Dutch banks: Rabobank Nederland, ABN-AMRO, Internationale Nederlanden Groep (NMB Postbank) and Mees & Hope. However, a number of smaller banks, such as Staal and Van Lanschot Bankiers, offer perfectly adequate services. The main banks operate networks throughout the country and, as with the major UK banks, there is probably little to choose between them.

184 *Living in The Netherlands*

Useful Addresses:

Rabobank Nederland (63 Mark Lane, London, EC3R 7NE; tel 071-488 2311) and *ABN-AMRO Bank* (101 Moorgate, London EC2; tel 071-638 2700) can provide details of their branches in The Netherlands.

De Nederlandsche Bank NV: (Central Bank) Westeinde 1, PO Box 98, 1000 AB Amsterdam; tel 020-5249111.

Using a Dutch Bank Account

Dutch banks seem to be able to offer every conceivable service except an efficient queueing system for the cashiers. The catch is that this does does not come cheaply. Bank charges are higher than in the UK and to avoid a nasty letter (and a charge) it is advisable to ask for an overdraft facility before going into the red. Official opening hours are from 9am to 4pm (or 5pm) and 7pm on late shopping nights. Branches are closed at weekends with the exception of special banks on the border, at the main train stations and airports.

The Dutch make no secret of the fact that they prefer payment in cash whenever possible and to accommodate this the number of cashpoints is growing rapidly; the use of credit cards and personal cheques is not as widespread as in the UK. The two forms of guaranteed cheque that are in common usage are *Betaalcheques* and *Eurocheques*. The former replaces what we would describe as a personal cheque and takes money direct from an account. The banks also operate *Acceptgiros*, which are invoices for goods or services, such as from the telephone or electric company. They have the look of a computer printout and state how much is owed. Simply sign the card (if the amount is correct), add your bank account number and send it to your bank for handling. Bills can also be paid by direct debit payments.

The Dutch Post Office (PTT) runs *Postbank* an alternative system that offers a variety of banking services throughout its 2,000 branches. PTT's cheques (*Girobetaalkaart*) can be used for purchases of up to Dfl 300 and the *Giromaatpas* to withdraw up to Dfl 500 from cashpoints.

The Currency

The Dutch currency uses the decimal system and the monetary unit is the guilder, which consists of 100 Dutch cents. Prices have the letters f, fl, Fl, Hfl or Dfl before the number. This abbreviation denotes the guilder unit and stands for florin, a relic of the earlier French monetary system. All Dutch notes have braille symbols in one corner so that the visually impaired can identify their value. The guilder became part of the European Monetary System (EMS) in 1979 and the current policy is to tie it to the German mark.

Coin value	Dutch name	Note Value	Colour
0.05	*stuiver*	5	green
0.10	*dubbeltje*	10	blue
0.25	*kwartje*	25	red
1.00	*gulden*	50	yellow
2.50	*rijksdaalder*	100	brown
5.00	*vijf gulden*	250	mauve

Transferring Funds to the Netherlands

For non-residents there are no restrictions on the import or export of currency.

The international *Swift* system, by which funds can be sent direct to the local branch of your bank, is one of the most efficient ways to transfer money to The Netherlands. Most Dutch banks will accept money through the *Swift* system and all transactions are logged with the precise time and date of transfer from the UK. The arrival of funds is guaranteed within two days.

Offshore Banking

One of the financial advantages of being an expatriate is that money can be invested in tax-free, offshore savings accounts. Many familiar names have established branches in tax havens such as the Isle of Man, the Channel Islands and Gibraltar. The facilities are as flexible as UK high street banking and range from current accounts to long-term, high interest earning deposits.

Useful Addresses

Nationwide Overseas Ltd: PO Box 217, Market Street, Douglas, Isle of Man; tel 0624-606095, fax 0624-663495.
Bradford and Bingley (Douglas) Ltd: 1st Floor, 30 Ridgeway Street, Douglas, Isle of Man; tel 0624-662883.
Abbey National: 237 Main Street, Gibraltar; tel 010-350 76090.
NatWest Expatriate Service: PO Box 12, 2nd Floor, National Westminster House, 6 High Street, Chelmsford, Essex CM1 1BL; tel 0245-355628.

Taxation

The Dutch are not a nation of tax evaders and foreign nationals would be well-advised to follow their lead. All taxes are administered by the *Rijksbelastingdienst*, a special department of the Ministry of Finance. Taxes are divided into direct payments (on income) and indirect tax (such as VAT, wealth tax or inheritance tax). In the case of direct taxes the burden of proof lies with the taxpayer. The tax year runs from January to December and all tax returns (*Aangifte biljet*) must be made by April 1. Failure to pay tax can result in fines equal to 5% of the amount due up to a maximum of Dfl 1,000. An incorrect tax return can incur a 100% penalty, and a deliberate attempt to mislead the tax authorities can lead to imprisonment. To avoid accidently falling foul of the Dutch tax authorities it is essential to get expert advice on the tax laws.

Income Tax

To encourage foreign investment the Dutch Ministry of Finance has set up what is known as the '35 per cent rule'. The rule allows foreigners to qualify for taxation on only 65 per cent of their gross salary.

Individual income tax is levied at rates of up to 60% of taxable income. Foreign taxpayers are classified as either residents or non-residents. Resident taxpayers are subject to tax on their worldwide income, while non-residents pay tax only on sources of income in The Netherlands. Residence is determined in accordance with an individual's principal place of residence and what the tax courts call 'durable ties of a personal nature'. Durable in this case means the closeness of the tie rather than the length of the stay. There are five separate income tax tariff bands with different tax-free personal allowances. The personal circumstances of the taxpayer such as marriage and income decide which band is applicable.

Tax Rate	Taxable Income
38.55% (13% tax + 25.55% national insurance premiums). For persons aged 65 years or more tax is charged at 20.3%	the first Dfl 42,966 (£13,310)
50%	the next Dfl 42,964
60%	any amount in excess of Dfl 85,930 (£26,600)

Self-employed EC nationals are entitled to a special Dfl 5,915 (£1,830) deduction if their net profit is less than Dfl 76,320 (£23,630). The minimum deduction is Dfl 3,815 if the net profit is more than Dfl 86,010. An extra deduction of Dfl 2,152 will also be made to an individual for the first three years of a new business.

Indirect Taxes

VAT: Value added tax (*Belasting op Toegevoegde Waarde — BTW*) is a general tax on goods and services. The standard rate is levied at 18.5%. A reduced rate of 6% is charged on certain basic necessities such as food, medicine, newspapers, passenger transport and non-alcoholic drinks. A special 0% applies to the export of goods from the The Netherlands.

Wealth Tax: This is not really a wealth tax, rather an asset tax (*Vermogensbelasting*). Individuals resident in The Netherlands are subject to a tax of 0.8 per cent, as of 1 January of each year. The taxable capital is the value of the taxpayer's net assets. These do not include such random items as food, furniture, objects of art and life assurance policies.

Inheritance and Gift Tax: Both gifts and inherited items are taxed at rates between five and 68 per cent depending on the relationship between the donor and recipient, and the amount. The inheritance tax (*Successierecht*) applies only to individuals who have died while a resident of The Netherlands. For a gift it is the responsibility of the donor and donee to make a declaration to the local Inspector of Registration and Succession (*Inspecteur der Registratie en Successie*). Non-residents are subject only to gift tax (*Schenkingsrecht*) on property (For a detailed account of inheritance tax see Chapter Five, *Retirement*).

Useful Addresses:

Inland Revenue: EC Unit Room S20, West Wing Somerset House, London WC2R 1LB; tel 071-438 6254.
The Tax Authority (Rijksbelastingen): Stationplein 75, 2515 BX The Hague; tel 070-3304000.

Health Insurance and Hospitals

The Netherlands has an excellent two-tier health care service comprising curative and preventative care. The former has the role of restoring people to health and encompasses hospitals, ambulances, nurses and GPs. The bulk of this provision comes from private organizations and is funded through insurance schemes. The state provides much of the preventative care through the Municipal Health Services and the Food and Commodity Inspectorates. It also pays for medical research.

The aim of preventative care is to both safeguard and improve the health of target groups (the old, people at risk and children). The emphasis is on education as well as precautionary measures such as school health programmes and screening for cervical cancer or cardio-vascular disease.

The E111
Anyone intending to move permanently to The Netherlands must register their change of address with the Overseas Branch of the Department of Social Security in Newcastle. They will be sent the paperwork required to obtain an E111 (allow one month for processing) which entitles all EC nationals to subsidized medical treatment in any Member State. The E111 covers emergency hospital treatment but does not include dental care, X-rays, specialist examinations, prescribed medicines and laboratory tests. It is advisable to take out private medical insurance for temporary visits to cover treatment not regarded as an emergency. The E111 is valid for three months and renewable on the proviso that the applicant still retains tourist and not resident status in the host country.

Medical Insurance
Health care in The Netherlands is funded through a number of insurance schemes. People with an income of less than Dfl 54,400 (£16,840) pay a monthly contribution to the state's Health Insurance Fund (*Ziekenfonds*) in return for which they receive medical, pharmaceutical and dental treatment, and hospitalization. (Pensioners, the young and the unemployed receive health provision free of charge.) Individuals paying into the *Ziekenfonds* usually take out a subsidiary insurance (*Aanvullende Verzekering*) which covers health expenses abroad and ante/post-natal services. A state-run scheme also exists that covers what are termed exceptional medical expenses (*Algemene Wet Bijzondere Ziektekosten* — AWBZ). The AWBZ provides treatment in recognized nursing homes, medical children's homes and institutions for the deaf, blind, handicapped and mentally ill. Under Dutch law anyone whose wage exceeds Dfl 54,400 must take out private medical insurance (*Particuliere Verzekering*). UK organisations such as the British United Provident Association (BUPA) and Private Patients Plan (PPP) offer a variety of international health insurance schemes. The advantage of taking out a UK policy is that it will cover the claimant for treatment costs incurred anywhere in Europe and not just The Netherlands.

Anyone intending to use the Dutch health service must be able to prove they are paying into either the Health Insurance Fund or a private medical insurance scheme. Therefore, it is advisable to have several copies made of your insurance certificate and hand out copies where necessary.

Useful Addresses
Dutch Health Service: Foreign Affairs Dept, Afdeling Buitenland van het Ziekenfonds (ANOZ), PO Box 9069, 3506 GB Utrecht; tel 030-618881
BUPA: International Centre, Imperial House, 40-42 Queens Road, Brighton BN1 3WU; tel 0273-23563, fax 0273-820517.
PPP: Philips House, Crescent Road, Tunbridge Wells, Kent TN1 2PL; tel 0892-512345.

Using the Dutch Health Service

The Dutch health service operates through its GPs (*Huisartsen*). To use the system (except in the case of extreme emergencies) it is essential to register with a GP as they sanction the use of ambulances and specialists, and authorize hospital admittance. A list of English-speaking GPs is available from Access (see below) or look in the telephone book under *Artsen — Huisartsen*. It is very important to note that hospitals are entitled to refuse to treat patients in a non life-threatening situation unless they are referred by a *Huisarts*. GPs hold surgeries, and carry out both house and hospital calls.

Mothers-to-be can choose either a midwife service (*Verloskundige*) or a gynaecologist (*Gynaecoloog*). The midwife service operates both at home and in hospitals, whereas gynaecologists work solely in hospitals. Hospital deliveries fall into two categories: at an out-patient hospital (*Polikliniek*), which means just 24 hours in hospital; or a maternity bed, which is provided for as long as is necessary. All new mothers are offered mother and baby home care (*Kraamverzorgster*). A seven-day 24-hour breast feeding information service is available on 045-324884.

Access: Access is an organization that offers free medical advice (as well as help on most everyday problems) in English. It is staffed by volunteers from the international community and offers a telephone information line (weekdays, 9.30am to 3.30pm), workshops and counselling.

Useful Numbers

Access: Bezuidenhoutseweg 125e, 2594 AE Den Haag; tel 070-3836161.
Cancer Information Line: tel 020-6644044.
Alcoholics Anonymous: tel 070-3600407.

Emergencies

If you are involved in or witness to a serious accident call an ambulance (*Ziekenwagen*) on 0611. In the event of a non life-threatening emergency such as a broken bone call your huisarts. He or she will make a house call and if necessary arrange for the patient to be taken to hospital. All Dutch hospitals have a casualty department (*Eerste Hulp Bij Ongelukken — EHBO*) for first aid and emergencies. To be admitted to a hospital you will require both your insurance card and doctor's notes. Your details will be recorded on an identity card (*ponsplaatje*) and used for reference if further visits are necessary. For minor ailments Dutch pharmacists are highly qualified and will probably be able to prescribe something for you. In The Netherlands two types of chemist exist. The *Apotheek* supplies prescriptions and over-the-counter medicines, whereas the *Drogisterij* sells toiletries, baby products and non-prescription medicines.

Social Security and Unemployment Benefit

Social Security

The Dutch social security system is one of the most benevolent in the EC and taxpayers are required to make no fewer than eight contributions. These total nearly

40% of their salary and are mostly withheld at source by employers. To qualify for social security benefits claimants must meet certain criteria:

Sickness Benefit: People unable to work as a result of sickness, disablement or an accident are entitled to up to 70% of their basic wage for up to 52 weeks. (The maximum amount is fixed at Dfl 274.01). For the first six weeks of unemployment the benefit is 100% of an employee's basic wage. Benefit is also payable for maternity leave of up to 16 weeks.

Disablement Benefit: Residents of The Netherlands (aged between 18 and 65) can claim disablement benefit if they are still 25% incapacitated after being unable to work for 52 weeks and had earned a minimum of Dfl 4,579.20 (£1,417) in the year preceding injury.

Disablement Insurance: If an individual is at least 15% unfit for work after 52 weeks of disability he or she is entilted to claim up to 70% of their former wage. The amount depends upon the degree of disability.

Family Allowance: Families are entitled to family allowance (*Kinderbijslag*). It is a quarterly payment and is payable for economic dependants up to the age of 17. Further payments are also made for students up to the age of 27. The allowance is calculated on the number and ages of the dependants. For example a family with two children, aged eight and 14, would receive Dfl 441.62 for each child.

Old Age Pensions: Anyone who reaches the age of 65 is entitled to draw a state pension. The average married couple receive Dfl 1,876 (£580) per month. Under EC rules state pension contributions in separate Member States can be combined. For further details see Chapter Five, *Retirement*.

Widows and Orphans: A widow or widower is entitled to funds if he or she has a child, has been incapable of working since the spouse's death and is aged 40 or more. An orphan receives funds up to the age of 16 (or 18 if disabled, and 27 if studying). Payments are made according to a sliding scale. For example a widow with a child receives Dfl 2,315 (£716) per month and a 14-year-old orphan will receive Dfl 783 monthly.

Unemployment Benefit

In general, the Dutch unemployment benefit system is open only to UK citizens who are made unemployed in The Netherlands. The benefit amounts to 70% of the claimant's most recent wage and is payable for at least six months. To qualify an individual must have worked for at least 26 weeks in the year preceding unemployment. If the claimant has worked for three years out of the last five he or she can claim the same benefit allowance for up to five years. (The income of the claimant's partner, if any, is not taken into account.) To apply for benefit it is necessary to register with the local labour exchange (*arbeidsbureau*) who will then contact the nearest Social Security office on your behalf. If you have received UK unemployment benefit for at least four weeks it is possible to receive up to three months' payments in The Netherlands. To apply, inform your local unemployment benefit office in the UK of your intentions and ask for the form UBL22. If you satisfy the conditions of transfer of benefit overseas a registration document will be provided by the UK authorities. This will enable the holder to sign on at the nearest *arbeidsbureau* once he or she is in The Netherlands.

Useful Addresses:

Ministry of Social Affairs and Labour (Ministerie van Sociale Zaken en Werkgelegenheid): (Zeestraat 73, PO Box 20801, 2500 Den Haag; tel 070-3715911) produces a leaflet comprehensively detailing the benefits available.
Department of Social Security: Overseas Branch, Newcastle Upon Tyne, NE98 1YX; tel 091-213 5000.
Social Insurance Information Centre: Rhijnspoorplein 1, 1091 GC Amsterdam; tel 020-5600955.

Local Government

Running parallel to the central government are two levels of local government: a provincial council/assembly (*provinciale staten*) and a municipal council (*gemeenteraad*). The Netherlands is divided into 12 provinces and 850 municipalities (*gemeenten*). Each province has its own *provinciale staten* and the members are directly elected every four years; the number is proportional to the province's population. Each council appoints a six-strong executive committee which is responsible for the day-to-day running of the province. The council also elects members to the Upper House of Parliament (*De Eerste Kamer* — First Chamber). A Commissioner (*Commissaris van de Koningin*) is appointed by the monarch and presides over the council.

The administration of each municipality is conducted by a municipal council, a municipal executive and a mayor (*burgemeester*). The council is largely independent and responsible for local administration, law and order, the fire service and civil defence. However, it is required to prepare and implement central government and provincial council decisions. The Crown appoints the mayor, for a six-year term, to preside over the executive and the council. Council members are elected every four years and foreigners legally resident in The Netherlands for five years or more are entitled to vote. Municipal councils are increasingly joining forces into unofficial regional authorities to tackle matters such as the location of industry, environmental issues, housing and transport.

Crime and the Police

The Netherlands has the second highest crime rate in Europe (the UK has the highest). Much of the crime is petty theft (24%) and to a large degree drug-related. Serious assault and rape are rare. The clear-up rate stands at about one-fifth of all reported crimes; a figure comparable with the UK. The Dutch authorities are endeavouring to crack down on crime. One notable success has been the fight against drink-driving. The number of convictions has dropped from 24,000 in 1980 to 15,000 in 1991. Another has been the battle against football hooliganism, which has been in decline since the late 1980s. Conversely, the drug problem in The Netherlands is hard to miss and on the increase. The police tend to turn a blind eye to the buying and selling of small quantities of soft drugs such as marijuana. However, the possession of more than 30g will be treated as an offence. The Netherlands also has a serious hard drug problem and pushers are dealt with severely.

The Judiciary

The legal system in The Netherlands is based upon Roman Law and there is no trial by jury. The justice organization is administered by a four-tier court system. The highest court in the land is the Supreme Court of The Netherlands (*Hoge Raad*). This heads a pyramidal court structure consisting of five Courts of Appeal (*Gerechtshof*), 19 District Courts (*Arrondissementsrechtbank*) and 62 Sub-district Courts (*Kantongerecht*).

Religion

The Dutch constitution guarantees freedom of religion and more than half of the population claim to belong to a recognized church. One-third are Roman Catholics (mostly concentrated in the provinces of Noord-Brabant and Limburg), one-fifth belong to the Dutch Reformed Church (Nederlandse Hervormde Kerk), and 7% to other Protestant groups. Dutch Catholics are regarded as among the most liberal in the world and as a result have often found themselves in conflict with the papal authorities.

Useful Addresses

English-speaking churches in the Netherlands:

Trinity Baptist Church: Pastor Stephen Smith, Bloemcamplaan 54, 2240 AA Wassenaar; tel 01751-78024.

The Church of St John and St Philip: Rev John Wallis, Ary van der Spuyweg 1, 2585 JA Den Haag; tel 070-3555359.

The American Protestant Church: Esther de Boer van Rijklaan 20, 2597 TJ Den Haag; tel 070-3244490.

International Roman Parish of The Hague (The Church of Our Saviour): Pastor Father David Buescher, Parish House, Ruychrocklaan 126, 2597 EN Den Haag; tel 070-3280816.

First Church of Christ Scientist: Andries Bickerweg 1B, 2517 JP Den Haag; tel 070-3636652.

English Reformed Church: Rev W. Geraint Edwards, Begijnhof 48, 1012 XV Amsterdam; tel 020-6249665.

Christ Church: Rev Canon John Wheatley Price, Groenburgwal 42, 1011 HW Amsterdam; tel 020-6248877 or 6952705.

Church of St John & St Ursula: Rev Father Marius Brands, Begijnhof 29/35C, 1012 WV Amsterdam; tel 020-6270260.

St Mary's Church of England: Pieter de Hoochweg 133, 3032 BG Rotterdam; tel 010-4764043.

The Scots Church Rotterdam: Rev J.E.Stewart Low, Schiedamsevest 121, 3012 BH Rotterdam; tel 010-4124779.

Social Life

The Dutch

The Dutch wear clogs, live in windmills and grow flowers. This is the tourist image which the Dutch themselves have done as much to promote as anyone. The underlying fact is unmistakable, however, the Dutch are a unique people and proud of it. Indeed this uniqueness begins with the fact that they have quite literally built their national identity. Over the centuries one-fifth of The Netherlands has been reclaimed from the sea and the land can be said to truly belong to them. To do this the Dutch have been both ingenious and pioneering; two traits that are as common today as they have ever been. However, the Dutch are not ones for boasting and tend to let their achievements speak for themselves. They are a commercially-minded small nation and having traded with the rest of the world for centuries are also proud of their adaptability and integration. This is amply shown in an exceptional tolerance towards others, especially in their liberal attitudes on sex and drugs. They also regard social problems as everyone's problem; an attitude evident in the benevolent social services available to the less fortunate in society.

Manners and Customs

The Dutch are generally a tolerant people but they do not believe in wasting time on trivialities. They tend to be very direct in their attitude which means they can sometimes be misunderstood as being rude and abrupt. Fortunately this is far from the truth and once friendships have been struck the Dutch can become very friendly and hospitable. The workplace is much less formal than UK counterparts and it is common practice for employees to be on first name terms. However, the Dutch generally guard their private life carefully and an invitation to their home is a mark of true friendship.

Making Friends

One of the most rewarding aspects of living in a foreign country is breaking down the barriers and forming lasting friendships. Cultural problems can make the process difficult but the Dutch often speak English very well so not knowing the language is no excuse. Perseverance is certainly the key and being accepted as a true friend can take a little time. But once the breakthrough is made the Dutch are a generous people and friendships will last a lifetime.

For those of you who need a rest from promoting cross-cultural links, the expatriate population in The Netherlands has established a large number of English-speaking clubs and societies in most major towns. They can often provide a friendly face and guidance on how to settle into your new Dutch way of life. A comprehensive list of expatriate social clubs is listed in the Chapter Five, *Retirement*.

Entertainment and Culture

There is a saying in The Netherlands that one works in Rotterdam, plays in Amsterdam and sleeps in The Hague. Anyone deciding where to locate would be well-advised to bear this in mind. The Hague does have some nightlife and Amsterdam has its quieter moments, but on the whole it is not far from the truth!

The Dutch believe that one of the key roles of art and entertainment is to improve the quality of life. The government is a keen supporter of this position and has gone so far as to encourage co-operation between artists and architects in the management of the environment. In a number of pilot schemes, such as that in the new town of Zoetermeer, near The Hague, teams of architects, planners, sociologists and artists have worked together to plan the aesthetics of new urban areas.

Art: It is virtually impossible to discuss the world of paint and canvas without mentioning at least one of the great Dutch artists. The names of Rembrandt, Hals and Van Gogh enjoy a revered international reputation. The Dutch are proud of this fact and take every opportunity to display famous works of art. The Netherlands has one of the highest numbers of museums and art galleries in proportion to its population in the world. Top of the list is the world-famous Rijksmuseum in Amsterdam which is home to Rembrandt's 'The Night Watch'.

Nightlife: Dutch nightlife can be divided into two distinct areas: Amsterdam/Rotterdam and the rest. The country's two largest cities offer everything from all-night bars to casinos, and nightclubs to live sex shows. The rest of The Netherlands does not have quite the same diversity and the nightlife is generally much quieter. The Dutch are happy to spend an evening at a restaurant or live music bar, or even entertain at home, rather than live it up at a disco.

Theatre: The theatre scene in The Netherlands is very active and an estimated 4,500 performances are staged every year. There are a number of repertory companies staging both classical and modern works. However, the government has been trying to promote more experimental companies which deal with subjects such as sexuality, drugs and women's rights.

Music: Traditionally, classical music has centred around the Dutch symphony orchestras, the two opera companies and three dance troupes which seem to be constantly in action. A number of major music competitions are held annually including the International Organ Competition in the St Bavo Cathedral in Haarlem, where Mozart once played. The Dutch are jazz freaks and there are hundreds of bars catering for live music throughout the country. Jazz festivals are common to several towns and each specializes in a particular style. The largest is the North Sea Jazz Festival held every year in The Hague.

Films and the Cinema: The Dutch were among the first to pioneer cinemas at the turn of the century and going to the pictures is still a popular pastime. The majority of films are foreign and are subtitled. However, the Dutch film industry has had recent international successes: *De Aanslag* (The Assassination) won an Oscar in 1987. A number of film festivals are held each year. The Rotterdam festival is held in February and Utrecht's takes place in September. All films are rated by the Dutch board of censors. The minimum age certificate (either 12 or 16) is always shown with the advert for a film and strictly enforced at the cinema. The letters AL (*alle leeftijden* — all ages) mean the film has no age restriction.

Sport

Sport is an extremely important part of Dutch life. One-third of the population belongs to an official club and and the same number again take part in sport purely for recreational purposes. Sixty separate sports have national organizations in The Netherlands. Cycling and angling are reckoned to be the two most popular pastimes, and tennis is second only to football in the number of official participants.

Football: Dutch football has the unenviable record of being regarded as producing the finest national teams never to have won the World Cup. In 1974 and four years later in 1978 the national side lost in the final. However, in 1988 The Netherlands did win its first international title, the European Championship. The Royal Netherlands Football Association has more than one million members and is by far the largest sporting organisation in the country. The Dutch league is one of the most competitive in the world and its leading clubs, Ajax (Amsterdam), Feyenoord (Rotterdam) and PSV Eindhoven rank among the best in Europe.

Ice Skating: Seventeen thousand competitors take part in The Netherlands' largest sporting event — the *Elfstedentocht* (the Eleven Towns). The race is organized annually (weather permitting) and participants skate 200 km along frozen canals between 11 towns in Friesland. The overall popularity of skating has risen dramatically in recent years. There are 5,580 miles of canals (available when frozen) but to meet the rising demand new rinks have been built in many major towns. Most of these have both a 400 metre track for speed skating and a separate area for ice hockey and figure skating.

Water Sports: The Dutch love the water and an amazing 600,000 sailing and motor yachts ply the country's waterways and canals. The Netherlands is well equipped to cope with the demand and has an abundance of facilities. Those include more than 1,000 marinas nationwide, with space for more than 163,000 moorings.

Fierljeppen: The Dutch have turned an unusual way of crossing canals into a bizarre type of sport. *Fierljeppen* has its origins in local traditions and is similar in principle to the pole vault in field athletics. However, rather than leaping over a bar and landing on a soft mat competitors use a long pole to vault over a wide ditch. It is unlikely to become an international sport but it is popular amongst the inhabitants of Friesland.

Shopping

The Dutch are by no means the most extravagant in the European Community and much of what they buy has a specific function. However, this does not mean fashion is ignored and they have a knack for combining it with quality. Shopping in The Netherlands is an easy and enjoyable pastime. The majority of city centres have extensive shopping facilities ranging from supermarkets and department stores, to street traders and small speciality shops. Food stores are generally open from 9am to 5.30pm on weekdays and Saturdays. Most shops are closed on Sunday. Many town centres hold a weekly market, which will probably have some of the more competitive prices, especially for fresh produce.

Dutch Food and Drink

The Dutch love to eat and drink. 'As many people, as many tastes' is a commonly quoted saying for the variety of products available. A number of favourite Dutch foods have already found their way onto the dinner tables around the world. Both cheeses and meats from The Netherlands have a reputation for the highest quality and need little introduction. The Dutch have a sweet tooth and are very fond of chocolate. It can take every shape and form, and Veghel is home to the world's largest chocolate factory. A brief mention must also go to the popular *Poffertjes*. These are made from an age-old recipe and resemble a small, light pancake.

The Dutch have a taste for both brewing and drinking beer. Not just Heineken, but Grolsch and Skol, are renowned for refreshing the parts others cannot reach. But these are just the more famous exports. Each town and even village produces its own special beer. The Dutch on average drink 90 litres of beer each and consume an estimated 100 million litres of distilled drinks every year. The most popular spirit is the colourless *Jenever* which accounts for more than half of Dutch sales.

Public Holidays

1 January	New Year's Day (*Nieuwjaar*)
April	Good Friday (*Pasen*)
April	Easter Monday
30 April	Queen Beatrix's Official Birthday
5 May	Liberation Day (*Bevrijdingsdag*)
May	Ascension Day (*Hemelvaart*)
June	Whit Monday (*Pinksteren*)
25 December	Christmas Day (*Eerste Kerstdag*)
26 December	Christmas Holiday (*Tweede Kerstdag*)

Retirement

No fewer than 10,000 UK citizens retire from work every week. Many may dream of a cottage by the sea or a villa in Spain, but unless they have some prior link few will contemplate moving to The Netherlands. Nevertheless should you consider The Netherlands for your retirement you will find the country has a lot to offer. One attraction is that the Dutch possess a high proficiency in the English language, although people should consider a commitment to learn Dutch necessary in the long run. The standard of living in The Netherlands is high, but so is the cost and it would be prudent to work out whether your budget would cover this. The health provision and public transport networks are excellent. The Dutch themselves make very good friends and there are also several well-established communities of working and retired Britons in and around The Hague and Amsterdam, so you won't be short of company. If you are fascinated by Dutch culture, The Netherlands has hundreds of museums and art galleries.

The Decision to Leave

Despite its many attractions, The Netherlands will never be quite like Britain so anyone contemplating a move must have a clear idea of what they are letting themselves in for. A successful relocation will require not just enthusiasm but a certain degree of adaptability. It is unlikely that anyone would decide to uproot and move to a country that they had never seen before. The majority of people who decide to settle in The Netherlands will probably have experience of the country from working there. However, living permanently in a land is not the same as either a short term stay or a holiday; especially on a pensioner's budget. It is advisable to consider living for a trial period, including a winter, in the area in which you wish to settle before making a commitment to stay permanently.

Residence Requirements

A statement from the Royal Netherlands Embassy in London declares that the Dutch authorities do not encourage additions to an already dense population and costly social services system. Since 1 January 1992 pensioners from EC Member States have been free to live wherever they wish in the European Community, providing they have adequate means of financial support. Anyone who intends to retire to The Netherlands will have to obtain a residence permit (*verblijfsvergunning* — see Chapter Two, *Residence and Entry*. The application will have to provide pension details, prove adequate health insurance and supply proof that individuals can support themselves. The residence permit entitles the holder to live and work in The Netherlands and will need to be renewed every five years. The most important criterion for being allowed to stay in The Netherlands is likely to be money. If you cannot show you have sufficient funds to support your stay, the Dutch authorities can ask you to leave.

Choosing and Buying a Retirement Home

The obvious point to remember about selecting a retirement property in The Netherlands is to choose something which is within one's financial scope. The majority of people will need to draw up a financial assessment based on their experience of the country to see if they can afford the expense involved in both moving abroad and the running and upkeep of a Dutch property. Also, anyone reliant on public transport (which in The Netherlands is pretty good) will need to bear in mind the proximity of shops, friends and health care amenities. Once you have decided on your new home you will need to follow all the procedures regarding the purchase of a property which are outlined in Chapter Three, *Setting up Home*.

Hobbies and Interests

Once you have settled into your new home, your thoughts will undoubtedly turn to socializing and the pursuit of interests you never quite had time for in the past. The Netherlands boasts many opportunities in this department. Gardening is a very popular pastime, but gardeners used to the inclement British weather will find a similar hardiness required. For lovers of art and history the Dutch have spent a lot of time and energy saving and displaying their rich heritage. There are no fewer than 350 museums to help you while away the time.

For those looking for a more active retirement cycling is a national pastime and cyclists have the use of several thousand miles of cycle tracks. The Dutch are also keen anglers and there is plenty of opportunity for both sea and coarse fishing throughout the country. For the dedicated walker The Netherlands may prove a disappointment as the country has very few hills. It also has the lowest percentage of woodland in the EC. But for gentle rambling both the coastline and acres of famous Dutch flower fields are areas well worth exploring. If all that sounds a little too strenuous what could be more relaxing than guiding a barge along the extensive Dutch canal network. There are also plenty of spectator events on offer, from football to fierljeppen.

Unemployment in The Netherlands is relatively high (4.4%) and the opportunities for obtaining work are correspondingly low. However, there is considerable scope for doing voluntary work, for which both expatriate clubs and the British Embassy can be useful sources of information.

Entertainment

The BBC World Service is without doubt in a class of its own and is an easy way of keeping in touch with home. Programmes and frequency charts can be obtained from London Calling, PO Box 76, Bush House, London WC2 4PH. Should you prefer to watch rather than listen the advent of satellite and cable TV means that BBC1 and BBC2 can be easily (and relatively cheaply) received in The Netherlands. The Dutch have an active theatre and music scene which provides something for everyone — see Chapter Four, *Daily Life*.

English-Language Clubs

Being resident in a country where both the language and the people are unfamiliar

198 Living in The Netherlands

can make the company of fellow expatriates very alluring. The Netherlands has a wealth of English-speaking, expatriate social and activity clubs. Whether you want to cultivate a dormant artistic ability or simply share a pot of tea and a gossip with fellow Brits the following list should provide a good starting point. (A more comprehensive list is provided by the British Embassy in The Hague.)

Amsterdam
British Society of Amsterdam: PO Box 7429, 1007 JK Amsterdam; tel 020-6479290.

English Speaking Ladies Club: Vrouwentrefcentrum, Hugo de Grootlaan 1, Uithoorn; tel 020-6475129.

International Women's Contact: Sonesta Hotel, Kattengracht 1, 1012 SZ Amsterdam; tel 02159-48116.

Royal British Legion: (Amsterdam Branch) Building 106 (1st floor), 1117 AA Schiphol-East; tel 020-6167971.

Breda
International Women's Club: Cafe Brauwers, Ginnekenmarkt, Breda; tel 076-100723.

Dordrecht
English Language Bond of Women (ELBOW): Community Centre De Keet, Dalymeyerplein, Dordrecht; tel 078-183681.

Den Haag
American Baseball Foundation: ABF Grounds & Clubhouse, Deylerweg 155, 2240 AC Wassenaar, c/o PO Box 133, Deylerweg 155, 2240 AC Wassenaar; tel 070-3470024.

American Women's Club: Nieuwe Duinweg 25, 2587 AB Den Haag; tel 070-3544171.

British Women's Club: Clubhouse de Societeit de Witte, Plein 24, 2511 CS Den Haag; tel 070-3461973 (10.30am to 2.30pm Tues, Wed and Fri).

The Decorative and Fine Art Society of the Hague (DFAS): Prinsenweg 97, 2242 ED Wassenaar; tel 01751-12283.

English Speaking Club: Scholeksterstraat 3, 2352 ED Leiderdorp; tel 071-418730.

International Art Club: Cultureel Centrum, Centrum Muzenhof Cor Gordijnsingel 4, Leiderdorp; tel 070-368 6743.

International Women's Contact: Congresgebouw, c/o PO Box 84404, 2508 AK Den Haag; tel 070-3558863.

Netherlands England Society: Gemeente Museum, c/o Gr. Hertoginnelaan 225, 2517 ET Den Haag; tel 070-3616891. (For details of branches throughout The Netherlands contact Van Meerkerkestraat 5, 2596 TN Den Haag; tel 070-3243272.

Netherlands International Yacht Club: Weteringpad by 28a, Woubrugge; tel 01729-8437 or 070-3470368.

St Andrew's Society of the Netherlands: Warenar Cultureel Centrum, Kerkstraat, Wassenaar; tel 071-173599 or 070-3776592.

Leiden
Leiden English Speaking Theatre Group (Lest): Postbus 85, 2300 AB Leiden.

Nijmegen
Foreign Exchange: Kraayenburg 94-15, 6601 PE Wijchen; tel 08894-11335.

Rotterdam
Pickwick Club of Rotterdam: Central Hotel, Kruiskade, Rotterdam; tel 010-4519498.

Utrecht
British Women's Club: British Anglican Church, Hoogendoorn Straat, Utrecht;
tel 03407-4924.

Pensions

If you became entitled to a state pension before leaving the UK there is no reason why it cannot be paid to you in The Netherlands. The important point to remember is that a UK pension will always be pegged at UK levels. This did at one time pose a problem for expatriates as the exchange rate between sterling and the guilder could effect the amount of money they received. Now that the UK has joined the European Monetary System (EMS) the chances of a severe devaluation have been reduced.

People who move to The Netherlands before reaching retirement age can continue paying national insurance contributions in the UK, in order to qualify for a British state pension, or pay into the Dutch social security to qualify for a combined pension. To claim a solely British state pension after retiring one must apply to the Overseas Branch of the DSS (The Overseas Branch, Venton Park, Newcastle-upon-Tyne, NE98 1YX; tel 091-213 5000) and ensure that your pension is delivered to a designated bank account each month. The normal procedure to claim a combined pension is for the British and Dutch authorities to exchange social security records and calculate the amount of pension payable by each country. Further details are given in the DSS leaflet SA29 — *Your Social Security, Health Care and Pension Rights in the European Community.*

Dutch pension payments are equal to 70% (for single people) and 50% (for married couples) of the minimum gross salary, multiplied by the number of years worked. The monthly gross pension payment currently stands at Dfl 1,346.90 (£417) for a single person and Dfl 938.11 (£290) each for a married couple.

Taxation

The DSS will not deduct tax from your UK state pension provided that you can prove you are resident in The Netherlands. In such a case payments must be transferred into a Dutch bank account and will be subsequently liable for Dutch income tax. A more complex situation arises if one spends time in both the UK and The Netherlands and for this it is essential to get professional advice. In particular you cannot completely escape UK taxes if you spend more than 183 days in Britain in the first year of obtaining residence abroad. People who intend to maintain connections with the UK must get professional taxation advice. Investments already established in the UK do not need to be altered and in most cases interest will be paid on deposits without any deduction of tax where one is non-resident. The Dutch tax year runs from January to December, whereas the UK tax year runs from April to March. The date of moving could affect one's tax liability.

The question of inheritance tax revolves around the fact of whether the deceased was domiciled in The Netherlands or the UK. If you apply for Dutch citizenship, do not vote in UK elections and have no property in Britain you have a good chance of escaping British death duties. However, the deceased's estate will then be liable for inheritance tax to the Dutch tax authorities. Wherever you end up paying death duties it will include worldwide assets. The heirs are required to file an inheritance tax return within five months of death and pay the tax within two months of the assessment. Taxes are levied on a sliding scale up to maximum rate for estates exceeding Dfl 1,332,407 (£412,510). The maximum rate paid by a spouse and children is 27%; for brothers and sisters it is 53% and; for distant relatives or unrelated persons it rises to 68%. A tax-free allowance is permitted to spouses on their first Dfl 466,342 (£144,380); children are exempt on up to Dfl 13,324 (£4,134) plus Dfl 6,662 for each year he or she is younger than 23. Parents are exempt on amounts up to Dfl 66,620.

Useful Addresses

Inland Revenue: Citygate House, 39-45 Finsbury Park, London EC2A 1HH; tel 071-588 4226.

Rijksbelastingen: (Tax Authority) Stationplein 75, 2515 BX the Hague; tel 070-3304000.

Offshore Banking

Anyone considering retiring to the Netherlands should take specialist financial and legal advice regarding their pecuniary situation. The majority of people even considering moving overseas have some capital to invest, or will have after selling their UK property. But it is worth remembering that any nest egg must last you the rest of your life so resist the temptation to splash out on the first opportunity that comes your way. For a retired British citizen not resident in the UK one tax-free investment opportunity would be offshore banking. A number of high street banks, building societies and merchant banks offer attractive, long-term (for more than 90 days) accounts through tax havens such as Gibraltar and the Channel Islands. The minimum amount of money required to open a deposit account ranges from £500 to £10,000. The interest rate is proportional to the inaccessibility of one's money. Interest can be paid monthly or annually and although the investor will receive much the same amount of gross interest either way, the monthly payments which bring with them a steady flow of income are more popular with retired account holders.

Useful Address

Nationwide Overseas Ltd: PO Box 217, Market Street, Douglas, Isle of Man; tel 0624-606095, fax 0624-663495.

Health

One of the drawbacks of retiring in The Netherlands is that there is no free National Health Service. Dutch hospitals and doctors provide excellent health care, but to receive medical treatment in The Netherlands you must have adequate health insurance. Unless you have paid into the Dutch Sickness Fund (*Ziekenfonds*) this will have to take the form of a private policy. It will be necessary to prove you have medical insurance not only to receive treatment but also to be issued with a residence permit.

Wills

Making a will can seem only one step removed from arranging one's own funeral. However, should you die intestate — without having made a will — in a foreign country the question of inheritance can become extremely complicated. Assets in the UK and The Netherlands (and elsewhere) will be treated differently. This will mean a minefield of inheritance laws for relatives to negotiate and the legal costs will almost certainly mount up. If you have not made a will then take the advice of a UK solicitor with experience of both the UK and Dutch legal systems.

If a UK will has already been made it may be necessary for it be to be reviewed. In The Netherlands a will must be drawn up by a notary public (*notaris*). A new will automatically renders all previous wills void under international law. However, a new will can still incorporate parts of the previous will if you wish. If you have assets in both countries it is necessary to draw up a will for both countries.

Death

Dying abroad can complicate matters in that one's relatives are not always on the spot to deal with the necessary formalities. It is therefore advisable to make your funeral wishes known in advance and preferably written down in a will. It is very expensive to have one's body shipped home for burial, so it might be worth considering making arrangements in The Netherlands itself. A death must be certified by a doctor and registered within 24 hours at the town hall (*gemeentehuis*) of the municipal council, with a valid death certificate and identity papers. The British Embassy can help with the arrangements.

SECTION II

Working in
The Netherlands

Employment
Business and Industry Report
Temporary Work
Starting a Business

Employment

The Employment Scene

Following an export-led period of growth and investment in the mid-80s the Dutch economy is almost certainly robust enough to emerge from the worldwide recession of the 90s in as good a shape as that of any other EC country. Revenue from natural gas production and positive government policies have shifted the emphasis away from defensive industrial practices. This has led to a spurt of modernization which has laid the foundations for future growth. The expansion and relative prosperity of the economy has produced a higher national income and virtually zero inflation, and has enabled the government to reduce the tax burden on businesses. Good labour relations have also played their part with employers and unions adhering to a policy of wage restraint. Unemployment fell gradually from 17% of the total workforce in 1983 to 4.4% in May 1992. However, it is expected to rise again and is still a cause for concern to the Dutch authorities. This concern is spelled out in a circular from the Royal Netherlands Embassy that stresses 'due to the high unemployment level jobs are not easily available'.

The number of people employed in agriculture and the manufacturing industry is in decline, while the demand for workers in the service industries (administration, tourism and catering) has steadily increased. Presently, 69% of the Dutch workforce is employed in the service sector, 26% in manufacturing and 4% in agriculture. In 1990 a nationwide survey revealed that 10% of the working population aged 18 years or older did shift work, 25% complained of high noise levels at work and 8% felt their working conditions were potentially dangerous. However, two-thirds of the workforce felt they had an opportunity to develop their skills in their job, 74% considered their job secure, 63% were content with the wage they received and one-third were satisfied with their promotion prospects. Almost 80% of the working Dutch population said that they enjoyed their work.

The overall prospects for the Dutch economy are bright. It is modern, efficient and leads the world in many areas of agricultural and technological development. There is no limit on the number of foreigners employed by or working in Dutch industry. Whether you intend to be an employee or an employer the Dutch economy looks certain to offer a wealth of opportunity.

Residence and Work Regulations

European Community regulations allow for the free movement of labour within the EC, and UK citizens do not require a work permit to work in The Netherlands. British nationals looking for employment can enter The Netherlands on a valid passport, but must apply for a residence permit (*verblijfsvergunning*) within eight days of arrival if they intend to stay and work for more than three months. The application must include a letter from your prospective employer stating the terms of the contract, salary level and proof that the company will pay your health insurance contributions. Further information on entry regulations to The Netherlands is given in Chapter Two, *Residence and Entry Regulations*.

Skills and Qualifications

Ninety-two professions have mutual recognition of qualifications between EC

Member States. This means that anyone who wishes to live and work in The Netherlands and whose profession is included in the 92 listed, is eligible to join counterpart Dutch professional associations and to continue in their line of work without having to take any kind of test or re-qualification training programme. The recognized professions include doctors, veterinarians, lawyers, nurses and architects. It is possible to get up-to-date information on the comparability of qualifications from the European Division of the Department of Trade and Industry (Ashdown House, 6th Floor, 123 Victoria Street, London, SW1E 6RB; tel 071-213 5354). In addition, the DTI publishes the booklet 'Europe Open for Professions'. You can also get direct comparison between UK qualifications and those recognized in The Netherlands from the Dutch branch of the National Academic Recognition Information Centre (NARIC). Call in at any Dutch job centre (*arbeidsbureau*) and ask them to contact NARIC on your behalf. Alternatively, your own professional association should be able to provide this and other useful information on transferring your skills to The Netherlands. A number of vocational qualifications in many areas including hotel and catering, construction and agriculture are also acceptable in The Netherlands. A fact sheet to aid comparability of skills is available from the Comparability Co-ordinator, Employment Department (Qualifications and Standards Branch — QS1, Room E454, Moorfoot, Sheffield, S1 4PQ; tel 0742-594144) or COLO (Centraal Orgaan Van de Landelijke Opleidingsorganen, AG Zoetermeer; tel 079-425699).

The DTI will issue individuals with a Certificate of Experience which guarantees that your qualifications are valid in other EC States. It is necessary to complete the application form EC2 and provide certificates and two references to prove your experience and training. An application costs £45, and a £10 charge is levied for any subsequent revisions. It is useful to remember that whatever line of work you are in, individuals looking for work in The Netherlands would be well advised to have their qualifications translated into Dutch. It is also important to note that in professions which involve dealing with the general public a knowledge of the Dutch language will almost certainly be necessary.

Sources of Jobs

Newspapers

UK Newspapers and Directories

Although an increasing number of overseas jobs are being advertised in the UK press it is unlikely that many people will find a job in The Netherlands this way. Where Dutch jobs are advertised it is likely that being UK-based is a requirement for employment. An exception to this is *Overseas Jobs Express* (available by subscription only from PO Box 22, Brighton BN1 6HX) which has a substantial *Jobs* section, as well as articles written by working travellers. Alternatively, a wide range of casual jobs, including secretarial, agricultural, tourism and domestic work, are advertised in the directory *Summer Jobs Abroad*, while *Teaching English Abroad* lists a number of schools that employ English-language teachers each year; both publications are available from Vacation Work Publications (9 Park End Street, Oxford OX1 1HJ; tel 0865-241978, fax 0865-790885).

International and European Newspapers

The concept of international newspapers is still relatively new in the publishing world. Publications such as the *European* and *The International Herald Tribune* circulate editions across several national boundaries and usually carry a number of job adverts.

Useful Addresses

The European: Orbit House, 5 New Fetter Lane, London EC4 1AP; tel 071-822 2002.

International Herald Tribune: 63 Long Acre Street, London WC2E 9JH; tel 071-836 4802.

Wall Street Journal: The International Press Centre, 76 Shoe Lane, London EC4; tel 071-334 0008.

Advertising in Newspapers

Those wishing to place advertisements in several daily Dutch newspapers, including *Algemeen Dagblad* and *NRC Handelsblad*, can contact Powers Overseas Ltd (46 Keyes Place, Dolphin Square, London SW1V 3NA; tel 071-834 5566). Adverts in *De Telegraaf*, the largest circulation newspaper in The Netherlands, can be placed through Publicitas Ltd (517-523 Fulham Road, London SW6 1HD; tel 071-385 7723, fax 071-381 8884). It is possible to advertise your skills in other publications. For a list of Dutch newspapers see Chapter Four, *Daily Life*.

Professional Associations

Many professional organizations do not officially provide information on working overseas. However, the majority will have had contact with counterpart associations in other European Community states, often during negotiations involving the reciprocal recognition of qualifications required by EC directives. Such associations, when pushed, should provide some individual help. Details of all professional bodies can be found in the directory, *Trade Associations and Professional Bodies in the UK*, available at most reference libraries. A list of the addresses of a number of the more mainstream professional organizations is given below.

Useful Addresses

Biochemical Society: 7 Warwick Court, Holborn, London WC1R 5DP.
British Computer Society: 13 Mansfield Street, London W1M 0BQ.
British Medical Association: BMA House, Tavistock Square, London WC1H 9JP.
Chartered Institute of Bankers: 10 Lombard Street, London EC3Y 9AS.
Chartered Institute of Building: Englemere Kings Ride, Ascot, Berks SL5 8BJ.
General Dental Council: 37 Wimpole Street, London W1M 8DQ.
Institute of Actuaries: Napier House, 4 Worcester Street, Gloucester Green, Oxford OX1 2AW.
Institute of Chartered Accountants: Chartered Accountants' Hall, Moorgate Place, London EC2P 2BJ.
Institute of Chartered Secretaries and Administrators: 16 Park Crescent, London W1N 4AH.
Institute of Civil Engineers: 1-7 Great George Street, London SW1P 3AA.
Library Association: 7 Ridgmount Street, London WC1E 7AE.
Royal College of Nursing: Henrietta Place, 20 Cavendish Square, London W1M 0AB.
Royal College of Veterinary Surgeons: 32 Belgrave Square, London SW1X 8QP.
Royal Institute of British Architects: 66 Portland Place, London W1N 4AD.

Professional Journals and Magazines

Many UK-based professional journals and magazines are considered world authorities in their field and can be a useful source of job adverts for The Netherlands. A comprehensive list of trade publications is published in media directories, such as *Benn's Media*, which are available from major reference libraries. For example *Farmers Weekly* and *Caterer and Hotel Keeper* carry positions in agriculture and the catering trade respectively.

Employment Organizations

One of the most useful and plentiful sources of temporary work is through private employment agencies (*uitzendbureaux*). These will be listed in the telephone book (*Gouden Gids*). They proliferate in large towns — there are more than 125 in Amsterdam alone — and among the largest are Randstad, Unique, BBB, ASB and Manpower. The Federation of Recruitment and Employment Services Limited (36-38 Mortimer Street, London, W1N 7RB; tel 071-323 4300) can provide the names and addresses of licensed UK employment agencies that offer work in The Netherlands. The *CEPEC Recruitment Guide* (available from CEPEC, 67 Jermyn Street, London SW1Y 6YN; tel 071-930 0322) is a useful guide to help you research the job market and it lists more than 550 UK recruitment agencies and search consultants.

The Dutch government operates the Centraal Bureau voor de Arbeidsvoorziening (Central Bureau for the Supply of Labour) which coordinates short-term summer jobs. A similar service is also offered by the UK-based Employment Service Overseas Placing Unit. Both accept applications for a number of summer vacancies in The Netherlands, but stress that individuals must not travel to The Netherlands prior to confirmation of a job placement.

Useful Addresses

Centraal Bureau voor de Arbeidsvoorziening: PO Box 437, 2280 AK Rijswijk, The Netherlands: tel 070-3130228.
Employment Service Overseas Placing Unit: Steel City House, c/o Moorfoot, Sheffield, S1 4PQ; tel 0742-596051/2, fax 0742-596040.
La Grouw Recruitment: World Trade Center, Strawinskylaan 601, 1077 XX Amsterdam, tel 020-6761666, fax 020-6732346.
ASB: Voorburgwal 146, 1012 SJ Amsterdam; tel 020-226666.
ASA: (students only) Singel 432, Amsterdam; tel 020-228444.
Management & Technical Recruitment Ltd: Suite D'Arcy Business Centre, Llandarcy, Neath, West Glamorgan SA10 6EJ; tel 0792-321202, fax 0792 321295.

SEDOC

SEDOC (Système Européen de Diffusion des Demandes d'Emploi Enregistrées en Compensation Internationale) is a network which exchanges employment information between EC member countries. Most UK employment services (job centres) should have access via a computer link to vacancy details held at the British branch of SEDOC (located at the Overseas Placing Unit, Department of Employment, Sheffield) and can supply details of any relevant opportunities. Unfortunately SEDOC is a little-used system which falls far short of its intended function. It is to be updated and renamed in 1993, and eventually incorporated into a pan-EC jobs data base that can be accessed from any EC country.

Job Centres

Dutch job centres (*gewestelijk arbeidsbureaux*), can be found in every major city and town. They offer job placement services, advice on employment in The Netherlands and help to prospective entrepreneurs. Under EC law these centres are obliged to assist foreigners, but do not expect them to bend over backwards to help. A full list of the addresses of *gewestelijk arbeidsbureaux* is available from the Centraal Bureau voor de Arbeidsvoorziening. The *gewestelijk arbeidsbureaux* in the major cities are located as follows:

Amsterdam: Singel 202, 1016 AA Amsterdam; tel 020-5200911.
Arnhem: Rodenburgstraat 25, 6811 HN Arnhem; tel 085-578111.
Eindhoven: Begynenhof 8, 5611 EL Eindhoven; tel 040-325325.
Groningen: Engelse Kamp 4, 9722 AX Groningen; tel 050-225911.
Haarlem: Jansweg 15, 2011 KL Haarlem; tel 023-156300.
The Hague: Troelstrakade 65, 2531 AA Den Haag; tel 070-3849511.
Leeuwarden: Tesselschadestraat 35, 8913 HA Leeuwarden; tel 058-977777.
Maastricht: Het Bat 12a, 6211 EX Maastricht; tel 043-211541.
Rotterdam: Schiedamse Vest 160, 3011 BH Rotterdam; tel 010-4039393.
Utrecht: W Dreeslaan 113, 3515 GB Utrecht; tel 030-737911.

The Application Procedure

If you decide the best way to sound out the Dutch job scene is to flood potential employers with speculative enquiries, make sure your enquiries are concise and polite. The Dutch are almost certain to reply to a letter and even if the answer is 'no' a polite enquiry may at least result in a word or two of advice so your effort may not be entirely wasted. Also, the Dutch do not have much time for trivialities; a creative flood of one's personal history will not be greeted appreciatively, so keep letters concise and to the point. It is advisable to send a c.v., whether the letter is speculative or in response to an advertised vacancy. An enquiry written in English will be understood, but if you feel it would be more effective in Dutch then the Institute of Translation and Interpreting (318A Finchley Road, London NW1; tel 071-794 9931) offers a freelance translation service for a fee of approximately £70 per thousand words. The list *Directory of Employers* at the end of this chapter is a good source from which to base a speculative job hunt.

Dutch business people are less formal than their UK counterparts, so at an interview dress should be smart, but of a casual rather than formal nature. It is polite to shake hands both on arrival and departure. As with job hunting in any country it is best to find out as much background as possible about the company to which you have applied. An interest based on facts and knowledge is likely to impress a potential Dutch employer. The *CEPEC Recruitment Guide* gives useful hints to help you research the job market, write letters and c.v.s, and negotiate interviews.

Types of Work

UK citizens are allowed to undertake both long- and short-term employment. In The Netherlands any work that lasts less than six months is considered temporary employment. Many short-term jobs are available because the Dutch do not want to do them; therefore, in manual jobs especially, expect poor pay and conditions. The minimum wage is about £150 a week (for over 23s) and employers are obliged to pay holiday pay which can prove a welcome bonus at the end of a contract. Under Dutch employment laws temporary work contracts must have an instant termination clause available to both parties. The Central Bureau for Educational Visits and Exchanges (Seymour Mews House, Seymour Mews, London W1H 9PE) publishes the book 'Working Holidays' and can provide a list of work camps in The Netherlands.

Teaching English

The Dutch population has a very high level of competence in the English language. Educated Dutch people are so fluent that the Minister of Education recently suggested that English should become the main language used in Dutch universities. There was an understandable outcry, but the implication for prospective English teachers is clear — this is not a country in which any old BA (Hons) degree enables you to step into a TEFL job! It is almost impossible to secure employment with a private language school without teaching qualifications and experience. Schools also tend to provide business English courses and will be looking for teachers with extensive commercial or government experience. The British Council in The Netherlands (Keizersgracht 343, 1016 EH Amsterdam; tel 020-6223644) can provide information on schools and work prospects in Amsterdam.

Language Schools

The Hague
The Hague Language Centre: PO Box 313, 2501 CH The Hague; tel 070-365 49 36.

Amsterdam
Amsterdam VNS Opleidingen: Willemsparkweg 191, 1071 HA Amsterdam; tel 020-6764220.*Berlitz:* Rokin 87-89 IV, 1012 KL Amsterdam; tel 020-221375/221376.
Bakker: Botticellistraat 38 II, 1077 GC Amsterdam; tel 020-6751664/6123456.
S.E.Belden: Bellamyplein 26, 1053 AT Amsterdam; tel 020-6162858.
Bressler's Business Language: Buiksloterdijk 284, 1034 ZD Amsterdam; tel 020-6334038.
Dinkgreve Handelsopleiding: Willemsparkweg 31, 1071 GP Amsterdam; tel 020-6761176.
Engels Taalinstituut: Prins Hendrikkade 136, 1011 AR Amsterdam; tel 020-6231302.
Feedback Taleninstituut BV: Koninginneweg 170, 1011 TC Amsterdam; tel 020-6716709.
International Language Consultants: PC Hooftstraat 57 II, 1071 BN Amsterdam; tel 020-6710051.
International Studiecentrum: Concertgebouwplein 17, 1071 LM Amsterdam; tel 020-6761437.
Koninklijk Instituut: Mauritskade 63, 1092 AD Amsterdam; tel 020-5688478.
Language Solution: Mrs S.Smit, Corellistraat 11, 1077 KP Amsterdam; tel 6574698.
NIBO: Hettenheuvelweg 16, 1101 BN Amsterdam; tel 020-5677777.
Pace Language Institute: Dale McCoy, J v Wassenaar Obdamstr 13, 1057 JP Amsterdam; tel 6167445.
Polytaal Nederland: E.J.B.Boermans, Mermedeplein 16, 1078 ND Amsterdam; tel 020-6648465.
St 't Leerpunt Amsterdam-Noord: Loenermark 243, 1025 SX Amsterdam; tel 020-6329262.

Studiecentrum ASR: Stadhouderskade 113, 1073 AX Amsterdam; tel 020-6760013.
F.C.Verhaaf: P. de Hooghstraat 96, 1071 EK Amsterdam; tel 020-6620192.
Vidilingua: 2e Nassaustraat 1b, 1052 BJ Amsterdam; tel 020-6824968.

Au Pair Work

It was not until 1986 that the Dutch employment laws officially recognized the au pair arrangement. The business is now above board and au pairs in The Netherlands enjoy good working conditions and a comparatively high rate of pocket money. Unfortunately, because the system has been up and running only for a few years, the demand for au pairs is still relatively small. Furthermore, day care provision for children with working parents is excellent and preferred by many Dutch parents to live-in childcarers. However, there is a demand for au pairs especially from families in Amsterdam, Rotterdam, The Hague and Utrecht. Positions are open to women and men aged between 18 and 30, and applicants must be able to commit themselves for at least six months. A standard contract stipulates that time must be given for the au pair to attend a Dutch language course (although a knowledge of Dutch is not necessary, except in more rural areas) and health insurance contributions must be paid by the host family. EC nationals do not require a visa, but will be required to sign an undertaking that they will leave the country within one year when registering with the local police (see Chapter Two, *Entry and Residence Regulations*). The application must include a hand-written letter of invitation from the host family setting out the au pair's rights and obligations, an undertaking to take out full health insurance and that the applicant has no criminal record.

A small number of agencies in The Netherlands deal with au pair placements. The Association of Dutch Au Pair Agencies will provide information on placements. A number of agencies in the UK and Europe also send a limited number of au pairs to The Netherlands.

Useful Addresses

Association of Dutch Au Pair Agencies: Mrs J. Hendriksen, c/o the association, Groningen; tel 050-422949.
Au Pair International: Bieslookstraat 31, 9731 HH Groningen; tel 050-422949.
Choice International: Millfield House, 904 Warwick Road, Acock's Green, Birmingham B27 6QG, tel 021-706 5963.
Exis (Au Pairs for Europe): (Postbus 15344, 1001 MH Amsterdam; tel 020-6262664) publishes a guide to being an au pair in The Netherlands.
Paragon Now Ltd: PO Box 1, Sutton Scotney, Winchester, Hampshire SO21 3JG.
Scattergoods Catering & Childcare Agency: Thursley House, 53 Station Road, Shalford, Guildford GU14 8HA.
Students Abroad: Elm House, 21b The Avenue, Hatch End, Middlesex, HA5 4EN.
Universal Care Ltd: Chester House, 9 Windsor End, Beaconsfield, Bucks HP9 2JJ.

Seasonal Work

Farming: Despite an increase in the area of land under cultivation mechanization in the agricultural industry has led to a fall in the number of people working on the land in the last two decades. A limited number of short-term placements (three months to one year) are available through the International Farm Experience Programme (YFC Centre, National Agricultural Centre, Kenilworth, Warwickshire CV8 2LG; tel 0203-696584). Applicants to the scheme must have at least two years training or practical experience in agriculture or horticulture. The NVEL (Dutch Union for Ecological Agriculture — Willemsvaart 304, 8019 AA Zwolle; tel 038-219855) may be able to help with information and contacts. Stichting de Kleine Aarde (Marta Resink 9, Het Klaverblad 1, Postbus 151, 5280 AD Boxtel; tel 04116-84921) is an environmental education and information centre. It has an intensive ecological garden and greenhouse and offers the opportunity to work in organic agriculture. The minimum stay is two months.

Bulb Picking: The agricultural industry does provide a wealth of jobs in the bulb fields (from April to October) which traditionally go to foreign workers. The Dutch tourist office (25-28 Buckingham Gate, London SW1E 6LD; tel 071-630 0451) produces a free map of The Netherlands showing the bulb growing areas. The centre for bulb picking has shifted from Hillegom to Noordwijk. Essential pieces of equipment are a tent and a bicycle, the latter to tour around the factories. Conditions can be poor, especially in the smaller businesses but food, accommodation and even beer are often provided free. Two recommended factories are M van Waveren (P.O.B. 10, 2180 AA Hilegom; tel 02520-16141) and Baartman & Koning (P.O.B. 27, AA Sassenheim; tel 02522-11141).

Tomato Picking: An alternative to bulbs is tomatoes. The trade is concentrated in Westland, near the villages of Naaldwijk, Westerlee, De Lier and Maasdijk. The season begins in mid-April and the hours are long — 5a.m. to 7p.m.

Tourism: The Netherlands attracts more than five million visitors every year and as a result the tourist industry employs large numbers of extra workers during the summer months. The best areas for finding work are Amsterdam and the coastal resorts of Scheveningen, Kijkduin (both near The Hague) and Zandvoort.

Secretarial Work

The opportunities for bilingual secretaries in The Netherlands are not overwhelming. The first obstacle is the ability of Dutch employees to speak English and secondly many positions are filled by qualified expatriates already present in The Netherlands. However, good secretaries are always in demand, especially by the business communities of The Hague, Rotterdam and Amsterdam. The Hague is also the seat of the Dutch Parliament and the International Court of Justice.

Useful Address

La Grouw Recruitment: World Trade Centre, Strawinskylaan 601, 1077 XX Amsterdam; tel 020-6761666, fax 020-6732346.

Medicine and Nursing

The Geneeskundige Vereniging tot Bevordering van het Ziekenhuiswezen (Postbus 9696, 3506 GR Utrecht) provides information on vacancies in Dutch hospitals. BNA International (3rd Floor, 443 Oxford Street, London W1R 2NA) recruits nurses for hospitals in The Netherlands. Contracts are for six months, with the possibility of a permanent post. RGNs and ENs must be qualified in either operating theatre or intensive care unit nursing; radiographers must have at least one year's experience. On obtaining an appointment it is necessary to apply to the Ministry of Welfare, Health and Culture (Public health section, Dr. Reijersstraat 10, Leidschendam) for a licence to work.

Voluntary Work

The majority of voluntary work available to British citizens in The Netherlands is co-ordinated through UK organizations. However, if you are already in the country you can make enquiries to SIW, Internationale Vrijwilligersprojekten (Willemstraat 7, Utrecht; tel 030-317721) or ICVD (Postbus 25, 1054 RH Amsterdam; tel 020-892735). The Head office of Universala Esperanto-Asocio, the organization for the enhancement of Esperanto, is located in Rotterdam (Nieuwe Binneweg 176, 3015 BJ Rotterdam; tel 010-4361539). A number of volunteers are required for six to 12 month periods. The main requirement is that applicants are fluent in Esperanto.

Aspects of Employment

Salaries

The average real earnings in The Netherlands grew by 5% in the late 80s putting the Dutch in seventh place in the EC in this respect. However, a survey in 1990 revealed that one-third of the Dutch workforce were unhappy with the wage they received. There is a legal minimum wage for all workers aged 23-65 and since 1 July 1989, this minimum has been set at Dfl 1,987.70 (£615) per month. After deductions this leaves a net monthly income of about Dfl 1,600. All wage contracts are reviewed at six-monthly intervals, and adjusted in accordance with the cost of living index. In recent years one-year collective labour agreements have tended to cover wage levels. Nevertheless, the Minister of Social Affairs is empowered to disallow agreements that are deemed contrary to the national interest and freeze wages if necessary.

The average monthly salaries for experienced and professional staff in The Netherlands are competitive with any other country in the European Community. For example administrative staff receive Dfl 4,200 (£1,300), engineers and accountants receive Dfl 7,000 (£2,167), and general managers Dfl 13,500 (£4,179). In general, men have higher incomes than women. This is partly explained by the authorities as being due to more women having part-time jobs which on average pay less than full-time employment.

A number of fringe benefits are used by Dutch firms to attract and retain staff. These include subsidized canteens and social clubs, a company car, and a supplementary payment (30% of wages) during sickness — the Sickness Insurance Act (*Ziekenfonds*) already covers 70%. A number of employers also pay a 13th month bonus at Christmas. A holiday allowance of 7.5% of annual salary is mandatory for monthly salaries of up to Dfl 5,960.

Working Conditions

According to official European Community statistics in 1991 the average working week in The Netherlands was 33.2 hours, the lowest in the EC. However, this is an overall figure (i.e. including part-time jobs). The actual figure for full-time employees is estimated by the Dutch authorities to be closer to 39 hours per week. Maximum working hours are restricted by law to eight and a half hours per day or 48 hours per week. Employers must obtain permits for overtime from the Labour Inspection Board and overtime is restricted for employees under the age of 18. The minimum holiday entitlement is 20 working days, although the more usual figure is 23 days, during which salary is fully paid. The working day commonly starts at 8am, and official business hours are 8.30am to 5pm.

Etiquette in the Workplace

Anyone working in The Netherlands for the first time will find a whole new set of business rules awaits them. The Dutch dislike pretentiousness and wasting time. Meetings rarely last longer than 45 minutes and as the Dutch do not mix business with pleasure, lunches are never elaborate affairs. In an apparent contradiction of efficient business conduct, the Dutch workplace is seemingly more relaxed than UK counterparts. Employees and employers are usually on first name terms, and dress is smart but casual. When dealing with the Dutch make sure you are punctual and straightforward. The local chamber of commerce will often act as a go-between, but once a name is given, it is quite acceptable to telephone a contact. Appointments should be confirmed in writing, but remember to communicate with the person by name; not to do so is considered rude. If a potential Dutch client agrees to see you it means he or she is interested in what you have to offer. If they invite you to lunch the deal is in the bag! Do not be late for a meeting and always hand out business cards. It is a common British trait to understate one's achievements. The Dutch are not ones to boast, but they will view this as a lack of commitment or take it literally. They are good negotiators, drive a hard bargain and make good business partners. Finally, always try to introduce yourself and say a few pleasantries in Dutch, have some knowledge of the Dutch Royal Family and avoid calling their country Holland, as this in fact refers to just two provinces in The Netherlands.

Trade Unions

Trade union membership is compulsory only in the printing industry, but approximately 40% of the Dutch workforce still belong to a recognized organization. The three main unions are the Federation of Dutch Trade Unions (FNV) — an amalgamation of socialist and Catholic associations, the National Federation of Christian Trade Unions (CNV) and, the Trade Union Federation for Staff and Managerial Personnel (MHP) — an association for executive and middle grade civil servants. A number of organizations also cover agricultural and retail trades. The Joint Industrial Labour Council helps to maintain good relations between employers and employees and acts as an arbitrator in industrial disputes. (The government is required by law to seek the council's advice on issues concerning wages, prices and social policies.) Dutch trade unions are not regarded as militant and do not normally strike to achieve their goals. The number of working days lost through strikes in recent decades has been small.

Women in Work

In recent years Dutch women have become more aware of their role in society and have challenged the traditional gender role pattern. From 1977 to 1986 a state secretary with special responsibility for equal rights was a member of the government. However, when the latest government came to power the position was abolished and the job now rests with the Minister of Employment and Social Security. An Interministerial Coordinating Committee on Women's Rights, on which all ministries are represented, coordinates overall government policy. Virtually all ministries have their own committees to deal with women's rights in relation to their own special fields.

In 1985 the government launched its Equal Rights Policy Plan which stated that 'equal rights for women is a fundamental and irreversible process to which Dutch society has not yet responded'. The objective of the policy was to transform Dutch society into a pluralist state in which men and women have equal rights, opportunities, freedoms and responsibilities. Nearly 40% of the workforce is now female (in 1975 the figure was only 27%). Women cannot be excluded from military service on the grounds of gender and there are approximately 2,500 in the armed services. The government is also considering extending national service to women.

Business and Industry Report

For the first time in nearly a decade Dutch unemployment figures are set to rise, investments in industry are set to fall and economic growth in 1992 is expected to fall to 1%; the lowest since the recession of the early 1980s. The message from the Dutch budget (*miljoenennota*) is that government spending in 1992 will be cut by Dfl 10 billion (£3.1 billion) resulting in a 30,000 rise in the jobless total to 525,000 and a 2.5% drop in corporate investment. The total Dutch national debt will reach approximately Dfl 359 billion (£111 billion) or 72% of the national income in 1992. Such gloomy forecasts for the next economic year do not on the face of it, augur well for the future. However, the ability of the Dutch to ride a storm, their pioneering spirit and the strong underlying foundations of the economy mean the prospects may not be as bleak as for some other EC countries.

The Netherlands has always been a strong advocate of free trade. It started with seafarers in the early seventeenth century and continued with the establishing of the Benelux Customs Union in 1948. Today this treaty is still regarded as one of the most advanced forms of international economic cooperation in the world. Since the Second World War, the Dutch economy has seen almost continuous growth; one of the key factors for this has been the establishment of the European Community. In 1957, one year before the Treaty of Rome, exports to Member States accounted for 41% of foreign trade. This figure has now risen to 73%. The removal of trade barriers produced a competitive market in which economies faced up to the challenges, or suffered the consequences of ignoring them. In the case of The Netherlands, industries rationalized and expanded to meet the new demands and the economy became very buoyant.

Before the first oil crisis of 1973, the Dutch economy flourished. Between 1960 and 1973, GNP rose by an average of 6% per annum, investment in industry increased 7% annually and the average unemployment rate was less than 2%. A second boom period in the mid-80s has been followed by the recession of the late 80s and early 90s which has again slowed the growth of the Dutch economy. However, entrepreneurs continue to invest and modernize, two factors that leave Dutch industry in a very healthy position for recovery. High-technology and service sector industries are expected to continue their fast growth into the mid-90s and will require skilled labour as a result. Dutch multinational companies will also provide good potential for UK job hunters. These include such household names as Unilever, Philips and petro-chemical giants Shell and AKZO. The big names may well promote Dutch interests worldwide, but small businesses are playing an increasingly important role in the Dutch economy. This is especially true in the agricultural and horticultural industries.

The following section provides an alphabetical guide to the most important Dutch industries. The current prosperity, or otherwise, of each sector is assessed with a view to its business and employment potential to the expatriate.

Aerospace

The Dutch aerospace business is dominated by Fokker. The former German company now flies the Dutch flag and is ranked fifth among the West's airliner manufacturers. Fokker employs more than 10,000 staff throughout The Netherlands and produces one plane every eight days. It has concentrated on the short-to-medium-haul airliners market and is regarded as a world leader in the small jet business. Air travel is continuing to expand faster than any other form of transport and Fokker's policy towards the future will mean a steady flow of jobs for aircraft designers, engineers and aviation experts. Fokker is also at the forefront of developing satellite and spacecraft technology and is an important participant in the European Space Agency.

Agriculture

The Dutch agricultural industry is worth Dfl 73 billion (£22.6 billion). Agricultural exports are worth Dfl 38 billion or roughly one-quarter of total Dutch exports. This is far above the 9% average export total for the European Community and makes The Netherlands a key component in the EC's Common Agricultural Policy. Dutch agricultural produce is renowned for quality and quantity, and The Netherlands is one of the largest exporters of farm produce to the rest of the world — behind only the USA and France. This is all a far cry from the latter part of the nineteenth century when The Netherlands was in the grips of an agricultural crisis. Ignorance and inefficiency meant farmers could barely feed their own families let alone the urban population as well. This remarkable turnaround was achieved thanks in part to the foundation of state-run agricultural colleges. Dutch production methods became a byword for intensive farming. Mechanization made the industry less labour intensive and the number of people working on the land dropped to a mere 4% of the population in the late 80s. However, the seasonal nature of agriculture means there is always a need for temporary workers in the summer. Many of these jobs traditionally go to foreigners.

The Netherlands produces three main crops: wheat, sugar-beet and potatoes. The potato accounts for the highest single yield and its annual harvest is nearly 1.5 million tonnes — 40% of which is turned into french fries for fast food restaurants. The phenomenal success of these establishments means the demand for potatoes is unlikely to abate.

The agricultural industry is highly intensive and many of the opportunities to enter farming lie in short-term, seasonal employment. However, the very nature of the intensive and high-technology farming industry has left The Netherlands with a need for expertise in an unexpected field. Intensive land use has emerged as an important cause of air, soil and water pollution and has forced the Dutch authorities to rethink its methods in two specific areas. Firstly, although The Netherlands is one of the EC's leading producers of meat and milk, by sheer tonnage its biggest product is manure. The 112 million-strong livestock herd produces a manure mountain at the rate of 80 million tonnes a year. A large amount is recycled, but much is unused and is being stored until a satisfactory way of disposing of it is found. Secondly, the use of herbicides and pesticides per acre of farmland is estimated to be the highest in the world. This has prompted the Dutch government to propose sweeping cuts in the levels used by farmers; by the end of the century it hopes to halve the use of pesticides. This cut will cost Dfl 2.3 billion to agriculture and the government's stated aim is 'to promote competitive, safe and sustainable farming'. These twin environmental problems now overshadow the undoubted success of Dutch agriculture. They need to be addressed quickly and a need for environmental experts is paramount.

Chemicals

The outlook for the Dutch chemicals industry is very bright. The two major multinationals that dominate the sector, AKZO and DSM, are among the most profitable in the world. Hard on their their heels are the likes of Shell and Unilever and internal competition alone is likely to keep the Dutch chemical industry at the forefront of worldwide development and production. The industry is centred on a modern, rationalized base around Europort, near Rotterdam. This provides companies with excellent transport links to worldwide suppliers and markets. The industry exports about three-quarters of production, accounting for 18% of all Dutch exports (or Dfl 27.4 billion — £8.5 billion). The greatest proportion of output comes from bulk chemicals such as fertilizers, caustic soda and plastics. Major foreign multinationals with a strong presence in The Netherlands include ICI and Dupont.

Electronics

The Dutch electronics industry is dominated by one name, Philips. This multinational company is synonymous with quality electrical goods and pioneering research. Philips invented the audio cassette, the compact disc and was one of the pioneers in the development of colour television. It employs 272,800 people in 60 countries and is ranked 29th on the list of the world's largest companies, achieving sales of Dfl 55.8 billion (£17.3 billion) in 1990. Last year Philips celebrated its centenary but the company is not resting on its laurels. It is constantly looking for scientists to develop new ideas and to keep ahead of the field for another 100 years it has undergone a radical management restructuring in the last decade. From its headquarters in Eindhoven to subsidiaries around the world Philips has rationalized, in its own words, 'to enable the organization to react more swiftly on developments in the world markets'.

Food and Beverages

The food and drink industry accounts for nearly one-fifth of the total turnover of Dutch industry. With the support of a highly productive agricultural industry Dutch food products, especially cheeses and meats, have become popular exports and are likely to remain favourites around the world. To maintain their place on the world markets the Dutch food producers cite quality and price-competitiveness as two major objectives. People's tastes can change rapidly and to combat this new brands are constantly being tried and tested. Quality, however, is something that is unlikely to change and to retain their reputation for the highest standards the government has established strict controls on the food industry. One project involves scientists at Wageningen University analysing every stage of the food chain from seed selection to the finished product on the consumer's table.

Heineken, Amstel, Grolsch and Oranjeboom are some of the more famous names in the brewing world. The beer industry boasts a long history and the Heineken Group can trace its roots back to 1592. Limburg is the brewing capital of The Netherlands and has no less than eight major breweries within its boundaries. Its oldest brewery is Brand which dates back to 1340. Dutch beer is served in more than 150 countries around the world and to maintain sales and continue expanding Heineken has recently agreed to build a new brewery in Ho Chi Minh City, Vietnam.

Tree management

Dutch woodland measures 4,400 square kilometres and has led foreign foresters to describe The Netherlands as 'a large garden with few trees'. Forestry in The Netherlands is far from profit oriented and has more of an aesthetical motivation. The Dutch people, many of whom live in urban environments, are anxious to improve their quality of life and tree preservation is seen as an integral part of this ideal. As cities continue to grow so will the need for environmental controls. Amsterdam and Rotterdam have an estimated 150,000 trees and each city authority spends Dfl 2.5 million (£770,000) annually on tree maintenance. Eight thousand trees in the major cities are on a protected list. Many companies operate protection and planting services. One such firm is Heidemij which specializes in the relocation of trees and operates a tree bank in Apeldoorn which has built up a stock of more than 1,000 trees. A Tree Foundation (*Bomenstichting*) has been established in Leiden to preserve trees and specialists hope new techniques developed at the institute will help to prolong the life of urban vegetation by up to 15 years.

High Technology

Dutch scientists are held in high regard in international circles and can claim to be world leaders in many areas of high technology research. Funding for development is given a high priority by both the government and private firms. Nearly one-fifth of research is directed towards health care; of this 60% is carried out by state-funded universities and institutes, and 20% by private companies. State-run establishments include the Central Laboratory of the Blood Transfusion Service, The Netherlands Cancer Institute and The Netherlands Institute for Health and Environmental Hygiene (vaccines). Private companies play an important role with Gist Brocades producing a quarter of the world's penicillin.

Horticulture

The humble tulip, which among other things has been described as a peculiar looking onion with an unpleasant taste, is at the heart of a thriving industry that employs 36,000 Dutch workers and had a record Dfl 6 billion (£1.86 billion) turnover in 1991. Dutch horticulture traditionally concentrated on salad products such as lettuce, cucumber and tomatoes, however, in recent years these have been increasingly overshadowed by the cultivation of flowers. Such is the extent of their success that The Netherlands can proudly boast the title of 'Florist of Europe'. To say the Dutch like flowers is an understatement and no shopping trip is complete without a visit to the florist. There is one florist shop for every 1,800 people; in the UK the number is closer to one florist per every 10,000. However, far from being just a decorative luxury, flowers are a multi-million guilder international business. The Dutch Flower Council estimates that 63% of the world's cut flowers and 51% of pot plants, or seven billion cut flowers and 530 million pot plants, are exported every year. At the centre of the industry is the Verenigde Bloemenveilingen Aalsmeer (VBA). It was founded in 1912 and is the largest flower auction centre in the world. It covers 500,000 square metres and every day 50,000 transactions sell 12 million cut flowers. The European Community accounted for 83% of total flower exports, with Germany alone receiving 43%. The fastest growing market for Dutch cut flowers is Japan, which rose by one-fifth to Dfl 73 million (£22.6 million) in 1991.

Hydraulic Engineering

More than half The Netherlands lies below sea level and Dutch engineers have had to battle for centuries to protect the population. A complex system of dunes and dykes now exists to protect the low-lying areas and pumping stations work day and night to drain the land. Through necessity the Dutch have been at the forefront of water control techniques and their expertise has been used throughout the world, from the Aswan Dam in Egypt to London's Thames barrier. Two projects have led the way in The Netherlands:

The Delta Project: On 1 February 1953 1,835 people lost their lives when large areas of the south-western part of the country were flooded. Today, all but two estuaries have the capacity to be closed to the sea. (The New Waterway and the Western Scheldt remain open to allow access to Rotterdam and Antwerp.) Across the mouth of the Eastern Scheldt Dutch engineers have constructed a storm-surge barrier that measures 3.2 km long. In stormy weather this can be closed.

The Zuyder Zee Project: Fifty years before the Delta Project a 30 km dam was built across the Zuyder Zee, connecting the provinces of Friesland and Noord-Holland. This transformed the area into an inland, freshwater lake (the IJsselmeer). Four huge polders (areas of reclaimed land) were drained and 165,000 hectares of new land were created for agriculture and housing. A planned fifth polder was scrapped due to the cost.

The Motor Industry

The leading vehicle manufacturer in The Netherlands is DAF (Doorne Auto Fabrieken), which concentrates mainly on the commercial vehicle sector. The company has lost heavily in the last two years (Dfl 228 million in 1990), but the acquisition of Leyland Trucks and a cut in its labour force means the company faces a much brighter future. Vehicles are exported throughout the EC and to many eastern European countries including Russia, Hungary, Czechoslovakia and Poland. Major foreign car manufacturers in The Netherlands include Ford, Saab Scania and Volvo.

Museums

It may seem odd to consider museums as an industry but they are a booming business with an annual turnover of Dfl 410 million (£126 million). The Dutch consider nearly any topic worthy of a museum and collections range from bee farming and bicycles to the tin can and taxes. Museums attract more than 20 million visitors every year and employ more than 10,000 people (about half are volunteers). Last year an estimated Dfl 300 million was spent on expansion projects. Hundreds of new collections have been started in the 80s swelling the number of museums to nearly 1,000 and the country's 'museum density' is expected to continue to climb.

Oil and Gas

The Netherlands' natural reserves of hydrocarbon fuels are an important factor in providing stability for the national economy. The country is the EC's leading producer and exporter of natural gas and the fourth largest producer of natural gas in the world. Gas supplies about half of the total energy needs and of the 77 billion cubic metres of gas annually produced, about 52% is exported. Oil makes up a further 40% of Dutch domestic energy requirements. Dutch oil wells already supply more than 7% of domestic needs and promising new fields have been discovered in the North Sea. The importance of processing and importing has declined but expertise to exploit new reserves is still needed.

Tourism

The Netherlands is the holiday destination for five million foreigners every year, making it one of the most popular countries in Western Europe for tourists. Amsterdam is one of Europe's top attractions and acts as the hub to the entire Dutch tourist industry. The clean and open nature of the northern provinces of Friesland and Groningen has long made them popular destinations for the Dutch. However, for those who do not want to 'get away from it all' a number of west coast beach resorts have developed, including Scheveningen and Zandvoort. These resorts provide a large number of seasonal jobs in the hotel and catering trades. Many foreign tourists have also traditionally been attracted to the bulb fields between Haarlem and Leiden for working holidays.

Transport

Dutch engineers have built the world's largest inland waterway system, transformed the bottom of the sea into land and pioneered both passenger and freight aviation. Today the country possesses a highly developed and versatile combination of transport services. Dutch carriers transport more than one half of the Rhine's cargo, Rotterdam is one of the busiest ports in the world and both it and Amsterdam have modern container terminals with large storage facilities. Dutch seaports in The Netherlands handle nearly 40% of all seaborne goods loaded or off-loaded in EC countries.

The railway system is one of the most efficient and comprehensive in the world. The modern electrified network is equipped with the latest rolling stock and provides a fast and regular service to all major business locations in The Netherlands.

Regional Employment Guide

In the *General Introduction* to The Netherlands, the main cities and regions were discussed with a view to residence. In this section, the regions are covered with a view to employment prospects in each area. The information provided will give some idea of the industries which are dominant and the type of jobs which are most readily available in each area.

THE NORTH
Groningen, Drenthe and Friesland

The three northern provinces continue to lag behind the rest of the country in nearly every category of economic development. To the casual observer the discrepancy is not readily apparent; the towns look as prosperous as in the south. But the gulf reveals itself in the statistics on unemployment, investment and economic growth. The north did prosper in the mid-80s but at a much slower rate than the rest of the country. The area fights a continual battle with regard to its perceived 'remoteness' from the rest of the country. A common joke told by northerners is that the distance from Amsterdam to Groningen is twice as far as the distance from Groningen to Amsterdam, thus emphasizing that the gap between the two is greater psychologically than in reality; it takes only two and a half hours to travel by train between these cities. A proposal for strengthening both the image and the power of the north was that the three provinces should join forces and form one 'super province'. This, however, is unlikely to happen.

The big stumbling block to the suggestion is Friesland which jealously guards its role as the protector of Frisian culture and language.

Despite the distance from the rest of The Netherlands the area has much to offer, especially in terms of the living environment. The levels of pollution are much lower than in the south and space is readily available for business and recreational purposes. The cost of land and property is cheaper and both energy prices and labour costs are lower than in the rest of the country. Businesses are increasingly taking advantage of these factors and the number of employment opportunities is correspondingly on the increase.

Groningen: The 'Top of Holland' is definitely the raw material capital of The Netherlands. The discovery of first salt in Winschoten in the 1950s and later gas at Slochteren in the 70s has twice stimulated growth in Groningen City, Slochteren and Delfzijl (which has the country's third largest seaport). More recently rich deposits of magnesium have been discovered and these are currently processed at Veerdam. Alongside agriculture, gas production and associated enterprises dominate the industrial nature of the province. Tourism also plays an important part in the economy with the area providing an easy escape for Dutch people from the rigours of urban life. At the turn of the century shipbuilding was second only to agriculture. Today the industry still survives but has undergone drastic reorganization and specialization.

Drenthe: Drenthe has large reserves of both gas and oil. One of the largest inland oilfields in Europe is located in Coevorden. The province provides virtually the entire gas needs of The Netherlands but with the current low world price for oil, oil production has been reduced to a minimum. Drenthe is the only one of the 12 Dutch provinces that has no direct association with either the sea or a major river. Metal and textile industries have a strong presence in Emmen and throughout the province the construction and chemical industries are two of the leading employers. Assen is the headquarters of Nederlandse Aardolie Maatschappij — the Dutch Oil and Gas Exploration Production Company. Drenthe has been successful in attracting foreign investment and leading foreign companies to locate in the province include Honeywell Computers and Saab Scania. Further information on Drenthe can be obtained from The Regional Development Institute for Drenthe (PO Box 142, 9400 AC, Assen; tel 05920-12547, fax 05920-10157).

Friesland: A black and white cow that takes its name from the province gives some idea as to the mainstay of the Friesland economy. The Frisian cow has a reputation for high milk and beef production and is reared worldwide. Friesland is dominated by agriculture and its farmers pioneered the centralization of dairy produce processing. Now with less than 5% of the Dutch population it claims production of 55% of cheese, 17% of milk and butter, and 75% of cattle exports. Much of the province is at or below sea level and as a result the area is also a key centre for the development and testing of hydraulic engineering. This includes the pioneering Zuyder Zee project. The Frisian people's battle to retain their identity has led to a flourishing traditional arts and crafts industry. The cultural theme combined with the coastline and recreational activities are at the centre of a growing tourist industry.

THE SOUTH
Noord-Brabant and Limburg

The south of The Netherlands has proved to be a remarkable economic success story. Twenty years ago the area was in terminal decline and much of the economy was based on coal. Today the provinces of Limburg and Noord-Brabant represent a remarkable turnaround in fortunes and are now showing the lead to the rest of the country.

Noord-Brabant: Noord-Brabant is the most industrialized province in The Netherlands and the centre of the Dutch electronics industry. It has the highest industrial output of any region in The Netherlands and is ideally located in the triangle between the German Ruhr-district, Antwerp and Rotterdam. Noord-Brabant's economy is growing and the area has attracted more than 250 foreign companies including Volvo, Hewlett Packard, ICI and Fuji. The economic centre of The Netherlands used to be the Randstad. However, this is no longer the case and due to a lack of space and inadequate infrastructure Noord-Brabant has been one of the areas to benefit most from the overspill of the main Randstad conurbation. The growth in industry is reflected in the fact that employment levels in the province are rising faster than the national average. The leading light behind the region's growth is the Brabant Development Company (*Brabantse Ont wik kelings maatschappij — BOM*). The main objective of BOM has been to strengthen and create businesses, through both investment and knowhow.

The city of Eindhoven is the driving force behind the province's economy. It is internationally renowned for its electronics and precision engineering sectors and is home to Philips' international headquarters. It also hosts the World Trade Centre for Electronics and the Centre for Micro-Electronics. Nearby Tilburg was once a thriving woollen/textile centre. This has long gone and the town now relies on a highly developed electronics base and is a leading service industry centre. The province's capital, 's-Hertogenbosch, (usually known as Den Bosch — 'the woods') is fast assuming industrial importance with a growing light industry zone. Further information on the province is detailed in the booklet *Noord-Brabant — The Business Gateway to Europe* (available from PO Box 90151, 5200 MC, 's-Hertogenbosch; tel 073-812820, fax 073-123610).

Limburg: Within two decades Limburg has been transformed from a depressed region to a fully fledged success story. In 1965 one in three of the workforce were dependent on the coal mining industry. However, worsening coal reserves and the discovery of gas fields in the North Sea sparked a turnaround that today leaves Limburg a thriving business region. The Dutch government invested Dfl 1.5 billion (£464 million) into Limburg in the 1970s which laid the foundations for success. What little mining that still remains is centred around Heerlen. The number of new high-technology and service industries that are setting up in the area has increased the demand for labour and unemployment has fallen to below the national average. The area's biggest employer is the chemical giant DSM with a 10,000-strong workforce. It accounts for one-quarter of the province's industrial output and invests nearly Dfl 925 million (£285 million) annually into its Limburg operations. Maastricht is the centre of a growing service sector that has taken advantage of its location on the borders of both Germany and Belgium. Two hundred foreign firms have settled there, making up one-fifth of the region's enterprise. One notable coup was the success in attracting Mobil Oil to build a Dfl 450 million plastic foil plant at Kerkrade.

THE WEST
Noord-Holland, Zuid-Holland and Zeeland

Two cities dominate the west of The Netherlands: Amsterdam and Rotterdam. This is the heartland of the Randstad and the number and variety of industries is too large to mention each individually. However, the area as a whole does have certain key industries.

Zuid-Holland: The famous bulb fields dominate the area to the north of Leiden. Millions of flowers are grown every year and provide the backbone to a multi-million guilder buisiness. Delft and Gouda are household names, for china and cheese respectively, but both now rely more upon light industry and service industries than the products for which they became famous. (Just three potteries continue the Delft line of blue and white china.) At the turn of the century Rotterdam was a small shipping and fishing community and during the Second World War the port and city were almost completely devastated. Today Europort is arguably the largest and busiest seaport in the world and handles nearly a quarter of a million ships a year. The port complex itself covers more than 5,300 acres of land and a host of associated industries have grown up to service the transport and storage sector. The Hague is the province's second largest city and is the seat of the Dutch government. It is also home to Royal Dutch Shell and N.V. Rubberfabriek Vredestein — the largest rubber group in the Benelux countries. A thriving tourist business has grown to meet the demands of the huge urban population. The seaside town of Scheveningen, which also has a large fishing fleet, is the equivalent of Blackpool in The Netherlands.

Noord-Holland: There are few areas that can offer as diverse an economic base as that around Amsterdam. Banking, tourism, manufacturing, petrochemicals, high-technology, telecommunications, farming and horticulture all play a significant part in the economy of Noord-Holland. Aalsmeer has the world's largest auction hall (*Verenigde Bloemenveilingen Aalsmeer*) which acts as the focus to the entire Dutch horticulture business. The Bennebroek-Lisse-Sassenheim area is the heart of the bulb fields that extend from Leiden to the southern limits of Haarlem, the nerve centre of the bulb industry. Amsterdam itself is a mecca to tourists and a thriving tourist industry has developed around the seaside resorts of Zandvoort and Noordwijk. The Dutch broadcasting industry is centred around Hilversum. Further information on Amsterdam is available from the City of Amsterdam Investment Office (Townhall, Amstel 1, 1011 PN Amsterdam; tel 020-5523536, fax 020-5522860).

Zeeland: Zeeland, as its name suggests, is a land of the sea. As a result industries aimed at both using and holding at bay the sea are thriving. The Delta project is probably the world's greatest hydraulic engineering feat. Agriculture vies with tourism as the region's biggest industry. Vlissingen is not only a popular summer resort but a working fishing and shipbuilding centre. Yerseke is the oyster capital of Europe producing 30 million Zeeland oysters in a good year.

THE CENTRAL AREA
Utrecht, Gelderland, Overijssel and Flevoland

Utrecht: This is the smallest of the Dutch provinces and its economy is overshadowed by the demands of its near neighbours. The province is sandwiched between the Randstad powerhouses of Amsterdam and Rotterdam and Germany. These are less than an hour's drive away and a host of industries have developed around Utrecht and Amersfoort to supply their needs. The province has many haulage companies and light industry manufacturers. A large number of service industries have centred upon Utrecht and the city also has the claim to fame that it is the world leader in holding trade and industrial fairs.

Gelderland: Gelderland is the largest of The Netherlands' 12 provinces and is split by the three great rivers: the Rhine, the Maas and the Ijssel. Both Arnhem and Nijmegen have become important centres for water transport and act as links between Rotterdam and Germany. The area has a reputation for pioneers and in Zaltbommel the Philips brothers first experimented with mass-producing electric light bulbs. Today Apeldoorn and Wageningen hold the pioneering mantle. The Dutch have few natural resources and Apeldoorn is the country's leading papermaking and recycling centre. Wageningen is responsible in part for The Netherlands' thriving agricultural industry. It is the seat of Europe's foremost agricultural university with 21 laboratories, 22 independent institutions and 10 associated concerns. Also located in Wageningen are the principal ship-testing laboratories where small-scale boats are tested under simulated trial conditions. Tiel is the headquarters of what is known as orchard-land (*Betuwe*), where many kinds of fruit including cherries, plums, apples and pears are grown.

Overijssel: Zwolle is the capital of a province that has many contrasts. The old towns of Blokzijl and Vollenhove have been turned from seafaring ports on the Zuyder Zee into specialist recreation and yacht-building centres on the IJsselmeer. The towns of Almelo, Enschede and Oldenzaal were originally the textile heart of The Netherlands. The decline in textiles has been offset by a growth in electronics and chemicals. Hengelo is the centre for metal industries and salt factories.

Flevoland: Flevoland was reclaimed from the sea and is The Netherlands' youngest province. Its very existence is testimony to Dutch engineering brilliance and the same innovative spirit pervades the whole Flevoland economy. The idea that Flevoland is a 'test case' has been translated into many areas of research and development. Its economy is growing at a remarkable rate and new industries, especially small concerns in the field of high technology, are setting up every day. The province has given a high priority to agricultural and agriculture-related technological research. It is Europe's most up-to-date farming region with more than 20 research institutes and experimental farms. NLR National Aviation and Aerospace Laboratory (with Europe's largest wind tunnel) at Noordoostpolder and De Voorst Hydrodynamic Laboratory at Kraggenburg. One other important growth industry is that of water sports and recreation. The IJsselmeer is a popular destination for both sailors and fishermen. A large number of businesses have developed not only to organize activities but also to design and manufacture new equipment. Further details can be obtained from *Provincie Flevoland:* Department of Economic Affairs, PO Box 55, 8200 AB Lelystad; tel 03200-72411, fax 03200-72590.

Directory of Major Employers

A full and detailed list of about 240 majority-owned British subsidiaries operating in The Netherlands is contained in the publication *Britain in the Netherlands*, obtainable from the Netherlands-British Chamber of Commerce (The Dutch House, 307-308 High Holborn, London WC1V 7LS) for £10 including postage. Also available is *The Netherlands-American Trade Directory* which offers a list of the American companies present in The Netherlands. The directory costs Dfl 230

(£70) and is published by the American Chamber of Commerce (Carnegieplein 5, 2517 KJ The Hague).

British Banks

Barclays Bank plc: Weteringschans 109, PO Box 160, 1017 SB Amsterdam; tel 020-262209, fax 020-266511.

Lloyds Bank plc: Hirschgebouw, Leidseplein 29, PO Box 3518, 1001 AH Amsterdam; tel 020-263535.

National Westminster Bank: P/A Van Lanschot Bankiers, Hoge Steenweg 27-31, 5211 JN 's-Hertogenbosch; tel 073-153911, fax 073-153188.

Dutch Banks

Algemene Bank Nederland BV: Vijzelstraat 32, PO Box 669, 1000 EG Amsterdam; tel 020-299111.

Amsterdam-Rotterdam Bank NV: Afdeling Rally Post 411, PO Box 283, 1000 EA Amsterdam; tel 020-289393.

Crediet- en Effectenbank NV: Herculesplein 5, PO Box 85100, 3508 AC Utrecht: tel 030-560911.

Bank Mees & Hope NV: Herengracht 548, PO Box 293, 1000 AG Amsterdam; tel 020-5279111.

NMB Bank: Amsterdamse Poort, PO Box 1800, 1000 BV Amsterdam; tel 020-5636481, fax 020-5636135.

Postbank NV: Haarlemmerweg 512, PO Box 21009, 1000 EX Amsterdam; tel 020-5849111.

Rabobank Nederland: PO Box 17100, 3500 HG Utrecht; tel 030-369111.

Insurance Companies

NV Amev International: Archimedeslaan 10, PO Box 2072, 3500 HB Utrecht; tel 030-579111, fax 030-522394.

Delta Lloyd NV: Sparklerweg 4, PO Box 1000, 1000 BA Amsterdam; tel 020-594111, fax 020-934100.

Equity & Law Levensverzekering: Korte Voorhout 20, PO Box 997, 2501 CZ Den Haag; tel 070-469262.

Kamerbeek Assurantiemakelaars: Bergstraat 9-11, PO Box 81, 3800 AB Amersfoort; tel 033-621044, fax 033-635631.

Nationale Nederlanden NV: Johan de Wittlaan 3, PO Box 29701, 2502 LS Den Haag; tel 070-581582, fax 070-581280.

Overseas Financial Services: City Office, Kettingstraat 2, 2511 AN Den Haag; tel 070-560199, fax 070-561458.

Sedgwick Nederland BV: Singel 323-347, PO Box 465, 1000 AL Amsterdam; tel 020-5516911.

Swiss Life Insurance Co: Apollolaan 153, PO Box 7007, 1007 JA Amsterdam; tel 020-733232.

Breweries

Allied Breweries Nederland: Ceresstraat 13, PO Box 3212, 4800 MA Breda; tel 076-252424, fax 076-252155.

Anglo-Dutch Ales Enterprise: 2e Sweelinckstraat 22, PO Box 51088, 1007 EB Amsterdam; tel 020-642652.

Grolsche Bierbrouwerij NV: Fazanstraat 2, PO Box 55, 7500 AB Enschede; tel 053-353570.

Heineken Brouwerijen BV: CAD 694, PO Box 500, 2380 BA Zoeterwoude; tel 071-814814.

United Dutch Breweries: Ceresstraat 13, PO Box 3212, 4800 MA Breda; tel 076-2523505, fax 076-252494.

Agriculture and Horticulture
Blanken Export BV: Heereweg 341a, PO Box 45, 2160 AA Lisse; tel 02521-19133.
Jan Kraats Export: Zijde 135, 2771 EV Boskoop; tel 01727-7206.
Krinkels Beplantings Mij. BV: Plantagebaan 58, PO Box 5, 4724 ZG Wouw; tel 01658-1851, fax 01658-2781.
Rijk Zwaan Zaadteelt BV: Burg. Crezeelaan 40, PO Box 40, 2678 ZG De Lier; tel 01745-3941.
Sion's Plant BV: Veiling Westland, PO Box 503, 2675 AE Honselersdijk; tel 01740-27644.
Westplant BV: Papedijk 1a, 2691 HE 's-Gravenzande; tel 01748-4731.

Estate Agencies
Healey & Baker BV: Jan van Goyenkade 13, 1075 AP Amsterdam; tel 020-737555.
Jones, Lang Wootton BV: Strawinskylaan 3103. 1077 ZX Amsterdam; tel 020-6612121, fax 020-6611566.
Pakoma BV: Wassenaarseweg 20, 2596 CH Den Haag; tel 070-469384.
Richard Ellis: Gebouw Hirsch Leidseplein 29, PO Box 19719, 1000 GS Amsterdam; tel 020-262691, fax 020-246305.

Chartered Surveyors
Chesterton International: Johannes Vermeerstraat 63, 1071 DN Amsterdam; tel 020-790313.
Nordic Estate Management: Daggeldersweg 7, 3449 JD Woerden; tel 03480-31757, fax 03480-31758.

Legal Services
Abeln CS Advocaten: Jan Luykenstraat 100, 1071 CV Amsterdam; tel 020-6641081, fax 020-6626818.
Barents, Gasille & Mout: Parkstraat 105, 2514 JH Den Haag; tel 070-648940, fax 070-651856.
Boekel de Neree: P.C. Hooftstraat 5, PO Box 2508, 1000 CM Amsterdam; tel 020-6641311, fax 020-710091.
Clifford Chance: De Lairessestraat 125, PO Box 5265, 1007 AG Amsterdam; tel 020-6641618, fax 020-769326.
Ekelmans den Hollander: J.J. Viottastraat 52, 1071 JT Amsterdam; tel 020-646666, fax 020-647617.
Nauta Dutilh: Weena 750, PO Box 20750, 3001 JB Rotterdam; tel 010-4170911, fax 010-4125266.
Rischen & Van Bellen: Haringvliet 86, Postbus 22096, 3003 DB Rotterdam; tel 010-4332777, fax 010-4047959
UWG Thole: Keizersgracht 561-563, PO Box 15724, 1001 NE Amsterdam; tel 020-264847, fax 020-203658.

Computer Services
Digital Applications International BV: Parkstraat 99, 2514 JH Den Haag; tel 070-624891.
Dutch Exp. Computer Services: Kampenringweg 45, PO Box 560, 2800 AN Gouda; tel 01820-70025, fax 01820-39946.
Dynamic Graphics International BV: Ambachtsweg 3, PO Box 25, 3950 AA Maarn; tel 03433-1941, fax 03433-1910.

European Channels: Prof. Gerbrandyweg 5, 2584 EC Den Haag; tel 070-553933.
Holland Automation International BV: Binnen Walevest 98, 3311 AB Dordrecht; tel 078-135666.
Logica BV: Wijnhaven 69, PO Box 22067, 3003 DB Rotterdam; tel 010-4330844, fax 010-4331447.
Sema Group Informatica BV: Van Houten Industrial Park 11, PO Box 143, 1380 Weesp; tel 02940-15441, fax 02940-13974.

Oil and Petrochemical Companies
Acheson Colloiden BV: Haven NZ 6, PO Box 1, 9679 ZG Scheemda; tel 05979-1303.
AFA Polytek BV: Indumaweg 1, 5711 EA Someren; tel 04937-3262.
BP Nederland BV: Frederiksplein 42, PO Box 1634, 1000 BP Amsterdam; tel 020-5201223.
Dorned BV: Herengracht 331, 1016 AX Amsterdam; tel 020-272466, fax 020-267875.
ICI Holland BV: Wijnhaven 107, PO Box 551, 3000 AN Rotterdam; tel 010-4171911, fax 010-4115560.
Pendy Plastic Products BV: Engelseweg 175, PO Box 313, 5700 AA Helmond; tel 04920-38835.
Plasticall BV: Dr C.J.K. van Aalstweg 8, PO Box 28, 1620 AA Hoorn; tel 02290-30324.
Polymar Groningen: Osloweg 19, 9700 GA Groningen; tel 050-120101.
Shell International Petroleum Mij. BV: Carel van Bylandtlaan 30, PO Box 650, 2501 CR Den Haag; 070-779111.
Shell Nederland NV: Hofplein 20, PO Box 1222, 3000 BE Rotterdam; tel 010-4696911.
E.Wethmar: Dukatenburg 82, PO Box 7028, 3430 JA Nieuwegein; tel 03402-51477, fax 03402-51403.

Pharmaceutical Products
Brunschwig Chemie BV: Butaanweg 8, PO Box 70213, 1007 KE Amsterdam; tel 020-113133, fax 020-137596.
Enzypharm BV: Soesterengweg 2-4, PO Box 54, 3760 AB Soest; tel 02155-12447.
Gist Brocades NV: Library Biotechnology, PO Box 1, 2600 MA Delft; tel 015-799111.
Glaxo BV: Wattbaan 51, PO Box 2190, 3430 CZ Nieuwegein; tel 03402-38244.
Wellcome Pharmaceuticals BV: Kobaltweg 61, 3542 CE Utrecht.

Media and Newspapers
Algemeen Dagblad: Marten Meesweg 35, 300 DB Rotterdam; tel 010-4066077/7211, fax 010-4066969.
Dagblad Trouw: Wibautstraat 131, 1000 AW Amsterdam; tel 020-5629444, fax 020-6680389.
De Telegraaf: Basisweg 30, 1000 EB Amsterdam; tel 020-5859111, fax 020-5852113/216.
De Volkskrant: Wibautstraat 148-150, 1000 BA Amsterdam; tel 020-5629222, fax 020-5626289.
NRC/Handelsblad: Marten Meesweg 35, 3000 DL Rotterdam; tel 010-4066077/7211.
Radio Nederlands: PO Box 222, 1200 JG Hilversum; tel 035-724211, fax 035-724352.

Printing and Publishing

Chevalier Printers: Nijverheidsweg 46, PO Box 210, 3340 AE Hendrik-Ido-Ambacht; tel 01858-7444.

Lochem Druk BV: Kwinkweerd 2, PO Box 77, 7240 AB Lochem; tel 05730-57654, fax 05730-51414.

Rohong Publishers: Lange Voorhout 46, 2514 EG Den Haag; tel 070-646134, fax 070-643947.

Trio Goemans BV: Parklaan 156, PO Box 256, 2170 AG Sassenheim; tel 02522-18584, fax 02522-17840.

Uitgevermaatsch. C. Misset BV: Hanzestraat 1, PO Box 4, 7000 BA Doetinchem; tel 08340-49911, fax 08340-43839.

Van Boekhoven-Bosch BV: Europalaan 12, PO Box 2035, 3500 GA Utrecht; tel 030-820911, fax 030-820311.

Wolters Kluwer Groep NV: Hoogoorddreef 5, PO Box 22981, 1100 DL Amsterdam; tel 020-5646360, fax 020-913551.

Management Consultants

Amsterdam Consultants: Locatellikade 1, 1076 AZ Amsterdam; tel 020-6627330, fax 020-6764071.

Coopers & Lybrand: Weenahuis Weena 151-161, 3000 CT Rotterdam; tel 010-4000400, fax 010-4331401.

Price Waterhouse: Koninginnegracht, 2514 AA Den Haag; tel 070-3108308.

Carriers and Storage

Combined Terminals Amsterdam VOF: Sardiniëweg 10, 1044 AE Amsterdam; tel 020-119555.

Continental Cargo Carriers: Puntweg 18, PO Box 374, 3200 AJ Spijkenisse; tel 01880-25088, fax 01880-25494.

DFDS Transport BV: Smirnoffweg 22-26, 3088 HE Rotterdam; tel 010-4286400, fax 010-4297180.

Dutch Air BV: Avio Trade Park, PO Box 75580, 1118 ZP Schiphol Airport; tel 020-6552444, fax 020-6534115.

Europe Combined Terminals BV: PO Box 7400, 3000 HK Rotterdam; tel 049-16911, fax 049-16115.

Forcom Commodities Forwarding BV: Waalhaven 4, 3008 EB Rotterdam; tel 010-4291966, fax 010-4290091.

Frans Maas Beheer NV: Noorderpoort, 5900 AZ Venlo; tel 077-597600, fax 077-547998.

Geest North Sea Line BV: Monsterseweg 117, 2690 AA Den Haag; tel 01748-13841, fax 01748-20327.

Maersk Nederland BV: Achterdijk 55, 3160 AD Rhoon; tel 01890-30700, fax 01890-30789.

Malenstein International BV: Galvanistraat 100, 6710 BH Ede; tel 08380-77111.

Nedlloyd Districenters: Lemelerweg 32, 1101 AH Amsterdam; tel 020-6912111, fax 020-6919741.

Nedlloyd Road Cargo: Van Maasdijkweg 5, 3008 AG Rotterdam; tel 010-4298200, fax 010-4282689.

Royal Nedlloyd Group NV: Boompjes 40, 3000 AL Rotterdam; tel 010-40007111.

Scanspeed Holland BV: Emma Goldmanweg 1, 5000 AS Tilburg; tel 013-625111, fax 013-631405.

Transport Centrale Gelderland BV: Binderskampweg 31, 6500 AA Nijmegen; tel 080-782800, fax 080-786228.

Transportgroep Brummen BV: Hazenberg 1, PO Box 150, 6970 AD Brummen; tel 05756-4545, fax 05756-1011.
Van Daalen Transport: Willem van Hooffstraat, PO Box 230, 2670 AE Naaldwijk; tel 01740-27541, fax 01740-28559.
Van Bennekum Hoekstra BV: 9c Keilestraat, PO Box 6634, 3002 AP Rotterdam; tel 010-4779122, fax 010-4777720.

Metal
Bolding Verpakkingen BV: Provincialeweg 200, PO Box 1037, 1500 AA Zaandam; tel 075-123105.
Borstlap BV: Zevenheuvelenweg 44, PO Box 5034, 5004 EA Tilburg; tel 03113-628628, fax 03113-628282.
Chubb Lips Nederland BV: Merwedestraat 48, PO Box 59, 3300 AB Dordrecht; tel 078-136144.
Elceestaal BV: Kamerlingh Onnesweg 28, PO Box 606, 3300 AP Dordrecht; tel 078-170888, fax 078-177204.
Gazelle Rijwielfabriek BV: Wilhelminaweg 8, PO Box 1, 6950 AA Dieren; tel 08330-29911.
Metaalcompagnie Brabant BV: J.F.Kennedylaan 59, PO Box 2, 5550 AA Valkenswaard; tel 0902-88333, fax 04902-43795.
Oostwoud International BV: Wageningselaan 38, PO Box 374, 3900 AJ Veenendaal; tel 08385-21211.
BV Staalindustrie: Industrieweg 4, PO Box 82, 7460 AB Rijssen; tel 05480-3805.
Uzimet BV: PO Box 19, 2600 AA Delft; tel 015-135395.

Civil Engineering
E.Blok BV: Kortenoord 29, PO Box 90, 2910 AB Nieuwerkerk a/c IJssel; tel 01803-3744.
B&S BV: Oranjestraat 59, PO Box 112, 4890 AC Rijsbergen; tel 01606-2139.
Hollandsche Beton Groep NV: Generaal Spoorlaan 489, PO Box 81, 2280 AB Rijswijk; tel 070-153911, fax 070-152408.
Polytex NV: Stephensonstraat 53, PO Box 100, 2000 AC Haarlem; tel 023-246824, fax 023-245114.
PRC Holding BV: Goudseweg 181, PO Box 1051, 2410 CB Bodegraven; tel 01726-19344, fax 01726-11902.
HCG Staalbouw BV: Westfrankelandsedijk 9, PO Box 212, 3100 AE Schiedam; tel 010-4279200.
Van Oord-Utrecht BV: Oude Haven 1, PO Box 15, 3984 ZG Odijk; tel 03405-97211, fax 03405-67553.

Starting a Business

The Dutch have a centuries-old tradition of successful trading. As early as the eighteenth century the very first stock exchange was established in Amsterdam and the Dutch East India Company had become a byword for worldwide mercantile prowess. Today Dutch business people are still at the fore and a new generation of global firms, such as Philips, Unilever and Shell, have helped to make The Netherlands one of the most commercially and technologically advanced nations in the world.

The Netherlands has for many years conducted an open-door policy vis-à-vis foreign enterprises and Dutch-registered companies can be formed by foreigners without difficulty. In fact, the Dutch government's policy of non-discrimination has been so successful that one-quarter of business investment in The Netherlands now comes from foreign sources. A number of professional activities are reserved for Dutch nationals and government monopolies are maintained in a few public activities, such as Dutch airlines and the postal service. The status of foreign-owned companies is generally the same as that of purely Dutch-financed enterprises. A number of tax and other investment incentives are offered to foreign companies and it is expected that the favourable attitude towards foreigners moving to The Netherlands will continue. (See below for the incentives available.)

For anyone considering setting up a business, The Netherlands has a number of further economic attractions. A low inflation rate (currently 4.4%) and a currency linked to the German mark combine to give a stable trading environment. The country also has an excellent communications and transport infrastructure. The Dutch workforce is highly skilled and it is not uncommon for people to speak three or four languages. The Netherlands is the result of the interaction of some of the most commercially alert minds of the last 300 years. Few merchants have traded like the Dutch and few peoples have the same profit and loss outlook on life uppermost in their minds. These qualities of commercial awareness mean The Netherlands offers potential entrepreneurs opportunities that are unrivalled in any other European Community country.

Procedures Involved in Buying or Starting a New Business

Preparation from Scratch

The Netherlands Foreign Investment Agency (*Commissariaat voor Buitenlandse Investeringen in Nederland* — *CBIN*), a division of the Ministry of Economic Affairs, provides financial and economic information to potential businesses. This includes help with project evaluation, implementation and location. Its services are free of charge, totally confidential and available from offices in The Netherlands and all Dutch embassies.

All new business ventures must be entered in the commercial register (*handelsregister*), which is also known as the trade register and register of companies, at the local chamber of commerce (*kamer van koophandel*). The register is open to public inspection and a prospective company is required to supply the following details: articles of incorporation (name, address and nature of business), the amount of capital investment, and details of capital, shareholders and directors. Firms must also register with the tax and social security offices. If an operation has the potential to cause damage or be a nuisance to its surroundings, it is necessary to apply for a permit under the Public Nuisance Act (*hinderwetvergunning*). The establishment of all companies must be published in the Official Gazette (*De Staatscourant*). Until all legal procedures have been completed the directors remain personally liable for any debts incurred by a new business.

Useful Addresses

Jordan and Sons Ltd: (21 St Thomas Street, Bristol BS1 6JS; tel 0272-230600, fax 0272-230063) offers research and administrative help to individuals setting up a business in The Netherlands.

Horwath Tax Holland: (Weerdestein 117, 1083 GH Amsterdam; tel 020-6612777, fax 020-6461248) provides a range of services to new companies including tax and legal advice.

Dutch Committee of the International Chambers of Commerce: Pr. Beatrixlaan 5, PO Box 95309, 2509 Den Haag; tel 070-3836646.

Association of the Chambers of Commerce: Watermolenlaan 1, PO Box 265, 3440 AC Woerden; tel 03480-26911.

Information Service of the Ministry of Economic Affairs: Economische Voorlichtingsdienst; tel 070-3798933.

Common Market Advisory Service for Business: Dalsteindreef 9, PO Box 112, 1110 AC Diemen; tel 020-901071.

Research Companies and Market Analysts

Veldkamp Marktonderzoek: Stadhouderskade 159, 1074 BC Amsterdam; tel 020-731125.

AC Nielsen Company: Amsteldijk 166, 1079 LH Amsterdam; tel 020-444972.

Orange Nassaulaan 25: PO Box 1075, AJ Amsterdam; tel 020-750071.

HORWATH TAX HOLLAND
Belgian & Dutch
International Tax Consultants

* Multinational team of advisors, including Dutch and Belgian tax lawyers
* Languages (fluent or mother tongue) — English, Dutch, French, Danish & German
* One of the best international tax libraries and most sophisticated international tax computer data base facilities in the Netherlands
* Specialists in international tax and related advice
* Excellent understanding of many foreign countries' tax laws and business culture
* Apart from tax advice we also assist with the formation of companies and their administration
* Extensive contact network throughout the world
* Located near Schiphol airport, Amsterdam

Contact: Ned Shelton (Head), Boudewijn Barre or Freddy De Petter.
Address: Weerdestein 117, 1083 GH Amsterdam, the Netherlands.

Tel: +31 20 661 2777   Fax: +31 20 646 1248

Or ask for our free brochure

Chambers of Commerce

In The Netherlands there are 36 local chambers of commerce, with 39 offices, covering the country. The chambers are statutory bodies and their main role is to promote trade and to supply detailed information about the industrial and commercial situation in a specific area. However, the extent to which groups can undertake research work on behalf of individual companies varies considerably between the chambers. They are generally unwilling to provide information on local employment opportunities. Anyone setting up a business in The Netherlands must register with the local chamber of commerce on arrival (see above).

Useful Addresses

Amsterdam Chamber of Commerce: De Ruyterkade 5, 1013 HH Amsterdam; tel 020-5236600.
The Hague Chamber of Commerce: Alexander Gogeweg 16, PO Box 29718, 2517 JH, The Hague; tel 070-3795795.
Rotterdam Chamber of Commerce: Beursplein 37, PO Box 30025, 3011 AA Rotterdam; tel 010-4145022.

Choosing an Area

After having a business idea and carrying out the necessary market research the next logical step is to decide where to locate. In the *Regional Employment Guide* (in Chapter Six, *Employment*) the general commercial base of the 12 Dutch provinces is discussed. The most dynamic regions are currently Noord- and Zuid-Holland, Noord-Brabant and to a lesser extent north Limburg. This does not mean, however, that the less commercially developed areas, such as Groningen and Friesland, should be ruled out. The Dutch government offers generous financial incentives to businesses choosing to locate in areas with weaker economies. The Netherlands is a relatively small country and possesses an excellent transport network. As a result no one area can be described as 'remote'. In addition, provinces away from the Randstad conurbation are generally less densely populated and less polluted. The type of enterprise envisaged will have a bearing on your choice of region. For example businesses reliant on expatriate clientele will almost certainly have to be near Amsterdam, The Hague or Rotterdam.

Useful Publications

Amsterdam Times: Monthly magazine providing visitors with business and entertainment opportunities in Amsterdam. Amsteldijk 126, 1078 RS Amsterdam; tel 020-6711177, fax 020-6751102.

Business Guide to The Netherlands: A guide to setting up business in The Netherlands. Published by Barclays Bank PLC, 54 Lombard Street, London EC3P 3AH.

Doing Business in the European Community: A useful guide to the world of EC business. Written by Paul Gibbs and published by Kogan Page Ltd, 120 Pentonville Road, London N1 9JN.

In Touch: Monthly Anglo-Dutch Trade magazine published on behalf of the Netherlands-British Chamber of Commerce. c/o The Dutch House, 307-308 High Holborn, London WC1V 7LS; tel 071-405 1358, fax 071-405 1689.

Roundabout: Monthly guide to what's on in The Netherlands. Postbus 96813, 2509 JE Den Haag; tel 070-3241611.

Window on the Netherlands: A monthly magazine aimed at the expatriate community. Contains articles of both a commercial and social nature. Published by Uitgeverij Cobbenhage BV, Treubstraat 1n, 2288 EG Rijswijk; tel 070-3995108, 070-3902488.

In addition to the above publications, international accountants Ernst & Young, Price Waterhouse and HLB Nederland Accountants and Consultants each produce their own free guides called *Doing Business in The Netherlands* which are available from their addresses below:

Ernst & Young: Marten Meesweg 51, 3068 AV Rotterdam; tel 010-4072222, fax 010-4552737.

Price Waterhouse: Strawinskylaan 3127, 1077 ZX Amsterdam; tel 020-5498200, fax 020-5498250.

HLB Nederland Accountants and Consultants: National Secretariat, Cronenburg 73, 1081 GM Amsterdam; tel 020-464011, fax 020-463251.

Raising Finance

British banks do not lend money to people contemplating setting up a business in The Netherlands, where the prospective proprietor intends to be resident abroad. However, Dutch banks will lend money to foreign businesses, and at a lower interest rate than their UK counterparts. Commercial banks can offer businesses overdraft facilities or cash loans for up to two years. Medium- and long-term loans are also available from the banks and specialist institutions such as the *Nationale Investeringsbank*. For a list of major Dutch banks see Chapter Four, *Daily Life*.

Alternatively one could investigate the potential of the Dutch government's business incentive schemes (see below).

Investment Incentives

In recent years the Dutch government has placed an increasing emphasis on balanced regional growth of the economy and to realize this, special incentives have been offered to firms locating in particular areas. The assisted areas broadly comprise the northern provinces of Groningen, Friesland, Drenthe, the northern part of Overijssel and the south of Limburg. Other regions of The Netherlands that experience a specific hardship (e.g. the closure of a factory) can also become eligible for assistance from time to time. The government has a very favourable attitude towards foreign investment and such enterprises are afforded the same rights as Dutch businesses.

Tax concessions: The rate of corporate income tax is reduced from 42% to 40% if a company's profit does not exceed Dfl 250,000 (£77,500). Foreign employees can qualify for the '35 per cent rule' which means only 65% of employment income is taxed by the Dutch authorities.

Regional incentives: To attract business investment to the economically weaker areas of The Netherlands the government has set up the Investment Premium Regulation (IPR). The IPR is a financial incentive given to companies that settle in specified areas. Regions and communities designated for this premium include: Groningen, southeast Drenthe, Friesland, south Limburg, Lelystad, Arnhem, Nijmegen and Wijchen. Three types of business development are eligible for a variety of IPR grants. Projects to establish or restructure businesses can obtain a grant of 25% of the capital investment, up to a maximum of Dfl 18 million (£5.5 million). The expansion of an existing business qualifies for 15% of the cost, up to Dfl 8 million.

Bonded storage: There are no free ports or fixed free zones in The Netherlands. However, the extensive and highly sophisticated transport network means that there are hundreds of bonded storage facilities that escape payment of import or excise duties, VAT, and agricultural levies. Goods stored in bond can undergo transportation, repacking, testing, bottling or mixing without being classified as imports subject to duties. Payment of levies becomes due only when the goods are cleared for use in The Netherlands.

Special-use company incentives: Special subsidies are awarded to Dutch and foreign firms that are researching or developing new products. The Subsidy for Technologically Innovative Business Projects (PBTS) programme was set up in 1986 to encourage developments in biotechnology, medical and information technology, and advanced materials. Amsterdam City Council has established an incentive programme to attract new businesses and cut unemployment in the city. For example, land on the western harbour was recently sold for Dfl 0.07 (2p) per acre and companies hiring 15 to 50 employees receive grants of up to Dfl 370,000 (£114,550). Ships that fly the Dutch flag qualify for incentives, provided the vessels are longer than 25 metres and spend one-third of their lives at sea.

Business Structures

Foreign investors can operate through a variety of business entities in The Netherlands. The types of organization most commonly used are a private limited liability company (*Besloten Vennootschap met Beperkte Aansprakelijkheid — BV*), a public corporation (*Naamloze Vennootschap — NV*), and a branch office. No one particular structure is favoured by Dutch business people.

Naamloze Vennootschap (Public Corporation)

To form a public company a minimum of Dfl 100,000 (£30,960) is required. In addition at least 20% of the authorized share capital must be issued, of which 25% must be paid for on subscription. There is no limit on the number of shareholders but the corporation cannot purchase more than 10% of its own shares. An NV must have at least two bodies — the general meeting of shareholders and the board of managing directors. A board of directors does not exist in The Netherlands, but an NV usually has a third body, the Board of Supervisory Directors. This oversees the management board. (For companies with a workforce of more than 100, and consolidated share capital and reserves of at least Dfl 22.5 million (£6.9 million), the appointment of a supervisory board is mandatory.)

To form a public corporation one person (either an individual or a legal business entity) participating in the share capital is required to execute a deed before a public notary. The notary will draw up a deed of incorporation (*akte van oprichting*), which includes the articles of association (*statuten*) — the company's details and its aims and objectives. The articles of association must be recorded in the trade register (*handelsregister*) at the local chamber of commerce (*kamer van koophandel*). The deed of incorporation must be submitted to the Ministry of Justice (Ministerie van Justitie) and if approved it will receive a declaration of no objection (*verklaring van geen bezwaar*). The decision will take on average two to three months to come through. If ministerial approval is not given an appeal can be made to the Council of State within one month. Once a declaration of no objection is received, the deed of incorporation is notarized and the details of the *NV* are published in The Netherlands' Official Gazette (*De Staatscourant*).

Besloten Vennootschap met Beperkte Aansprakelijkheid (BV): A *BV* is usually subject to less stringent requirements than an *NV*. A sum of Dfl 40,000 (£12,380) is required to set up a private company. One or more individuals (or companies) need to sign the articles of association in the presence of a public notary. They must also provide proof that the Dfl 40,000 is deposited in a Dutch bank account. (It is useful to note that the money can be immediately withdrawn.) The deed of incorporation must be approved by the Ministry of Justice before the company can be established. The cost of the process for both an *NV* and a *BV* will normally include a 1% capital issue tax, and the fees payable to the public notary, the chamber of commerce, the bank receiving the capital and the Ministry of Justice. An *NV* can be converted to a *BV*, or vice versa, provided such a change is approved at a shareholder's meeting, the deed of incorporation is modified to accommodate the change and the Ministry of Justice issues a declaration of no objection.

Branches: It is common for foreign companies to begin operations as a branch. A new branch must be recorded in the register of companies, giving information concerning both itself and its parent company (including the parent's articles of association). The foreign parent is held responsible for all liabilities and obligations of its Dutch branch.

Partnerships: Three types of partnership are permitted in The Netherlands: general, professional and limited. A general partnership (*Vennootschap onder Firma — VOF*) must be formed by contract and its details must be registered with the local chamber of commerce. Professional partnerships (such as lawyers and accountants) are known as *Maatschappij*. A limited partnership (*Commanditaire Vennootschap*) is essentially the same as a VOF but has one or more limited partners. No annual accounts need to be published. The three partnerships do not actually exist as legal entities in the eyes of Dutch law and each partner is individually liable.

European Economic Interest Groupings (EEIG): An EEIG is a new supranational legal vehicle designed to encourage cross-border co-operation in the European Community. An EEIG must have at least two members that maintain head offices, residences or main activities in different EC member states. Virtually any individual or company can join an EEIG and it is particularly useful for pan-European activities that are too costly for one company to engage in alone. A contract needs to be drawn up, but need not be in the form of a notarial deed. The contract must then be registered with the register of companies.

Co-operative Societies: A co-operative society is an association of persons that allows for the free entry and withdrawal of members. Its name must contain the word *coöperatief* and must give some indication of its objectives, for example buying and selling dairy products. In addition the name must include certain initials to indicate the liability of its members; WA, unlimited liability; BA, limited liability; or UA, no liability. Co-operatives are frequently used in such trades as agriculture and horticulture, and are formed to represent the interests of its members collectively, rather than earn profits for an investor. It is a legal entity and is founded by a notarial deed.

Others: Most importers appoint a commercial agent to handle their entry into the Dutch market place. Agents in general cover the whole country. No special legal or tax provisions apply to offshore companies. An ordinary Dutch company may, of course, have foreign activities such as investments in foreign subsidiaries or obtain foreign-source interest or royalty income.

Ideas for New Businesses

The Dutch are very successful business people, so opportunites in many established trading areas are few and far between. For example competition in the fields of food production and the food retail business, flowers and plants, precision engineering and electronics is likely to be very keen.

Teaching English: Despite the fact that the Dutch have a good command of the English language there is always a demand for teachers especially in the field of business English. There is therefore scope for opening a language school or private tutor agency.

Sport and Recreation: The majority of the Dutch population lives in urban areas and the Dutch have an increasing amount of leisure time at their disposal. Sports and recreation are therefore playing an increasingly important role in Dutch life. New businesses are being established to cater for the demand especially in the field of water sports. Both instructors and equipment are in short supply around the IJsselmeer and along the west coast. Adventure holidays and golf are two other forms of activity that are expanding rapidly and at the moment much of the expertise comes from abroad.

Estate Agents: Although a number of British estate agents have made successful ventures into the French, Spanish and Italian markets the National Association of Estate Agents has no member that deals specifically with Dutch properties. There is no shortage of estate agents in The Netherlands itself, but an increasing number of people are contemplating a move and there is definite potential in consultancies to help and advise people before they travel.

Tourism: Amsterdam dominates the Dutch tourist industry. However, outside the country's capital city there is tremendous scope for development of small family hotels and restaurants, and other tourist facilities. Friesland and Groningen are becoming increasingly attractive to both Dutch and foreign visitors.

Third World Crafts: The Dutch are mirroring the trend of many Western Europeans and showing an increasing fascination with Third World arts and crafts. The fad is likely to get stronger and suppliers are in demand.

Antiques: A long tradition of displaying heritage in museums is as strong as ever and at the last count nearly 1,000 museums were registered in The Netherlands. However, a rising affluence level means many Dutch households are investing in antiques. Dutch tastes are predominantly centred around the history of The Netherlands, but more and more interest is being shown in British and other European items.

Exporters

The Dutch desk of Exports to Europe Branch of the Department of Trade and Industry in London (DTI, 1-19 Victoria Street, London SW1H 0ET; tel 071-215 5103, fax 071-215 5611) and the regional offices (see below) provide help and information to potential exporters to The Netherlands. It offers market information, reports on specific companies and current details on tariff rates and import procedures. Fees are charged for most of these services. The DTI publishes a number of general booklets aimed at individuals planning to set up a business abroad. These include *Financial Services*, *Company Law Harmonisation* and *Starting a Small Business*. In addition, the free quarterly magazine, *Single Market News*, is a good source of business news and regulations concerning the single market. All of these publications are available free of charge from the DTI hotline on 081-200 1992. The DTI's Export and Market Information Centre Library (Room 150, First Floor, Ashdown House, 123 Victoria Street, London SW1; tel 071-215 5444) is open from 9.30am to 5.30pm Monday to Friday and visitors are required to sign in with a business address.

Useful Addresses

DTI Regional Offices:

DTI *South East:* Bridge Place, 88/89 Eccleston Square, London SW1V 1PT; tel 071-215 5000.

DTI *North West:* Sunley Tower, Piccadilly Plaza, Manchester M1 4BA; tel 061-838 5000.

DTI *West Midlands:* Ladywood House, Stephenson Road, Birmingham B2 4DT; tel 021-212-5000.

Northern Ireland Office: Industrial Development Board, IDB House, 64 Chichester Street, Belfast BT1 4JX; tel 0232-233233.

Scottish Office: Industry Department for Scotland, Alhambra House, 45 Waterloo Street, Glasgow G2 6AT; tel 041-248 2855.
Welsh Office: Industry Department, Cathays Park, Cardiff CF1 3NQ; tel 0222-825111.

Running a Business

Employing Staff

Contracts: Employment contracts must be written and drawn up in accordance with Dutch labour laws. The Civil Code defines a contract as 'an agreement in which the employee undertakes to carry out work in return for wages, during a certain period of time'. Contracts are normally indefinite, although fixed-term contracts are in use. Trial periods can be specified, during which time contracts can be terminated without notice by either side. The minimum notice period is normally one week for each year of service, up to a maximum of 13 weeks. For workers aged 45 or over there is an additional week for each year they have worked beyond 45. The maximum number of weeks is 26. Employers wishing to terminate a contract, other than by mutual agreement, must obtain approval from the Regional Labour Office. Dutch employers are increasingly using casual, external labour on contracts for outwork (work from home), contracts for temporary employment (six months maximum), on-call commitments and freelance agreements. In each of these cases the employer and the employee have the right to terminate the contract at any time or, in the case of on-call contractors, ignore it.

Trade Unions: Although trade union membership is not compulsory about two-fifths of the Dutch workforce belongs to a labour organization. The Netherlands has three trade union organizations, two central employers' organizations representing large trade associations and some multinationals, two central organizations for medium- and small enterprises and three farmers' unions. Union leaders do not tend to regard strikes as a means to achieve a goal and the number of days lost through strike action in The Netherlands is small.

Labour Relations: Companies with more than 35 employees must set up a Works Council (*Ondernemingsraad*) to advise employers on certain labour matters (see below). Structured companies (*structuur vennootschappen*), NVs and BVs with more than 100 employees or more than Dfl 10 million capital reserves, must appoint a Supervisory Board (*Raad van Commissarissen*); this supervises the Board of Management on behalf of employees and must have at least three members. In companies with less than 35 staff members, the management is obliged to meet with the whole workforce at least twice a year. Works Councils must be consulted on such matters as mergers, closures, a firm's change of location and important reorganizations. Managements must obtain the consent of a Supervisory Board on decisions regarding pensions, insurance, profit sharing, working time and holidays, work safety, promotions, training, and the handling of complaints. In 1945 the Joint Industrial Labour Council was set up to handle labour agreements at national level. There is also a 45-strong Socio-Economic Council comprising: 15 members appointed by the employers' organizations, 15 by union groups and 15 independent experts appointed by the Dutch government. The government is required by law to seek the advice of the council on all major issues concerning wages, prices and social policy negotiations.

Employee Training: The Dutch government provides financial assistance for the training of labour. For approved training programmes, employers are given grants for wage costs of employees during training, the cost of the training course and travelling expenses.

Wages and Salaries: The statutory minimum wage is currently Dfl 1,987.70 (£615) per month or Dfl 458.70 a week for workers aged 23 and over. The minimum wage for younger employees is based on a percentage of the full minimum wage. The band ranges from 30% for 15-year-olds to 85% for 22-year-olds. In common with many other European Community countries, employees are often paid an additional month's salary ('the thirteenth month') in December. Dutch firms also use a number of fringe benefits to attract and retain staff. These include subsidized canteens, pensions and savings plans, company cars and supplementary payments of 30% of wages during sickness (the Sickness Insurance Act pays 70%).

Social Security Contributions: The Netherlands' social security system is governed by numerous different acts and has developed over several decades; as a consequence it is very complex. In broad terms it can be grouped into two categories — national insurance and employee insurance. The national insurance comprises contributions towards old age pensions, the widows and orphans fund, major medical expenses, disability benefits and child benefits. The premiums are paid solely by employees and are incorporated into income tax payments. The employee insurance programme requires payments from employers as well as employees. This covers sickness benefits, unemployment benefits, disability insurance and compulsory health insurance. Payments are withheld at source and paid in advance each month to the Industrial Insurance Board.

Paid Holidays: The legal minimum holiday is 20 days a year and a minimum holiday allowance of 7.5% on annual salaries, of up to three times the minimum wage, must be paid. There can also be as many as nine statutory holidays in a year (see Chapter Four, *Daily Life*).

Taxation

The principal taxes in The Netherlands are corporate income tax, personal income tax and VAT. A tax return (*belastingaangifte*) is due within six months of the end of a company's financial year. The authorities issue a provisional tax assessment in March, based on the average taxable income of the company during the two previous years. A double taxation treaty is currently in force between The Netherlands and the UK.

Corporate Income Tax (*vennootschapsbelasting*): A two-tier system of corporate income tax charges 40% on taxable profit up to Dfl 250,000 (£77,400) and 35% on all taxable profit in excess of Dfl 250,000. Companies controlled in The Netherlands and established under Dutch law are subject to tax on their worldwide income. (This also applies to subsidiaries.) Branches of foreign firms are taxed on profits derived in The Netherlands and income arising from the sale of Dutch real estate.

Individual Income Tax (*inkomstenbelasting*): Taxable income is the aggregate amount of net income or profit arising from employment and profits. The rate of income tax ranges from 13% to 60%. Foreign nationals can be eligible for the '35 per cent rule', which means income tax is charged only on 65% of an individual's earnings. Capital gains from the sale of shares representing a substantialinterest are taxed at a flat rate of 20%.

Value Added Tax: VAT is referred to as BTW (*Belasting Toegevoegde Waarde*) or OB (*Omzetbelasting*). The standard rate is 18.5% and business registration can take up to six months. There is a reduced rate of 6% for designated essential goods and services, such as foods, books and water, and a zero rate for exports. Transactions in real estate (including rental and leasing), medical and educational services, banking, and postal services are exempt from BTW. Prostitutes must pay VAT at 18.5% after the Ministry of Finance ruled that they, like other entrepreneurs, were liable not only for income tax but also for sales tax. However, written receipts are not necessary and businessmen who visit prostitutes cannot write-off the extra VAT levy against tax.

From January 1 1993 all inter-business cross-border trading within the European Community will be subject to VAT in the country of purchase, rather than the country of origin. To aid the process the European Commission is spending more than £6 million to set up a Community-wide computer network — the VAT information exchange system (*Vies*). A company selling a product to an EC business customer will tap into *Vies* check the customer is VAT registered, and dispatch the goods. The buyer will have to declare the purchase on his or her periodical VAT return. At present a single administration document has 50 boxes to be filled in and checked by customs officials.

Property Tax: For property transfers, a transfer tax (*overdrachtsbelasting*) of 6% is levied on the value of commercial and private property. This transfer tax also applies to the movement of shares in real estate companies. In both cases it is the purchaser who is legally responsible for filing a tax return.

Other: Excise taxes are levied on beer, wines, spirits and soft drinks; on tobacco products; on alcohol-containing substances; on sugar and sugar-containing products and on petroleum products. A capital issue tax of 1% is levied on the formation of a company or any increases in share capital. A special consumption tax is applied to personal cars. There is a net wealth tax of 0.8% and a gifts and inheritance tax is levied at rates of 5% to 68%, depending on the amount bequeathed and the relationship between the donor and the recipient.

Legal Advice

The prospective business person in The Netherlands is almost certainly going to need specialist legal advice, both in the purchase or setting up of a business and in future operations. This applies no matter how large or small the business is. Although there are some UK lawyers with a knowledge of Dutch law most small business needs will be best served by a local firm. Dutch legal specialist Van Beuningen & van Beurden is an English-speaking practice that offers advice and help on the Dutch legal system.

Useful Address

Van Beuningen & van Beurden: Lange Houtstraat 37, 2511 CV Den Haag; tel 070-3560850/3645817, fax 070-3615050.

Accountancy and Auditing Advice

Dutch law requires all businesses to keep financial accounts in such a way that the liabilities and assets can be determined at any time. Financial statements should be prepared and signed within five months of a company's year-end for *NVs* and

BVs, or within six months for other business organizations. Under Dutch law the books of account and records, financial statements, and incoming and outgoing correspondence of an enterprise should be retained for at least ten years. These records can be kept in any form, including on mechanized and electronic systems. The annual accounts should include:
1. balance sheet
2. directors' report
3. income statement
4. audit report
5. a statement detailing the appropriation of profit or loss
6. full accounts of subsidiaries not already included
7. a description of any third-party rights to share in the company's profits
8. a statement of any events with significant financial consequences that have arisen after the financial year

Large- and medium companies are required to prepare full financial statements whereas small firms are required to file only abridged balance sheets and accompanying notes. A company is defined as medium in size if it conforms to two of the following criteria: 50-249 employees, annual net turnover of Dfl 8-35 million (£2.5 to £10.8 million), and assets of Dfl 8-17 million (£2.5 to £5.3 million). A small company should conform to two of the following: 49 employees or less, turnover of less than Dfl 8 million, and assets of no more than Dfl 4 million. Large companies are those which do not meet these criteria.

Auditing: Audits (the formal examination of accounts) are compulsory only for large- and medium-size companies. They must be carried out by independent qualified Dutch accountants or by individuals recognized by the Ministry of Economic Affairs (Ministerie van Economische Zaken) on the basis of qualifications obtained abroad.

Directors' Report: The directors' report should discuss the results of the company's operations and give expectations about the future course of the business, giving special attention to finance, personnel and investment. Information in the directors' report should not conflict with any data given in the annual accounts.

Useful Addresses

Price Waterhouse Nederlander, & Vooren: Koninginnegracht 8, 2514 AA Den Haag (PO Box 30439, 2500 GK Den Haag); tel 070-3108308.
Moret Ernst & Young: GH Betzweg 1, 3068 AZ Rotterdam (PO Box 488, 3000 AL Rotterdam); tel 010-4072222, fax 010-4552737.
HLB Nederland Accountants & Consultants: National Secretariat, Cronenburg 73, 1081 GM Amsterdam; tel 020-464011, fax 020-463251.
Price Waterhouse Publications Department: 32 London Bridge Street, London SE1 9SY; tel 071-939 3000.
Ernst & Young Publications Department: Melrose House, 42 Dingwall Road, Croydon, Surrey CR0 2NE; tel 071-928 2000.

Luxembourg

Living and Working in Luxembourg

General Introduction
Residence and Entry Regulations
Setting Up Home
Daily Life
Retirement
Employment
Temporary Work
Business and Industry Report
Starting a Business

General Introduction

Destination Luxembourg

Mention Luxembourg to most people and probably the first thing that springs to mind is the radio station of the same name. That is hardly surprising in view of the fact that Luxembourg plays only a minor part on the world stage. But those who take time to discover one of Europe's smallest countries will not be disappointed.

Throughout history Luxembourg has held an important geographical and cultural place in Europe's development. It was founded in the tenth century and ruled in turn by Burgundy, Spain, France and Austria from 1448 to 1815. In 1867 the Congress of London decided that Luxembourg should become an independent state, and it was placed under the collective guarantee of the signatory powers. Despite being neutral Luxembourg was overrun by Germany in both world wars and ended its isolation in 1948 when it adopted a customs union with Belgium and The Netherlands (the Benelux Union). From that moment its 390,000 inhabitants have played a central part in European affairs and been at the forefront of forging peaceful economic unification in Western Europe. The Grand Duchy is a constitutional monarchy and as a founder member joined the then EEC and EURATOM in 1957. Today its capital Luxembourg-Ville (a.k.a. Lützelburg) is the home of the Secretariat of the European Parliament, the EC Court of Justice, the European Investment Bank, the European Court of Accounts and for three months of the year it is also the meeting place of the Council of Ministers of the European Communities.

Political and Economic Structure

The key to Luxembourg's development can be found in its historical roots and a long tradition of economic co-operation with neighbouring countries. To some extent this has been both forced and a necessity but today its commitment to the success of the EC has resulted in the Grand Duchy playing a pivotal role in the Community.

Economy

Luxembourg's economy was built on the back of the iron and steel-making industries and for a period in the early 70s it suffered a setback owing to a decline in demand. A radical change of direction has seen the economy steadily break free from a dependence on heavy industry and move towards a lighter industrial base. The result is a diversified manufacturing sector that incorporates plastics, chemicals, textiles, mechanical engineering, electronics and a modern, rationalized iron and steel industry. In the wider economy banking plays a key role. Luxembourg is now best known as a financial centre, and as a base for banking and investment services. A love of money and a favourable fiscal climate have attracted more than 150 foreign banks, including the ill-fated Bank of Credit and Commerce

International (BCCI). Although not as famous as its Swiss counterpart, the importance of banking to the Grand Duchy is evident from the fact that the industry employs 15,993 people — or one out of every 12 of the Luxembourg workforce.

The people are hard-working and strikes are virtually unheard of — virtues which combined with successful diversification have produced an economic growth rate in recent years above the EC average. Luxembourg now boasts relatively low unemployment (1.5 per cent of the workforce) and low inflation (2.8 per cent per annum) — proof of the economic stability of this little country.

Government

Luxembourg is a constitutional and hereditary monarchy currently under the watchful eye of Grand Duke Jean, who exercises executive power through a 12-strong Council of Ministers (akin to the UK's Cabinet) led by the President of the government (Prime Minister) Jacques Santer. There is also a Council of State, nominated by the monarch, comprising 21 members, which acts as the supreme administrative tribunal but has limited legislative functions. Primary legislative authority is through the Chamber of Deputies (reduced to 60 in number in 1989). General elections to this chamber must be held at least every five years using a system of proportional representation, which has tended to produce coalition governments made up of members of two of the three large political parties; the *Christian-Social Party (PCS)*, the *Socialist Workers' Party (POSL)* and the *Democratic Party (PD)*. The *Christian-Social Party* has played a key role in all the post-war governments with the exception of 1974-79. The present coalition between the PCS and POSL, under the leadership of Jacques Santer, came to power in 1984 and despite a reduced majority in 1989 is expected to exhibit traditional Luxembourg political stability and remain in power until at least June 1994. Several minority parties exist including two green groups who collectively hold four seats.

Geographical Information

This tiny nation measures just 999 square miles and on most maps even a shortened version of its name, LUX, scarcely fits within its borders. Luxembourg is land-locked, lying to the east of Belgium and sandwiched between France and Germany. The population has risen slowly but steadily in the last 50 years and currently stands at nearly 400,000. The rise can be explained in part by the number of non-Luxembourgeois nationals, some 109,600 at the last count. This proportion of aliens is the highest in Europe, and twice the number of second-placed Switzerland. The Portuguese account for the biggest single group (41,769) followed by the Italians (19,831). These two groups, who were largely brought in to supply the iron and steel-making industries, now fill unskilled and manual positions. The British community totals 3,375 and the largest non-EC group is the Yugoslavs at 2,325. Luxembourg-Ville accommodates one-fifth of the population, 78,900, and Esch-sur-Alzette ranks second with 25,000.

Climate

Nobody goes to Luxembourg for the weather — the climate is very similar to the UK, temperate, with cool summers and mild winters. The average annual rainfall is approximately 32 inches; early winter is the wettest time of the year. Snowfalls are frequent between December and March.

Climate at Luxembourg City — 1951 to 1990

	Jan	April	July	Oct
Temperature degrees celsius (degrees fahrenheit)				
— Average	0.8(33.4)	8.3(46.9)	17.5(63.5)	9.5(49.1)
— Maximum	9.5(49.1)	22.0(71.6)	30.7(87.3)20.7 (69)	
— Minimum	-9.5(14.9)	-2.2(28)	6.9(44.4)	-0.4(31)
Relative humidity (%)	89.0	74.0	73.0	86.0
Hours of sunshine	38.6	158.7	200.5	94.7
Rainfall(mm)	69.0	50.6	62.9	63.8

Regional Guide

The Grand Duchy has two natural regions, to the north the Oesling (one-third of the country) and the Good Land (two-thirds) to the south, and is split into 12 administrative cantons. For our purposes the country is easily divided into four separate parts:

LUXEMBOURG-VILLE

The valleys of the Alzette and Pétrusse rivers meet to make the setting of Luxembourg-Ville one of the most dramatic in Europe. The capital is tiny — smaller than Bath — and broadly divides into four distinct sections. The old centre is situated on the northern side of the Pétrusse, high on the small central plateau of the old fortifications. It is made up of a tight grid of cobbled streets and Gothic houses, and is a lively, pleasant area to live. The new centre is on the opposite side of the river connected by the Pont Adolphe and Pasarelle bridges to the old quarter. It must be said this is the less attractive part of town and is home to some of the city's sleazier aspects. The third area, the Valleys, covers the land from the river banks up to the old centre. Finally, to the east, the fourth area, situated on the plateau of Kirchberg, is the home of the European Community Institutions. Most of the medieval city was destroyed in 1554 and much of the older part was rebuilt in the seventeenth century. The city was renowned for its awesome defences but the once impenetrable barriers were partly dismantled in 1867, giving an open feel today to many areas in the city.

THE SOUTH

The Moselle and Industrial Southwest

The south of Luxembourg is generally regarded as the least picturesque region containing much of the Grand Duchy's industrial base around Esch-sur-Alzette. The area was built on mining and iron/steel production and has the scars to prove it. At nearby Rumelange the old industrial remains have been turned to advantage and the *Musée National des Mines* operates guided tours 1000m down in a disused mine shaft. The one redeeming feature is the Moselle river and 25km of vineyards that constitute Luxembourg's small but quality wine industry.

THE CENTRAL AREA
Echternach, Ettelbruck and Diekirch
North from the capital the undulating countryside gives way to stunning hills and woodland. Much of the area around Ettelbruck and Diekirch suffered heavy damage in late 1944 during the Battle of the Bulge and many monuments mark where those who fell are buried. To the east, towards Germany, Echternach is the main centre of what is known as Little Switzerland.

THE NORTH
Esch-sur-Sûre, Clervaux, Vianden and Wiltz
Much of the northern part of Luxembourg lies in the Ardennes region with its fairy-tale castles. Vianden is the main centre through which the booming tourist trade from neighbouring countries reaches the region. In 1871 Victor Hugo exiled himself to this delightful town which has recently seen its eleventh century castle restored to its former glory. Clervaux lies in the far north of the country and the town's castle, dating from the twelfth century, forms part of a centuries-old defence structure. To the west the picturesque towns of Bourscheid, Esch-sur-Sûre and Wiltz nestle in the beautiful wooded scenery.

Residence and Entry Regulations

The Current Position

The cosmopolitan nature of Luxembourg's population is testament to its willingness to accept foreigners. More than one-quarter of the population are currently non-Luxembourg nationals and the figure is set to continue rising.

Requirements for British Citizens.

UK citizens need only a full British passport — which must be endorsed with the words 'Holder has the right to abode in the UK' — to stay in Luxembourg for up to three months (a visitor's passport is not sufficient for those taking up work). Passports issued after 1 January 1983 should have the words British Citizen on page one.

Residence Permit

To extend a stay beyond three months, UK citizens must obtain an Identity Card for Foreign Nationals. To apply, contact the Police des Etrangers and provide the following five documents: proof of identity, (usually a passport, but a driving licence is sometimes accepted), a *Déclaration Patronale* (proof of sufficient means of subsistence or employment contract), a *Déclaration de Départ* (a reference from your previous place of residence that you are of good character), a medical certificate issued by a Luxembourg doctor and a certificate showing proof of residence in Luxembourg. The card is valid for five years and is renewable.

Entering to Work

The Grand Duchy is subject to European Community regulations concerning the free movement of labour. As a result holders of a valid UK passport can freely enter the Grand Duchy to look for employment; a work permit is not required. However, to work continuously for more than three months it is necessary to obtain the Identity Card for Foreign Nationals. The application to the police should include a letter from your employer stating the terms of your contract (such as the salary and the duration). This acts as the *Déclaration Patronale*.

Entering to Start a Business

The Grand Duchy actively promotes business within its borders and treats foreign entrepreneurs in the same positive manner as it does its own. The above terms for entry and residence cover individuals entering the country with the aim of setting up a business. All industrial and commercial activities require a government permit, issued by the Ministry of Small and Medium Businesses (Ministère des Classes Moyennes). To qualify applicants need to show professional qualifications and experience in the field they wish to trade, and evidence of good standing and solvency. For detailed information on how to start trading see Chapter Seven, *Starting A Business.*

Non-EC Nationals

Visas to visit Luxembourg for less than three months are not required for persons from the United States, Canada, New Zealand, Australia, Israel, Singapore, Japan, Malaysia and nationals from Member States of the European Free Trade Association. Other visitors must obtain an entry visa, which is valid for tourist and business purposes. An *Autorisation de Séjour Provisoire* (residence/work permit) is required by non-EC nationals intending to work or stay longer than three months in the Grand Duchy. It is issued only if employment has been secured and at least one month should be allowed for processing. An applicant must be in possession of the permit before travelling to Luxembourg. The application for the permit must be made to the Luxembourg Embassy of the applicant's country of residence. It needs to include five completed application forms, three recent passport photos and a *Déclaration Patronale.*

Useful Addresses

Luxembourg Embassy: 27 Wilton Crescent, London, SW1X 8SD; tel 071-235 6961.
British Embassy: 14 boulevard Roosevelt, 2450 Luxembourg; tel 29 86 4.
US Embassy: 22 boulevard Emmanuel Servais, 2535 Luxembourg; tel 46 01 23, fax 46 14 01.
Luxembourg Embassy: 2200 Massachusetts Avenue, NW Washington DC 20008, United States of America; tel 202 2654171.
Police des Etrangers: Ministère de la Justice, 16 boulevard Royal, Luxembourg.
Administration de l'Emploi: 38a rue Philippe II, 2010 Luxembourg, tel 47 68 55-1.

Setting Up Home

Moving to Luxembourg is not as common an occurrence as moving to other EC countries and it is even rarer to buy a property there. As a result UK agencies are not geared towards such a move and little can be done from the UK. In Luxembourg estate agents exist and the British Embassy (and expats) will offer advice.

How do Luxemburgers live?

Luxemburgers tend to live in small, rather than extended, family units. The majority (71.7%) buy rather than rent property and the trend towards purchasing homes remains upwards, especially the practice of buying a plot of land and building one's own house. The standard of living is high and Luxemburgers rarely go without when it comes to the comforts of life. The quality of accommodation is very good and most Grand Duchy homes are fully equipped with the everyday domestic appliances.

Finance

Mortgages can either be arranged through UK or Luxembourg-based banks. The type and number of home loans on offer are virtually the same as in the UK, but in the Grand Duchy applicants are subject to strict financial checks and insurance is a must.

Purchasing Property

The procedures for buying a property in Luxembourg are very similar to those in the UK. The greatest number of properties are advertised in the *Luxembourg Wort* newspaper (Wednesday and Saturday) and through estate agents (*agents immobiliers*) — the largest two being Rockenbrod and Immosol. 'For Sale' signs (and 'To Let' signs) are never displayed and a property survey is not required, but conveyancing must be carried out by a bona fide public notary. The standard of housing is high, but so is the cost. In Luxembourg-Ville expect to pay more than in the countryside. A deposit equal to one-quarter the price of the property is payable as well as high agents' fees.

Useful Addresses

Rockenbrod: 16 boulevard Royal, 2449 Luxembourg; tel 47 55 23 (to buy) or 47 55 21 (to rent).
Immosol: 14 avenue de la Liberté, 1930 Luxembourg; tel 22 55 33.

Renting Property

Renting is still a popular choice in the Grand Duchy, especially on a short term basis. Furnished accommodation is not easy to find and Luxembourg-Ville itself is the most expensive, with prices one-third more than in the rest of the country. The easiest and quickest way to find a house is through estate agencies, which can cost two or three months' rent. Leases are generally fixed for three years, short term leases of just a few months are rare and require a deposit of one month's rent or more. Unfurnished means just that and light fittings, curtains or rods, carpets, kitchen cupboards and domestic appliances are not included. Furnished flats or houses for rent tend to include absolutely everything from furniture and fittings to lights and linen. Apartment buildings follow the German style of architecture with windows that can be opened in two directions and a communal laundry room in the basement.

Utilities

In Luxembourg-Ville gas, electricity and water are supplied and connected by one authority, the Recette Communale, which means bills, sent monthly, are charged on the same invoice. CEGEDEL supplies electricity to the rest of the country, with bills sent on a quarterly basis. Piped gas is available in Luxembourg-Ville, and the central and southern areas of the country; other regions rely on bottled supplies. For rural water connections contact the local *Administration Communale*. The domestic electricity supply uses three types of two-pin wall plugs: round pins with no earth connection, round pins with earth connections, and flat pins with earth connections. Enquiries concerning the installation of new telephone lines or the renaming of old ones should be directed to the state-owned telecommunications company P and T. A charge will be levied for reconnection and monthly rental, in addition to the cost of the calls. Details of the telephone service can be found in the front of the telephone book — of which there is only one — on the green-edged pages. Dustbins are emptied everywhere once a week but only garbage placed in bins or the correct refuse sacks will be removed. A collection of larger items is held every month in the city and every three months in other parts of the country.

Property-related Taxes

The Net Worth Tax is payable at 0.5 per cent but an allowance against tax is made at LF 100,000 (£1,690) for each member of a household. In addition, the municipalities charge a tax on land and buildings, based on the standard value (usually well below market value) of property. The tax is paid by the owner. Estate duty is payable on inherited property where the net value exceeds LF 50,000 at rates up to 15 per cent, depending on the net value and the relationship between the deceased and the beneficiary. Heirs in direct line to the deceased are exempt from succession duties.

Removals

The cost of moving is high, so take the minimum. Conversely buying new items in Luxembourg will be expensive, so take exactly what is needed. EC law states that legitimate household items can be imported duty free. Pets can be taken into the Grand Duchy (provided vets' reports and export and import certificates are in order). Rabies vaccinations are compulsory for dogs and cats. A number of companies specialize in removals to Europe and can advise on the red tape involved.

Useful Addresses

Arthur Pierre Removals: Tovil Green, Maidstone, Kent ME15 6RJ; tel 0622-691330, (or Brusselssesteenweg 344, Overijse, B-3090 Brussels, Belgium; tel 02-6877610, fax 02-6873730).

Scotpac International Moving: Security House, Abbey Wharf Industrial Estate, Kingsbridge Road, Barking, Essex IG11 0BT; tel 081-591 3388, fax 081-594 4571.

The British Association of Removers: (3 Churchill Court, 58 Station Road, North Harrow, Middlesex HA2 7SA; tel 081-861 3331) produces an information leaflet for anyone contemplating removals overseas.

Ministry of Agriculture: (Animal Health Division, Hook Rise South, Tolworth, Surbiton, Surrey KT6 7NF; tel 081-330 4411) gives advice on importing pets.

Daily Life

Living in a new country normally means learning a new way of life, but in the case of Luxembourg it's more than that. Combine German efficiency with French flair, add a little essence of Belgium, a touch of *je ne sais quoi* from the Grand Duchy itself and you have the recipe for Luxembourg life. Foreigners make up more than a quarter of the population and tourism attracts more than four times the country's own number each year, mainly to the north and the Ardennes region. Needless to say the country is as cosmopolitan as anywhere in the world. But the people are rightly proud of what they have achieved and they are forever saying so. *'Mir woelle bleiwe wat mir sin'* is the national motto and inscribed everywhere. It means quite simply 'We want to remain what we are'. Spend time living and working here and you too could find yourself echoing these sentiments.

The Languages

The native tongue in Luxembourg is Letzeburgesch. It is spoken throughout all walks of life but is very difficult to learn. However, Luxemburgers have adopted both French and German, and English is widely understood in the capital. French is the official government and administrative language, German, on the other hand, is associated with the less educated sections of the population, and is the language of the press and churches. Everyday conversation is usually conducted in Letzeburgesch.

Schools & Education

Three schools in the Grand Duchy are English-speaking: St George's School, the American School of Luxembourg and the European School. St George's takes children from three to nine years, and fees range from LF 156,000 to LF 261,000. The other two take children from the age of four to the end of secondary education.

Education in Luxembourg is compulsory between the ages of six and 16. Children leave primary schools at 11 and move to one of three establishments: the *Lycée*, which is considered the stepping stone to university, the more practical and vocational based *Middle School* or the *Ecole Complémentaire*, which treads a line between the two. Luxembourg does not have what we would call a university, but the *Centre Universitaire*, set up in 1969, offers one-year courses that include law, humanities, sciences, and teaching, as preparation for entry into other European universities.

Useful Addresses

St George's School: 55 rue Demy Schlechter, 2521 Luxembourg-Bonnevoie; tel 48 29 10. (Also c/o British School of Brussels, Leuvensesteenweg 19, 3080 Tervuren, Belgium; tel 02-7674700, fax 02-7678070.)

European School (Ecole Européenne): 23 boulevard Konrad Adenauer, 1115 Luxembourg; tel 43 20 82, fax 43 67 38.

American School of Luxembourg: 188 avenue de la Faïencerie, 1511 Luxembourg-Limpertsberg; tel 47 00 20.

Ministère de l'Éducation Nationale, 6 boulevard Royal, 2449 Luxembourg; tel 4 79 41.

Centre Universitaire: place Auguste-Laurent, 1921 Luxembourg (science), 162a avenue de la Faïencerie, 1511 Luxembourg (for other subjects).

Media & Communications

Newspapers/Books

Five daily newspapers are on offer in the Grand Duchy and one-third of Luxemburgers buy one every day. The papers cover a wide political spectrum from the communist *Zeitung vum Letzeburger Vollek* to the democratic (and most widely read) *Luxemburger Wort.* The tabloid as we know it does not exist, but a ready supply of French and German papers fills the gaps. The English-language *Luxembourg News* is the newsprint bible for the expat population.

Television/Radio

Luxemburgers like television and there is an estimated one TV set to every three persons. Viewers are spoilt for choice and can tune into stations from France, Germany and Belgium. Most villages even have their own satellite dish to add yet more programmes. There is a no more widely-known radio station than *Radio Luxembourg.* UK listeners can tune in only via satellite these days but in the Grand Duchy it is going from strength to strength. It is part of the *Compagnie Luxembourgeoise de Télédiffusion* and broadcasts programmes in French, German, English, Dutch, Italian, Portuguese, Spanish and Serbo-Croat.

Telephone/Post

Telephoning Luxembourg is relatively easy as there are no area codes. Simply dial 010-352 and the number required. To phone home to Britain dial 0044 and the number, minus the first 0 on the STD code. The emergency number is 012 which covers police, fire, ambulance, duty chemists and locksmiths. The state-owned postal service is as quick and efficient as anywhere in the EC. Charges are slightly higher than in the UK.

Useful Address
Main Post Office: 8 avenue Monterey, Luxembourg-Ville; tel 4 76 51.

Transport

Roads

To get around, a car is almost essential, and if you are a Luxemburger two is the norm. A total of 5,091 road kilometres, including 78.5 kilometres of motorway,

St. George's School Luxembourg

International English-speaking Primary School
offers an excellent
British style education from age 3.

Contact : Mr E. Milnes, Headmaster
Rue Demy Schlechter 55
L-2521 Luxembourg - Telephone : 48.29.10

comprehensively cover the Grand Duchy. The use of lead-free petrol is increasing and the majority of cars are brand new. Parking is at a premium in Luxembourg-Ville so taxis are a popular option. Alternatively the town's bus service is a cheap and easy way to get around. For travelling further afield hitch-hiking is acceptable and on the small roads getting a lift is relatively easy.

Railway

Rail travel in the Grand Duchy is clean and on time, but limited. The Luxembourg National Railways network links the capital to Esch-sur-Alzette in the south, to Wasserbillig (and onto Trier and Koblenz) in the east, and Clervaux, Ettelbruck (branch line to Diekirch) and Kautenbach (branch line to Wiltz) in the north. Luxembourg-Ville is on the main line from Ostend-Brussels to Basel: eight express trains run daily in each direction, and the journey to Brussels takes less than three hours.

Air

Luxembourg is easily accessible from Europe by land but a quarter of a million air passengers still use its main international airport, Lux-Findel, every year. It lies three miles east of Luxembourg-Ville and from here the national carrier Luxair operates three flights a day to London. British Airways has one scheduled daily service.

Useful Addresses

Luxair: Aéroport de Luxembourg, 2987 Luxembourg; tel 43 61 61.
British Airways: European Bank and Business Centre, 6th Floor, 6 rte de Trèves, 2633 Senningerberg; tel 34 83 47, fax 34 82 69.

Banks and Finance

The personal banking system is similar to that in the UK. The majority of banks offer personal services including deposit and current accounts, loans, mortgages and insurance. There is no restriction on foreign nationals opening accounts, but the banks will require proof of identity and a letter of introduction from your UK bank. Accounts can be opened in the UK or in the Grand Duchy and no restrictions apply on money transfers.

Useful Addresses

Kredietbank SA Luxembourgeoise: 43 boulevard Royal, 2953 Luxembourg-Ville; tel 4 79 71, fax 47 26 67. (London office: Founders Court, Lothbury, London EC2R 7HE; tel 071-600 0332.)

Banque Internationale à Luxembourg SA: 2 boulevard Royal, 2953 Luxembourg-Ville; tel 45 90 1, fax 4791 2010. (London office: Priory House, 1 Mitre Square, London EC3A 5AN; tel 071-623 3110, fax 071-623 5833.)
Banque et Caisse d'Epargne de l'Etat Luxembourg: 1 place de Metz, 2954 Luxembourg; tel 4015 3515/3519.
Lloyds Bank: 1 rue Schiller, 2519 Luxembourg; tel 40 22 12.

Taxation

Indirect taxation in the Grand Duchy is renowned for being lower than in its neighbours, which means goods and services are somewhat cheaper. The taxauthorities are the *Administration des Contributions Directes et des Accises* (income tax, excise duties and municipal business tax), the *Administration de l'Enregistrement et des Domaines* (VAT, stamp and registration taxes), Customs and the Communes (ground tax and tax on salary). People spending more than one tax year outside the UK are not liable to pay tax on earnings but will still be liable for tax on savings accounts and investments in Britain.

Income Tax

There are no special income tax rules applicable to foreigners and the rate is split into three categories: single; married couples without children and non-residents; and married couples with children. Income tax is levied on a sliding scale from 15% to 50%. Category one has the steepest rise, the other two groups have the same ceiling but the increase to the top rate is not as steep.

VAT

The standard rate of value added tax (*taxe sur la valeur ajoutée* — *TVA*) is 15%. However, the rate is currently under review and an intermediate rate of 12% has been set during 1992. No VAT is levied on banking, exports, postal services, certain social and cultural activities, insurance, and the transfer and letting of property.

Health Insurance and Hospitals

The Luxembourg health service is good and almost entirely private. Insurance premiums are normally paid by employers but it is advisable to take out extra private insurance. There are no private hospitals as such and the majority of hospitals are run by the state. The service is funded by the *Caisse de Maladie* (sickness contributions). An Elll entitles visiting British citizens to treatment, but they must be resident in the UK. Details are available from the DSS Overseas Department (Newcastle upon Tyne NE98 1YX; tel 091-213 5000.)

Social Security and Unemployment Benefit

Luxembourg's comprehensive social services system is administered by semi-public bodies (*caisses*). The two major benefit areas are pensions (old age and disability) and family allowance, and health (doctor and dentist fees, some convalescence and prescription charges). There is no provision for opting out, but all contributors benefit irrespective of nationality.

The unemployment fund is financed via supplementary income tax and a special unemployment tax. To qualify applicants must meet the following criteria: have worked in Luxembourg for 26 weeks (except students), be involuntarily out of work, domiciled in the Grand Duchy, and between 16 and 65 years of age. Unemployment benefit is 80 per cent of the average monthly gross salary for the three months preceding unemployment, but not more than 2.5 times the minimum salary for an unskilled worker, and payable for 12 months.

Useful Address
Common Centre of Social Security: 125 route d'Esch, 1471 Luxembourg; tel 49 92 01.

Local Government
Central government has most power in the running of the country. Each commune has its own local council or *conseil communal*, elected by the residents, which deals with local issues. The majority of the wider-ranging issues, such as taxation, roads, transport and utilities, are centrally controlled.

Crime and the Police
Luxembourg has one of the lowest crime rates in the EC and it is not uncommon for Luxemburgers to leave cars unlocked. Burglaries and petty crime do exist but more violent offences are very rare. The Grand Duchy's police are armed but are relatively few in number.

Religion
The practice and hold of religion has been on the decline this century, but the overwhelming majority of Luxemburgers (97%) still profess to be Roman Catholics. Religious instruction is taught in schools, but in the higher grades there is a choice between Catholic doctrine and a lay course in ethics and morality. Freedom of worship is an old tradition and both the Protestant pastor (Reform and Augsburg churches) and chief Rabbi are paid by the state, as are the RC priests.

Useful Addresses
Archbishop of Luxembourg: Most Rev Fernand Franck, Archeveché, 4 rue Génistre, BP419, 2014 Luxembourg.
Anglican Chaplain: Rev C. G. Poole, 44 boulevard de la Pétrusse, Luxembourg.
Chief Rabbi: Joseph Sayag, 15 boulevard Grande-Duchesse Charlotte, 1331 Luxembourg.

Social Life
Outwardly Luxemburgers appear unfriendly and a little distant but once friendships have been struck this can give way to a surprising openness. There are of course a number of little rules and quirks to remember. Hand shaking is very common, on meeting and parting; punctuality is also very important and if invited to someone's house it is customary to take flowers or chocolates for the host or hostess.

Entertainment and Culture
Luxembourg is not famous for its night life and much of the partying is at the

instigation of the foreign communities. In the capital, the White Rose and the Pub in the Grund are just two bars under the English influence, and the Pygmalion has an Irish flavour. Beer is relatively cheap in the Grand Duchy and there are plenty of local brews to choose from, including the oddly named Henri Funk.

Thanks to active encouragement the arts are positively thriving in Luxembourg, as can be seen from the number of galleries, theatres and other cultural activities that abound. The number of professional artists is relatively small — expressionist painter Joseph Kutter and photographer Edward Steichen are two international exports.

● The new music scene is not particularly vibrant but the classical variety is the first love of the true Luxemburger and every village and town has at least one band or a choral group. Cinemas are the popular form of entertainment among the younger generation and most films are subtitled rather than dubbed.

Football is the nearest any Luxemburger gets to becoming excited about sport but the Grand Duchy's amateur team do not win many games and a draw is cause for national celebration. Needless to say attention is focused more on the German and French leagues.

Public Holidays

1 January	New Year's Day
March/April	Easter Monday
1 May	Labour Day
May	Ascension Day
May/June	Whit Monday
23 June	National Day
15 August	Assumption Day
1 November	All Saints' Day
25 December	Christmas
26 December	St Stephen's Day

Additional holidays are observed on Shrove Monday, in February, Carnival Monday in March, Biergerdag (Luxembourg-Ville only) in September, and All Souls' Day on 2 November, these are not official, but many businesses close and services may be curtailed. Shops and firms traditionally close in the afternoon on Christmas Eve. If a public holiday falls on a Saturday or Sunday the following Monday is observed instead.

Retirement

Luxembourg cannot guarantee sun, sea, sand and sangria, but it does have beautiful countryside and a slow, relaxed way of life to offer those in retirement. Subject to meeting Luxembourg's entry and residence qualifications (see Chapter Two, *Residence and Entry*) one of the biggest disadvantages of retiring in the Grand Duchy will undoubtedly be the cost of living. A UK pension will not necessarily make ends meet and this should be taken into consideration. To arrange for pension funds to be transferred contact the Overseas Branch of the Department of Social Security. Private health insurance is a must as a National Health Service as such does not exist. The language could also prove to be a stumbling block, and a good knowledge of either German or French would be strongly advisable. To avoid legal problems making a will is recommended. For further details the Department of Social Security produces the booklet *Your Social Security, Health Care and Pension Rights in the EC* (available from DSS Overseas Branch, Newcastle upon Tyne, NE98 1YX).

On the plus side the country is beautiful and the standard of living very high; also the English-speaking expatriate community (in excess of 3,000) is well-established and very helpful. Their experience can make all the difference to a successful integration into the Grand Duchy's way of life.

English-Language Clubs

British Ladies' Club: c/o E. Turner, 15 Haupeschhaff, 6910 Roodt/Syre; tel 7 77 44.
British Businessmen's Club: c/o Plumpton, Morgan & Partners, 3 rue Guillaume Kroll, 1027 Luxembourg-Ville; tel 40 63 58.
Cricket Club: 8 rue Jean Engling, 1466 Luxembourg-Ville; tel 43 16 94.
Hockey Club: 31 rue de la Libération, 8031 Strassen; tel 31 25 20 (men), 31 rue Eugène Welter, 2723 Howald; tel 49 34 18 (women).
Rugby Club: 47a rue de Hobscheid, 8422 Steinfort; tel 39 95 43.
Squash d'Or: 404 route d'Esch, 1471 Luxembourg-Ville; tel 48 01 40.
New World Theatre Club Asbl: 23 rue J. F. Kennedy, 7371 Helmdange; tel 33 96 71.

Employment

The Employment Scene

With an area of just 999 square miles and a labour force of 165,100 the Grand Duchy obviously offers finite employment opportunites. However, a constant demand does exist for skilled labour. Luxembourg has one of the lowest unemployment rates in the EC, currently 1.5 per cent, a figure that is expected to continue edging down. The biggest difficulty for anyone seeking employment will be the lack of a good knowledge of French and/or German, as both are in common usage and essential in commerce and industry. As far as obtaining work is concerned speculative enquiries can be made to firms in Luxembourg but it is advisable to make sure the company will be interested in the skills you can offer and that you correspond in either French or German. A full list of British companies in the Grand Duchy is available from the Luxembourg Embassy in London.

Residence and Work Regulations

As a member of the European Community Luxembourg is subject to community regulations concerning free movement of labour, and UK citizens do not require a work permit. A passport is sufficient to stay for up to three months; beyond this period an Identity Card for Foreign Nationals is required (see Chapter Two, *Residence and Entry Regulations*).

Sources of Jobs

Newspapers

The job sections in newspapers can provide one of the most up-to-date sources of employment and also advertise your own particular skills. The English language *Luxembourg News* carries a well-read jobs column and adverts in Luxembourg's largest circulation daily, *Luxemburger Wort* can be placed through London-based publisher representative *Publicitas Ltd*. Do not expect to find too many jobs in UK papers' sits vac columns, and if there are any, being UK based is likely to be a requirement. The specialist bi-monthly *Overseas Jobs Express* publishes a wide and diverse number of employment opportunities in Europe.

Useful Addresses

Luxembourg News: 34 avenue Victor Hugo, 1750 Luxembourg.
Luxemburger Wort/La Voix du Luxembourg: 2 rue Christophe Plantin, 2988 Luxembourg, or c/o *Publicitas Ltd:* 517-523 Fulham Road, London SW6 1HD.

Professional Associations

The majority of professional associations cannot give information on working overseas. The nature of Luxembourg's economy means that most demands for employees will be in banking, computers, EC offices and secretarial work. However, it must be stressed that the highest qualifications are required and UK associations are not employment agencies. Details can be found in the directory,

Trade Associations and Professional Bodies in the UK, available at most libraries. In Luxembourg a number of business groups can offer advice on employment.

Useful Addresses

European Parliament Recruitment Service: Bâtiment Robert Schuman, Plateau du Kirchberg, 2920 Luxembourg.

Luxembourg Chambre de Commerce: 7 rue Alcide de Gasperi, 2981 Luxembourg; tel 43 58 53.

Confédération du Commerce Luxembourgeois: 23 Allée Scheffer, 2520 Luxembourg; tel 47 31 25.

Centrale Paysanne Luxembourgeoise (agriculture): 16 boulevard d'Avranches, 2980 Luxembourg; tel 48 81 61.

Teaching English

Three schools are English-speaking but the thirst (and ability) to learn foreign languages means the need for private tuition is widespread. Only Luxembourg nationals can teach in state schools but private establishments may have vacancies. Further information on teaching English overseas is available from The European Council of International Schools (21b Lavant Street, Petersfield, Hants GU32 3EL), and the British Council (Overseas Educational Appointments Department, 65 Davis Street, London WIY 2AA).

Au Pair Work

There is no special agency that deals with the placement of au pairs but positions can be found through general employment agencies. A potential employer must obtain an *Accord Placement Au Pair* from the Administration de l'Emploi. This is the contract specifying the conditions of the au pair's stay and is signed by both parties. It will require the host family to affiliate the au pair to the social security system and if the au pair falls ill they must guarantee board and lodging, and medical treatment. The contract must be concluded before travel to Luxembourg.

Useful Addresses

Manpower-Aide Temporaire: 19 rue Glesener, 1631 Luxembourg; tel 48 23 23 (general).

Bureau-Service: 2 allée Leopold Goebel, 1635 Luxembourg (office work).

Officenter: 25 boulevard Royal, 2449 Luxembourg; tel 47 25 62 (temporary office jobs).

FM Recruitment: 6 Conduit Street, London WIR 9TG (catering).

Cercle de Coopération et d'Aide au Développment du Tiers Monde: 5 avenue Marie-Thérèse, 2132 Luxembourg (voluntary work).

Choice International: Millfield House, 904 Warwick Road, Acock's Green, Birmingham B27 6QG; tel 021 706 5963 (au pair).

Luxembourg-Accueil-Information: 10 Bisserwe, 1238 Luxembourg; tel 4 17 17 (general and au pair).

Centre Information Jeunes — Youth Information Centre: 76 Boulevard de la Pétrusse, 2320 Luxembourg (student and au pair).

MBR Services: BP19, L-7701 Colmar Berg; tel 85 94 74 (farming).

Eurocamp: Edmundson House, Tatton Street, Knutsford WA16 6BG.

Aspects of Employment

Salaries

A minimum salary rate for employees is fixed by Grand Ducal decree; for a worker without a family it is LF 36,819 (£620) per month, and LF 37,934 for employees with a family. The rate increases 20 per cent for skilled/qualified staff, and is reduced to 60, 70 and 80 per cent for workers aged 15, 16 and 17-years-old respectively. Wages are normally index-linked and a 2.5 per cent rise in the standard-of-living index results in an equal rise in remuneration from the following month. What we would regard as fringe benefits, such as canteens and company cars, are not normally provided. Overtime has to be authorized by the Minister of Labour (Ministre du Travail) and is paid at rates between one and a quarter to two times the normal rate, or equivalent holiday is given.

Working Conditions

The standard working week in Luxembourg is 40 hours. Employees are not expected to work on Sunday but it is not uncommon for senior staff to work at weekends. Annual paid holiday of 25 days is obligatory and special leave is always granted for marriages, births and deaths. Maternity leave is provided for eight weeks before birth and up to 12 weeks post-natally. A new mother can take a year's maternity leave and must be re-employed by priority in an adequate position.

Trade Unions

Strikes are very rare and industrial relations in Luxembourg are excellent thanks to extensive conciliation arrangements from the shop floor right up to national level. By law, employees are required to have their say either on the boards of large companies (more than 1,000 employees) or in the form of works' councils for smaller firms.

Women at Work

Unfortunately Luxembourg is no exception when it comes to women occupying senior positions — there are very few. However, more and more women are working in the Grand Duchy and constitute 34 per cent of the current workforce compared with only 23 per cent in 1970. The banking sector employs the highest number of women, 48 per cent, but the jobs are for the most part at the bottom of the employment hierarchy.

Business & Industry Report

Luxembourg is a small, industrially developed country essentially reliant upon foreign markets. Following the ravages of the Second World War it can claim to have achieved a mini economic miracle and today boasts one of the strongest and most stable economies in the world.

Banking & Finance

Banking is big business in Luxembourg, accounting for more than 15% of the country's GDP. The state-owned Banque et Caisse d'Epargne de l'Etat is the country's oldest financial institution, founded in 1856. A favourable financial climate and a veil of banking secrecy have seen the number of banks rise to 185, out of a total of 200 eligible worldwide to open up in the Grand Duchy. But experts are uncertain about the future as EC laws have eroded some of the financial benefits and loopholes previously offered by the Grand Duchy.

Media & Communications

The country has no state-owned TV broadcasting company but it is still responsible for the audiovisual diet of more than 120 million Europeans, mainly through the *Compagnie Luxembourgeoise de Télédiffusion (CLT)* and *Société Européenne des Satellites (SES)*, whose satellites carry *BSkyB*. In 1931 the Luxembourg government granted *CLT* permission to broadcast from its territory, and the company now transmits 10 radio stations (including *Radio Luxembourg*) and six TV channels.

In 1988 a programme of tax-breaks was established for film-makers in what was described as an attempt to create a European Hollywood. By the end of 1991 $20 million had been spent attracting several small productions, but the project is still in its infancy.

Iron and Steel-Making

The iron and steel industry has undergone massive modernization and rationalization in the last 20 years. In 1970 the industry accounted for nearly one-third of Luxembourg's GDP. Today the total is nearer 11 per cent, of which the giant ARBED accounts for ten of the 11% and employs one in 25 of the Duchy's population. The savage cuts inflicted upon the industry have turned vast losses in the early 1980s to handsome profitability in 1991. Three-quarters of production is aimed at foreign markets and as the EC develops ARBED is expected to join forces with a European rival.

Manufacturing Industry

Japanese electrical giant TDK is responsible for the largest ever investment in the Grand Duchy. Its LF 7 billion (£118 million) factory, creating 600 jobs, is the jewel in the crown of Luxembourg's rapidly expanding light industry sector. Manufacturing has seen its GDP share drop from 43 to 25% in 20 years, but a push to diversify away from iron and steel has sparked a flow of companies and money into the country. In 1990 and 1991 LF 16 billion (£270 million) and LF 18 billion (£300 million) respectively were estimated to have been invested in the manufacturing industry, and forecasts are that this level of investment will continue.

Tourism

An estimated 800,000 tourists visited Luxembourg in 1990 attracted by the stunning ruins of medieval castles such as Clervaux, Vianden and Wiltz and footpaths/hikes through beautiful wooded countryside. The majority of visitors reportedly treat Luxembourg as a stop-off point to other destinations in neighbouring countries. This apparent under-exploitation means the industry has plenty of room to grow.

Useful Addresses
Office National du Tourisme: 77 rue d'Anvers, BP1001, 1010 Luxembourg.
Luxembourg National Tourist Office: 36/37 Piccadilly, London W1V 9PA; tel
    071-434 2800.

Starting a Business

As one of the European Community's most economically successful countries Luxembourg has proved that size does not matter. The Grand Duchy is geographically and culturally where France and Germany meet. But as far as its economy is concerned identification with either of these countries is a thing of the past. The country is well placed for the growth of the EC's single market, with low inflation (2.8% per annum), a proven record of strong economic growth and a highly trained workforce.

Procedures Involved in Buying or Starting a New Business

Creating a New Business

A government permit is required to set up any industrial/commercial venture. This is issued by the Ministry of Small and Medium-sized Businesses — *Ministère des Classes Moyennes*. (A company is classed as small if annual turnover is less than LF 160 million (£2.7 million) and it has less than 50 staff. A medium-sized firm has a turnover not exceeding LF 640 million and no more than 250 employees.) In all cases the applicants must prove themselves to be of good standing, which usually requires professional qualifications and proof of experience. Applications must be accompanied by a registration stamp for LF 1,000. All new businesses must notify the Commercial Court's trade and companies register (*Registre de Commerce et des Sociétés*). In addition public and limited liability companies must appear before a notary and execute the *Acte de Constitution* (detailing the ins and outs of the company). Also all firms are required to register with the local VAT office within 15 days of starting, the *Registre aux Firmes* and join the Chamber of Commerce. The overall cost is not cheap, but most of the initial registration fees are tax deductible. The registration tax is 1% of the subscribed capital, notarial fees are a proportion of this capital. It costs between LF 14,000 and LF 74,000 to register in the Official Gazette (*Mémorial*) and registration with the *Registre aux Firmes* costs between LF 2,400 and LF 4,800.

Useful Address

Jordan and Sons Ltd: (21 St Thomas Street, Bristol, Avon BS1 6JS; tel 0272-230600, fax 0272-230063) can offer legal and administrative advice to individuals considering setting up a business in Luxembourg.

Buying an Existing Business

No restrictions exist on foreign ownership, monopolies and acquisitions or mergers, other than those laid down in EC competition law. Commercial estate agencies (*agences immobiliers de commerce*) provide listings of firms for sale. For a limited liability company the transfer of shares to outside parties requires the consent of shareholders holding at least three quarters of the share capital. For public companies the transfer of bearer shares is effected by delivery of the share certificates. The transfer of registered shares must be recorded in the register of shareholders.

Business Structures

Six types of business entities exist in Luxembourg, of which the commonest two are the public company *Société Anonyme (SA)* and the private limited liability company *Société à Responsabilité Limitée (SARL)*. An *SA* must have a board of at least three directors, two or more shareholders, and a minimum capital on formation of LF 1.25 million. The capital must be fully subscribed and at least 25% paid up. A *SARL* is limited by Luxembourg law to at least two shareholders and no more than 40, but public issues of bonds and shares are not permitted. The company is managed by one or more managers, subject to corporation tax and commonly used for medium-sized businesses. The others are the general partnership *Société en Nom Collectif (SENC)*, the limited partnership *Société en Commandite Simple (SECS)*, the *Société en Commandite par Actions (SECA)*, and the co-operative society *Société Coopérative*.

Finance

A host of financial institutions in the Grand Duchy offer a wide choice of services. The privately-run *Cedel* clearance payments system provides for the administration and settlement of primary and secondary market transactions in international securities, bonds, equities, euro-commercial paper and notes. The system has more than 2,400 participants in 60 countries, and can also help to organize overdraft facilities. International payments can be made via the *SWIFT* network.

Investment Incentives

The Luxembourg government has stated that investments should promote the creation, rationalization, extension or reorientation of firms. It promotes a diverse development programme which does not discriminate between foreign and national investment, although preference is given to high technology ventures. To this end the Société Nationale de Crédit et d'Investissement (SNCI) was set up. The SNCI is financed by state grants and can offer loans. It also takes up shareholdings in SA and SARL companies having a commercial or industrial objective. The government itself provides cash grants of up to 15% of the total investment for research projects, and also interest rate rebates (on loans from subsidized credit institutions) on the cost of training, environmental protection, construction and market studies. On the export front the Comité pour la Promotion des Exportations Luxembourgeoises offers interest rebates on loans financing the export of goods. For the first eight years of trading 25% of the taxable income may be exempted from tax. Investment credit tax can be carried forward for four years and credits are available and may be deducted from corporate income tax. All government-organized incentives are to be modified at the end of 1992.

Ideas for New Businesses

Two sectors stand out head and shoulders above others as areas of potential growth — manufacturing and finance. Foreign investment is positively welcomed by the government. Tourism is expected to continue growing and the advantageous fiscal laws also mean establishing holding companies is as popular as ever. Other areas that are popular include health foods and recreation, and third world crafts.

Running a Business

Employing Staff

The labour force is skilled, well-educated and adaptable, and in addition the country has both skilled and unskilled labour from neighbouring EC countries. Contracts are usually a matter of collective agreement but employers must draw one up for each individual employee. The notice required on the employer's side ranges between two to six months, on the employee's side it can vary from one month for those with less than five years' service to three months for those with more than ten years. Severance pay is from one to three months' wages for manual workers with five years or more service. Non-manual workers are entitled to one month's salary for five years' service, rising to 12 months for more than 30 years in the job. The working day is eight hours but a flexible approach allows start and finish times to vary. Overtime is frequent, but regulated by the government. Employees are entitled to a minimum of 25 days holiday each year.

Conciliation arrangements at both factory and national level mean employer-employee relations are very good. Worker representation is required on the board for firms with more than 1,000 employees. Companies with more than 15 employees must provide workers' councils, which advise and conciliate in disputes. The law regarding the minimum wage depends upon an employee's age, skills and family circumstances.

The social security system operates a comprehensive scheme and firms are liable for certain contributions. Sickness insurance is contributed at a rate of 2.4% for non-manual workers, and 4.35% in respect of manual workers. Employers and employees alike pay 8% to the State Pension Scheme. The employer is expected to fund the family allowance scheme by contributing 1.7% of salary (1.65% for temporary staff). Accident insurance is payable from 0.5% to 6% of salary depending upon the degree of risk in the occupation, and the unemployment fund is financed by company contributions, equivalent to 2% of corporate income.

Taxation

For foreign firms one of the key elements of the Luxembourg tax system is its tax-free treatment of holding companies. They are exempt from taxation on profits, capital gains and interest and dividend distributions. The heirs of non-resident shareholders are not subject to death duties or inheritance tax. The only tax liability is a 0.2% annual subscription tax on equity. As a consequence there are more than 7,000 holding companies based in the Grand Duchy. Other businesses, however, are considered resident for tax purposes if the registered office or central management is in Luxembourg. Resident firms are subject to several principal taxes on worldwide profits, but non-resident companies are liable only on Luxembourg source profits.

Corporation tax is levied on a sliding scale from 20% on the first LF 400,000 (£6,750) of profits to 33% on profits above LF 1,312,000 (£22,143). Non-resident companies are entitled to a reduced rate where worldwide profits do not exceed the top rate. Municipal business tax is applied at a rate of 4% on profits, subject to a multiple of between 1.8 and three depending on the area. The standard rate of VAT is 15%, however, the charges are currently under review and an intermediary levy of 12% is in force (see Chapter Four, *Daily Life*). Banking, exports, the postal services, some sanitary, educational, social and cultural activities, insurance and the letting of property are exempt from VAT. Income Tax, which includes investment earnings, ranges from 15% to 50%. Capital gains are taxed as income but are only subject to half the relevant rate. Tax is withheld from earnings and firms are required to provide the authorities with details by 1 March.

Accountancy and Legal Advice

By law accounts must include the balance sheet, the profit and loss account before deductions and the proposed appropriation of profit (or treatment of loss) in the latest and preceding years. In addition a journal for the entry of day-to-day transactions and a record for the annual registration of the inventory of assets and liabilities are required. Auditing standards published by the *Union Europeénne des Experts Comptables (UEC)* apply in the Grand Duchy where they do not contravene local laws. Independent auditors (*Réviseurs d'Entreprises*) prepare accounts for large and medium-sized firms, while smaller companies are looked after by statutory auditors (*Commissaires aux Comptes*).

The prospective business person in Luxembourg would be ill-advised not to seek specialist legal advice on setting up a business. The Luxembourg Embassy in London can provide a list of English-speaking solicitors in the Grand Duchy.

Useful Addresses

Thielen & Korn Avocats: rue de Nassau, 2213 Luxembourg-Ville; tle 44 62 41, fax 45 42 33.

DTI Information Centre: 1-19 Victoria Street, London SW1H 0ET; tel 071-215 5444.

Luxembourg Press and Information Service: 43 boulevard FD Roosevelt, 2450 Luxembourg; tel 47 83 21.

Luxembourg Chambre de Commerce: 7 rue Alcide de Gasperi, 2981 Luxembourg-Kirchberg; tel 43 58 61.

Belgium-Luxembourg Chamber of Commerce in Great Britain: 6 John Street, London WC1N 2ED; tel 071-831 3508.

Jordan and Sons Ltd: (21 St Thomas Street, Bristol BS1 6JS; tel 0272-230600, fax 0272-230063) offers help and advice to individuals setting up a business in Luxembourg.

The Law Society: Foreign Lawyers Department, 50-52 Chancery Lane, London WC2A 1SX; tel 071-242 1222.

Appendix 1

Personal Case Histories — Belgium
Michael Ingham OBE

Michael Ingham is 51 years old and the Managing Director of De Keyser-Thornton NV/SA, an international shipping and forwarding agency based in Antwerp. After leaving school he went to the University of Madrid for a while and then started to work for a shipping business in Madrid. Subsequently he joined United States Lines, a shipping multinational, and was head of their European operations for eight years. He took over De Keyser-Thornton from his father in 1977, and built it up into a major international business with offices in France and West Africa. He was the President of the British Chamber of Commerce in Brussels from 1989 to 1991 and is now the President of the Council of British Chambers of Commerce in Europe, an organization based in the UK. He has also been a member of official Belgian Trade Missions all over the world. He was appointed an OBE in 1991.

How did you find Belgian red tape?
There are very strict formalities to be followed in Belgium and it is essential to have a local to help you deal with them. Everything has to be re-done, for example your driving licence, and then there are things which are quite alien to British people, such as having to carry an identity card.

How were you able to build up your business?
The late 1970s and early 1980s were years of great expansion in the port of Antwerp, which is one of the world's major ports. We were able to expand by following the increased cargo throughput. De Keyser-Thornton was founded in 1853, but since 1977 it has expanded about one hundredfold. We have now set up companies in France and the Ivory Coast, and deal with leasing, forwarding, warehousing, discharging, repair of containers and so on.

How about Belgian workers?
While the cost factor is greater here than in the UK, the same workload can be done with far fewer people. I would have to employ two or three times as many workers to run the same business in Britain. Belgian workers have a high reputation for efficiency and hard work and this is entirely justified.

What advice do you have for someone starting a business in Belgium?
There are three main points. The first is to get to know the local customs. The second is to understand the mentality of the people. And the third, is not to try to impose British working practices on the locals. Because of the social laws, it is very difficult to get rid of workers, so you are looking at a long-term commitment. If you make mistakes in this area then they can be very expensive indeed. You must also be aware of the language differences. If you speak French in Flanders or Dutch in Wallonia then you can forget about doing any business. Languages have always been important to me; I grew up speaking German, English and French, and later learnt to speak Spanish and Dutch.

How do you find social life in Belgium?
It is difficult to get into the Belgian scene, but once you make friends they are

very loyal. Although I work in Antwerp, I have always lived in Brussels. A lot of interesting things go on there, and of course there is a great mix of nationalities.

Peter Burnett

Peter Burnett is 52. He read economics, Spanish and French at Cambridge, and then worked for the Ministry of Agriculture in the External Relations Section for 10 years. He has worked for the Council of the European Commission in Brussels since 1970 and specializes in translating from Spanish, French and Italian into English.

How did you find Belgian bureaucracy?
If you work for the EC you won't have many problems. The EC looks after its workers very well. I pay my taxes to the EC, so things are rather simplified. On the other hand, I have to pay for my rubbish collection. In the past there have been occasional problems when the communes have tried to levy taxes they were not entitled to. EC workers evidently have advantages over other workers, and as a result there is a certain amount of envy of our status.

Was it difficult to find work?
After university I worked for the Ministry of Agriculture and developed an interest in translating agricultural policy documents coming from Brussels. Eventually the chance arose to work for the European Commission itself and I started work there at the beginning of 1970. I was involved in translating not only the texts of the negotiations for Britain's entry, but also press releases and other information, which even at this time had to be put out in English. These days I translate a wide variety of texts, whose subject matter can be legal, economic, scientific or whatever.

What are opportunities like now?
With the expansion of the EC the workload for translators has grown enormously and there is a steady demand for them. Interpreters are even more in demand. People choose to be either interpreters or translators. The interpreters are much more extrovert, more like actors, while translators are introvert backroom people. There are now specialized courses for translators and interpreters at British universities. It's not enough to have language skills, however. You need to be able to understand the content of the texts. You may find yourself working all night with the people who are drafting the texts or with legal experts. It can be very strenuous.

The likely growth area in the future will be in Scandinavian languages and Finnish, since these are the countries entering the Community next. Later on there could be a demand for Eastern European languages. In general there are not enough Britons working at the EC. Some of this shortfall is being compensated for by Whitehall training 'parachutists', preparing certain new recruits specifically for jobs in the Commission.

How do you find social life in Brussels?
I knew The Netherlands and France quite well but Brussels was confusing. I couldn't recognize the local dialect as being French or Dutch. Brussels people don't have a clear identity and this makes them insecure with foreigners. This seems to be less of a problem with people in other Belgian cities. I tried to integrate myself into the local community from the start rather than mixing with expatriates

all the time. These days I spend time with all sorts of nationalities, in particular Italians.

Have you any advice for those thinking of taking the plunge?
Learn Dutch if you don't know it and get your family to do likewise. That can open many doors and iron out many problems in Belgium. Buy a house or a flat as soon as you can before land prices get out of hand. Otherwise, good luck!

Appendix 2
Personal Case Histories — The Netherlands
Eileen Brown

Eileen Brown is 68 and has lived in The Netherlands for 24 years. She and her husband left England in 1953 and after spells in Uganda and Canada finally settled in The Netherlands — and she says they have no intention of leaving. Her husband was a chemical engineer with Royal Dutch Shell and retired eight years ago. For several years Eileen undertook voluntary work for charity in The Netherlands. She lives in The Hague. We asked her:

How easy was Dutch red tape in practice?
There were no problems at all with red tape and officialdom. The paperwork was at a minimum and I found the Dutch authorities to be most helpful and efficient.

Was it difficult to retire?
After 24 years living and working here it seemed quite natural for us to stay on in our retirement. There were no problems with the authorities and it was simply a matter of registering our change in status. Someone from the pensions office of the Dutch Social Security Department came to see us. He was very helpful and did all the necessary paperwork for us to receive our British pensions. I now receive small British and Dutch pensions.

How do you find living and working in The Netherlands compared with other countries?
I pay more taxes than I would in the UK but the services are excellent. Public transport, buses, trains and trams, are highly efficient. Medical facilities are good and virtually covered by our private health insurance. Shopping is easy and the food is delicious. There are even Marks & Spencer stores in Amsterdam and The Hague. Also, for those British goods one just cannot live without, there is a constant stream of traffic by expats to and from the UK.

How do you find the social life and the Dutch?
We lead a busy and enjoyable social life with both Dutch and British friends. I joined a golf club 20 years ago and I would certainly recommend anyone to join a social group. The types are almost too numerous to mention and include the British Women's Club, the International Women's Club and the Netherlands-England Society — the latter has branches all over Holland. Almost without exception, any sport, hobby or cultural interest is available.

What is your advice for those thinking of taking the plunge?
I would advise any newcomer to live in or near The Hague, Rotterdam or Amsterdam, where there are large international communities. The added bonus over moving to France, Italy or Spain is that the Dutch like to speak English. However, this must not be taken for granted and people intending to stay for a long period should be prepared to learn Dutch.

Elisabeth Cox

Elizabeth is 39 and moved to The Netherlands four years ago. Married to a civil servant, she had little choice in going but has since fallen in love with the place. Elizabeth is involved with an English-language magazine and although she officially handles the publication's finances and advertising, describes her role as generally 'mucking in'. The couple live in Benoordenhout, a pleasant leafy suburb of The Hague, which is within walking distance of the beach.

How easy was Dutch red tape in practice?
I was fortunate enough to bypass much of the bureaucracy of moving. My husband was transferring jobs and much of the paperwork was done for us. From what I can gather it was straightforward enough and the Dutch authorities were co-operative.

Was it difficult to find work?
Finding work does not appear easy unless one is recruited from Britain. The majority of people I know secured a job before coming to The Netherlands. I would not advise people to arrive 'on spec'. Standards are very high. Most Dutch people speak at least two foreign languages and are highly educated. Quite frankly, anyone who speaks only English is hardly likely to impress an employer. I was lucky enough to be involved with the magazine virtually from the start and I found the Dutch authorities very helpful towards the business.

Was it easy to find accommodation?
It is relatively easy to find accommodation. Many local makelaars (estate agents) have lettings departments for foreigners and are very helpful. However, finding affordable rented accommodation is another matter. Rents are high compared to purchase prices, so for longer term stays I think it is better to buy. Dutch houses are generally well built, warm and comfortable. Prices are cheaper than UK equivalents.

How do you find the social life and the Dutch?
Mixed! The Dutch are very family oriented and tend to entertain in restaurants rather than at home. On the whole it is rare to be invited to a Dutch person's home. The Dutch tend to dine at about 6.30pm and go to bed correspondingly early.

What is your advice for those thinking of taking the plunge?
Get a job first, then go. Also, the standard of living is very high but be prepared to pay for it. The taxes are horrendous!

Index of Advertisers

Vacation Work also publish:

The Directory of Summer Jobs Abroad...£6.95
The Directory of Summer Jobs in Britain...................................£6.95
Vacation Traineeships for Students..£6.95
Adventure Holidays...£4.95
The Teenager's Vacation Guide to Work, Study & Adventure.............£6.95
Teaching English Abroad...£7.95
Work Your Way Around the World...£8.95
The Au Pair & Nanny's Guide to Working Abroad.........................£5.95
Working in Ski Resorts — Europe...£5.95
Kibbutz Volunteer..£5.95
The Directory of Jobs and Careers Abroad...................................£7.95
The International Directory of Voluntary Work..............................£6.95
The Directory of Work & Study in Developing Countries..................£7.95
Live & Work in France...£6.95
Live & Work in Spain & Portugal..£8.95
Live & Work in Italy...£7.95
Live & Work in Germany..£8.95
Travellers Survival Kit: South America......................................£10.95
Travellers Survival Kit: Central America.....................................£8.95
Travellers Survival Kit: Cuba..£7.95
Travellers Survival Kit: USA & Canada......................................£8.95
Travellers Survival Kit: Europe..£6.95
Travellers Survival Kit: Soviet Union & Eastern Europe...................£8.95
Travellers Survival Kit to the East...£6.95
Travellers Survival Kit: Australia & New Zealand..........................£8.95
Hitch-hikers' Manual Britain..£3.95
Europe — A Manual for Hitch-hikers...£3.95
The Traveller's Picture Phrase Book £1.95

Distributors of:

The Summer Employment Directory of the United States £9.95
Internships (On-the-Job Training Opportunities in the USA)..............£15.95
The Directory of College Accommodations £4.95
Emplois d'Ete en France...£6.95
Jobs in Japan..£9.95
Teaching Tactics for Japan's English Classrooms...........................£5.95

Vacation Work Publications, 9 Park End Street, Oxford OX1 1HJ
(Tel 0865-241978. Fax 0865-790885).